Praise for
Milspeak Creative Writing Seminars

Writing your thoughts on paper as Sally taught us to do and then sharing them is a great way to help other people who might just need one word that you have written to answer a question in their mind.

—Kathryn Evans Parker, Member of the Military Family, Milspeak Writer

Although I have had some publishing success, the Milspeak experience, and in particular, Sally, encouraged me to explore new directions in my writing via the Milspeak seminar format, providing me with a structured approach to reading and critiquing my work along with fellow participants.

—Vivian Bikulege, Member of the Military Family, Milspeak Writer

One of the wonderful things about writing is the cleansing process that it invokes. Writing "Time" was as much a soul cleansing as the months after 9/11 .... The balance of mother and Marine is delicate. Fear of failing either the Corps or my children is constant and that sense of failure precariously looms in the distance.

—Sondra Meek, Veteran of the War on Terror, Milspeak Writer

An old, retired sailor, I had begun writing a life history for my five grandkids, knowing how my forbearers had shied away from giving me any information. .... Sally put us all to work on one-another's works to produce readable copy.

—Jack Hayes, Korean War Veteran, Milspeak Writer

Knowing that my fellow writers had also been around the military for years made it possible for me to tell my story.

—Charlotte Brock, Iraq War Veteran, Milspeak Writer

D1453700

When Sally's creative military writing workshop confronted me, I dared to try it! I had nothing to lose! I had been dead for thirty-five years and still got to work everyday.

—Bernard "Moe" Haagensen, Vietnam Veteran, Milspeak Writer

To really write a story you have to be honest with yourself.

—Monica Greer, Member of the Military Family, Milspeak Writer

If I never get a check for something I write, it's O.K. I've been well paid already, in self-awareness and the lifting away of a blanket of guilt.

—F.P. Siedentopf, Vietnam Veteran and Cold War Veteran, Milspeak Writer

My Milspeak classmates gave me the courage to unravel the ball of disillusionment that was held inside my soul, to let the poison of hurt pour out onto the paper thus releasing it from my heart.

—Debra A. Pochie, Member of the Military Family, Milspeak Writer

I hope this story does some justice to those who send loved ones into combat areas and have to worry quietly and wait for their safe return. Being a Marine did not make it any easier. I had a particularly good idea of the situations my son was getting into. I appreciate my son sharing this account with me and allowing me to share it with others. This story should reach an extremely broad audience and my hope is that it inspires many conversations between military members and their families.

—David Charles, Cold War and War on Terror Veteran, Milspeak Writer

MILSPEAK

MILSPEAK

Warriors, Veterans, Family, and Friends
Writing the Military Experience

Edited by Sally Drumm

Press 53
Winston-Salem, NC

Press 53
PO Box 30314
Winston-Salem, NC 27130

First Edition

Cover design by Kevin Watson
Cover photograph Copyright © 2009 by Crystal Ann Floyd

The editor gratefully acknowledges the following publications:

Marine Corps Gazette first published MajGen Matthew P. Caulfield's speech, "A
Battalion Remembers" online at http://www.mca-marines.org/gazette/

Riley, Atsuro. "Hutch" Published in *Poetry*: December 2007, V.CXCI:3. Will be
included in *Romey's Order*, forthcoming in 2010 from the Phoenix Poets series of *The
University of Chicago Press*.

McClanahan, Rebecca. "Children Writing Grief"; Published in *The Southern
Review*, Volume 34, Number 1

Brock, Charlotte. "Hymn." First Publication: *The Gettysburg Review* 21:3. Autumn
2008. Anthologized in: *Powder: Writing by Women in the Ranks from Vietnam to Iraq*,
edited by Lisa Bowden and Shannon Cain. Kore Press, 2008.

Hayes, Jack. "The Fez." First Publication: *The Graybeards: Official Publication of
The Korean War Veterans Association*, 21:3

"The Art of Theater No. 11" Copyright © 1997 by *The Paris Review*, reprinted with
permission of The Wylie Agency LLC.

Printed on acid-free paper
ISBN 978-0-9824416-2-6

Dedicated To

F. P. Siedentopf
Master Gunnery Sergeant
United States Marine Corps (Retired)

Hutch

—by way of what they say

From back when it was Nam time I tell you what.

Them days men boys gone dark groves rose like Vietnam bamboo.

Aftergrowth something awful.

Green have mercy souls here seen camouflage everlasting.

Nary a one of the brung-homes brung home whole.

Mongst tar-pines come upon this box-thing worked from scrapwood.

Puts me much myself in mind of a rabbit-crouch.

Is it more a meat-safe.

Set there hid bedded there looking all the world like a coffin.

Somebody cares to tend to it like a spring gets tendered clears the leaves!

Whosoever built it set wire window-screen down the sides.

Long about five foot or thereabouts close kin to a dog-crate.

A human would have to hunch.

Closes over heavy this hingey-type lid on it like a casket.

Swearing to Jesus wadn't it eye-of-pine laid down for the floor.

Remembering the Garner twins Carl and Charlie come home mute.

Cherry-bombs 4th of July them both belly-scuttling under the house.

Their crave of pent-places ditchpipes.

Mongst tar-pines come upon this box-thing worked from scrapwood.

From back when it was Nam time I tell you what.

—Atsuro Riley

CONTENTS

MCWS 8

FOREWORD

Silences
(After Tillie Olsen)

by Michael Kobre

In 1962, in a talk at Radcliffe College, the writer Tillie Olsen, author of a slim masterpiece of short fiction *Tell Me A Riddle,* gave voice to generations of men and women who, like herself, had struggled to break through the silences that oppressed them. For Olsen, whose career as a writer had been interrupted for decades by the need to work and take care of her children—she'd even walked away from a contract to have a novel published when she was in her twenties—the subject was personal too. "I have had a special need to learn all I could of this over the years," she said, "myself so nearly remaining mute and having to let writing die over and over again in me."

As Olsen noted, there were many kinds of silences: from the work stifled by the same sort of everyday demands that had thwarted her own writing—the silences of harried men and women living divided lives as "part-time, part-self persons"—to the experience of writers silenced by censors or indifferent audiences or repressive governments or their own unquenchable doubts. Olsen even counted among the silenced people whose "lives never came to writing . . . those whose waking hours are all struggle for existence; the barely educated; the illiterate; women. Their silence the silence of centuries as to how life was, is, for most of humanity."

Olsen's talk would later be published to much acclaim in expanded form as a book, *Silences,* in 1978, and over the years it's become a classic in Women's Studies and to anyone who cares about what is all too often, for far too many, a struggle to write. Yet in addition to all those unnatural silences that Olsen describes, there's another kind of silence too that so many of the writers gathered in this volume have broken: what Sally Drumm in "Scars on My Heart" calls "the traditional silence about military life." A silence imposed by a professional culture in which voices, when they're raised at all, are told to speak through formal channels, in measured cadences that always recognize a chain of command.

So it's all the more astonishing, I think, the stories they tell now. The fearless candor. The sacrifice. The honor of their profession. The enduring bonds between them. And, yes, as Sally and others gathered here acknowledge, the scars too. In the introduction, Sally writes of Milspeak's "potential to build the civilian community's understanding of military life"— and as someone who's never served, a college professor for nearly 20 years, part of a world that's about as far removed from military culture as possible, I can attest that the voices heard in this collection have at least increased this civilian's understanding of that life.

But it's as a civilian also, invited to raise his voice alongside these others, that I have to acknowledge my own kind of silence. The silence, I mean, of someone who stands by and watches from a distance, the complacent silence of all of us who take for granted the commitment and sacrifices of the men and women of the military and their families. In the last few years particularly, shocked by the 9/11 attacks, roused to anger and fear, we all participated in a march to war that went too fast. And then, when it became painfully clear that the mission hadn't been accomplished as quickly and easily as we expected, when the men and women of the military were ordered to serve multiple tours of duty and the rest of America was told to go shopping (on bad credit, as we've learned since), war, for too many of us, was something we watched on television. It was a handful of minutes on the news filled with foreign names and a grinding repetition that never seemed to resolve anything, a long, shapeless parade of horrors that was happening far away to someone else. We watched for a few minutes, tried to take in the ebb and flow of violence and the shifting alliances, sometimes shook our heads and voiced words of outrage, then changed the channel.

Which is why the stories gathered here are so important.

There's something about an image on the screen that for all its precise resolution keeps us at a distance, that instills a kind of familiar passivity learned from long hours consuming entertainment. But words on a page, the voices we hear in our minds, those are different. When we read we're active participants in a transaction between writer and reader. We imbue those words with life and in so doing embrace something of the lives they describe. The boundaries of self become a little more porous. And so maybe then if civilians like me—on-lookers mostly, the beneficiaries of others' sacrifices—could only listen carefully enough to the voices heard in these pages, well, maybe we too could be shaken out of our own silences.

INRODUCTION TO MILSPEAK

Scars on my Heart
by Sally Drumm

I.
Why Milspeak?

Eighteen years into my military service to the United States of America, I was denied the right to lead a group of Marines into a South American country on an undercover drug surveillance mission. The EC-7 mission would take several active duty members from various branches of the military—controllers, interpreters, medical personnel, and communications personnel—deep into the Amazon jungle to a radar site atop a 5600-foot mountain for three months. The official message requiring my removal from the team read: "...due to cultural differences, request team be composed of male personnel only to avoid possibility of sexual harassment...." I was infuriated that sexual harassment policy initiated after the Tail Hook incident (Naval aviators demeaned themselves and made national headlines by groping women in a Las Vegas hotel) was being used against military women when the policy had been designed to protect us.

My only recourse was to request mast, an official, documented request to take my problem to the chain of command for resolution. In the Marine Corps, request mast is not undertaken lightly by most of those who use it to resolve problems. The process begins with the commanding officer hearing the problem. Each commander in the Marine's chain of command is given the opportunity to solve the problem. If no one in the direct chain of command can resolve the problem to the Marine's satisfaction, the Marine can send a letter stating her case to the Commandant of the Marine Corps.

In 1996, as I contemplated requesting mast in order to be allowed to do the job I had trained eighteen years to do—a job I was being denied simply because I was a woman—I remembered my first fight to be trained as the first enlisted woman in my military occupational specialty in 1978, and I remembered every other moment in my eighteen-year fight for equal recognition as a Marine. The list of exclusions due to gender is endless, and runs from mild to outrageous to sublime. For many years—and during the first six years of my enlistment—women were outlawed from firing weapons or qualifying at the rifle range because money was tight. We were not allowed to deploy with our units because women weren't allowed in the field or aboard ship. We were ordered to always wear skirts in formation and forced to live in barracks away from unit barracks because that was where all the women on base lived, often behind high walls or rolls of concertina wire. As one supervisor, an enlisted Marine who had become a warrant officer, told me in 1986, "You're nothing but a token Marine."

Two female junior-enlisted Marines were to accompany me on the EC-7 mission, women who worked for me and were trained by me, women who deserved the opportunity to lead when their time came. By 1996, I had also served two tours—more than four years—as a drill instructor. From 1978, when I began active duty, through 1991, when I left the drill field for the second time, I had witnessed and been part of the development of woman recruit training from a focus on image development to a focus on warrior training while preparing hundreds of women for Marine Corps duty.

I was not about to turn tail and run just when the going got a little rough with the United States State Department. Also, my unit (and units in all military branches) was suffering the effects of a mandated force drawdown—a consequence of Americans' perception that their military had outgrown its usefulness after the Berlin Wall came down. Resulting personnel shortages demanded that I do my part. More importantly, as a staff noncommissioned officer, a gunnery sergeant, my being excluded from a key leadership position made training junior Marines of all genders a hypocrisy that undermined my authority, therefore undermining subordinates' respect for me.

I requested mast to air my grievance over a denial to leadership that I read as an institutional devaluation of my years of service and of my ability to lead as a staff noncommissioned officer, and because, in being excluded from the EC-7 mission, I was reliving the first years of my military career in its last years. The mirror was unbroken. As a woman, I will never be anyone's idea of the perfect Marine, but I had served my country as well as any man for eighteen years and I had earned the right during those years to lead the EC-7 team into South America. I didn't want another woman to have to go through what I had experienced between 1978 and 1996. In requesting mast in 1996 I wasn't fighting only for myself, but for all military women. This fight began for me in 1978, still hadn't been won in 1996, and remains to be won.

When I talked with my commanding officer about the EC-7 situation, he told me that requesting mast was unnecessary and promised to do his best to right the situation. This, I knew, was a way to keep my request mast proceedings undocumented and off the record. A few days after our talk, my CO gave me the news: the Marine Aircraft Group and Wing Commanders had been unable to change the ruling—the State Department, overlord of the EC-7 operation, was the rust in the hinge. I took matters into my own hands, disregarding standard procedure for request mast, and sent the Commandant of the Marine Corps an email stating my case. The Commandant responded on March 19, 1996:

> GySgt Wyndham, Thank you for standing up to be counted. You did and you counted. Your commandant thanks you. While the team leader for the group [...] will be an officer [...] the restrictions against women being members of the team have been rescinded by [...] (who originally requested them). Our Marines— all of our Marines—are deployable worldwide on a moments notice. I know that—I saw the effectiveness of our woman Marines when I was CG 2nd FSSG in Desert Shield and Desert Storm. You, of course, know that. Stick to your guns, Gunny.
> Semper Fidelis, C. C. Krulak, Commandant

Although an officer was assigned to lead the team for the first time since recurring EC-7 deployments had begun and I wouldn't be the EC-7 team leader, I would be the staff noncommissioned officer in charge, the officer's-in-charge right-hand woman. Two additional women would accompany us: one woman from my unit and a medic. My commanding officer and the Group and Wing commanders were furious with me for going over their heads to the Commandant with "my" problem. My direct supervisor kowtowed to his senior officers via email, and I played along. In apology, he wrote: "Gunnery Sergeant Wyndham is totally satisfied with the attention she received on this issue, but at the same time realizes that there was a better way to initiate her concerns." "Attention" I received? This was a minimalization of my concerns, making my request for equal recognition as a leader seem completely personal, but there was no doubt in my military mind that I had won a major battle in the fight for equality. Others' underestimation of my will to make right a wrong had paid off once again, but winning the battle proved more costly than expected.

While in South America on a shaved-flat mountaintop, I fell many times on cloud-covered pathways built with logs harvested when the mountain was topped to make way for system equipment. Log trails wound between radar, equipment vans, and hastily built log shacks used for living and eating. Many mornings I stood at the edge of the mountain to watch vast masses of cloud rise from Amazon jungle below. Those of us on the deployment spent seven days on watch on the mountaintop and seven days in a small village twenty minutes by helicopter from the mountain—the site was accessible only by chopper.

During one of my stays in the village, Pedro, one of two helicopter pilots, crashed into the mountain during a heavy fog. All aboard were killed, none of them from our detachment, all of them visiting dignitaries. My officer-in-charge was away in a distant city meeting with State Department officials. After informing the State Department of the disaster by telephone, a young enlisted Marine interpreter and I went to the airfield to meet with the South American general in charge of the radar site. I extended our condolences and offered to help in any way. Later that evening, I was warned that the general was seeking my arrest for spying. Fortunately, the misunderstanding was resolved by the State Department.

Soon after the crash, I returned to the mountaintop. I stood my watches at the radar console. I ate my meals with the South American officers and troops in a wooden shack where meals were served on cloth-covered tables set with nice china. At night, I slept alone in a steel van positioned below the radar site and reached via a steep stairway of slippery log steps. A few weeks before the deployment ended, one last fall seriously injured my back by jamming the end of an upturned log into the small of my back. I didn't realize how badly I was injured until later that night. During my twelve-hour watch I became nauseated, my stomach began cramping, and I felt as though I was dying. The South American doctor on site asked me to lie on a rack in his hooch. We shared little of each other's language.

After explaining as best I could that I'd experienced a serious fall, he asked me to lie on my stomach and pull down my cammie trousers. I trusted him completely—my pain was immense; he was kind and gentle. He discovered a huge and growing bruise on my lower back, diagnosed nerve trauma, and gave me an injection. To this day I have no idea what the syringe contained, but the contents relieved my pain. The next day, I was flown down to the village by helicopter and never again returned to the mountaintop.

Upon my return to the States, my back injury caused me to become one of the walking wounded, an active duty Marine who is considered a sick bay commando because he or she cannot heal. The injury or illness affects command readiness. The injured Marine is just "taking up space." Often, coworkers and the system treat us walking wounded as though our injuries and limitations are psychological. Always, we walking wounded are treated as a liability to mission accomplishment.

During the last two years of my career, the fight to make it to retirement was difficult. Being one of the walking wounded was embarrassing. I felt as though my back injury was a punishment for fighting for my rights as a woman Marine, capable and more than qualified to lead but denied leadership because of gender. I endured injections in my spine under x-ray and underwent every form of physical therapy. Each time I tried to run even a short distance to keep up with the pack, I was unable to walk for days afterward. Despite a doctor's letter requesting I remain in the rear, I was deployed to Gulfport, Mississippi, to work atop a Bauxite mound where The System, the tangle of cables, computer vans, and radars used by controllers in a Marine Air Control Squadron, was emplaced. I had to be returned from the deployment early because climbing and walking on that coal-like mound immobilized me. I believed this assignment was punishment for forcing my way into the EC-7 detachment, but every ordeal, every moment of pain, was worthwhile, despite the physical damage to my body and the political damage to my career.

On my return to Marine Corps Air Station (MCAS) Beaufort from the Bauxite Mound, I received permanent change of station orders to Marine Air Control Squadron 24 (MACS 24) at Dam Neck, Virginia. In response, I submitted my retirement package and removed myself from promotion rolls. Because I expected to receive a small disability rating for my back injury, I followed the advice of an Old Salt when submitting my retirement package. I listed on the Veterans Administration form all injuries and scars received during my military career: the seven-inch scar on my left forearm incurred during a drunken car wreck that nearly killed my best friend; the three-inch scar on my right knee from kneeling while drunk on a broken glass; the three-inch scar on my right hip where the bone graft had been harvested to heal my broken left arm a year after it was broken; and the six-inch scar above my Mound of Venus where my uterus, fallopian tubes and ovaries had been removed from my body in 1984 when long-term problems with my reproductive organs were interfering with military readiness. I was given a choice before that surgery: have the surgery or be discharged from the Corps. I chose surgery and duty over the sense of personal well being that comes with knowing that one day you might have a child. A month after that surgery, while still on convalescent leave, I received my first set of orders to the drill field.

There was no place on the VA's form to list the scars on my heart.

Shortly after I retired from active duty on February 5, 1998, I received a letter from the Veterans Administration in response to my application for disability. The news was stunning: I was assigned a 60% disability rating in a two-paragraph letter. No VA representative contacted me. No one advised me how to proceed with my life as a disabled veteran. I could still walk, talk and possessed all my fingers, toes, and eyes. I felt undeserving of the disability rating and totally confused by it. The VA had assigned 10% each for my back problem and for carpal tunnel syndrome in my left hand, the result of wearing a cast for more than a year. Civilian doctors employed by the military medical system in 1985 kept telling me my arm would heal. After threatening to contact my senator in Illinois, I was sent to Bethesda Naval Hospital for my first appointment with the Naval doctor who performed a bone graft from my hip to my arm. Fifteen months after breaking my arm, the cast came off for the last time; the steel plate that ran the length of my ulna remained. An additional 10% disability rating was assigned because I had a spouse, a husband; my third—military life is as hard on relationships as it is on the body. A 50% rating was assigned for loss of my reproductive organs. This 80% percent total was refigured by some mysterious formula into a 60% total service-connected disability rating.

After receiving this news, I went into a depression that lasted weeks. Feeling undeserving was only part of the problem. I read the 50% rating for my 1984 hysterectomy as an admission that the operation had been unnecessary, that it was all a mistake, that my ability to bear children had been stolen from me. Perhaps this was a misreading on my part, I thought, so I read the paper over and over, trying to find a way to believe I was a 60% disabled veteran.

Finally, I decided I would never speak about it again, that this was just another part of life's plan for me, a plan more often ambiguous than clear. This self-imposed silence lasted many years; I am breaking it now. It is a silence shared by many disabled veterans who feel they are at the mercy of a health care system and a military system that will make them suffer if they speak out. If we speak of disability we are often misunderstood, often unemployed, and often left feeling ashamed and undeserving. If we speak of disability we are often viewed as taking advantage of the system. Many disabled veterans believe their silence is expected in order to honor their service, that to speak out is disloyal. Ours is a silence that speaks of both self-denial and a public denial of our value to society, of our ability as disabled veterans to be contributing members of society. In its worst form, this denial is a silencing of the disabled veteran's right to exist in a world where the value of Beauty often suppresses the value of Life. The very word *disability* in all its forms, with its demeaning prefix, *dis-*, provokes negativity in definition: *dis*card, *dis*miss, *dis*may.

In my own state of denial, I went about my after-service life struggling to establish a career in landscape design. I hadn't yet accepted my physical limitations. While on active duty, I had studied horticulture at the local technical college and planned to build a career in landscaping following retirement from the Corps. After injuring my back, I couldn't let go of the dream—there had to be some way to become a landscape designer. This was something I could do sitting down without the physical labor involved in landscaping: I could draw designs and find people to create them. It was a ridiculous fantasy. As in the military world, I would have to earn my title in the civilian world—that meant physical labor in landscaping if I were to become a credible designer.

For nearly a year, I drew beautiful plans and performed the hard work of carrying them out. There were many days when back pain made walking difficult. Lifting and digging were out of the question. I forced myself to do the work anyway, inventing ways to limit stress on my back. My chiropractor was my best friend—I have paid thousands of dollars to him over the years; he keeps me walking; his service is not covered by my military medical benefits. My husband Pete often helped me with landscaping jobs. Pain was my constant companion. Finally, at the end of a $20,000 job that involved hiring many people to do the work I couldn't do, I admitted to myself that I was a failure. There was no way a landscaping career could work for me. The beating my body had taken during my twenty-year run with the Marines had finally registered in my heart and mind.

I applied for administrative jobs, but remained unemployed. How could I not reveal to potential employers that I am a 60% disabled veteran with a back problem?

One morning in 2000, I woke up and fell head on into a tremendous anxiety attack. If something were to happen to my husband Pete, I wouldn't be able to support myself, to continue to live in our home, or to maintain our quality of life. We live on a small island near Beaufort, on an acre of ground purchased from my mother-in-law. Pete, a self-employed carpenter, built our home on the shore of Lucy Point Creek. Jets from the Marine Corps Air Station often circle overhead. Rifle fire from Parris Island echoes across the marshes on Friday qualification-day mornings. We watch the sunset from our deck beside the river. Each day, one of us asks the other, "Do we really get to live here?" Fear of economic insecurity has been a driving force in my career choices. My employment history began in high school with a job waitressing that bought me my first car, a green 1964 Rambler American, a tank of a car that I lived in before I wrecked it in 1977—everything I owned fit in the trunk with room to spare. Waitressing transformed into a job cooking following a skin-of-the-teeth graduation from high school. Then it was bartending, working in an Easter grass factory, working in an old folks' home, and finally, unemployment prior to enlisting in the Corps on December 22, 1977.

On the morning of my anxiety attack, my employability was limited. Military job skills don't easily translate into civilian skills. In my case, more than 2000 dogfights and a keen understanding of air-to-air tactics earn zilch in resume points. I was as unemployable or less so than when I enlisted in the Corps. How could I explain a 60% disability to a potential employer? Who wants to hire someone with a history of back problems? Was I going to have talk about my lost reproductive organs to explain my disability to employers for the rest of my working life? I couldn't even wait tables. I figured I'd end up a greeter at Wal-Mart, but even that would be iffy because standing for any length of time is always a chore.

Following retirement from the Corps, I didn't enjoy the opportunities that men I had worked with in the military enjoyed. Many of them retired into positions in the defense industry, often due to contacts made through the military's Good Old Boy network. I've never been in that network and I've always been proud that no matter the obstacle set before me, I could find a way around it on my own. But finding that way around had gotten me right where I found myself that morning in 2000—dependent upon a man, my husband, for my welfare, a position I never wanted to be in because of a long history of abandonment that began with my father abandoning me when I was a child.

Certainly, I did have retirement and VA disability pay. Each dollar of disability pay was offset dollar for dollar by a reduction in retirement pay. I had retired as a gunnery sergeant/E-7. In 2000, I was receiving less than $18,000 a year in retirement and disability benefits. My husband, a self-employed carpenter, made a little more. Our combined incomes allowed for a simple lifestyle. But if his pay were lost, if he were injured, could we survive?

My only option was to return to college and earn a degree that would make me employable. It never occurred to me that military stereotypes or disability might possess potential to destroy what I could create of myself with an education. Once I have a plan, I am unstoppable. If a door closes in my face, I will find the back door, the side door, the trap door, the mouse hole. Through my local university, I discovered that I could become a librarian in four years if I worked hard. A university counselor suggested I contact the VA for education assistance, even though I had paid into the Montgomery GI Bill program and had $16,000 in education benefits in reserve.

The drive to the VA office in Columbia, South Carolina from Beaufort, South Carolina is about two and a half hours up I-26. I prepared for my meeting with a VA education specialist by keeping my expectations low. Also, I had prepared a full brief, including a proposed course schedule, on achieving my education goals in four years despite having accumulated only 17 credit hours toward a degree in horticulture. Later, I would discover that the many service schools I had attended and my active service would earn an additional three credit hours toward a degree—20 years, three credit hours. During the drive to Columbia, I further prepared for my first meeting with a Veterans Administration official by not expecting a positive reception. During the drive back to Beaufort, I cried—not in sorrow, but for joy. The VA had agreed to fund my entire education. They would pay for tuition and books, and also provide a living expense stipend. I felt as though I'd just won the lottery. I also felt guilty as hell.

Who was I to receive this kind of treatment? I still had my fingers and toes. I could walk most of the time, short distances anyway. I could pay for this myself, with my GI Bill benefits and a second mortgage on the house. But who was I to turn away this kind of help purely out of false pride? The voice of reason won out.

The VA made few demands of me. I had to give up $1200 paid into the Montgomery GI Bill plan and my benefits under that plan, maintain a B average, meet regularly with a counselor, and complete my education within four years. I did all they asked and more—I maintained an A average despite family illnesses, changes in counselors, tuition payment snafus, and wading without a compass through a culture, Academia, I had never before experienced. I completed a four-year Bachelor of Arts in Interdisciplinary Studies degree in two years—the twenty credit hours accumulated during active duty covered my electives.

During my last undergraduate semester, I applied to University of South Carolina's Master of Library and Information Science degree program. While I was waiting for a reply, I received a flier in the mail from Queens University of Charlotte, North Carolina announcing a low-residency program for a Master of Fine Arts in Creative Writing degree. Queens' two-year low-residency program meant I could pursue a career in writing without having to move from Beaufort or endure a long separation from my husband. Writing was what I had always wanted to do, long before I enlisted in the Corps. I applied to the Queens program, creating my application portfolio from essays written during my undergraduate studies in literature and philosophy. Upon learning of my decision to pursue a master's degree in creative writing, Dr. Carl Eby, one of my undergraduate literature professors, asked if I had ever read Annie Dillard. My answer was no—I had never heard of the memoirist and essayist or of her creative nonfiction, the primary genre I would study at Queens. I went to Queens intending to learn to write better essays and somehow find a back door into a journalism career, the profession I had wanted to pursue before I enlisted in the Corps.

My husband was unsettled by my decision to change course from library science to creative writing—what kind of job would a degree in creative writing earn? I filled his head and mine with visions of adjunct teaching and freelance writing assignments. Internally, I struggled with the idea of the sensible thing (librarian) butting against the fantasy (writer). I'd always chosen the sensible thing—at least since 1977, when I'd enlisted in the Corps. I decided to take a chance on myself and follow the dream. I threw the dice; they've yet to land.

My VA counselor, newly assigned to my case after my original counselor—a woman—moved to a new VA location, didn't like the change of plan, either. We argued in his office in Columbia over my decision. He wasn't sure the VA would fund the program. Fine, I told him, I'll take out a second mortgage.

"Let's not go there, yet," he said.

"You need to tell me today if you won't fund this. I need to make arrangements now if the VA won't fund this."

"Well, uh, I, uh—"

"Look, if you don't know, go ask your supervisor."

"Don't tell me what to do."

"This is my life and I've got a right to a say in it...and what about that sign?" I pointed to the VA's "Roadmap to Excellence: Planning the Journey" poster hanging on the wall.

ROADMAP TO EXCELLENCE
Planning the Journey
VBA Mission Statement

"The mission of the Veteran's Benefits Administration, in partnership with the Veterans Health Administration and the National Cemetery System, is to provide benefits and services to veterans and their families in a responsive, timely, and compassionate manner in recognition of their service to the nation."

"We are dealing with veterans, not procedures—with their problems, not ours."

—Omar Bradley-1947

Our vision is that the veterans whom we serve will feel that our nation has kept its commitment to them; employees will feel that they are both recognized for their contribution and are part of something larger than themselves; and taxpayers will feel that we've met the responsibilities they've entrusted to us. Courage, honesty, trust, respect, open communication, and accountability will be reflected in our day-to-day behavior.

"You're not going to use that against me, are you?" my counselor asked.

"Yes. I'm holding you to it...and I'd like a copy of that before I go."

"Okay, okay," he said, and left the office.

When my VA counselor returned to his office, his answer was yes—the last two years of my self-devised educational program would be VA funded in 2003 as promised when my journey toward excellence began in 2001.

As I left my counselor's office, he asked, "How's your kids?"

"I don't have any."

Nearly two years would pass before the relevance of his comment about "kids" sank home in my brain-housing group.

I began the Queens writing program in May 2003, two weeks after I graduated magna cum laude from University of South Carolina. I worked hard at Queens, struggling with all I didn't know about creative writing, which was everything. I had never taken a creative writing course or studied writing formally, but I had written poetry, short stories, and plays from the moment I learned to write my name. Fortunately, I'd studied literature, philosophy, and anthropology as an undergraduate, my instructors had required me to write seriously on my subjects, and I'd fallen in love with research. So I didn't come to the table empty-handed.

What I wasn't prepared for was the alienation I experienced during each of my five residencies at Queens. I had brought that alienation on myself, and it was directly related to my lack of social skills, craft skills, and my choice of subject matter: alcoholism, addiction, ostracism, death, family dysfunction, military life. For me, writing is pointless unless I address subjects important to humanity. My subjects were too deep and dark and my ability to write too poor. Readers cringed when faced with my work and found my experiences strange and unbelievable.

Once again, I was an outsider in my chosen community. I made only one lasting friendship in the military and made none among students during my tenure as a Queens' student. My mother told me each time we talked that I would never finish graduate school, and "Don't be too disappointed if your plans don't work out." My husband was bumming because reading, research, and writing had become my locus of activity. My VA counselor and I weren't getting along, either. Tuition payments to Queens were consistently late. A constant stream of email and phone calls ensued and interfered with my studies, with me as middleman between the VA and Queens. My counselor always said he would fix the problems but didn't— not until my fifth and last semester at Queens.

My VA counselor and I met for the last time in a classroom at Technical College of the Lowcountry, where my horticulture study had begun in 1994 and ended in 1996. He began our meeting by apologizing for the payment trouble. He went on to explain that he had in fact been intentionally hard on me. Why? He had worked for a woman in the Air Force who had treated him like dirt. This woman, my counselor told me, had intentionally had a hysterectomy so that she could receive disability after she left the service. She had children before she had the surgery.

My counselor thought I had done the same thing—sacrificed my reproductive organs to earn a VA disability rating. I was shocked—why would anyone intentionally rip out her guts to get disability? The notion was beyond my range of thought. In fact, I had no idea that loss of reproductive organs rated disability until my rating determination letter arrived in the mail—I wouldn't have included the hysterectomy on the VA form if the Old Salt advising me hadn't said to include every injury, every scar, every ache and pain. Everything wrong about how my counselor had treated me—from asking how the kids were to holding up tuition payments to making me pay for my books in graduate school—finally made sense. I forgave him as I have so often been forgiven for assuming something about someone else. We went on with our meeting.

My student days came to an end with writing a thesis and graduation from Queens University of Charlotte in May 2005, 29 years after graduating high school. My thesis was an overly long, jumbled and nearly incoherent account of my military career. But something good came of writing that scramble. I better understood my position in military and civilian society, as well as the position within those cultures of the people I had served with. My outsider status gained new meaning. Pride in my accomplishments during military service was restored to me. My perspective changed. Writing about my life set me free of the past. Researching my life to write about it helped me to better understand my family, the military, and my place in the world.

Developing and leading Milspeak Creative Writing Seminars is my response to my military experience, to my experience as a disabled veteran, as a woman in the military, as an alcoholic, as a student and as a teacher, and as a writer. Milspeak is an expression of gratitude for all I have been given by my country, its citizens, and the Corps—developing and leading Milspeak is my way of giving back and a way of providing a forum for other military people to break the traditional silence about military life.

II
Writing as a Healing Art and The
Warrior Poet in American Literature

Today's military writing is evolved from a long tradition. *The Iliad*, the Greek poet Homer's epic revelation of war's devastation upon both civilian and warrior, stands out as the first example of military experience translated into literature. In what may be the most poignant metaphorical moment in literature, wild, tormented youth—Achilles—is approached by humble, wise, old age—Priam. The two reconcile their differences in a record-breaking moment of peacemaking. Imagine youth meeting old age over the body of middle age to settle the score between waste of time and waste of life. Both learn the power of forgiveness, both are guided by a power greater themselves to create something greater than themselves. Although centuries separate then from now, writers still attempt to answer the question posed by Homer in *The Iliad*: What hold has higher law in human affairs? The answer is still out there. Writers search for this higher law with every word placed on paper, attempting to confirm or deny its existence through deeper understanding of the human experience.

The Iliad is important not only as literature or as historical, spiritual, and cultural record. Homer's epic also holds a key to understanding the warrior's psychological dilemma. Identified by Dr. Jonathan Shay in his groundbreaking book on the subject, *Achilles in Vietnam: Combat Trauma and the Undoing of Character,*[1] Achilles' actions in response to the death of his brother-in-arms represent the first literary characterization of Posttraumatic Stress Disorder (PTSD).

PTSD was known as Soldier's Heart during the civil war. Who better epitomizes the condition than the character Ashley Wilkes in *Gone With the Wind?* Following WWI, Ernest Hemingway captures the PTSD-afflicted soldier in Krebs, protagonist of "Soldier's Home." T.S. Eliot renders the devastation by war of a generation in his epic poem, *The Waste Land.* Joseph Heller's Yossarian in *Catch-22* encapsulates the imagination of the 1960s peace movement. Tim O'Brien speaks for the infantryman in Vietnam through *The Things They Carried.* Sometimes a writer helps an entire culture or nation assimilate a shared experience, as Margaret Mitchell did with the Civil War in *Gone With the Wind.* Writers sometimes fictionalize personal military experience while trying to make sense of events that happened at ticker tape pace. The result is often amazing, artful, and entertaining, as is the case with Pat Conroy's autobiographical novel, *The Great Santini.*

I have never been diagnosed with PTSD, but I now know that I began experiencing symptoms early in my life. Heavy drinking was self-medication, my way of taking the edge off the brutality I have experienced since childhood. Members of emergency response teams tell me they believe everyone experiencing trauma suffers some degree of PTSD. From experience, I have learned that writing about a traumatic event and/or its aftermath is one way of coping with the mental, emotional, spiritual, and physical syndrome known as alcoholism, and its sibling, PTSD. The two conditions often surface together. Whether or not one is diagnosed with PTSD, writing about traumatic experience diminishes the power of the event to control the future. When the traumatized places him- or herself into the action as a character at a safe distance from the event, either in time or space, the true nature of the event is realized and lessons the sense of survivor's guilt.

Narrative writing has a long history of use as therapeutic, or healing, tool. Perhaps the warriors of old were aware of the healing power of storymaking and storytelling. Maybe that is why literature as we know it today was built by the contributions of many Warrior Poets, why the plots and characters of ancient poems and treatises reappear in today's works, and why so many of today's filmmakers retell Warrior Poets' stories.

The Warrior Poet tradition reaches far into the history of civilization. The Fianna, a band of Gaelic forest warriors led by Finn MacCumhaill, existed two thousand years before the advent of Saint Patrick. These warriors were not aristocrats, but fighters in the trenches, each of them required to memorize the oral history of the clan and its many poetic cycles before becoming one of the Fianna. Finn MacCumhaill, sometimes known as Finn McCool or just Finn, fathered the better-known Irish hero Oisin. Finn is recognized as a hero in Ireland and Scotland. He is sometimes identified as a giant and his men as a clan of giants. Among the Irish, it is believed Finn, like Britain's King Arthur, sleeps in a hidden location and will awaken when needed by his people.[2] Joseph Campbell, the renowned mythologist, relates a story of one of Finn's men, the giant Caeilte, engaged in conversation with St. Patrick:

> Patrick said: 'Was not he a good lord with whom ye were; Finn MacCumhaill that is to say?' Upon which Caeilte uttered the following tribute of praise:
> 'Were but the brown leaf which the wood sheds from it gold,
> Were but the white billow silver;
> Finn would have given it all away.'
> 'Who or what was it that maintained you so in your life?' Patrick asked; and the other answered: 'Truth, which was in our hearts, strength in our arms, and fulfillment in our tongues.'[3]

In defining the Warrior Poet, consider the many ancient Greek and Roman warriors who wrote. Among them stood Homer and Marcus Aurelius, a Roman Emperor who died fighting barbarians on the Danube frontier. Consider any of the many Warrior Poets of many nationalities and eras that you have met through reading: Chinese, Egyptian, African, English, French, Italian, Swedish, Icelandic, Norwegian, American, et al. Imagine their shared qualities: military experience, literary excellence, historical significance, all of them engaged in a search for meaning, and you have met the Warrior Poet: e. e. cummings, Robert Graves, Thomas E. Lawrence, George Orwell, Joseph Heller, Norman Mailer, Leon Uris, Ernest Hemingway, Kurt Vonnegut, Tim O'Brien. Try to imagine literature without these writers, and your definition of Warrior Poet will be complete.

Milspeak writers continue the Warrior Poet tradition by capturing the world of the moment while exploring what science and history cannot: "the human heart in conflict with itself."[4] This phrase of Warrior Poet William Faulkner's is the beating heart of memoir, and of military memoir in particular:

> Our tragedy today is a general and universal physical fear so long sustained by now that we can even bear it. There are no longer problems of the spirit. There is only the question: When will I be blown up? Because of this, the young man or woman writing today has forgotten the problems of the human heart in conflict with itself which alone can make good writing because only that is worth writing about, worth the agony and the sweat.[5]

I use Poet in describing writers of military memoir in the broadest sense: that language is poetic; that creative writers use the poet's tools; that prose, too, can be poetic; and that the literary genres as we know them today, divided and subdivided, still share a common foundation in written language used as communication between inner and outer worlds. Creative nonfiction is a hybrid genre as is memoir, as is poetry, as we know the genres today. Lyric essays, like "Life as Dream," and "Hymn," written by Milspeak writers Yvonne Green and Charlotte Brock, are poetic by nature.

Milspeak writers also continue the traditions of American Literature. Ralph Waldo Emerson, a major influence on American Literature, wrote in his essay "The Poet" that "cause, operation, and effect" go by many different names, including "the Knower, the Doer, and the Sayer" or "the love of truth, the love of good, and the love of beauty." "The sign and credentials of the poet are," Emerson continues, "that he announces that which no man foretold. He is the true and only doctor; he knows and tells; he is the only teller of news, for he was present and privy to the appearance which he describes."[6] Milspeak writers bleed words to describe the military world they have experienced, often in hopes that what they have learned will benefit someone just beginning the journey on a road the writer has traveled. Purists and critics might abhor my use of Poet to describe writers of military memoir, but every writer in the role of language smithy is a poet.

Emerson writes in "The American Scholar" that "Life is our dictionary":

I embrace the common, I explore and sit at the feet of the familiar, the low. Give me insight into to-day, and you may have the antique and future worlds. What would we really know the meaning of? The meal in the firkin; the milk in the pan; the ballad in the street; the news of the boat; the glance of the eye; the form and the gait of the body; —show me the sublime presence of the highest spiritual cause lurking, as always it does lurk, in these suburbs and extremities of nature; let me see every trifle bristling with the polarity that ranges it instantly on an eternal law; and the shop, the plough, and the ledger, referred to the like cause by which light undulates and poets sing; —and the world lies no longer a dull miscellany and lumber room, but has form and order; there is no trifle; there is no puzzle; but one design unites and animates the farthest pinnacle and the lowest trench.[7]

Who can better reveal the everyday in American military life than those who have lived it? Our present day Warrior Poets sing new chants and old while they run in formation. These warriors memorize history, customs and courtesies in boot camp and read from professional reading lists. Today's Warrior Poets are rapping, singing, writing verse, blogging, publishing books, and participating in Milspeak Creative Writing Seminars. So doing, they aren't just finding their voices by writing the truth about their military experiences; our Warrior Poets continue an ancient tradition of honoring the past by keeping it alive in the present. Beyond being a catch-all for the historical and cultural details of military life that might otherwise be lost, Milspeak's most important achievement is bringing together military people from all military branches, all generations of veterans and retirees, members of the military family, and civil service employees. By being inclusive rather than exclusive, our stories have the potential not only to heal wounds of memory, but also to build the civilian community's understanding of military life.

III
How Milspeak Works

Milspeak Creative Writing Seminars (MCWS) is a series of workshops developed for military people who want to write about their experiences. MCWS grew from a shared idea. Several veterans attended the Queens University of Charlotte creative writing program with me. During graduation residency in May 2005, three of us talked about what was next. We agreed we'd like to do something to help veterans, a writing workshop, or something like that. Creating a writing workshop for combat veterans wasn't as difficult as you might think. The Milspeak program is a hybrid of the Queens' creative writing program. That program depended upon a weeklong residency each semester for craft seminars and manuscript critiques, a well as serious and lengthy reading prior to residencies, and an email manuscript exchange to develop writing craft among pod members. Each pod was assigned a writing instructor for the semester. Instructors were published authors and usually held teaching degrees. Each month of the semester, pod members exchanged a new piece of writing for critique by their pod and the pod instructor. MCWS is organized the same way, but in my initial plan writers workshopped one story from idea to final draft through a six-week process. Adapting the Queens' program to the military lifestyle also ensured that the workshop would not become a burden on participants by taking up too much precious off-duty time.

Milspeak is a simple creative writing program designed as an outreach program focused on teaching combat veterans to use narrative writing to assimilate the wartime experience. The program introduces military people to the writing process, helps them understand their own writing process, and transforms their writing. While undergoing the creative process that occurs during each MCWS, participants' understanding of their own experience is transformed. In undergoing the creative process that unfolds during each MCWS, in re-seeing the facts of experience, old fictions of memory can be set aside. The only requirements for participation are membership in the extended military family, an idea for a true story about military life, a willingness to try writing memoir or personal essay, an email account, and access to a computer and a printer. Participants do not pay a fee, although there is minor cost involved in printing manuscripts. I do not receive monetary compensation for my work with Milspeak.

My initial proposal for the Milspeak program called for two one-hour meetings a week over a six-week span. The first workshops were held during lunch, from 11:45 a.m.–12:45 p.m. on Tuesdays and Thursdays. MCWS now meets twice year on five Saturday mornings from 9:00 a.m. to 12:00 p.m. Each MCWS begins with distribution of a flier designed to draw participants, who respond by sending a one-paragraph email to me that explains why the writer wants to attend. A Welcome email and the MCWS Handbook are delivered via email to participants prior to the first workshop (Welcome emails and the handbook are posted on the program website: www.milspeak.org). Delivering the Welcome Email and handouts early allows Milspeak writers time to prepare before Seminar Saturday. During Seminar Saturday, the basics of creative writing and creative critiquing are taught. On Second Saturday, a guest author is invited to speak to MCWS writers about the writing life. Following Second Saturday, writers submit first drafts via email to me. I then distribute drafts to workshop participants for critique. During Third Saturday, Workshop 1, critiques are discussed and suggestions for revision are offered. Revised manuscripts are again routed through me for distribution and critique. During Fourth Saturday, Workshop 2, a roundtable critique discussion offers writers suggestions for revision. On Fifth Saturday, Celebration Saturday Read & Chow, participants come together with family and friends for a potluck breakfast, and final draft manuscripts are read aloud. Each Milspeak writer is also invited to publish his or her work in the Writers Gallery of the Milspeak website. Other opportunities for publication are discussed during each seminar, but writers must do the work to publish to a wider audience.

Since September 2005, Milspeak writers have gathered twice a year to write memoir in a classroom at Marine Corps Air Station Beaufort. A sign above the classroom whiteboard reads, "Blackbird Zone." The sign is a museum piece, as is the SR-71 Blackbird, a spy plane decommissioned several years ago. Milspeak writers' works are artifacts as well. Each memoir is a carefully crafted reminiscence, the telling of a memorable moment in a military life, a personal, cultural, and historical record, a work of art crafted through sweat and anguish for a reader, and has the potential to foster greater understanding of military life among the civilian community. Sadly, these writers' hard-wrought works are often overlooked by a publishing world more often interested in spectacle than in matters of the heart meeting mind over the body of a written page.

Military life isn't all blood-and-guts combat tours. The majority of service members and veterans—there are millions of us—never see a day of combat. Milspeak writers' topics cover the gamut of military life: from caring for a dying veteran to acknowledging the impact of one life upon another, from the drudgery of daily operations to the excitement of enlisting or enlisting someone else. Service members' families' stories, too, are often forgotten or overlooked by the publishing world. The trials and terrors of being the family member of a service member are no less in principle than those experienced by the hardened combat veteran. Civil Service workers supporting operations aboard bases and beyond are the silent million. Their sacrifice is great and their story is untold.

In Milspeak Creative Writing Seminars, these members of the military family are finding a voice, but many participants believe their stories are unimportant. From capturing the sound of rounds fired down range, to humming a song in desperate times, to remembering words spoken by someone lost and brought to life from memory at just the right moment, Milspeak writers are discovering that writing is not only hard and valuable work, but like any art form, it is also one of the healing arts with an ancient past. They are learning that exploring the details of a military life can be salve on an open wound, a balm that allows the future to unfold, not only for the writer but also for the reader. In a country at war, everyone, military or civilian, has a war story to tell and a wound to heal—the story each of us is running from or running down, the brutal truth of loving and losing, of dying and surviving.

Yours is the story only one person can tell.

What follows in this anthology is a narrative thread that begins each chapter and leads to memoir written by Milspeak writers who have participated in MCWS 1 through MCWS 8. The narrative tells the Milspeak story, including my experience developing Milspeak, my findings on Milspeak's accomplishments, and my understanding of the program's potential to assist military people positively assimilate their experiences. In this anthology you will also find memoir and essay by guest contributors who have given time and effort toward developing Milspeak, mentoring Milspeak writers, and serving as MCWS Guest Writers. Each of us has reached into the abyss of meaning and returned with boon, a measure of experience to be shared with you. Caeilte of the Fianna might say, "Truth is in our words, strength is in our pens, fulfillment in sharing our stories with you." In this anthology you might come face to face with your own fear, or your own story. Perhaps, your perspective on military life will be changed by these stories, as mine was. And maybe, if you are a military person struggling to find your place in the world, you will find a way home in the words of these writers, as I have. When Milspeak began, I never imagined the writers I met would lead me home to a sense of belonging in the military family I never felt part of and abandoned when I retired.

Notes:
1 Shay, Jonathan, M.D., Ph.D. *Achilles in Vietnam: Combat Trauma and the Undoing of Character*. New York: Touchstone, 1994.
2 Finn's story is related in many texts. The Fenian Cycle lives in tales like the story of Tristan and Isolt and James Joyce's *Finnegan's Wake*. This version of Finn's story is paraphrased from Internet sources, *The Celts* by Nora Chadwick (Folio), as well as *The Masks of God: Creative Mythology* by Joseph Campbell (Penguin Compass).
3 Campbell, Joseph. *The Masks of God: Occidental Mythology*. New York: Penguin Compass, 1968. 471-472.
4 Faulkner, William. 1949 Nobel Banquet Speech. From *Nobel Lectures, Literature 1901-1967*. Ed. Horst Frenz. Amsterdam: Elsevier Publishing Company, 1969. Downloaded at http://nobelprize.org/nobel_prizes/literature/laureates/1949/faulkner-speech.html.
5 ibid.
6 Emerson, Ralph Waldo. "The Poet." *The Norton Anthology of American Literature*. Fifth Edition, Vol. 1. Nina Baym, General Editor. New York: W.W. Norton & Co., 1998. 1144-1159.
7 Emerson, Ralph Waldo. "The American Scholar." *The Norton Anthology of American Literature*, Fifth Edition, Vol. 1. Nina Baym, General Editor. New York: W.W. Norton & Co., 1998. 1112.

MILSPEAK

MCWS 1

06 September – 14 October 2005

Guest Writer: Richard Peabody

Participants:
Gary
Lu
Dusty Pack
David
"N" – the Narrator

Beside the common incidents of life, it should tell us of his studies, his mode of living, the means by which he attained to excellence, and his opinion of his own works.

—James Boswell discussing Dr. Samuel Johnson's comments on biography from "September 22," in Thomas Boswell's *The Journal of a Tour to the Hebrides with Samuel Johnson, LL.D.*, Riverside Edition, 1965, p. 270.

ANYTHING HELPS

Following graduation from Queens University of Charlotte, I placed great pressure on myself to complete three after-graduation projects: finding employment as a teacher, revising my graduate thesis into a memoir for entry in Middlebury College's 2005 Bakeless literary competition, and developing an unfunded military writing workshop. Bakeless submissions were due in November. I spent my first summer off from school racking my graduate thesis from 500-plus pages to under 300. At one point, I sent a not-quite begging email to Ian Pounds, the Bakeless competition administrator, asking if a manuscript five to seven pages over the 300-page limit would be disqualified. "Please enter. I'll accept your manuscript," he replied.

As for teaching, I had quickly learned that my MFA degree would allow me to teach only basic composition and survey of literature courses as an adjunct instructor. Neither of the two colleges in my area offers creative writing degrees, and had not offered creative writing classes during my undergraduate studies. My new credentials added value to my resume, but lack of academic teaching experience made me noncompetitive for a fulltime position locally or elsewhere. University of South Carolina Beaufort (USCB) did offer me the opportunity to teach two courses during the Fall 2005 semester. I had never before written a course syllabus, and found the research to prepare syllabi for two courses required time, lots of time. Later, the two courses I'd prepared and had been scheduled to teach at USCB were cancelled; then another was sent my way—a week after classes began. What a jolt into teaching! When the pressure grew too intense, I'd imagine how much easier becoming a librarian would have been and how much better the pay would be. As an adjunct instructor during the Fall 2005 semester, I earned $1,500 for four months work. Adjuncts are paid only for time spent in the classroom, usually three hours per week per course. I was paid nothing for the many hours spent developing the courses, preparing for class, or for working with students and their writing, not to mention the hours spent counseling students and performing the many other administrative tasks required by institutions of higher education. I hung onto my hope that adjunct work would somehow translate into a fulltime teaching position, if I had the opportunity to prove myself worthy of my colleagues' respect.

In fact, this capable Marine was terrified of failing to succeed in all three post-graduation projects. I was moving from point A to point B on the road toward excellence simply because each "next step" seemed to be the next right thing to do, and because I believed I was the person who could accomplish the mission. Maybe that's arrogant; maybe it's healthy self-confidence. I needed a good measure of both. Trying to complete my three projects at once was either crazy-ambitious or just plain dumb. I've been accused of both. Fortunately, naïveté is damned good armor against cynicism and the fear of new beginnings, particularly when facing the challenge of starting an unfunded writing program. Had I known in 2005 what I know in 2009—that nearly all of my time would be consumed by my three projects—I might not have continued any of them. I was often frustrated and overwhelmed by the work I was doing. I felt incompetent and inadequately prepared to teach writing to college students or military people. This insecurity was compounded by a self-enforced lack of emotional connection to the military.

After my retirement in 1998, my contact with the military was nil except for the occasional visit to medical or the commissary. Even going grocery shopping at the commissary was avoided unless family visits meant buying extra supplies. I had wanted to walk away from the military forever—no retirement ceremony for me, no membership in the American Legion, no happy hours spent at the Staff Noncommissioned Officers' Club slogging brewskis with Old Salts. I'd had enough of military life and rejection by my military peers to last several lifetimes. My favorite retirement gift is an 8 1/2 by 11 inch paper with a coffee mug stain, yellow footprints, and yellow cane prints. My last names from marriages and divorces are listed: Ginter, Flacco, Ginter, Wyndham, Drumm. Marines I worked with during my last tour of duty signed the paper. The top of the framed paper reads: *Walking Papers,* milspeak for discharge papers. When I retired after twenty years of military life, I effectively divorced the military and was more than ready to walk away with no intention of looking back. Putting myself back among military people by creating a writing program for them was a challenge, a risk I wasn't sure I wanted to take or could handle emotionally.

But writing about military life for my graduate thesis had healed some of my old emotional wounds, our country was at war, and Marines I had trained were serving in Iraq and Afghanistan. Writing had proved a positive experience for me, so I thought it could be a positive creative outlet for the stress and angst of the war experience veterans carry, an experience that often sits untended in a broken place. It could also work for noncombat veterans like me, who encounter tremendous stress during active duty. Our adjustment dilemma upon return to civilian life often goes unrecognized. I had learned plenty about angst during my ongoing recovery from alcoholism. Much of my military career had been affected by my attempts to drink away emotional pain. Truthful writing had allowed me to recognize the successes too often hidden in the disappointments of my military career. In 12-step recovery meetings, I had learned about giving back. One way of doing that is to sponsor, or mentor, those new to recovery. I thought the same principle could be applied to assisting military people with memoir writing in a workshop setting.

Although accepting my disabled status remained troubling and I lacked combat experience, I wanted to reach out to veterans in any way I could. Military people love stories, writing, and poetry, they love sharing their stories with others, and writing had helped me come to terms with my own military experience. No matter their writing skills, I believed that military people would be able to turn an idea into a worthy essay or memoir by using the workshop method—if I could do it, they could, too. Military people will give their all to achieve their goals and they are trained to be systemic thinkers. Teach them a process and success will follow. Would they accept what I offered? I didn't know, but finding participants for a creative writing workshop would not be a problem. A large participant pool exists in Beaufort's Tri-Command area (where I also live), which includes Marine Corps Air Station (MCAS) Beaufort, Marine Corps Recruit Depot (MCRD) Parris Island, and Beaufort Naval Hospital (BNH). Personnel from the Beaufort Triangle were deploying regularly in support of Operation Enduring Freedom in Afghanistan and Operation Iraqi Freedom in Iraq, what I call Gulf War II; Desert Storm is Gulf War I in my milspeak dictionary.

I wasted no time making the memoir workshop a reality. Within a month of graduating from Queens University of Charlotte, I had developed a six-week writing workshop program for war veterans, had put the plan in writing, and was prepared to present it to anyone who would listen. I had no funds to create the program, so finding a place to meet, a way to get the word out, and gaining support from the military community could prove a major stumbling block. I decided to tackle all three problems at once by contacting social services at MCAS Beaufort. I expected a negative response or a run-around, and wasn't disappointed. Social services suggested I contact the Station Education Officer. I figured that office would also redirect me, that no one would be interested sponsoring the workshop, and that it would die before it had a chance to live. I was wrong. The Education Officer agreed to a meeting.

David Ellard gave me a big smile and extended his hand when we met in his tiny office at the back of a classroom in the MCAS Beaufort education building. David is a bear of a man: brawny and intimidating despite his kind eyes and smile. We shook hands and squeezed into his closet-sized office. I knew he didn't have much time to spare. David's position requires the work of three people, as is usually the case with any position in the military and civil service.

I launched into my proposal without wasting a minute. The workshop, I told David, would be a basic introduction to craft, writing guides, and writing resources. Its goal to open war veterans' minds to the possibility of writing as an act of meaning making for an experience that can seem meaningless and brutal. Although methods of debriefing and de-stressing combat veterans had improved since the Vietnam War, the many Reagan-era combat operations, and Gulf War I, the passage of time always has something to add to war veterans' angst. Writing might help with that. If the program worked, it might serve as a model for similar programs at other military installations.

David asked why I would volunteer my services.

I wanted to help war veterans, I answered, and I wanted to give back in return for the education I had received. I didn't want to be paid, not even if pay was offered. The workshop could be held without cost to the government. Leading the workshop would help me, too, by giving me creative writing teaching experience. Building a memoir workshop for military people seemed a worthwhile expenditure of time and energy for them and for me.

David asked me to email my written proposal to him. By the next day, June 14, 2005, the proposal was on his computer, and David immediately began gathering support for the workshop from his superiors at Marine

Corps Community Services (MCCS). As soon as he received permission to proceed, he began figuring the marketing angle—how to get the word out. David asked me to write up a program summary for a flier, which he then created and distributed through the MCCS web-newsletter, *Happenings*. David has continued this practice for each MCWS. The workshop could not have happened without David's belief in the value of the Milspeak program or without the support of MCCS. David has been Milspeak's staunchest supporter. He did the hard work of paving the way through military red tape and publicizing the program by getting us space in *Jet Stream*, the MCAS Beaufort newspaper and in *The Boot*, the MCRD Parris Island newspaper. To keep MCWS growing, David and I discuss learning points after each seminar: what worked, what didn't, and what we could be doing better. This process is similar to but simpler than the way it's done in the Corps after every mission; in business, this practice is sometimes referred to as post-mortem.

David and I agreed that the workshop should not be marketed as therapy, but that we should make counseling contact information available to participants. David believed that if we advertised the workshop as a therapeutic tool, no one would sign up. So did I. This was my introduction to the newest form of an old stigma associated with combat stress-related issues, mental health issues, and addiction issues within the military. Not because David held a negative attitude toward recovery—his outlook was quite positive, but both he and I recognized that many military members will not seek help with problems with living associated with anything termed mental health for fear of repercussions.

In the military, problems with living—anger, missed work, depression, lack of sociability, problems at home that seep into work, sadness and crying, argumentivity, harshness, and the myriad symptoms that signal deeper issues—affect command readiness; in the civilian community, profit is affected. In both the civilian and military communities, supervisors and co-workers often do not realize that acknowledging problems with living and seeking treatment frequently leads to better job performance. It is considered cost effective to avoid hiring someone with such a history, or to let a troubled employee go, rather than to address underlying causes of surface symptoms associated with problems of living. Most employers, military and civilian alike, do not want to get involved, a natural and expected response to the problems of others. Secrecy becomes a way of life for employers and employees.

My experience in recovery from alcoholism and seeking therapy during active duty taught me that a long history of negativity toward therapy and rehabilitation services haunts the military—seeking help can be a career-ender. For exactly this reason, many military people will not admit to having problems adjusting to home-life after war or to civilian life after military service. The Clinton-era slogan "Don't Ask; Don't Tell" has become a catchall phrase for many aspects of military life, and seems to include combat experience and its aftermath. Silence about military life, particularly combat, is traditional in the military. The roots of this tradition are the belief that silence is courageous, that problems equate to malingering, that talk will result in accusations of war crimes, and that civilians will mistake war tactics for murder, in large part due to misunderstanding created between military and civilian communities during the Vietnam War Era. The density of the resulting silence often leaves military people feeling they have no recourse for their problems that will not negatively affect their careers in the service and afterward.

As Milspeak has evolved, so has my understanding of the rehabilitation climate in the military. Those who seek help with trauma are still more often considered malingerers, or whiners, or walking wounded, than they are thought of as responsible people seeking help for real problems with living. This enforces the stereotypical notion that recovery leads only to failure. The stigma attached by military members to mental health and addiction issues is equaled in the civilian world—many civilians hide problems with living in order to preserve their jobs, and many employers will not hire people who have been treated for addiction or mental health problems. In our society, stories about slips in recovery overshadow success stories creating a climate of distrust for those in recovery. Life is already too complicated without having to bear someone else's burden. And yet, when we look the other way, it hurts all of us.

Days before MCWS 1 began, I saw a shaggy man sitting on the curb at the entrance to the parking lot of the Wal-Mart Superstore. He was holding a sign, "Anything Helps." I tried to look the other way, but while I waited for an opening into traffic, my eyes kept cutting back to him. He didn't look like homeless people I'd seen at Okinawa, Japan or Pataya Beach, Thailand. In Japan, as in Beaufort, the homeless were well hidden. Dashing into traffic from hiding places beside the road to beg, Okinawan homeless looked like hermits or impoverished monks—long shaggy hair, a piece of ragged cloth tied with a rope around a famished body, sandals fashioned from cardboard strapped to their feet with string. In Thailand, the homeless were more obvious. Lepers sat on newspapers, their wounds pasted over with scraps of newspaper. A mother once held her baby up to me from where she sat on a curb: she, swaying and holding both a cup and the infant out to me; me, bending over to drop some American Green into her cup, and noticing the child was dead, long dead.

In Washington D.C., where I had attended 12-Step meetings as an in-patient participant in the military's addiction rehabilitation program at Bethesda Naval Hospital, I once met a homeless woman over the sinks in the women's restroom at the National Cathedral. It was wintertime. We were both attending a 12-step meeting at the National Cathedral. Both of us wore heavy coats. It was 1985. Christmas. I was getting sober for the first time since 1972, when I was fourteen and began drinking and drugging.

The old woman and I washed our hands over our separate sinks. We looked at each other in our separate mirrors. I tried not to stare. She looked at me in the mirror, opened her huge coat, smiled a toothless smile, and said, "I don't keep bottles in here no more," while nodding to the many pockets lining the inside of her coat. She closed her coat, turned away from me, and walked out the door.

I stood transfixed. It wasn't because of what she had said or done. I wanted to be as free from addiction as she seemed to be. I was twenty-seven years old, a disgraced drill instructor, a seven-year Marine, and I wanted what the old homeless woman had—freedom from alcoholism. Two years and seven months later, on July 15, 1988, my thirtieth birthday, I picked up the next drink. Seven years later, on January 28, 1992, while stationed in Okinawa, I finally got sober.

You don't see many homeless in Beaufort, a small city with a huge veteran, active military, and reservist population. The story goes that the cops take the homeless to jail; sometimes the Salvation Army pays for a night in a hotel. If the cops see them again, the homeless person is escorted out of town to Gardens Corners at the intersection of US 21 and Highway 17. One way leads to Savannah, Georgia; the other leads to Charleston, South Carolina. Both those cities have halfway houses, addiction centers, and VA hospitals. Beaufort doesn't.

Outside the Beaufort Wal-Mart Superstore on that August morning in 2005, I pulled my Explorer to the curb and rolled down the window.

"You a veteran?" I asked the stringy-haired man holding the "Anything Helps" sign.

"Yeah, Da Nang," he replied.

"Here, take this." I handed him a ten-dollar bill, all the cash I had in my wallet.

"Are you sure?" he asked.

I waved off the question, and asked, "What are you doing out here?"

"Just got out of jail this morning. I got a alcohol problem. Cops kept my car and my dog. My gear, too. I gotta get some gear."

"Look," I said, "I'm a Marine and an alcoholic. There's a meeting at 12 at Alano Hall in Port Royal. 12th Street. Go there. Those guys will help you. And even if you tried getting sober before, try it again. Use that money for food, not booze."

Getting sober takes years, and many tries, but it's possible. Even for Vets like us.

He said thanks, and I drove off to finish my shopping. I didn't even know his name—I hadn't asked—but I was crying as I drove away because I couldn't pick him up and take him to the meeting myself. My emotion was anger, not sadness. It was the injustice of being a woman in our society, the injustice of not being able to help a man because I am a woman, the injustice of futility, of being a woman. I was angry because I couldn't let Anything Helps get into my car without risking my safety and later being told, "You know better." That sense of unfairness felt worse than looking the other way, and I feel it everyday in all I do. Instead of shopping that day, I did what I could and drove to a friend's house, a guy, an alcoholic in recovery, and told him about the Vet on the curb. He went after Anything Helps, to take him to the meeting, to get him off the street, but he was already gone when my friend arrived.

Veterans like "Anything Helps" are why I started Milspeak. My father, a WWII and Korean War Veteran, died homeless.

My mother, brother, and I were separated most of our lives by my father. He divorced my mother when I was two years old. He retained custody of my brother, Byron, who grew up in military academies, served 22 years in the Navy, and helped our father as long as he was allowed to. I met my father only four times in my life, twice as a child after the divorce and twice as an adult. My brother Byron and I didn't get to know each until we were stationed together in 1980, by coincidence, in Hawaii. My father was sexually abusive to me; he was violent and physically abusive toward Byron and our mother. None of us learned of our father's death until six months after he died. The news came in May 2003, on the week of my graduation from University of South Carolina, and two weeks before my first residency at Queens University.

Early into my work on my graduate thesis, my brother informed me that years before our father's death on August 23, 2002, he had been diagnosed schizophrenic by the Veterans Administration. This news motivated me to send for our father's military and medical records—I was concerned I might develop schizophrenia and I wanted to know my father's story, a story he never shared with me. The string of correspondence I received stretched from my father's days as an eighteen-year-old enlisted soldier in WWII to his GI Bill college days at Notre Dame, on through his days in the Korean War as an officer engineer, into his life as a merchant marine, and later, into his life as a ferryboat diesel mechanic in Washington state. The single element stringing his days together was my father's bitterness. This hostility was evident in his correspondence to military authorities and VA representatives, and born of a $75 debt he felt the government owed him from his college days. His records said nothing about schizophrenia, but said plenty about his bitterness. His records also reflect his homelessness, his inability to obtain and retain employment, and the Veterans Administration's refusal to grant disability pay. Throughout years of correspondence, my father continued arguing the $75 due him by the VA. My father, unable to express his frustration on all counts, grasped the frustration he could understand—a $75 payment still due.

While researching my father's life, I came to understand him, the man who had so affected my life in a negative manner. In recognizing his obsession with the past, I recognized my own. Something else was at work in the story my father's military records and awards tell, something my father refused to acknowledge—his inability to cope with problems of living, what I believe is the result of posttraumatic stress syndrome. It is a problem we share. I have learned to cope by undergoing therapy, by attending 12-Step meetings and trying to live the 12 Steps. I survive by reading, writing, and learning, by opening rather than closing my heart to others, and by reaching out to others no matter how often I am turned away. What would it have taken to release my father of his obsession? Payment of the $75? Or recognition that he too was lost, as so many are, in the syndrome that is posttraumatic stress disorder? He was never diagnosed, but his pattern of symptoms fits the pattern of posttraumatic stress syndrome.

How many other veterans from our country's many wars and conflicts have been misdiagnosed? PTSD is a new name for an ancient condition, a psychological wound that no longer warrants a Purple Heart for combat veterans. Too many of our veterans from wars past are left without recourse by laws structured to help only veterans of more recent wars and those either still on active duty or those that receive disability ratings. What about the men and women who serve for a few years only to discover they have no benefits after receiving walking papers? Despite the many problems of an overwhelmed military benefits system, if veterans do not reveal their suffering to those responsible for evaluations, how can they be helped?

In researching my father's life while writing my thesis/memoir, I came to know him. In addition to his records, I also sent for a set of his medals and awards. Have you ever seen a WWII Victory Medal? The ribbon is a rainbow with a river of red running through the center. Nike, the Roman goddess of victory, looks to the right and stands with one foot upon a helmet, symbolic of Mars, the Roman god of war; together they symbolize the end of war. Behind the helmet beneath Nike's right foot, the sun bursts forth symbolizing the dawn of peace. Nike holds a broken sword in her hands, the hilt in her right hand, the blade in her left. On the coin's other side, "United States of America—1941-1945" forms a circle. Within the circle, a feather separates two phrases: "Freedom From Fear and Want," and "Freedom of Speech and Religion," recalling the Four Freedoms humanity cherishes and is willing to die for. Perhaps you have seen this medal. To hold this medal is to hold a nation's beating heart in your hand.

Reading the symbols on my father's twelve medals and awards is like reading a Tarot spread. To meditate upon them is to see my eighteen-year-old father leave the family farm in Oklahoma to enlist in the Army Air Force. It is to see him, an aircraft mechanic and gunner, flying across Africa and Italy, to see him operate the top turret position in a combat zone and to see him fly 23 combat missions in B-25 and B-26 aircraft with the 12th Air Force based at Corsica. To meditate upon his medals is to see him awarded a battle star for meritorious action in combat, to see him leave the service five years older and begin college, and to see him become an Army officer. It is to see him on the bloody fields of Korea, to see him meet my mother upon his return from those fields of death and to see them love each other for awhile. It is to see him divorce her and me, to see him, in 1966, apply to attend school at Mid-Western Broadcasting School in Chicago dreaming of becoming a broadcaster, to see his dream die, to see him molest me on Christmas Eve1967, to see him fail himself and his family, to see him apply for Veterans Benefits in 1997, to see "Homeless" and "No Degree" listed on his application, and to see him find no recourse for his problems with living.

To witness the death of a dream is perhaps the most felling blow a human being can experience. For my father, that blow resulted in obsessing over a $75 debt, the rock he pushed uphill every day of his adult life. His obsession eventually killed him. When my father died, the van he lived in and all possessions in it disappeared. All that I have of my father's story is in his records and his awards—symbols of a life. To meditate upon those medals and awards is to see my father die homeless, broken, and alone. To see Anything Helps sitting on a curb at the Wal-Mart Superstore is to see my father sitting there. To help him is to help my father. Even in death, my relationship with my father continues to grow through writing. He has been an important teacher by showing me what sort of person I do not want to become, and by showing me that the results of an overburdened veterans' care system were as dismaying to him as they were to me and to those who have followed. To me, my father's obsession represents a failed system, a system too overworked, underfunded, and understaffed to provide the care veterans need.

Too many young lives—and with them the lives of their family members—are slipping through the cracks because the Veterans Administration is suffering a form of bureaucratic PTSD. The system has yet to admit the vastness of its dysfunction, a dysfunction that began long before its mistreatment of Vietnam Veterans and Gulf War I Veterans. When Gulf War II ends and a few years have passed, Gulf War II Veterans will discover what other veterans already know—when your war or your service ends, your benefits diminish, the system you to turn to for relief is dysfunctional and suffers from its own trauma. These veterans will also feel as I have felt: that speaking about the system's problems is disloyal and dishonorable. They are taught that to suffer in silence is courageous.

For women warriors, the demand for silence about what they endure is an unspoken requirement for membership in the military. No one knows how the wartime experience is going to affect women veterans in the long run. A cadre of women vets from Gulf War II will probably join the ranks of Anything Helps. Which model of assimilation will they use to unravel the web wartime experience has spun, entangling the spirit in despondency? Will they seek to resolve the conflicts of the human heart in Homer? In Achilles? In Odysseus? Or in Lara Croft? At the very least they will find, as I have, that the ambivalence of their position within ranks, always the outsider because of gender, constantly under the pressure of being perceived as disloyal simply for being Other-than-male[1], is emotionally and spiritually excruciating. Perhaps writing about their military experience will help these women veterans understand their experience, as writing my thesis/memoir has done for me. Perhaps they will learn that demanding equal treatment is not traitorous.

Meeting Anything Helps moved me beyond my insecurities about starting Milspeak by making me realize how a new generation of war veterans might benefit from the support of a writers' organization. "The principle of change," the linguist Ferdinand de Saussure wrote, "is based on the principle of continuity."[2] In Milspeak workshops, seasoned veterans come together with young veterans and find strength in each other. Wars end; the problems created by war never end. Vietnam War Veterans taught us that the real battle unfolds here at home, years after war ends, when there is time enough to examine in memory past events that occurred at ticker tape pace. MCWS 1 was an opportunity to learn if we veterans can fight that battle together by writing together.

The group of twelve writers who responded to the MCWS 1 flier was composed of active duty Marines and Sailors, military family members, and civil service workers. In each sign-up email, the writer included a paragraph about him- or herself and reasons for wanting to participate.

Dear Ms. Drumm,

I am very interested in taking part in your seminar but will be on my honeymoon until the 23d of September. If there is space available and a pre-planned late arrival to the class is permitted, I'd like to take part in your seminar. I flew the CH-46E assault support helicopter in Iraq and Kuwait prior to and throughout the first seven months of OEF. Thank you for your time.

Good Day Ms. Drumm, I am contacting you in regards to the upcoming Creative Writing Seminar Sep. 6 - Oct. 14. I am very interested in attending. I have been working on a book for the past year and a half. I would be further along but, I have done two combat tours with 3/4 in that time plus a move to Beaufort. I have a good friend who is published with which I have confided my story. He feels it is very good and needs to be finished. Now that my life is a little slower here in the "slow country," I am re-prioritizing my goals putting this book on top. I would really appreciate a spot in your workshop please. Thank you for your time and have a great day!

Good Morning,

I received the information about the Creative Writing Class from my CWO4, he thinks it is a wonderful idea and so do I. I would like to attend the class to broaden my horizons. I have taken English 1 and 2 in college and find English to be my best subject. It would be very interesting to hear the guest speakers and maybe get the names of some good books to read in my spare time. Thank you for your time.

Mrs. Drumm,

My husband told me about a writing class that was coming up that I am very interested in attending. All my life all I've ever wanted to be was a writer. It's about the only thing that I am passionate about. I know that there is limited space in the class but I would work hard and listen with a open mind if I am about to take the course. I am sure that I could benefit from the class. I love to write but some times is hard for me to put pen to paper and express my thoughts. I just need so additional instruction. As I said before writing is the only thing that I am even half way decent at and I still need help with that. I hope to here from you and be sitting in your class soon. Thank you so much for reading my email.

After reading these and many other emails, my fear of placing myself back among military people vanished because these writers wanted what I was offering—the workshop wasn't a crazy idea. The emails also reminded me why I had so loved being a troop leader. These combat veterans, wives, and civil service employees, all members of the military family, were so earnest, so humble. They were thanking me for my time, for reading email! How could I not invest my energy to make their writing workshop into something worthy of their time? One thing I soon learned—military people who sign up for MCWS are just like everyone else: they are yearning for someone to listen to their stories without passing judgment. What matters is getting those stories into the open, uncovering the truth, and providing a safe haven to share traumatic experience. These, not therapy, were the goals of the writing workshop. I am not a therapist, but I do know from experience that finding your voice and having your say is sometimes enough to improve quality of life. In Milspeak workshops, I don't analyze writers; I interpret their writing. We wear civilian clothing and not our rank. In workshop we are writers with military experience, not officers leading and troops following.

Most Milspeak writers have not had formal training in writing as craft, and most of their writing and critiquing work is done at home. Critiquing others' writing is a difficult skill for Milspeak writers to learn. For help, I turned to Rebecca McClanahan's excellent advice in a critique handout given to her writing students. Rebecca, one of my graduate school writing instructors, allowed me to use a modified version of her handout. MCWS handouts were combined by David Ellard prior to MCWS 5, and are now distributed as the Milspeak Handbook. Delivering the Welcome Email and Handbook early allows Milspeak writers time to prepare before our first meeting.

Some of the handouts and the format for Milspeak were developed with assistance from others of my Queens writing instructors. Not one of these professionals ever said, "You can't do this." They also didn't tell me how complicated I was making everything. My naiveté in 2005 served as armor by shielding my hopes of success for Milspeak, and for my writing and teaching future. My teachers knew I had to learn for myself whether or not I was a teacher and a writer. I try to practice this philosophy with Milspeak writers. I didn't realize when Milspeak began how difficult developing and leading a writing program for military people might be, but, in large part, my twenty-year military career was spent developing and leading training. How much more difficult could developing a writing program be than training Marines to do a hundred things at once? Knowledge is power: give a service member a process to follow and the job will be done. Tell a Marine an objective is impossible to achieve, and you have a major battle on your hands. That's why they say, "Tell it to the Marines."

Richard Peabody, publisher of *Gargoyle* magazine, emailed shortly before MCWS 1 began to tell me that he was planning a reading tour. My writing was first published in *Gargoyle*. I had stayed in touch with Richard, who is also a poet, fiction writer, and anthologist. I invited him to stop in Beaufort to speak to Milspeak writers. To make the stop at MCWS worthwhile, poetry readings at USCB and a local bookstore were arranged. The Milspeak tradition of asking a guest writer, someone with publishing success willing to share his or her experience of the writing life, to join us began with Richard. When Hurricane Katrina destroyed New Orleans and much of the Gulf Coast days before MCWS 1 began, Richard's readings were transformed into a mini-fundraiser for Long Beach, Mississippi, Beaufort's adopted sister-city. Long Beach was devastated by the storm. When an email interview I held with Richard was published in *Lowcountry Weekly*, an arts and entertainment newspaper, I included the information about our mini-fundraiser for Long Beach. I plastered Beaufort with fliers announcing the event.

Although MCWS 1 began with a list of twelve names, only five writers attended the first workshop. I read first drafts carefully, provided marginal notes, my interpretation of the piece, and suggestions for revision in a note to each writer. This element of the Milspeak program remains unchanged.

Dusty Pack, Gulf War II Veteran and enlisted man, wrote about the challenge of climbing what seemed to him the tallest tree in his state when he was seven years old. Another Gulf War II Veteran, Alexis, wrote about a place called Enchanted Rock where she had made the decision to attend Annapolis. David, a former recruiter and military investigator, wrote about a day in his life trying to make recruitment numbers in a world of opposing forces: Family, Work, Self. Lu, wife of a Gulf War II Veteran, thought she might write about fear, and explained that her fear was greater when her husband left for boot camp than when he left for Iraq. Gary, a detective who hadn't been able to attend the workshop, emailed his story, a staccato narrative about a journey to a murder scene, the investigation, and of trying to make sense of one human being's acts of aggression against another.

Of the five writers who submitted first drafts, only Lu showed up for the Tuesday workshop of our second week. It seemed the first MCWS might be the last due to lack of interest. I tried to hide my disappointment, but Lu seemed to feel let down, too. While we were discussing her memoir, a man dressed in swat team gear raced into the classroom pointing a brown guard mail envelope in my direction.

"I can't attend today," he said. "I have to investigate a death across the street."

Ah-ha! —The detective who hadn't yet attended a workshop but had emailed his work. "You must be Gary?" I asked.

"Yes, yes, and I'm really sorry, but I have to run. Here," he said, pressing the envelope into my hands. "This is my revision. I brought copies for the other people in my group."

"Thank you. That's so thoughtful. Well, I'm glad to meet you." My words fell into the open doorway where Gary had been standing.

Remember, wherever you are with your writing, it is okay.

Milspeak writers and my twenty college students were invited to attend Richard Peabody's poetry reading at the USCB Performing Arts Center. All would have gone well, had I not flustered the USCB Chancellor with my fundraising plan. Via a flurry of email, I realized that the Chancellor thought I was trying to undermine her own Katrina Relief fundraising efforts, which I knew nothing about as an adjunct. Adjuncts were not in the university's information-for-faculty loop and were not included in faculty meetings. Two things happened. Adjuncts were added to the faculty mailing list and I never again taught at USCB. Only one faculty member attended Richard's reading. This was a cold introduction to university politics. Richard's reading at the bookstore went better, although the owner almost cancelled. She was just opening the store and worried that Beaufort's conservative population would shun her business if she hosted a liberal poet's reading. Richard's reading at the bookstore raised about $125 for Katrina Relief, which I handed over to an aide in the Mayor's office. Fortunately for my teaching career, a USCB English professor recommended me to Technical College of the Lowcountry.

Anything helps as life goes on for each of us, our journeys unfolding like oars clattering from a rowboat caught up in the outgoing tide, each of us attempting to make meaning from experience while time slips by. Years after Hurricane Katrina, the people of the Gulf Coast are still clinging to the oars; their lives remain battered. "It isn't for the moment you are struck that you need courage, but for the long uphill climb back to sanity and faith and security," Anne Morrow Lindbergh wrote of her personal battle to overcome adversity.[3] This statement holds true for disaster victims, for warriors, veterans, their families, and for fledgling teachers, writers, and writing workshops. Revising our lives after disaster is perhaps the hardest and most rewarding work we will ever do.

Milspeak received good news during MCWS 1. NEA (National Endowment for the Arts) began "Operation Homecoming" in 2002. The project was designed to collect in a national archive the personal stories of Gulf War II Veterans and their families. A group of distinguished authors sponsored by NEA visited several bases and spoke with military personnel about the program and writing. I didn't learn about the program until Richard Peabody told me about it and suggested I contact NEA for help with Milspeak. After sending several emails that went unanswered, the NEA sent program brochures and CDs for Milspeak writers. In a way, I'm thankful that NEA didn't offer financial support. Since its inception, Milspeak has operated without funding or overhead. In the Corps we say: "Can do, Make do"—Milspeak embodies this spirit.

Beatrice Figueroa, a salesperson at Pearson Longman publishing, also helped Milspeak grow by sending ten copies of Catherine L. Hobbs' book, *The Elements of Autobiography and Life Narratives*. It's a small book, handy and complete. Of the many requests to publishers for materials to share with Milspeak writers, only Beatrice responded. In fact, Beatrice's was the *only* response to dozens of emails I sent to publishers. The books were lent to MCWS 1 writers. I asked them to sign their names inside the front cover and return the books when workshop ended. Signing the books became a Milspeak tradition.

A mentor also entered my life while Milspeak was coming to life. Tristine Rainer, founder of Center for Autobiographic Studies (CAS), and I began corresponding shortly after she received my fan letter thanking her for writing the book, *Your Life as Story: Discovering the "New Autobiography" and Writing Memoir as Literature*. Her book was helpful in revising my thesis. Tristine and CAS were important to Milspeak's development. During the first two years of Milspeak's evolution, the CAS website provided a home on the Web for Milspeak writers. Because of website exposure, several people contacted me to ask if they might use the program as a model for their own workshops with veterans. I always say yes. I've never felt I own Milspeak. Continuing the workshop is a calling, work that I love that gives me purpose, adds something positive to the lives of others, and continues to show me how to be a better writer, teacher, and person.

Tristine encouraged me, inspired me, and shared her thoughts with me on teaching at a time when I was devastated by Lynn Freed's article, "Doing Time: My Years in the Creative-Writing Gulag."[4] The subjects of Freed's article were MFA students, MFA programs, and the narrator's relationship with both. Her take on the environment wasn't positive—her article stated that too many poor writers were getting into one of too many MFA programs. These poor writers were creating 500-page theses for their programs. Freed, an MFA program instructor, reported she was worn out by all the traffic. At the time I read the article, Freed the Narrator angered and devastated me for many reasons. I was one of those 500-page thesis writers. I was one of those pitifully amateur writers struggling to publish.

Lynn Freed's article helped me understand why many doors remain closed when I knock on behalf of Milspeak and Milspeak writers. Rejection isn't personal—it is über-personal, collateral damage of class warfare. I have encountered the psyche of both the academic and publishing cultures reacting to the presence of the wanna-be, the modern Other who hasn't worked, struggled or dwelled in the bowels of academia or journalism long enough to warrant respect for their pitiful writing projects, never mind dreams of publishing and full-time teaching positions. Bias is alive, well, and thriving in America. No matter its origin, bias is equally damaging to victims and perpetrators. Both are often unaware of the role bias plays in breaking the bridge of human relations, separating those who could learn from each other. In 2005, I was just stepping into the flame of rejection, and already I understood that help would be difficult to find. But I believed that anyone who wanted to write could write well if they learned to by using the workshop method, and worked hard. Without realizing at the time what I was doing on many different levels, to develop and lead Milspeak has been an experiment in nurturing writers from any social or economic class. The work of Milspeak writers is proof that nurturing can produce good writing from any social or economic class.

Anything Helps.

I needed all the help I could get—the workshop idea seemed destined to die with MCWS 1. Only three writers attended MCWS 1 during our fifth week. Attrition was understandable, no matter how disappointing. Revising is hard work, writing is revising, and I was an inexperienced, demanding teacher stumbling through my first experience as a workshop leader. The initial workshop plan had fallen apart during MCWS 1's first meeting. My idea of what would work for the writers differed from what actually did work. We did talk briefly about *Jarhead*, which was on the initial seminar schedule. No one wanted to read the book. Both the book and the film had been the subject of scathing commentary by military people who spread their contempt through the Internet. The controversy found its way to my desktop. What was it they found to fear in *Jarhead*? Reality? In the book-length memoir by Anthony Swofford, a Marine gets out of the Corps following Desert Storm, kills himself, and his friend suffers survivor's guilt. Survivor/Narrator finds release and solace through writing about the time the friends served together and the pressures they endured. Did the book and the film diminish the reputation of the Corps? Will my own writing and that of Milspeak writers receive such rejection? If so, let it come. Have your say. Throw your stones—label the work narcissistic, solipsistic, ignorant, uneducated. Above all else, find your voice. Say your truth. Your words will fall like leaves on the magnolia-scented night.

Of the three writers who stayed with MCWS 1, Lu, the wife of a young enlisted Marine, veered away from writing directly about fear to writing about a ghost story her grandfather had told many times during her girlhood. But Lu, who was pregnant, grew tired of revising her work and stopped attending workshop. Dusty Pack, who always came to workshop in desert cammies, seemed to sweat sand from every pore. He struggled to revise his piece, a self-questioning, reflective, rite of passage memoir. The heart of this piece was "I wonder...how my life would have turned out if I never climbed that tree." Thinking back on climbing a huge tree, his biggest childhood accomplishment, "N" the Narrator questions his actions as an adult, his involvement in war, and reflects upon his tree climbing adventure in search of an answer. The theme is lost innocence. Thematic conflict emerges from the dynamic between what N wanted as a boy and discovering what he has lost and gained as a man. His is the story of finding a way to be the hero in his own life, what Charles Dickens suggested is the primary work of every human being.

I have searched for Dusty Pack, who attended our last workshop, a celebration of accomplishments and a read aloud of final drafts. I invited him to read from the last draft he workshopped. He declined. I felt responsible for his frustration. I had asked a lot of him and of all the writers. We had workshopped a memoir from idea through five revisions during our six-weeks together. The writers were asked to revise over and over, to re-see their work through the eyes of a reader. They had come to MCWS with an idea for a story. They had worked hard. When they left, they had a story in mind, if not in hand. But losing Dusty Pack still bothers me. His email addresses no longer exist. Did he finally conquer the dervish that left the scent of hot sand in his trail?

Two Davids appear in this anthology, David Ellard and David Charles. David Ellard, my Marine Corps Community Services liaison, continues to assist in developing Milspeak. David Charles' MCWS 1 memoir about a day in the life of a recruiter reflects on the conflict between Corps' values, family values, and personal values. The theme is maintaining integrity in the presence of the values and expectations of others. At the end of his day, does N find Corps' family values imperfect? Is creating the perfect family possible? Or has N found that despite the flaws he finds in himself and others, perfection is not only an unreasonable demand that others have placed on him, but also an onus he has placed on others and himself in particular? In answering this question, N completes the hardest task of all, achieving self-acceptance. David's piece in this chapter was initially titled "Numbers," but numbers were a thing to be ignored as MCWS 1 came to a close. David, with his talent for dry humor, was the only writer to submit a final draft for MCWS 1.

Notes:

[1] Consider Emmanuel Levinas: *Totality and Infinity*. Trans. Alphonso Lingis. PA: Duquesne Univ. Press, 1969.

[2] Saussure, Ferdinand de. *Course in General Linguistics*. Charles Bally and Albert Sechehaye, eds. Roy Harris, Trans. LaSalle, IL: Open Court, 2002. 75.

[3] Quoted in *Each Day a New Beginning*, "September 10," Hazelden Foundation, 1982.

[4] *Harper's* vol. 311, no. 1862 (July 2005): 65.

REACH OUT IN THE DARKNESS

By Richard Peabody

I first met Sally Drumm via Martin Seay, a gifted fiction writer who'd been one of my Johns Hopkins students. She sent me a wild creative nonfiction piece, which I printed in *Gargoyle* #48. After an interesting correspondence Sally invited me down to Beaufort, SC for a couple of readings she'd cobbled together at the university and a local bookshop, with the added enticement of a workshop at the Marine Air Base. I stitched together a mini-tour including gigs in Charlottesville, and Charlotte, NC. Everything dovetailed nicely around a literary festival at Florida State in Tallahassee.

Now, when I agreed to all of this I kind of figured I could handle anything. I'd taught middle school kids, college freshmen, high school students, and grad school. While I'd never taught any military types, I'd always been good at breaking the ice by giving students exercises and making them write to my prompts. But the more time I had to think about the workshop on my drive down Interstate 95, the more I wondered if I wasn't the wrong guy for the job.

My only dealings with the military had been a year of college ROTC at Ohio University during the Kent State era, when I'd walked to class stoned out of my mind while in uniform only to be greeted by hippie chicks who asked me, "How many babies did you kill today?" I was stunned that they couldn't tell I was stoned just like they were. And hell, I needed the ROTC Aid to go to college. All of this came apart a few weeks later when I had younger Ohio National Guardsmen training their rifles on me.

The morning after the Kent State shootings, the governor of Ohio had closed all Ohio colleges and commanded that out-of-state students must be across the border within 24 hours. In that pre-cell phone era every single student at Ohio's numerous colleges reached for the phone to call home at the exact same moment crashing everything. My roommate and I walked uptown through broken glass and pepper spray to the main drag, where Athens' two streets intersected. We were stunned by the damage—broken glass, boarded up windows, rubble, you name it. And there were guardsmen every 12 feet.

We crossed the street to go to the bank to withdraw some money in those pre-ATM days, and since there was no traffic, crossed mid-street. We were about three steps onto the blacktop when the Guardsmen turned their weapons on us. Somebody shouted, "Halt." Strange when you realize we had short hair and didn't look that different from any of them. A couple privates walked out into the street and forced us back to the "Don't Walk" sign at gunpoint. I was so angry I was shaking. One of the kids dared me to fight by giving me a finger-wave "C'mon" with his left hand. I think that was the first time in my life I really wanted to kill someone. When the light changed to "Walk" they allowed us to cross. But everything had gone sour.

Needless to say that was the end of ROTC for me. I wound up being a pretty good shot, but worthless at marching or giving orders. At the time, the fact that I knew more about military history and tactics than any of my ROTC professors appalled me.

So the idea of having anything to do with Marines was near anathema.

So, what happened? Well, I was older than most of the folks in my class at the base. Sally had prepped them on my work and me. They were as passionate as she was about writing and all pumped up. I had exercises prepared for these men and women, but what I remember is an intense group driven by desire to complete stories they felt had to be told. This was 2005 and post 9/11 Bush America. I had a chip on my shoulder having driven down from the belly of the beast that is Washington, D.C. with my "Bush is a Punk Ass Chump" bumper sticker on the back of my van. What I ended up doing was giving them an intro course on the "ins and the outs" of the NY publishing world as I'd experienced it. I don't want to rain on people's parades, but so many beginners want to be Stephen King by tomorrow—to rack up instant fame, fortune and immortality—that it's tough to be the chief purveyor of truth. I talked a lot about alternative publishing, agents, sending stories to literary magazines, and the marketplace. The group asked intelligent questions and possessed that rare combo of energy and experience that seemed promising. Some of them were raw beginners but others had the spark that could ignite something meaningful. All of them were searching for a place in the tribe of writers.

In the end my fear and loathing was all smoke and mirrors. These were folks just like any I've encountered anywhere else—students like those in my classes since I began teaching back in 1985. I did as I always try to do—teach students self-reliance, steer them to the info they'll need to market themselves, feed them as many tips and short cuts as I can in the time allotted, and if I can't talk them out of this crazy business, give them a swift kick in the pants and give them permission to submit their work.

Sally has identified other members of the military tribe who are most like herself—hungry for words, dying to share stories, anxious to get into print, or just hoping to sort out their thoughts and experiences. My role as always is to kick-start engines, point them toward the bright lights, and let go of the steering wheel. In the end I'm grateful for the experience. While it was nothing like I expected, I think I'm the wiser for participating.

ALWAYS FAITHFUL

By David Charles

I stepped into the recruiting office at 5 p.m. and was greeted by "What'cha got?" belched out by the Master Gunnery Sergeant in charge of the station. I disrespectfully thought of him as "the old sergeant" or "the boss salesman." I didn't like what he brought to the Marine Corps uniform that we wore daily.

"Not much success yet. I'm working on it though," I replied, trying to stay positive. The day's nearly fruitless efforts flashed through my mind. Like most days of the past several months, seven days a week, I arrived at work about 7:30 a.m. knowing I could look forward to working until after 10 p.m.

"Working? Only one of your appointments showed up and you disqualified him like it was cool!" said the old sergeant. Cutting off my reply, he continued, "If you didn't make appointments with disqualified people, you wouldn't have to work so hard and maybe you could put your three bodies in the Marine Corps this month!"

"You know I screen them right before making appointments," I protested. "I can't help it if they turn out to be druggies, criminals, stupid or just plain broken when they sit down for a complete screening and I get them talking. But wouldn't you rather I screened them out during the initial interview than to have them disqualified after we've spent days or weeks on them?"

"Don't tell me you're working when you know it's results that count!"

The old sergeant was bellowing as if he had an itch in a bad place today.

"What I would prefer is that you got your three appointments, you had them show up, you gave them a good interview, you made them want to join the Corps, and you got 'em processed and in the Corps! Use your investigator stuff to convince them to say yes, not to say they are disqualified! Maybe then you could get home to that family of yours at a reasonable hour!" He about-faced and marched back into his office.

I walked to my desk. Shake it off and make these phone calls count, I thought while I got the marketing lists back out. But my mind wandered.

Being assigned to recruiting from my usual job as a criminal investigator was both good and bad. As an investigator, I wasn't afraid to talk to people and ask them questions, but as a recruiter I seemed twice as likely to find out the prospect was disqualified. Once a successful screening was done, I smoothly conducted the interview because I had interviewed so many people as an investigator. Still, I felt I had to be honest. As an investigator, I had success reading people and getting them to tell the truth. As a recruiter, I had success getting them to tell me what they thought they needed and then explaining to them how the Corps could meet that need. One out of two interviews ended with the qualified prospects saying they wanted to join the Corps. As an investigator, I had been awarded two Navy Achievement Medals. As a recruiter, the medals and awards pinned over my heart on my starched staff sergeant's uniform only helped with my public Marine image. Despite the advantages that being an investigator brought me as a recruiter, the biggest effect of my investigative skills on recruiting duty was a wide path of disqualified prospects left in my wake.

A recruiter's tasks are based on statistics. Mine went something like this: To get three new people with signed contracts each month, I needed five people to pass my thorough screening and say they wanted to be Marines. You may wonder why the stats demanded I get five prospects to become applicants each month. Two of them would not make it into the Corps. The reasons for that were: Parents are often pro Marine Corps until their young Johnny or Molly say they want to join. Molly and Johnny themselves sometimes have second thoughts of their own and they wonder if they can actually handle being a Marine; after all, I am honest with them about what it is like. Finally, the MEPS (that's the military entrance processing station) would occasionally find health problems even the applicant didn't know about.

Getting back to those tasks based on statistics, stay with me now as I get through how the numbers worked out. To get the five applicants to say they want to be Marines, I needed to interview ten prospects that could pass tough screening. To get those ten, I needed twenty to show up for an appointment and allow the screening. To get those twenty, I needed appointments with about fifty people who I had initially screened. That's because so many of them chickened out and never even showed up for their appointments. To get those fifty appointments, I had to approach and talk to a lot of people.

I talked to those people either on the telephone or in person, what we called daily recruiting activities. Those activities included about 200 telephone calls each day, and, getting back to this day at a little after 5 p.m., I'd made about seventy-five phone calls (not counting the disconnected or wrong numbers), and about ten area canvasses, which actually meant obtaining contact information of qualified prospects at high schools, businesses, restaurants and various other locations. I'd also made six contacts (not counting those immediately disqualified or who refused to give "follow-up" information); and three "home visits," knocking on doors at homes where someone had shown some interest in enlisting in the Marines in the past. I'd made all three home visits that day with the usual lack of success; they no longer lived there. All those daily recruiting activities were supposed to result in three appointments for the next day, every day. Making all those "numbers" was occasionally impossible, especially the "three appointments for the next day."

I looked back at the lists and decided to make a head call before a telephone call. Cause sometimes, that old sergeant just made me want to shit!

"Slacking off again? Get busy and sell someone on the Corps!" bellowed the old sergeant. He didn't even know what the real Marine Corps was like anymore. He had been on recruiting duty for sixteen years, and he was out of touch with reality, judging by the half-truths I heard him spouting to prospects: Boot camp isn't as hard as people think it is; You only work eight hours a day on average, once you get to the fleet; You'll get a promotion every two years on average, and every six months at first. He was not familiar with the truth or he chose to ignore the truth. Either way, his way was not my way.

"You know you're not going home until you have an interview and three appointments for tomorrow!" the old sergeant regurgitated.

When I returned to my desk from the bathroom, the old sergeant was heading out the door with his Bible. According to the recruiters who had been there longer than I, that was no Bible study he was going to! He was off to another affair. It seemed prospects weren't the only people he enjoyed lying to. Scuttlebutt was he had a former mistress at home for a wife and a new mistress on the side. I was just glad he was leaving. Excuse me but my career job was as a criminal investigator. I know trash when I smell it! Integrity was very important to me as a husband, father, investigator, and Marine. This grungy, old fart of a salesman wouldn't know integrity if it poked him in the eye.

The old sergeant was the guy I had to call every night to get approval to secure—to leave work, to go home at night. I had to call the boss, the old sergeant, and report my numbers every evening. During each call, I could expect to receive a lecture about my sorry performance, unless I had actually enlisted someone in the Corps that day. The old sergeant was a taskmaster who genuinely enjoyed pushing my buttons.

After almost five hours of talking to people on the phone and going out and talking to people at malls, stores, and various other public places, I felt done for the day. I made the required 10 p.m. phone call to the boss without three appointments for the next day, expecting another demoralizing lecture.

"What'cha got?"

"Four appointments, two for tomorrow."

"Keep looking," he huffed. "Go out and find a good appointment for tomorrow. Call me at eleven."

The next call was to my wife, Marty, the third call to her that day.

"I don't know why you don't just come home," she said. "It would be better if you were sent overseas again. At least then I didn't expect you home."

Until I began recruiting duty, we had thought my time overseas without the family was the worst thing we were going to face besides combat.

Dragging ass, I continued to approach people around 7-Eleven stores and such, acting like I just happened to be stopping by on my way home from work.

At 11 p.m., I made the next required call to the old sergeant.

"What'cha got?"

"I talked to some more people to call back over the next couple days but all the legitimate businesses are closing up."

"You are going to stay out there and canvass the bars until you make that appointment with a qualified applicant! And don't secure until you've got one!" he ordered.

I called home for the fourth time.

"I still don't understand why a thirty-year-old staff sergeant in the Marine Corps can't come home at a reasonable hour." Marty moaned. "This is stupid. Just come home!"

I canvassed about three or four rank, stale bars. Each reeking with odors that reminded me of my alcoholic, chain-smoking, family-abandoning father. I avoided the mumbling, stumbling drunks who called out, "Marine, come join me for a drink." I watched men in their early twenties turn their backs when they saw me approaching their pool tables. Some of them saw me as a shark in their swimming hole and dove for cover. I was more like a lifeguard, offering to lift them out of their fetid water, only they couldn't see me underneath the pressed uniform with expert shooting badges, personal decorations, and the famous dress-blue trousers with scarlet "blood-stripe" down the seams. Enlisted Marines shedding their blood at the Battle of Chapultepec had earned the blood-stripe. Only non-commissioned officers and staff non-commissioned officers are given the honor of wearing blood stripes on their uniforms. I felt the only blood a recruiter feared shedding was that of his career if he strayed from honesty and was caught fraudulently enlisting someone who was disqualified. Over the next two hours, I managed conversations with about five prospects that seemed to recognize me for what I was without the fear of being caught.

Finally, a little after 1 a.m., I struck up a conversation with a prospect destined to become the required appointment. He was a healthy-looking man in his early twenties. He appeared only slightly under the influence of the untold drinks he had consumed.

"Yes," the prospect said, "I would like to find out more about the Marine Corps."

I waded in further, "... but not everyone can be a Marine." I listed the things that keep men out of the Corps: drugs, health problems, lack of education, inability to pass written and physical tests, and on and on.

The prospect replied positively each time with things like: I wouldn't want to be in the Corps with people on drugs either; I don't have a problem with that; I'm good there. He answered each disqualifier with a qualifying remark.

As I discussed the importance of Marines, the prospect interjected, "I've always thought of joining the Marines."

I paused.

"What are you doing when you get up tomorrow?" I asked.

"Not much, why?"

"Well I'm about to get out of here, but why don't we get together around two o'clock so I can tell you more about the Corps," I suggested.

"Sounds good," He said.

After ironing out the details and writing down his contact information, I finally left the musty tavern and drove home, exhausted and sweaty. The smoke and stale booze clung to my uniform and drifted through the car, evoking memories of winter car rides with my smoking father, Canadian Mist on his breath, my three brothers and me squeezed in the back seat with the windows rolled all the way up.

I opened my window to let in a breeze. I could not wait to get a shower and then get some sleep. Unfortunately, my home was half an hour away. It seemed like a good idea when Marty and I chose it, but it was too far from the office considering my already too long day. While no castle, it was far more appealing than the rusted, modified, mobile home of my childhood, where the addition made of scrap wood was better than the original trailer. My modest, three-bedroom house was a block away from the beach to make it as nice as possible for my family.

I eased into the dark, quiet house about 2 a.m., trying not to disturb our children.

"Where have you been?" Marty asked, sounding half asleep.

I was undressing as I went through the bedroom and into the master bath. My dress shoes landed just inside the bedroom door. My dress-blue trousers landed on top of a dresser, the blood stripe gleaming in the dim light. My sweaty uniform shirt hit the floor by the bathroom door. "You know where I've been, out looking for an appointment as ordered." I said, and my underwear hit the bathroom floor.

"I hate you being out so late! Who in their right mind is going to try to make appointments all night? You always take your shower in the morning. What's really going on?"

She sounded angry and hurt.

I couldn't hide behind orders tonight. I didn't say a word. My day was all talk, too much talk with too many people, Marines at work, students and staff at schools, workers at businesses, any people wherever I found them, ultimately, even malcontents in the bars. My job as a recruiter was to become known, to build a positive reputation with each body I met, whether in person or over the telephone, and put the eligible bodies in the Corps. The only people that didn't seem to matter to the Corps were my family. I wanted my tour as a recruiter to end, but it wouldn't for two more years.

This doesn't make any more sense to me than it does to Marty, I thought as I stood in the shower. No one in a bar after eleven is in any shape to really commit to a next day appointment. Hell, after tonight I'm not going to be in any shape to conduct an interview anyway! The water I had dreamed of rained down on my body but brought no relief.

"You always take your shower in the morning. What smell are you trying to hide?" Marty called out while I was drying off. The fragrance of soap replaced the smell of sweat and cigarette smoke on my body, but I still felt dirty and the acid taste in my mouth was growing stronger.

I climbed into bed. Marty was silent, but her almost imperceptible movements told me she was crying. I thought she wanted to know if I have some honey on the side like the old sergeant, but I didn't want to have to deny it—if I were enough like the old sergeant to be unfaithful, I would have just lied about it like he did. Marty's back was to me. I placed a hand on her shoulder. She immediately shrugged away from my touch. It was only a slight movement and yet, it hurt like a slap. I just lay there with nothing right to say.

The glowing numbers on the clock said it was a short night before I had to get back up and start another recruiting day. Instead, the night dragged on forever. I did not rest. My mind buzzed with numbers and conversations from the day, recruiting numbers I may not be able to reach and swarms of disappointment lying in wait for me to fail: the old sergeant wanting to make quota; prospects wanting to become a Marine without any sacrifice; Marty wanting me to give more time to the family like I always had before recruiting duty; everyone expecting me to live up to their image of a Marine; the disappointment I would feel if I allowed such pressures to grind me down like my father or the old sergeant. My wife could not understand why I just didn't lie to the old sergeant and come home when I was ready to.

That's when it struck me. That was what the old salesman wanted, too.

The old sergeant wanted me to lie. If I gave up my integrity, he could get more contracts out of me. If I bent my morals in his direction just once, he could get me to do it in any situation. I was technically a very good recruiter; we both knew it, but technically proficient was not good enough.

A prospector can do everything right and end up with no gold in his pan at the end of the day. I had done everything right and still ended up empty-handed—disqualified prospects were no good to anybody. A recruiting boss may not want his recruiters to get caught frauding people into the Corps but he is willing to risk it to make his station's mission. Like a grunt in a battle, one blown-up, caught-cheatin' recruiter in the battle to meet the numbers is an acceptable casualty of war. I was not going to be an integrity casualty of this war. Recruiting was a job I was ordered to do, but I still had a family to provide for and a career to get back to after the recruiting war ended. I am not my father. I am not the old sergeant. I am still the man of my house, a husband, a father, a Marine, and an investigator as well as a recruiter. I was resolved.

I didn't know how, but I wouldn't give that up.

MCWS 2

24 January – 23 February 2006

Guest Writer: Warren Slesinger

Participants:
Gary
Debra
Melissa
Anthony
"N" The Narrator

Theoretically, perfectly, what one wants to do is put the protagonist and the audience in exactly the same position. The main question in drama, the way I was taught, is always, What does the protagonist want? That's what drama is. It comes down to that. It's not about theme, it's not about ideas, it's not about setting, but what the protagonist wants. What gives rise to the drama, what is the precipitating event, and how, at the end of the play, do we see that event culminated? Do we see the protagonist's wish fulfilled or absolutely frustrated? That's the structure of drama. You break it down into three acts.

—David Mamet; interview by John Lahr in *The Paris Review*, No. 142.

MEETING THE MINOTAUR

During our MCWS 1 debrief, David Ellard and I decided to try holding MCWS 2 at Parris Island Marine Corps Recruit Depot. David emailed the flier to units in the Tri-Command area. I placed a free ad in *The Beaufort Gazette's* "Happenings" column. We hoped for a bigger turnout, although I limited participation to nine writers, with combat veterans having first priority for seats. Nine writers were all I felt I could manage alone as a workshop leader. We continued the lunchtime workshop schedule, meeting on Tuesdays and Thursdays, days of the week that did not interfere with my Monday/Wednesday teaching schedule. David and I both felt that holding the workshop at lunchtime would make attendance more convenient for active duty participants. The workshop schedule was reduced from six weeks to five weeks. Maybe less time with the same piece of writing would be better for the writers. Before we met, MCWS 2 participants were asked to read Tristine Rainer's *Your Life as Story: Discovering the "New Autobiography" and Writing Memoir as Literature.* This reading would provide common ground for craft discussions.

Eight writers signed up for MCWS 2; three attended the first workshop.

Anthony, a twenty-year Marine still on active duty, had studied journalism in college for three years before joining the Corps. When contacting me about participating in the workshop, he mentioned that he had already written an unpublished autobiographical novel about two very important years in his childhood. He balked at writing memoir. I explained that addressing the facts of his life as they actually happened would make him a better novelist. Writers who deal point blank with issues of the past by writing according to nonfiction standards of truth are better equipped to prevent those same issues from acting out subconsciously, taking over the lives of their fictional characters. This made sense to Tony, who agreed to try writing memoir.

Melissa, a Department of Defense employee who works at Parris Island, also writes fiction. For MCWS 2, Melissa decided to write about the moment she first realized her mother was a cancer patient. Breaking through denial is always difficult, no less difficult is trying to capture that moment of clarity in words.

Our third participant, Debra, a Marine first sergeant and Iraq War Veteran, was working as the senior enlisted woman in a woman recruit training company. Always beyond busy, she kept to the regimen of writing. Debra chose to write about being a member of a convoy launched from Kuwait just after Hussein's 48-hour warning ran out. Her story recounts the first days of her journey into the desert and the convoy's encounter with an enemy tank regiment during the worst sandstorm in a hundred years.

We moved through revision after revision during the next four weeks and wrapped up our fifth workshop week with a visit by Warren Slesinger. Warren, poet and retired publishing executive, is perhaps best known among writers and graduate students for editing *Spreading the Word: Editors on Poetry* with Stephen Corey, editor of *The Georgia Review*. In *Spreading the Word* "editors of twenty literary magazines discuss the philosophy and practice of selecting poems."[1] Warren had given me a copy of the book when I was a student in his fiction course at USCB.

An accomplished poet, Warren began his talk with a question: "Why would someone write a poem?" He mentioned Gregory Orr's work often. Orr has written of his tumultuous personal battles following his brother's death. When they were children, Orr accidentally shot and killed his brother. Warren quoted Orr as saying that writing poetry is an attempt to work the interplay of order and disorder. In reworking events of the past through application of imagination combined with craft, the power relationship between event and self is changed. Self as poet masters the disorder that almost overwhelmed by reestablishing order through taking charge of the imagination. This reestablishment of order from chaos can also be achieved through writing memoir and personal essay. This principle underwrites narrative's value as an effective healing tool for wounds of memory. We also held a lively discussion about poet William Wordsworth's ideas on the writer's inward eye being the inner place of tranquility. Poet Robert Frost's idea of writing as a stay against confusion was mentioned. Orr's, Wordsworth's, and Frost's thoughts apply to combat veterans writing to assimilate the wartime experience.

Warren then read a few of his poems before opening the floor to further discussion. He spent a great deal of time on the road during thirty years in the publishing world. His poems centered on family and his sense of apartness and unity, a sensibility shared by military service members. Warren choosing Orr's work to bring to the group was brilliant. Coincidentally, two workshop participants had already chosen to write about family in their essays, and Debra's piece speaks of the family bond formed among military members in combat.

MCWS 2 writers received final critiques on works-in-progress during the fourth week, so final changes to their essays were a surprise revealed at the read aloud held in a classroom at MCRD Parris Island. Milspeak writers work hard during the five-week workshop. Reading their lives as text is possibly the hardest task of all. It's one thing to write for yourself, but it is a different beast to discuss your work among other writers and to read your finished work to others. At Queens University, I learned how trying that experience could be.

Queens' students held a reading at a local tavern during each residency. The aftertaste of years of drinking infused the place's dark brick interior: beer sloshed from mugs onto brick, Kahlua engrained in wooden tables, wine stains blotting the floor. The microphone for our readings stood at the end of a long dark tunnel of a room beyond the bar; and yes, each time I entered the place I felt like Alice looking into the rabbit hole of my past as a practicing alcoholic. The room was uncomfortable for me, but even more so was the discomfort of reading my work to a group of peers who were actually judges in the guise of students. I forced myself to read anyway, my body and voice shaking, my eyes watering, the words sometimes impossible to see. At times, I could barely speak so I shouted like a drill instructor, holding up before those many judges the contents of my heart. It was cathartic, exhilarating. It taught me to not give a damn what anyone thought of my voice, my work, my story.

It is a story only I can tell.

In those student readings, I learned not to ignore the value of my own work as I, my Self, had been devalued so many times in life. I learned that I, the writer, have the final say in my work, and that if I didn't believe in my work, no one else would. I wanted Milspeak writers to experience that moment of meeting the Minotaur in the labyrinth. The read aloud at the end of each workshop cycle provides it, and has become a Milspeak tradition. I met the Minotaur during MCWS 2 via a different route, in the labyrinth of memory.

Coming to Parris Island for each workshop began changing my relationship with the place where I had spent more than four years as a drill instructor. Maybe this was because Debra was on the drill field at the time. She shared many stories about changes to female recruit training. For instance, I had no idea that Women Marines were no longer called Women Marines and are now called female Marines or just Marines. More importantly, Debra taught me how a new generation of women warriors was holding up during wartime.

I often arrived early for workshop. Debra might be there to teach me more about how life had changed for military women during the eight years that had passed since my retirement. Being on Parris Island twice a week and interacting with Debra was stirring my own past to life in unexpected ways. Debra surprised me when she mentioned she had been a recruit during my first tour on the drill field. While Debra was training to become a Marine at Parris Island in 1985, I was an inpatient training for sobriety at Bethesda Naval Hospital. If Debra had known the truth about my past, would she want anything to do with me? By not sharing the reality of my past with Debra, I was hiding myself, protecting myself, and protecting Milspeak from being tarnished by my past. Was this dishonest? Was I sparing Milspeak writers the truth of my past to keep the focus on their writing or to keep the focus off my past? By not sharing who I really am was I taking away their right to make an informed decision about participating in Milspeak?

Sometimes I drove onto Parris Island early to travel the roads I used to run and march with recruits. Driving those back roads before workshop meetings was my stay against the confusion I felt during MCWS 2. The rappelling tower, gas chamber and rifle range are landmarks along Parris Island's back roads. Revisiting these old haunts was my way of reordering memory, a way of establishing my relationship with a place that had greatly affected me, a way of aligning my past with my present. I needed to face those landmarks, to re-see them, to re-design them and my place among them in the society of memory. I needed to prove to myself that mistakes can have positive outcomes, even at Parris Island where mistakes can cost lives. This is after all the greatest fear every military person knows, that a mistake will result in loss of someone else's life. This fear drives the service member's willingness to place the value of others' lives above his or her own. This valuation of life, the hierarchy of value in combat, is instilled in each recruit, male or female, during boot camp—your life is more valuable than my own.

As a Drill instructor during my first tour from 1984 to 1986, everything about woman recruit training was different from my boot camp experience in 1978. The daily uniform for recruits was camouflage utilities instead of Air Force blue slacks and light blue cotton shirts. Silky running shorts, T-shirts with a big USMC across the front, and name brand running shoes replaced skort PT gear and white canvas tennis shoes. Physical training had intensified. Conditioning marches of up to twelve miles resulted in a straggling gaggle of cammies and boots carrying packs on their backs—drill instructors enjoyed coming up with just the right combination of gear to be carried in recruits' packs. Recruits' 1978 tea parties, trips to Fripp Island for Dinner Out, and trips to the Beaufort museum were eliminated, although classes on wearing make-up and poise and etiquette were still considered important aspects of a woman recruit's training in 1984. As a recruit, I had spent one day playing softball as a field exercise during training in 1978. Although male recruits spent ten days learning field skills, between 1984 and 1986 each series of women recruits spent only three days in The Field—the abandoned runways at Page Field on the backside of Parris Island—marching from field skills Courses A to Z. The area was surrounded by forest, swamp, river, and ocean. Talk of gators kept recruits in their tents at night. Talk of raccoon invasions kept them from smuggling food into those tents.

I worked only two platoons before my alcoholic lifestyle rendered me useless as a drill instructor, a Marine, and a human being. While on break following the graduation of my second platoon, I crashed my car during a blackout. My best friend nearly died, my right arm was broken, and I was reassigned to the Academics Section, where it was my duty to teach recruits customs & courtesies, history, and alcohol awareness classes. I was also assigned to Level 1 and 2 alcohol abuse classes and faced the possibility of a court-martial for drunk driving. When local authorities dropped charges against me, the command dropped court-martial proceedings. I was also sent to a Curriculum Developers Course at Camp Lejeune, North Carolina. Upon my return from the course, I became part of the team of woman recruit trainers who rewrote the curriculum that translated women's training into warrior training paralleling men's training. I tried to stop drinking, but couldn't on my own, despite my best intentions and the alcohol classes I had attended. Maybe because I couldn't stop lying to myself and everyone else. Maybe because I was in denial. Maybe because I was incapable of being honest with myself.

I requested treatment for alcoholism after waking up in jail on September 23, 1985 following a blackout drunk. When I awoke, I was gagged and wearing a straitjacket and ankle shackles. I hung in my cell like a banana in suspended animation by chains running from the cell bars to my ankle shackles and by a leather tong attached to my straitjacket under my neck and to the cell's back wall. I couldn't move or scream. I was surrounded by complete darkness—internally and externally. All I could do was bounce my butt against the cell floor and wait. To this day, I do not recall the gag, straitjacket or shackles being removed from my body. After my jail experience, I asked for inpatient treatment because, for the first time in my life, I feared myself, what I might do in the next blackout. In treatment, I was able to accept that I am an alcoholic and to unravel many of the secrets of my past that had kept me living in a vicious cycle of shame, guilt, denial, and drunkenness. I left the drill field seven months sober and grateful for a second chance to have a military career through sobriety. I never wanted to drink again. But following all that had occurred as a result of my drinking, to have "Successful Tour" stamped in my service record book felt like a lie. I asked for my second tour on the drill field to make up for all that went wrong during my first tour. My second tour was intended to prove to myself that I could do It, whatever It might be, and It could be done successfully while sober.

When I returned to the drill field in 1987, fourteen months after my first tour ended, many changes were occurring to recruit training. The lesson plans I had written during my first tour were being put into action. All recruits fired for qualification at the rifle range. Recruits drilled with rifles and we DIs carried swords. Basic Warrior Training began for women. One of my platoons was the first to go through this extended training that introduced many aspects of male recruit training; including the feared Confidence Course and the Infiltration Course, where TNT charges set by DIs simulated bombs being dropped near recruits low-crawling through mud with their M-16 rifles in hand. Our time in the field was extended to two weeks, with a few days spent on A-Line firing .50 caliber machine guns, SAWs, AT4s and grenade launchers. I had never before done any of these things as a Marine.

One day during my second tour on the drill field, I was driving along the road between the rappelling tower, gas chamber and rifle range when an AV8B Harrier fighter jet dropped out of the sky; the pilot ejected low and into a grove of pines. I watched him fly across the sky in his ejection seat and slam into a tree. It happened so fast. I didn't stop. I couldn't believe my eyes. I reported what I had seen when I arrived at my destination—I can't remember where that was. I was told that it wasn't a mirage. The pilot had died instantly. I began drinking again, two years and nine months after completing rehabilitation treatment. It wasn't just the pilot dying and my not stopping to help him that caused me to drink again. My life was filled with stress: a major sting operation to find homosexuals was underway; DIs disappeared daily; each week we who remained were called into a classroom and told to give up information about suspected homosexuals. The Sergeant Major hated me; I was constantly in his office. I could do nothing but stand at attention while he screamed at me, spit flying from his mouth, anger shooting from his eyes. There was a trial. I was called to testify on behalf of one of the DIs. I testified against the Sergeant Major, told of his pulling us into a classroom each week to berate us, to force us to make accusations against others to save our own skins—I refused to do that. I cried the entire time spent on the stand. We no longer were called to the classroom each week. The Sergeant Major never stopped hating me. As a Senior Drill Instructor (SDI), I was working far more than 120 hours per week. My DIs called me Dragon Lady behind my back. Sometimes there were only two of us to work a platoon. Within a day or two of seeing the plane drop out of sky, I found my husband engaged in sex with a stranger, a younger woman, one of many he pursued. I was 29. When I found them together, my face was covered with camouflage paint and bug juice; I had been in the field with recruits doing night maneuvers. I had no time to go to 12-Step meetings. DIs dropped daily from platoons, dropped from sight, disappeared. Those who said they would serve again with homosexual DIs were relieved of duty and terminated from military service. Our Series Chief Drill Instructor was one of those—I never saw her again. I took her place in the series hierarchy, assumed her duties, mostly administrative duties for both platoons, and continued my own duties as SDI. My waist became so small my headgear could have fit around it. I became a closet drinker. I went through the motions. I hid my drinking from my recruits, the DIs and officers I worked with, and my husband. I lied to myself about it. I forgave him, but I couldn't forgive myself. He hadn't wanted me to go back for a second tour. When I left the drill field for the second time in 1990, I left part of me there. Something burnt out in the engine that runs me and I've never been able to repair it. This is the dead zone in me. But while I was there in the dead zone, I did my job. I did it well, even when I was hung-over. I hid those, too. I felt as though I had rappelled into a pit and someone had pulled the rope up before I hit bottom. It was dark in there.

During my second tour as a drill instructor, I experienced severe symptoms of PTSD. I didn't realize this was happening at the time. This realization occurred while I was leading MCWS 2, along with the knowledge that recurring memories of a terrible time had caused me to avoid Parris Island for so many years. But during MCWS 2, my fear of Parris Island was vanquished. Maybe because of Warren's talk I began to understand myself better, and to better understand why I am so drawn to writing. Maybe because Debra accepted me as I am. I felt safe among the MCWS 2 writers, safe enough to drive by my old haunts, stop, reflect, and find solace in imperfection, in the knowledge that even mistakes can have positive outcomes—

Parris Island's forty-foot tall rappelling tower, a steel and wood behemoth with no way down except by rope represented a major obstacle to both DIs and recruits. Every recruit was required to negotiate this obstacle twice in order to graduate from boot camp. A spiraling staircase through the tower's center leads to the rappelling platforms. No one walks down those steps. Two trips up that staircase and two rappels, one for the wall and one for the free fall, were required of every DI and recruit. DIs jumped before the recruits arrived. DIs who refused to jump were excommunicated from the league of recruit trainers. Drill instructors working atop the tower jumped one more time when the day's work with recruits was done. A day's work on the rappelling tower meant snapping in more than a hundred recruits and motivating them to jump twice from the Tower, even when I was hiding a hangover.

From my perch atop the Tower, I wait for the flow of recruits to my station to begin. On the ground below me, my platoon stands in one big formation. Nearby, recruits from our sister platoon receive instruction on how to tie the Swedish seat that will soon be connected to an aluminum rappel hook for the long walk up and the short flight off the Tower. It's another glorious Marine Corps day and I feel fine, minus the throbbing headache from the night-before's vodka and cranberry juice. I keep my bottle with a pistol in the cabinet above my stove; both are hidden from my husband behind cooking oil and a can of Crisco. With each drink I take, I pray for the courage to put down the bottle or pick up the pistol. I am too cowardly to do either.

A leather belt and tether connects me to the Tower. I've learned to enjoy the slide-ride in my insides when I look down, even when I'm hungover. Baking in the sun, wooden planks lining the Wall rappel station groan. A serpentine flow of recruits clings to the stair rail while clanging up the Tower stairs. Soon we are snapping rappel hooks and sending recruits into space, each launch accompanied by murmurs of "You can do it, Recruit," and "No Pain; No Gain."

"Left foot first, Recruit," I say to Private Archer, who doesn't seem scared at all for a change. She must have figured out what it's all about—"OOH-RAH MARINE CORPS."

Archer begins shouting before she jumps: "MARINE CORRRRRRR—"

The breeze is hot with the smell of steel burning rope and rope burning goatskin gloves.

The Freefall Station steel-arm juts above my head and over the edge of the platform, where another recruit will soon be swinging. On the ground, the rappel rope is in the gloved hands of a belay DI. She stands prepared to break the recruit's fall by pulling the rope away from the Tower, if the recruit freaks out and fails to break on her own. Archer manages to negotiate the break. Okay. Sweat beads on my face, falls from my nose. I wonder if it smells like vodka. Between the ground and Tower, the rope runs double over the Freefall arm. Archer, dangling thirty feet above ground, must be feeling the wind in her toes. She makes her way to the ground by break and fall.

"Next recruit, UP!"

"Private Mitchum REPORTING FOR RAPPEL, MA'AM!"

"Ready, up," I say into the air. Mitchum moves into position at the edge of the platform beneath the Freefall arm. "Well, don't that beat all, you actually got it right this time."

"Yes Ma'am!"

"Safe Seat," I shout over my shoulder in the direction of the Series Commander, the officer in charge of recruit training and the safety officer for our Series. Accidents are far between, but the occasional recruit breaks the occasional arm or ankle.

Running the double-rope down the front of Mitchum's body, I double loop it through the rappel hook on the front of her Swedish seat, locking the rappel hook before placing the rope in her gloved right hand at waist level. "Mitchum, RIGHT hand behind your back, LEFT hand at chin level, both hands stay ON the rope."

"Aye-aye, Ma'am!" The smell of fear-sweat shoots from her body as she pulls the rope behind her back with one hand and grasps the rope at eye level with her other hand.

"Call the belay, Mitchum."

She is a frozen cube of human flesh and blood, leaning her face against her left hand, eyes squeezed shut, mumbling a prayer.

"Say it, Recruit." My words have no edge.

"Private Mitchum On Rappel," she whimpers.

"SERGEANT SANDERS ON BELAY," my DI partner shouts from below.

Mitchum's shaking gloves are her only movement.

"Come on Mitchum, you can do this. Just one thirty-inch step with that good old left foot, always the left foot first. You can do it, Recruit, just step and go. Once you clear the platform, just pull that right hand hard against your back and you'll get the scenic tour."

Mitchum shivers. She's been a fucking problem all through training. She can't align the gear under her rack, she can't iron, she can't spit shine, she can't swim, she can't run—

"WHY ARE YOU HERE, RECRUIT? ANSWER ME NOW!" We aren't supposed to holler at recruits on the Tower, but Mitchum is in a state of shock anyway. Something has to make her move—

"ANSWER UP, RECRUIT!"

"Ma'aaam..." she bleats like a goat.

"What? Why are you here? Tell me, Recruit." I say this with sugar. Snap personality changes sometimes scare them into moving, like the idea of Hell before hearing the crackle of fire.

"Ma'am, this recruit has never been able to complete anything in her life. This recruit has always been told she's dumb...just like the SDI knows, Ma'am...and this recruit WANTS TO FINISH JUST ONE THING IN HER LIFE, MA'AM!"

"Recruit, why do you suppose I'm standing here in one hundred and ten degree heat chatting away the afternoon at your private garden party in the sky?"

"Ma'am, this recruit does not understand why the SDI would waste time on this recruit."

"You get *this* through your head and *you* file it away in that gear locker *you* call a brain and *you* get it once and for all and right now. Private—I spend time on you because YOU ARE ME, and I'm a fighter, been one all my life. That freefall is the reward for all the crap I ever had to put up with. *I earned that scenic view,* Mitchum, and I'm taking that step and chasing the wind, Mitchum, cause when I get wherever the wind takes me, I'm gonna be free, Mitchum, *free—even if it's only for one second,* so I'm gonna count to three, Mitchum, and at 3, I'm gonna put that left foot forward and shout Marine Corps all the way. You got that Mitchum?"

"AYE, AYE, MA'AM"

"1...2...3...STEP!"

"MARINE CORRRRRPS!"

"Break, Mitchum, RIGHT HAND IN YOUR BACK!"

Jesus, thank God for Sanders on belay.

"NEXT RECRUIT UP!"

Mitchum will be back up for her second jump. Maybe she'll have more fun the second time down, riding the red wall, her back to the sky, legs stretched out front, feet bouncing against wall, butt pointed down, head pointed up, her body a tiny L, falling, falling—

In fellowship with Milspeak writers, I see my own struggle to move beyond my limitations as a military person, a writer, and a human being. When I work with Milspeak writers, I stand with them every step of the way through the workshop process, no matter what is going on in my life. We come together to make our shared dream of becoming writers a reality. During the read aloud, Milspeak writers finish one thing they've always wanted to finish—writing a complete story and sharing it with others. For me, the joy is in learning as much from them as they do from me. Together we form a safe zone where the past loses power to harm the present.

Moments of clarity, understanding the past, capturing that moment for a reader—these themes ran the course of our five weeks together in MCWS 2; these themes run the course of the writing life. It is a happy coincidence, one of life's great small things, that Warren's talk centered on everyday heroism. That others might find a new source of courage in their stories inspired these writers. Melissa found that not only was her writing improved as a result of participating in the workshop, but so was her understanding of her past. We discussed emotional flooding during our first week, so she was mentally prepared for that onrush of reliving the past emotionally. We both agreed, though, that nothing could adequately prepare a writer for placing herself back into a difficult time, except knowing her reasons for putting herself there. Melissa and I likened this experience to Joseph Campbell's vision of the Hero's Journey[1]—we face the obstacles and challenges of writing to share our experience, strength, and hope with others who have encountered or will encounter the same, but we also take the risk of writing to better know ourselves. We go into the abyss to bring back the Boon: the truth only one person can give, the lesson of experience. I felt especially close to Melissa; we had much in common. Just before MCWS 2 began, my aunt had died of lung cancer. Her husband, my uncle, died on the evening of her memorial service. Melissa's, Tony's, and Debra's memoirs are statements of proof that everyday heroism exists in very real terms in everyday life, something we seldom recognize in each other or in ourselves.

Notes:
[1] *Spreading the Word: Editors on Poetry*. Stephen Corey and Warren Slesinger, Eds. Beaufort, SC: The Bench Press, 2001.
[2] Campbell, Joseph. *The Hero with a Thousand Faces*. NJ: Princeton University Press, 1973.

MY OWN DEFINITION

By Warren Slesinger

In the late 1980s, I was dealing with the problem of writer's block. I was trying to stimulate a thought by looking up the definition of a word in the dictionary, when I realized that the listings (if used selectively) often formed a pattern that I could use myself: a "definition" that enabled me to generate a sequence of associations and contain them in a structure that relied more on verbal synopsis than syntax. I used numbers instead of stanzas for a structure that looks like a real definition.

Sometimes a single word has several meanings, so I did not feel confined by the form. Quite the opposite: I could make "free" associations as long as I connected them, but I am not an experimental writer. I am more likely to observe a process or consider a problem; the more "personal," the better. Perhaps the most accessible poem of this kind is the following:

MARGIN

Margin (mar.gin) n-s. 1. The space on a page
beyond the main body of the text. 2. A pause
in the thought process between the seen and
the sensed. 3. The edge of vegetation that extends
from the pine barrens to the tidal flats, a wetland
the eye is hesitant to enter; its nature to remain
separate from Nature, its guiding intelligence a step
beyond the physical reality of so much salt marsh:
the sun a shadowy white against the green tussocks
of cordgrass, the flight-dragging feet of the egrets,
the sagging planks of a spindly pier; sameness
in a sinuous maze of stalks and blades; the heat
seething with insects, a glittering swarm; numberless
fiddler crabs scuttling down identical holes; dull hunks
of gurgling mollusks in the gleaming muck; so much

seepage that a stream curves and cuts through the silt
to the sea, a glimmering expanse. 4. The broad surface
of an observed phenomenon from which an inference
is drawn: Science assumes a subject in fact and form,
but its origin remains half-hidden in the *margin*.

This was written a couple of years ago when I was taking a Master Naturalist
course and using a field guide. Each week the class would meet with an
instructor who helped us identify the plants and animals in a habitat
(piedmont, sandhills, coastal plain). In this case, it was a short physical
distance from the road and a short visual distance from the description on
the page to the place itself: a saltwater marsh on the coast of South Carolina.
But I realized that I needed to take an imaginative leap to comprehend
the complexity of an ecosystem.

Of course, a "margin" is literally "the space on a page / beyond the
main body of the text," but the difference between what is described
("seen") and what is beyond words ("sensed") is the "physical reality" of
the place itself, which explains "a pause in the thought process."

Nevertheless, I began with "the edge of vegetation that extends / from
the pine barrens to the tidal flats" because I wanted to deal with the way
we turn whatever we see into words; especially, "if the physical reality" is
comprised of "a sinuous maze of stalks and blades; the heat / seething
with insects"—not to mention an occasional alligator or snake.

No, it is easier to do what human beings usually do: discover, name,
and wonder about the world at large and the origin of life.

We assume that it came from the sea, that" shimmering expanse"
that serves metaphorically as the "broad surface / of an observed
phenomenon from which an inference / is drawn." But we do not know
how or when it arrived on land, where the "margin" is a tidal zone that
teems with life as well as a margin of knowledge that remains "in fact
and form" a mystery.

As you will see, I am not as serious in some of the definitions that I
offer as evidence that the form is flexible enough to cover a wide range of
subjects.

GARDEN

Garden (gar.den) n-s 1. A plot for
the cultivation of plants, i.e., fruits, flowers,
and vegetables for household use: a *garden*
white and green with blossoming pole beans
and cabbage butterflies among the rows
of rounding leaves. 2. Of a familiar kind:
a quote from the *garden* of a favorite poem.
3. Commonplace: your *garden* variety
of that squatty amphibian with the warty skin:
an interloper that sits on its tailless
and terrestrial rump, its webbed toes spread
in the freshly spaded dirt; the image
of bug-eyed immobility until the mouth opens,
and the tongue is flipped with a snap
of satisfaction at the tip. 4. The poem: "a real
toad in an imaginary *garden*."—Moore.

GLASS

Glass (glass) n-es 1. A miracle that occurs
in the mineral world when a white-hot mass
of silicates, oxides and potash fuses to form
a bright and brittle substance that is clarity
itself: a thin, square, rigid pane of *glass*.

2. Collectively, a structure comprised of
panes: the *glass* in the greenhouse was
clouded with the closeness of livings things.
3. A mirror made by backing glass with
a silver coating: "Art is Nature with a *glass*
by a tranquil stream."—Walpole. 4. A device
for use in a gallery: With *glass* at eye and
and catalog in hand, he peered at the pinkish flesh

of "The Bathers" by Rubens. 5. An object
made wholly of glass; hence, its contents:
Before he sipped the bubbles of champagne,
he raised his *glass*: "To Life!"

"Vapor" is an example of how military people might use definitions to
break down the writer's block wall, when writing about the Middle Eastern
experience. My own wartime memories have dimmed with time.

Write while you can, when you can.

VAPOR

Vapor (vay.por) n-s. Something
in the air: a mixture of suspended matter
that makes it difficult to see down a street
in Baghdad. 2. A mist with a man in it.

Vaporize (vay.por.ize) v. 1.Only
to convert into a vapor with the heat
of a high explosive. 2. To detonate a mess
of manhood high-strung on hate.

Vaporous (vay.por.us) adj.1. What
is collecting in a cloud of Middle-Eastern
malice. 2. Rising from a blast of body parts
on the same old ground.

HAIR TODAY, GONE TOMORROW

By Melissa Ellis

"Mookie, I want you to wash and roll my hair before you leave," Ma said, for what was probably the third time.

"Ok, Ma," I replied with a sigh, finally giving in.

I don't know how it happened or even remember when it did, but I had become the designated shampoo and roller girl. Maybe it was because I was the youngest and, being the last one to live with her, had gotten the chore through a process of elimination. However, even after I'd moved away, doing Ma's hair was still my job. Luckily, I didn't really mind. The simple act of wash, rinse, repeat had a soothing affect on me.

After ushering her to the kitchen, I cleared the counter to give us more room and bent her over the edge of the sink. I began by wetting her hair, pouring the shampoo into my palms, and then slowly massaging bubbles into her hair. Ma had never made a fuss about her hair, but she had always been meticulous about its care. I can't remember ever seeing it unkempt, unless it was being washed or rolled. Hair care was only one of the many consistent things in Ma's life.

A single mother after the unexpected death of my father, she had taken a job as an elementary school custodian and had kept that job for as many of my twenty-four years as I could remember. Ma never talked about Daddy's death. Never. The little that I do know about him came from my sisters, my brother, and random conversations that I was never directly involved in. My father's existence is almost as unreal to me as his death because I was only about two when he was killed. Leaving a card game, he'd been stabbed and had died instantly. Although there were rumors of who had murdered him, no one was ever arrested or charged for the crime that robbed five children of their father and a woman of her husband. By all accounts, Ma had remained strong through the entire ordeal and had simply done what needed to be done. None of us had ever seen tears and she never discussed Daddy with us. She had simply done what needed to be done. She had taken that custodial job and picked up Daddy's share of the responsibilities as if they had always been her own. With her mother's help, she continued to take care of us, while also paying the bills for the small trailer we called home.

Ma had chosen to live in our small mobile home even after all of us, my brother and sisters and me, were grown and on our own. Until recently, that is. Less than a year before, she had decided to move into a small apartment instead. Now that her children were grown, she'd said, it was time for her to live her life for her. Renting the apartment had been her first step towards total independence. Even so, I couldn't help but remember all of the times I'd done this same job in that small mobile home.

Having been Ma's designated shampoo girl, it's funny that role was never reversed. I can't remember a time when Ma had washed my hair. Raised by my grandmother for most of my childhood, it was she who had cared for my hair until I was old enough to do so myself. I was small enough to lie face-up on the counter as Grandma washed my hair. Even then, the process had a calming effect on me. Grandma talked to me the whole time. She told me how pretty and thick my hair was. She now wears wigs to disguise her thinning hair, but in her stories, she had no need for them. Back then, her own hair, as she always reminded me, was as thick and beautiful as mine. Those moments always left me feeling beautiful and I suspect her memories of her own hair left her feeling the same way.

Other than the actual location, Ma's apartment kitchen hadn't changed much from the trailer kitchen. The faded yellow curtains, the heavy cast iron skillet that always remained on or near the stove and the wooden handled silverware had all made the journey from the trailer to the new apartment. The toaster sat in the same proximity to the sink as it had in the trailer, as did the fancy wooden breadbox. Her recipe box still sat atop the refrigerator and the dishtowels hung across the lower cabinet door. It felt as if Ma had simply picked up the old kitchen and moved it to the new apartment.

In the trailer, I had been forced to wash Ma's hair in the bathroom sink because there simply wasn't enough room to do it in the kitchen. She'd hated that, mainly because it hurt her neck to bend down so far. The bathroom wasn't much bigger than the kitchen, just less cluttered — no water bucket next to the stove and no dish rack next to the sink to get in our way. We couldn't stretch out by any means, but I had always managed to give Ma a good shampoo, massaging the foamy bubbles into her hair, scratching her scalp and protecting her eyes from the shampoo. Remembering those days, I smiled, but as I maneuvered my hands over Ma's head, her hair began to come out. Not the occasional stray strand or two that one would expect during a routine shampoo, but handfuls of her hair were everywhere - wrapping around my fingers, swirling in the sink and gathering in the drain.

"Ma," I said, my voice shaky despite my effort to be strong, "your hair is coming out."

Her spine stiffened.

"A lot of it, Ma."

In silence, I rinsed what was left of Ma's hair, unable to resist watching as it slowly swirled down the drain. A million things went through my mind - shock, anger, sadness, uncertainty. What must she be feeling? What, if anything, could I do or say to make it better? I was terrified. How could I comfort someone who I imagined being ten times as terrified because this was actually happening to them?

After what seemed like hours, Ma's mostly-bald head was wrapped in a towel as I quietly followed her to the bathroom where she stopped before the mirror. She removed the towel. We stared at her reflection, taking in the remaining wispy patches that looked more like peach fuzz than hair and the smooth baldness of her head. I noticed a weakness in her eyes that I hadn't seen before and a tightness in her mouth; the kind that comes from trying to hide a pain that was impossible to hide.

"We knew this was gonna happen, right?" I asked, trying to sound soothing.

She nodded, but her eyes lacked conviction.

"It's gonna be all right, Ma," I said, trying to smile. "It's gonna grow back, just watch."

Her weak smile failed to reach her eyes. Without a word, she replaced the towel around her head, walked back to the kitchen, and proceeded to clean up. Just as she had when Daddy died, Ma carried on as if nothing had happened. She took the shampoo back to its proper place, wiped down the counters and cleaned the sink. Neither of us spoke, although there was much I wanted to say and do.

I wanted to hug her, lay my cheek atop her head, and tell her that it would be all right. I wanted to cry with her, wanted her to know that she wasn't alone. But my family's relationship had never been a physically close one. We weren't the type of family who hugged or said, "I love you." We rarely showed our feelings, relying instead on an unspoken understanding and the connection that came with being family.

It didn't seem right to dote on her. Unsure what else to say or do, I quickly gathered my things and left the apartment. My brother's apartment was in the same complex and I made the short trek to his place in a fog. I entered the apartment where my brother and sisters were playing a game of cards. Grimly, I told them the news.

"She won't want everybody making it a big deal," one sister said.

We all agreed and decided to leave Ma alone to deal with it.

"It" was a really inadequate word for what was happening to our family, but none of us had the desire or the courage to admit what "it" really meant. I, however, had a more physical image of "it" because as Ma's hair had fallen through my fingers, I had seen her not only as I always had—as a mother, provider, role model—but in her new role as a cancer patient. My mother passed away a few months later, a mere six months after being diagnosed with lung cancer. She was buried wearing a wig.

OPEN WOUNDS

By A. M. Yallum

I swung my legs off the bed, sat up, and rubbed the sleep from my eyes. With the exception of the box springs and bare mattress that I sat on, my room was completely void of furniture. The glass in my bedroom window had been busted out for the better part of a year, and although it was morning, the summer heat had already intruded into my room with suffocating humidity. Since our ancient crumbling apartment building had been built in the 1920s it was without air conditioning, and the only relief we had from the summer heat anywhere in the apartment was from a small noisy fan my mum used in the kitchen that was caked with grease.

From outside all was quiet and only the occasional rumble of a car engine could be heard as it accelerated up the road. I strained my ears. The absence of laughter or voices carrying the guttural dialect indigenous to the poorer towns and boroughs around the City of Pittsburgh told me that the neighborhood kids that I loafed with had not yet come outside to play. From across the hallway, the boisterous sound of my sisters arguing and my mum threatening them if they didn't stop told me immediately that Jake was not home.

I emerged from my room and scampered across the hall to my sister's room. My oldest sister Mindy was on the bed, humming loudly to herself while pretending to read an *Archie* comic book. Doreen was trying to scream over her to get a point across. The louder and more irritated Doreen got, the louder Mindy hummed to drown her out. Finally, her frustration becoming too great, Doreen rose from the floor where she had been reading her own *Betty and Veronica* comic book. She stepped menacingly towards Mindy.

"Wha'cha fight'n about?" I interrupted. They both stopped their bickering and looked over at me as I walked into the room. Mindy spoke first.

"Bra Bra, who ya think's prettier, Betty or Veronica?" She asked, placing an emphasis on Betty's name.

"I heard dat! I heard de way ya said Betty. Dat ain't fair. Bra Bra always takes your side." Doreen was increasingly agitated. Mindy, on the other hand, sat calmly on the bed looking at me and smugly waited for my answer.

"Betty's way prettier," I lied. "Veronica's ugly."

Doreen's entire body quivered with rage. "I hate ya!" she spit. "I hate yinz both!"

The level of her anger put us both on guard.

"Yinz both make me sick," she finally hissed pushing past me as she stomped out of the room.

Mindy and I looked at each other and sighed. We knew our sister, and we knew what she was capable of when she became this angry. Although Doreen knew she was over matched, we knew from experience she would be willing to chance a beating from us for the few good kicks or scratches she would inflict in return. Doreen and I were both considerably shorter than Mindy, but everyone said she and I were the same height. Doreen always insisted venomously that she was taller than me. Whenever I challenged her to stand back to back, she snubbed me by saying she wouldn't put her head against my dirty hair if I were the last person on earth—she insisted she didn't want to end up with head lice. She was five pounds lighter than me and wiry and when I was on good terms with her, she was a valuable ally to have on my side. On several occasions, she had come to my aid in schoolyard fights. Doreen was fearless towards any of the kids in school or our neighborhood, and could probably fight better than most boys her age. However, if anyone happened to get on her bad side, then they better be looking over their shoulder. No one could hold a grudge like Doreen. She was unpredictable, vindictive, and downright dangerous. Mindy and I understood that for a little while at least we would have to be on guard because chances were that at some point during the day Doreen would probably try to exact retribution.

I can't be sure why Doreen was different than Mindy or me. She was the middle child and my mum said that was the reason she was the way that she was—but I didn't believe it. I think it had more to do with Jake.

Jake was my mum's live-in boyfriend. He dominated every aspect of our lives and when he was home, we were wary about speaking above a whisper for fear it would invite a hard slap to the back of our heads. At six foot one, he was intimidating. He was a powerfully built man who roamed about the apartment usually wearing nothing more than a pair of boxers.

He had cruel black eyes that were totally void of humor. His thick nose narrowed hawk-like in front of his naturally aggressive face and he blew it incessantly into a snot stained hanky he always carried with him. Like many Italians, his skin was dark and thick, and his huge forearms and massive biceps sported a number of vulgar tattoos that rippled and jerked when his muscles flexed. He was a man who had few friends and was hated and feared by most. For whatever reason he had a dislike for people and he rarely spoke to anyone. When he did speak, his voice was deep and threatening and commanded instant obedience and fear from my mum and my sisters and me.

I think it was the beatings that we frequently got from Jake that affected Doreen differently than Mindy and me. I guess Mindy and I viewed it as something in our lives that was beyond our control that we had to cope with as best we could, so we just accepted it. Doreen on the other hand could not seem to come to terms with it, and the fact that she could do nothing about it just plain made her mean.

It was like the puppies that our neighbor Rocco Deluca got a couple of years before. He named them Caesar and Max and would beat them for no good reason or for any little bit of mischief they got into. As the dogs grew, Max developed a genuine distrust for people, and would skittishly run away when one of us approached the fence and only after considerable coaxing could we get him to come to us to be petted. Caesar on the other hand would walk right up to the fence and wait for us when he saw us approaching. Though most times he would wag his tail, there was no telling what he would do. Sometimes he would allow us to reach over the fence and pet him, yet other times he would unexpectedly and viciously lung at the fence too try to rip our arms off. This was kind of the way Doreen had become.

Our three-story apartment building faced out over the neighborhood. It was built of red brick that had dulled over the years. We lived on the third floor in the middle apartment and except for an old crazy man named Lloyd who lived next door to us playing his trumpet at all hours of the day and night, the rest of the apartments had long been abandoned and were in an advanced state of decay. There were two cement porches that ran the length of the building. The kitchen to each apartment opened up to the porches, and from one end, leaning over the wrought iron railing, the back of Costa's store could be seen.

Unable to find any of my friends from the neighborhood, I retraced my path across the old graveled parking lot and headed for home. I glanced up at our apartment. The kitchen door was pried open with one of our wobbly kitchen chairs. I could see movement in our kitchen and as I got closer to the apartment building the song 'The Duke of Earl' drifted down from our kitchen radio to meet me.

The back of Costa's grocery store was at the bottom of the black metal steps stretching two floors up to our apartment. The entire area was covered in sawdust. The butcher shop was located to the rear of Costa's store, and there was always a thick layer of sawdust on the floor that filled the store with the tantalizing aroma of newly cut wood and fresh raw meats. Every evening the old sawdust was swept through the back door and replaced for the next day. Next to the backdoor, Mr. or Mrs. Costa had stacked empty boxes, the insides coated with wax smeared with a film of raw fat, ripe with the smell of freshly packed meats. There were also wooden crates pungent with the scent of salted fish, and plain boxes with the lingering smell of Italian cookies. I held these boxes to my face and inhaled deeply until my stomach growled. Hoping to find some hidden treasure like a ball of twine or unopened cookies that had been smashed in the box during shipping, I began to rummage through the cache of debris.

I set boxes and crates to one side as I dug into the pile. I found nothing worth keeping. I straightened to leave.

My head exploded with pain. Brilliant specks of white light flashed before my eyes. I dropped to my knees cringing in pain. The scenery around me began to blur. I pressed my hand against the top of my pounding head. A warm wetness oozed through my hair and fingers, down my face, and into my eyes. Squinting, I saw my hand covered in blood. I heard the faint clicking of hard shoes as they sprinted away on the cement porch above me. I couldn't seem to focus. Everything was foggy. My heart pounded in my chest from panic and confusion. What had happened? I reached for the ground to steady myself. My hand brushed up against a large chunk of brick that lie next to me.

I heard someone whistling. The back door to Costa's store opened, and Pete Costa wearing a butcher's apron stepped outside carrying an empty box. He moved in slow motion and if it weren't for the pain in my head, I probably would have laughed at his outlandish movements. He looked over at me, started to smile, but stopped abruptly. He rushed over, snatched me up in his arms, and started up the metal steps to our apartment.

"Josephine! Josephine!" He screamed.

My body went limp and it jerked and jolted as Pete climbed the steps. I felt nauseous. My mother's voice sounded hollow and distant.

"Oh God, Oh God! What happened to 'em?" She cried. I shut my eyes and the voices around me merged into one just before the blackness overtook me.

Someone was wiping my face. I opened my eyes and blinked to focus. I was staring up at the large crack that ran through our living room ceiling. My mum was wiping me down with a wet rag. Someone had removed my blood soaked shirt and pants. They lay crumpled on the wooden floor near the couch. I felt my mum's fingers gently parting my hair as she inspected the wound on my head. The panic from before had subsided. The last hint of fog melted away. Mr. Costa and my mum were talking.

"Are ya sure, Josephine?" Mr. Costa was saying. "Dat gash on his head is pretty nasty. It could use some stitches. It ain't a problem. I could put 'em in ne car an run 'em over to de hospital."

"Thanks, Pete, but I think he'll be okay. De bleed'ns stopped an 'nat." She looked over at me worriedly. "If it looks like he ain't no better in a couple hours, I'll send one of de girls to come git ya."

They both walked out into the kitchen. "Okay, Josephine, I'll be down stairs in ne store if ya need me, but don't ya let'em sleep for the next few hours," Mr. Costa warned.

His footsteps echoed across the linoleum floor in the kitchen as he made his way towards the back door. On the cement porch, they changed to a clicking sound before fading away down the back steps.

It's funny the things that you think about in times like that. This was the only time I could remember hearing another man's footsteps, except for Jake's, inside our apartment. Jake's footsteps were slow and deliberate and threatening. Mr. Costa's footsteps carried a feeling of normalcy that had a calming effect on me.

My mum came back into the living room and knelt beside me. She wiped at the large gash on my head. Her hand was shaking. She noticed me looking up at her.

"Bra Bra, what happened? Who did dis to ya?" She asked.

"I dun' know, Mum, I was just stan'in 'nar, and den my head started hurt'n an nats all I 'member." I answered.

"How ya feel'n now? Are ya still dizzy? Is your head hurt'n?"

I nodded. "A little."

"God knows we can't afford no hospital bills, but if we gotta git you to de hospital, den we will. Okay?" She feigned a smile.

"Okay," I said.

I glimpsed Mindy over by the kitchen passage way. She had been crying and was clearly worried for me. I smiled weakly at her. Then I noticed Doreen standing on the far side of the living room by a window. She was staring at the floor. She was plainly scared, but it was not the same fear and concern I saw on Mindy's face. Doreen's fear carried something else. Something I had seen all too often before. My eyes followed hers to the floor and came to rest on her hard, buckled shoes.

IN THE DESERT

By Debra Sharkey

At 2100 on the evening 15 February 2003, my unit held a formation at the barracks aboard Marine Corps Air Station, Cherry Point, North Carolina, for accountability and saying our final goodbyes to our loved ones. We were on our way to the APOE (aerial point of exit/entrance) to board the plane that would fly us to Kuwait International Airport in the Middle East. I was a Gunnery Sergeant filling the billet of the Company 1stSgt. I had only been with this company for two months before we deployed and often thought to myself, Do I really know what I am doing? I had one hundred eighty Marines and sailors in my company. My Company Commander, and my Company Executive Officer were already forward deployed, so I was in charge of the company. We as a unit needed to be at the APOE four hours prior to departure, to complete the flight manifests.

On 16 February 2003, I departed Cherry Point, alert, clean and feeling somewhat sad because I was leaving my husband and my dogs, but at the same time I was anxious to start this adventure. In a few months, my husband would also say goodbye to his son, who was joining the Marine Corps.

We were flying into Kuwait not on a military transport plane but on a huge Continental Airline's plane. It was an awesome plane. I couldn't believe that we were going to fly to Kuwait in such comfort. The flight crew cheered as we boarded the plane. It really made you feel as though you were already a hero. We flew to an Air Force airbase in Germany, I can't exactly recall where, but it was very cold outside. We sat for many hours in that airport because we were told they needed to ensure there was enough fuel in Kuwait to fly the airplane out of that country after we were dropped off. It was the same day the Daytona 500 race was on television. To my surprise, never being much of a race fan, it was hard to believe how involved I was in that race, knowing it was going to be the last bit of TV that I would see for months. We didn't find out who won the race for several days. By then it was no longer important because too many other things were more important.

It took us approximately 20 hours of flying to get to Kuwait. I was sitting in First Class and thought it was weird that my first experience sitting in such luxury was on my way to war rather than to vacation. The flight crew kept us entertained with movies, they were playing games with the troops, and one of the male stewards got a high-and-tight hair cut from one of the sergeants on the plane.

Kuwait International Airport first appeared as any other airport, at least until we deplaned and boarded buses that took us to the staging area to receive our ammo, a full combat load, and our rules of engagement class prior to the convoy north on buses. As I arrived at the staging area, I could see hundreds maybe even a thousand Marines and sailors waiting for the same things as me. Some were dressed in the tri-colored cammies, but many more were dressed in the Marine Corp's new desert camouflage uniform. There were bunkers surrounded by numerous layers of sandbags and a small tent to get a cup of coffee. While we were waiting in the staging area, the NBC alarms went off and we all put on our gas masks. Maybe it was just a drill, I am not really sure, but I was relieved that I was able to do it so calmly. Minutes turned into hours and hours felt like days. Finally, after all tasks had been accomplished, we received the go ahead to board the buses that would take us into the desert.

As I stowed my gear and got settled into my seat, the bus commander gave a safety brief. We were told to keep the curtains covering the bus windows closed and not to look out. Our last instruction was to make a Condition One weapon, which means putting a round in the chamber and keeping the weapon on safe. For all of us on that bus, it was the first time other than being on the rifle range that we ever had our weapons loaded with rounds that could be used in the defense of our lives. The atmosphere on the bus changed. It became very real to me as to why we were there.

We rode in the bus approximately two hours before we turned off the highway and drove for several miles out into the desert. There wasn't much at all to see as far as landscape, although it was interesting to me since I had never seen the desert before. There were several people that we passed, desert people walking on the side of the road as we drove by. Where were they coming from and where were they going? There wasn't anything around for them to be going to or coming from. As we approached what would be Camp Workhorse, you could see a large berm within a berm. Many of our unit's Marines were already there, flown out of North Carolina on different days. Once again our unit was becoming whole. This was the place we would call home until we went north into Iraq.

Back in the States on 18 March 2003, in a televised address at 0100, Mr. Bush, my Commander in Chief and President of the United States, gives Saddam Hussein 48 hours to leave Iraq or face invasion.

In the desert we were broken down into three groups: two FARP Teams (Fueling and Rearming Point) and a FOB (Forward Operating Base) element. The two FARPs were named Chicken and Sofa. The officers in charge of these two teams were pilots and those were their call signs. The FOB was called Pegasus, a white horse with wings and the logo for our squadron. Our squadron nickname was The Workhorses.

On 18 March 2003, somewhere around 1100, my S-3 Officer, Major Tappa, read the speech given by President Bush to us. It was being read to us because we didn't have any television like some of the more established bases did. Our camp was being used as a staging area, and we still lived in primitive conditions. Everything we had done prepared us for this moment: NBC (nuclear biological and chemical) drills, rehearsing tactics to be used in case of an IED (improvised explosive device) exploding near our convoy, and perfecting numerous other tactics that would be needed when we crossed the border into Iraq.

To mentally prepare for our mission, we sat in a large informal gathering on the berm and did a large sand table walk-though of our mission. The walk-through reminded me of an episode of *Friends*. They are all in England when Ross is getting married. Joey and Chandler are touring London. Joey doesn't really know how to orientate a map so he puts it on the ground and stands on it. Well, this is what we were watching: the convoy commanders standing in a map of Iraq drawn in the sand. The FARPs would move north one day apart from each other. The FOB element would move out on the third day when the war started. The FARP teams would leap frog each other and were to fuel the helicopter gun ships in support of the RCTs (regimental combat teams) as they moved through Iraq. The FOB was to move up to an airfield in the town of An Numaniyah. We learned the names of the routes we would be taking and the names of FARPS other than our own along the way. Highways were named after football teams. For instance, Highway One, the main highway through Iraq, was called Tampa and the highway that ran parallel to it was referred to as Dallas. As the mission was read to us, each of the FARP team commanders walked through the large sand table to show how the mission would move. The FARP sites were named after baseball stadiums: Pac Bell, Qual Com, Wrigley, and finally Three Rivers, the FOB that would be located in An Numaniyah. After the mission brief, as each team prepared to leave, we felt somewhat invincible.

On 23 March 2003, the night before we left, we slept in the staging area on cots or in the vehicles—wherever you found space to sleep. We were issued extra ammo, and the SNCOs had the option of carrying grenades. I had two grenades and I immediately named them Mac and the Holy grenade—Mac was my buddy and when all else fails use the Holy grenade. We spent many hours that night in and out of the bunkers because of SCUD missile attacks. There wasn't much sleep that night; however, this, I think, is the first time since we left North Carolina that the twitch in my right eye became annoying. I first noticed this twitch in my eye sometime before we left to fly to this miserable place, but can't say I know when it started; it was just there. It stopped sometime after I returned home.

On 24 March 2003, FOB element Pegasus departed the safety of Camp Workhorse, rolled up Highway One, and crossed the border into Iraq. The first sign you see is of a camel with one line drawn through it, the international sign meaning no camels were allowed into the country.

On the second day into our convoy, the morning sky was a different color than I had ever seen before. It was blood orange red. If I could imagine what the sky in hell would look like, I would picture this. As we started out, a sandstorm began and continued to strengthen. Visibility was good but getting worse. The humvee I was traveling in didn't have any doors, so there wasn't any protection from the elements. As the day went on I was covered in sand. A scarf on my face kept the sand out of my throat.

We encountered what were probably army solders who had ditched their uniforms and opted for civilian clothing. One of our security vehicles stopped these men and searched them. Hidden on their bodies were several AK-47 rifles broken up into separate operating groups. During this encounter, my company commander radioed the convoy commander and asked how far after the bridge was our left turn. The turn happened to be only two hundred yards after the bridge. We were two miles or so down the road. Our convoy was now split up. We missed a turn we were supposed to take but because of the blinding sandstorm, you just couldn't see it. Our convoy was heading in two separate directions.

The humvee I was traveling in raced to the front of the convoy to stop forward movement. We told the lead vehicle driver what had happened, and that now we had to turn a large, heavily loaded convoy of tactical vehicles around on a very narrow road. It was done quickly and with purpose. We eventually had our convoy back together despite the sandstorm, We continued to try to maintain visual sight of the vehicle directly in front of us while maintaining a safe distance, but we also continued to travel at a higher rate of speed than conditions allowed.

Although we had hurried, that night we were forced to halt our convoy on the side of the road and endure a night of freezing cold, driving rain in enemy territory. We had traveled only 28 miles in 14 hours. During one of the many NBC classes we were given prior to our departure, I vividly remember the sergeant who gave the classes telling us to keep our MOPP suits as clean and as dry as possible so that the charcoal lining in the suit wouldn't break down as quickly. Well, with no doors on the humvee there was little hope of keeping my suit dry. I prayed that one night of pouring rain wouldn't doom my suit.

All the vehicles were positioned on the sides of the road. Two 7-ton trucks mounted with MK-19s were positioned at the front and rear of the formation. On our flanks were several hardback humvees mounted with M2s. During the night, we were on 50% alert. I was on radio watch so that my company commander could get some sleep and then we would trade off after a while. Things did not stay quiet long.

Radio silence was broken when the forward radio operator came on and said a low rumbling noise was coming our way. Within minutes, he came across again with the same message. Marines were starting to get out of their vehicles to listen, preparing themselves for the worst. Many weapons did not function because they were so packed with sand from that day's storm and we had no way to clean them. As the rumbling continued to approach, we were as prepared as we could be for whatever was to happen. It was evident that we were going to have some kind of confrontation. The night was so dark you could not see your hand in front of your face. The darkness in the desert is the darkest you will ever see. You could actually wave your hand in your face and feel the breeze from your hand but not see your hand.

It was the scariest night I spent in Iraq, not knowing what was going to become of us. Somehow, from somewhere, we felt a lot of prayers coming our way. The next day we found out we had gotten forward of the regimental combat team due to the sandstorm and were deep into Iraqi Army territory. An Iraqi tank division passed us, but never saw our convoy on the roadside. It was the darkness that provided us with camouflage. All of us had lived through the worst sand storm in 100 years and a near miss by an enemy tank column. For the next several days, we would see the aftermath of war: oil lines burning, dead Iraqis, and the death of one of our own.

MCWS 3

21 March – 20 April 2006

Guest Contributors:
Shawne Steiger
Dinty W. Moore
Tom Sheehan
Lisa Kahn Schnell
Bob Cowser, Jr.
Rebecca McClanahan
Ian Pounds
Jillian Schedneck

There it lay, a tranquil sea or lake without water, if such a simile be admissible, with the day going down upon it: a few birds wheeling here and there: and solitude and silence reigning paramount around. But the grass was not yet high; there were bare black patches on the ground; and the few wild flowers that the eye could see, were poor and scanty. Great as the picture was, its very flatness and extent, which left nothing to the imagination, tamed it down and cramped its interest. I felt little of that sense of freedom and exhilaration which a Scottish heath inspires, or even our English downs awaken. It was lonely and wild, but oppressive in its barren monotony. I felt that in traversing the Prairies, I could never abandon myself to the scene, forgetful of all else; as I should do instinctively, were the heather underneath my feet, or an iron-bound coast beyond; but should often glance towards the distant and frequently-receding line of the horizon, and wish it gained and passed. It is not a scene to be forgotten, but it is scarcely one, I think (at all events, as I saw it), to remember with much pleasure, or to covet the looking-on again, in after-life.

—Charles Dickens, on first seeing Looking-Glass Prairie, where now exists Highland, Illinois. In *American Notes for General Circulation*, Ch. XIII: A Jaunt to the Looking-Glass Prairie and Back: http://ebooks.adelaide.edu.au/d/dickens/charles/d54an/chapter13.html

THE TROUBLE WITH WRITING

A writer is like a recruit: the trouble with writing is as great as the trouble with boot camp. Every male recruit's life as a United States Marine begins the same way: get off the bus and stand on the yellow footprints to receive a dressing down. This first of many "Hurry up and wait" Training Day moments of infamy is like a writer's life filled with many stops and starts. Writers answer their calling via many beginnings, but always they need and find someone to help lead the way. Writers find mentors; recruits find drill instructors.

On January 3, 1978, three years after the Vietnam War ended, I arrived at Parris Island, South Carolina, for recruit training. I sat waiting for I knew not what on the bus that had carried us from the Charleston airport, the hub of congregation before our midnight run to Parris Island. Having enlisted only two weeks before my ship date, I was clueless as to what might follow. During my first moments at Parris Island, I stared out the bus window, watching as men lined up on the yellow footprints painted on the road beside the curb. Soon the men were slouching away under a browbeating handed out by a wiry guy wearing a Marine-green uniform and a Smokey, Drill instructors' signature headgear. Then a woman in a Marine uniform—light green shirtwaist, dark green skirt, black oxfords, and green coal scuttle-shaped hat—boarded the bus and told the hundred or so expectant faces looking up to her to line up on the sidewalk.

No yellow footprints for us. We woman recruits were ferried to our next stop, Woman Recruit Training Command (WRTC), aboard a cattle car—a stale sweat-smelling metal box-on-wheels lined with benches and attached to a truck cab. We traveled toward WRTC along Parris Island back streets in the hour before dawn. I didn't notice the "Where It All Begins" sign hanging across Boulevard de France between the visitor's center and the post office, but that sign would become etched in memory during my recruit training and my years as a drill instructor. Although the sign still hangs today, thirty years after I completed recruit training, the slogan has been changed to something more generic and less meaningful to me: "Where the Difference Begins"; as if to say the world is in a constant state of revision, like recruit training and writing.

Upon my arrival to Parris Island, I didn't even notice the palmettos lining the avenue that led to WRTC—I was too busy thinking about the Dress Blue uniform I planned to be wearing when I left the Island. This was my new beginning, and I was going to be the best Marine ever—the Honor Graduate, the only recruit in those days who left the Island wearing Dress Blues. Recruits, like writers, always hope to be Number 1 in their profession, no matter denials of aspiration. Writers' new beginnings take form as edits and revisions. We learn violence of craft as we polish ideas into final drafts. Sometimes the polishing is never finished, as Walt Whitman discovered in writing the many versions of *Leaves of Grass*, his epic poetic work.

Upon our arrival to WRTC, we recruits were ushered into a classroom. I sat at a schoolhouse desk filling out paperwork and answering multiple choice and fill-in-the-blank questions while pondering urinalysis, a thing I had never before encountered. "Pregnant or using drugs?" they asked at intake, while shoving a small, clear plastic bottle with a gold cap in my direction. I answered, "No," and hoped for the best on both counts. Hope was all I had. This is as true for writers as it is for recruits, at least until training is completed. Most writers begin their work with little more than an idea and the hope that hard work will result in publication.

When I joined the Marine Corps in December 1977, nothing much was working out for me. Adrift in my small Midwestern hometown with no center to my universe, I survived by waitressing, piece working in factories, cooking in diners, cleaning nursing home rooms, and living in my car. I had a feeling that even the American Dream, the idea that hard work could change my future, was a lie I had been bottle-fed along with the goat's milk my father had insisted my mother feed me as an infant. Like me, many writers struggle to make a start from humble beginnings and continue the struggle with their writing during bits of time snatched away from hours working a job to pay the bills. Writing seldom pays monetary rewards.

Right then and there in the classroom, I realized that having worn a brown corduroy dress and brown leather heels on my ship date was naïve. Other recruits had received more than a short list of what to bring to boot camp from their recruiters. Many of the recruits had received instruction on the essentials of military life during regular meetings with their recruiters. Some recruits had already been doing physical training, or PT, as I soon learned to call exercise. I felt the grandest fool in the history of recruit training, but I could hardly blame my recruiter. Desperate for a job, I had enlisted on my recruiter's promise of a job and a keg of rum. As a writer, I've often felt the fool after submitting my best work for publication only to have it rejected, later discovering how error-riddled my manuscript had been, or how silly it seemed when compared with others' finer works.

My platoon was processed through the fundamentals of recruit life under the guidance of forming DIs. We recruits wouldn't meet our training DIs until our third day aboard WRTC. The forming DIs moved us from building to building along catwalks, above-the-ground walkways between the WRTC compound's raised-foundation buildings. Stumbling along from place to place, I noticed that hitting the heels of the recruit ahead of me initiated a domino effect in the undefined herd of female flesh. The Great Herd moved blindly toward gear issue and chow, each recruit part of a chain reaction, wobbling, tottering, shoving her toes into the heels of the recruit ahead. Publishers' slush piles of rejected work come to mind, bin after bin of refused manuscripts piled one atop the other, bound for the Great Dumpster of Unpublished Works.

My feet hurt terribly in the heels and the dress was a nuisance. Thank God, by the end of the first day we had received our initial gear issue, including uniforms. We were hurried to change into blue cotton slacks, light blue short-sleeved blouses, dark blue button-front sweaters, blue canoe-shaped hats called covers, and spiffy white canvas tennis shoes worn with white socks. Marine-green zip-front field jackets and web belts hung with a canteen attached to the belt by clips on the Marine-green cloth canteen cover completed the uniform. When a writer's work is finally accepted for publication, and redressed by an editor and the fact-checking staff, it often ends up reading completely differently from the original submission.

Throughout training, we were trucked from place to place in cattle car after cattle car, each carload smelling more strongly of sweat equity than the last. Our first stop on Forming Day 2 was classification testing. This was an exercise in redundancy—I had already taken the required tests and was guaranteed a position as an air control electronics operator in the A7 occupational field, a job I knew nothing about. Any job other than cooking was fine with me. I raised my hand and made my point absolutely clear to the Marine administering the test: I could see absolutely no reason for being retested—didn't he understand that I was tired and had a headache? He replied that I had enlisted only for the A7 job field, and my test score would determine my specific duties.

"But that's not what my recrui—"

"Sit down, shut up, pick up that pencil, and fill in those circles—I don't care what your recruiter said." That test administrator was similar in many ways to editors I've worked with: "Do you want this published? Then accept correction."

The recruits nearest me gave me that "Stop making life worse for us" look. But someone had to stand up for individual rights. Still, at that moment I began to wonder if my recruiter had lied to me about more than the keg of rum he had promised, a keg of rum I'd yet to receive—that eighth wonder of the world remained as elusive as its seven sisters. Maybe my recruiter had lied about my job as an air control electronics operator, too; maybe I would still end up a cook in the Marines. *Maybe my work will never be published—*

I shut up and took the test.

Later that day, at the Chamber of Horrors known to all recruits as Medical, Series 1 stood in line waiting to receive the first set of a long series of inoculations spread across eight weeks of training. Each of us held The Recruit Guidebook open before our eyes. The Guidebook seemed to be the only thing that mattered to everyone except me—I hated studying and hadn't known that boot camp would mean memorizing endlessly long passages of Marine Corps history, uniform regulations, and inspection procedures. As a writer, I've found many guidebooks, some written as creative works, others written as textbooks: MLA-Style, APA-Style, Chicago-Style—

"Do Not Lose That Guidebook, Recruits," the forming DI commanded. "That's your Bible. And you better get that stinkin' rank structure memorized by evening chow. Maybe your real DIs'll give you a little credit for having a brain. Say it. You got nothing else to do but wait for them sailors to give you shots. Get on it. You, Recruit—Don't even think about talking to those males. STAND UP STRAIGHT. Say it...NOW."

The long line of recruits stretching into an alien horizon came to life with one voice: "Aye-Aye Ma'am. Private-E1-Breathe, Private first class-E2-Breathe." On and on we recited—no, shouted—each title and pay grade directly from the Guidebook. From private to private first class, lance corporal to corporal, sergeant to staff sergeant, the mysterious titles leapt from our mouths until we reached the top of the enlisted rank structure: "Sergeant Major-E9, Breathe, Ma'am."

"It's a good thing we put the 'Breathe' in there Recruits, 'cause if you weren't told to breathe, you'd forget to breathe, every single half-civilian one of you out there—and believe you me, when we get through with you there won't be one-sixteenth civilian left in you. You give a hundred and ten percent; you get back a hundred and fifty. You get what you give and nobody gives a dog-gone what you did before. Now...who runs the show, Recruits?"

"Ma'am, the officers, Ma'am," we fired back some of the hype aimed our way at every turn on the catwalk. The forming DIs seemed to truly enjoy washing our befuddled brains with military knowledge, just as writing instructors fill their students' minds and time with endless writing exercises on description, character, and plot. My DIs pontificating on what "My Marine Corps" meant to each of them was a nonstop frontal-lobe attack morning, noon, and night. So, too, the endless reading lists writing instructors assign and student writers must master.

"Recruits, who gets the job done?"

"Ma'am, the troops, Ma'am."

"The Troops make it happen. Don't you forget it. And don't you forget you can't do it alone. Let me repeat that: YOU CANNOT DO IT ALONE. Now recite the officers' rank structure, Recruits, and make it pronto, the bluebells are comin' with their spears."

Like a writer's aching pen-hand or typed-out fingers, we recruits were no less sore. Our upper arms swollen from shots, we returned to the squad bay to pack our civilian clothing and any contraband items in our suitcases. After locking and labeling the suitcases, we watched as the life we used to know was herded away in a cattle car. It was all headed for storage in a warehouse at a mystery location, like so many drafts of a life story shut away in a file drawer. While we recruits were watching our pasts roll away, the forming DIs continued talking—they never stopped talking, just as a writer never stops writing—assuring us that Parris Island was a real island surrounded by acres of alligator-filled swamp at the edges of alligator-filled rivers that led to an alligator-filled ocean. DIs are as skilled as writers at using the power of imagination as means to an end. Of figures of speech, DIs know no end.

There were only two ways off Parris Island. Either recruits graduated and were sent on to their "A" schools for basic training in their new jobs or they were kicked out for failing to pass the markers on the roadmap to Graduation Day. Our forming DIs rattled off the long list of ways a recruit might be exiled forever from Parris Island and the Corps: mental problems, physical problems, failure to pass the physical fitness tests, failure to pass the academic tests—

Failure? Kicked out? Not me! Not ever!

Writers, too, write until they drop; no matter how many times they are warned failure awaits their efforts to bring a work to life.

As the DIs droned on, their list of possibilities for failure as endless as the turns in the river beyond our barrack's portholes, my concerns grew about the contraband camera locked in my footlocker. But there it stayed as the cattle car rolled away, and as forming days grew into training days, that camera recorded a snippet of each day—a group of women in sweat gear climbing over stalls in the head; a group of women engaged in field day, a day of playing battle ball and softball, of eating C-Rats and hot dogs in the ball field, of smoking the single cigarette that came in the boxes of food left over from Vietnam, the boxes packed with waterproof matches, salt and pepper, coffee, sugar and creamer packets, a single paper napkin and a single cigarette, the C-Rat cardboard boxes neatly packed with cans containing edible sustaining grit, John Wayne can-openers, plastic cutlery and a single piece of chocolate shit-disk candy we recruits thought had been formulated to counteract negative effects of the gritty food.

On the third day of forming, our real training began when our forming DIs handed us off to our permanent escorts on our guided tour of Parris Island—namely, our platoon DIs. One of these three tour guides looked tough and one looked like a librarian (Any teachers or writing instructors come to mind?). The third DI's face appeared to be covered with all the make-up she owned; the starch intended for her uniform seemed to have been sprayed onto her blonde curls. The librarian introduced herself as Staff Sergeant Raines, our Senior Drill Instructor, claiming direct responsibility for our training and for the conduct of the other two DIs. Her assistant assassins of the civilian in each recruit were Sergeant Harkor, more Incredible Hulk than woman, and Sergeant Crays, that starched and made-up blonde version of Linda Carter channeling Wonder Woman.

A recruit is powerless to do anything except follow the recruit in front of her from TD 1 (Training Day) to Graduation Day. So it goes for writers from idea to publication. There is always anxiety of influence for both recruit and writer to contend with—how can any writer ever expect to out-write the masters that came before? How can any recruit expect to outperform her DIs?

We recruits had the right to make head calls, to three hots (meals) and a cot (rack) each day, to send and receive mail, and to enjoy one hour of free time each weekday with four hours free time allowed on Sundays. As a teacher and a writer, I've enjoyed far less free time than any recruit! For us recruits, those 10 hours of free time a week were not free, but were spent catching up on spit-shining, Irish pennant cutting, ironing in preparation for another inspection, and studying the cursed Recruit Guidebook in preparation for another test (or publication submission).

I hadn't expected to, but I enjoyed the force-fed structure and discipline of recruit training, and I've enjoyed applying that discipline to writing. As a recruit, I wanted more than ever to be the number one recruit, the Honor Graduate, the very best recruit in the platoon, the one who wears the Dress Blue uniform home. From the beginning of training, I was absolutely certain that I would be that recruit. As a writer, the longer I work my craft, the more skilled I become, and I always hold out hope that someday my work will be published.

When the person responsible for enlisting me told me that no one cared what I had done before enlisting, I believed. For the first time in my life, it didn't matter that I was the child of a broken home, raised by my mother and grandparents in tiny Highland, Illinois during the 1960s, when broken home families were outcasts from the larger community. For the first time in my life, it didn't matter that I'd grown up next to a dump, in a house where stock cars racing on a nearby track hummed me to sleep. I believed I could be the best Marine recruit ever to tread the catwalk—I could be Number 1 if I worked hard. No less is my belief that if I work hard as a writer, my work will be rewarding.

We recruits came to know our drill instructors a little better as one or the other of them shouted us awake each morning at 0445 with her rendition of "Reveille, Reveille, get out of the rack! It's another glorious Marine Corps morning!" Each night, we were ordered into the rack by 2045. At the end of each glorious Marine Corps Training Day, Taps sounded: *Day is done, gone the sun, from the lakes, from the hills, from the sky, All is well, safely rest, God is nigh.* But silence never fell with the last tape-recorded bugle note piped through the compound. An anonymous recruit would begin singing the Lord's Prayer. Recruits throughout the compound joined in rounds until every platoon in WTRC was singing the Lord's Prayer, the chorus carrying a thousand wishes across the dark sky and away from our world of tears. We writers, too, shed a world of tears, the result of our characters' conflicts and our own, the result of frustration, rejection letters, indifference, and sometimes, of flat-out being ignored. Sometimes our work results in emotional flooding, and memory feels real once again. In those moments, we remind ourselves that the past is past, that "Now" is a safety zone where the past can no longer harm us, and that we have a purpose in sharing our memories with others through writing. A writer must always know her purpose and her audience just as a recruit knows her family in the stands on graduation day.

At boot camp, everything between reveille and the Lord's Prayer gradually took on a sense of routine. Yet never was routine quite routine, remaining always a degree more fantastical than reality, as if I were adrift in someone else's dream, or a character in a novel. Every waking hour was a training hour and not a minute of eight weeks training time was wasted. This is also true for the writer who covets every moment for writing, and finds characters and books taking over life. The writer is never grumpier than when living interferes with writing.

The DIs appeared everywhere, whenever least expected. Like editors and publishers transforming a manuscript or a writer—despite the latter's objections—my drill instructors were relentless, fire-breathing Hellcats always on the watch for refusals to train, scheming fresh horrors to transform our civilian brains into military minds 24-Hours a day. When The Three Hellcats were not in our faces inflicting their wills and the regulations of the Corps upon us, they hung out in their office, the Hellcat Hut, with the blinds drawn. We recruits were certain they were peeking through the slats to catch a recruit at loose ends, fresh reason to tear brains in two with Hellcat hobgoblinry. For writers, Hellcat critics maul our best intentions by finding the loophole missed in revisions, threatening extinction for writer and work following publication.

Each morning, during the fifteen minutes between 0445 and 0500, we made head calls, brushed teeth, combed hair, and dressed in our blue utility uniforms. We placed on our feet the black socks and black leather spit-shined oxfords that had replaced our spiffy white socks and white tennis shoes after our forming days ended. In 1978, the female Marine utility uniform—blue slacks and light blue blouses—looked nothing at all like the green male Marine utility uniform: Vietnam War-era sateens heavily starched and pressed and worn with black leather jungle boots. The men's uniform, and the stated difference of ours, is like a writer's work built upon past works—an echo from another world.

Standing at the position of attention in front of our racks at 0500, we forty-nine recruits were ordered to "Square away the squad bay." Writer, you must keep your workplace and your mind free of rubble.... Scurrying about, bumping and trampling each other in the rush to empty GI cans, we swept the floor and squared away the head before morning chow. Screeching and ordering us lesser minions about, our guide and squad leaders quickly became Napoleons intent on conquering the WRTC world. Memories of writers' conference and graduate school workshop sessions filled with too full-of-themselves writers are no less stressful. And those ideas—my God, how they trample a writer's psyche on their way into the world!

At 0515, we were once again standing-by in front of our racks, recruits and racks lined up two-by-two, we recruits ready to carry out the Plan of the Day: learning to stand perfectly still at the seven-point position of attention. As if from thin air, Sergeant Crays appears with an ironing board, and begins fifteen minutes of instruction on ironing a cutting crease in the sleeves of the light green Service "A" uniform blouse. Sergeant Crays, who always looks as though she had just unrolled her hair and freshly applied her pound of make-up (like a writer who gets it right each time with the first draft), obviously believed our best interests were served only by our metamorphoses into cookie-cutter versions of herself. Only then would we be ready for the great adventure that followed boot camp, what she and other DIs called "being a woman in a man's world."

Being a woman in a man's world was a new term for me. I immediately resented the phrase upon presentation in the first of many image development classes. Being an emerging writer in the midst of accomplished authors is a similar experience. At every turn, we women recruits were force-fed lessons on how to adapt to the Corps, including: "You might not be accepted by the men right away, Recruits, but you can definitely do a better job than them by always wearing your uniform proudly, maintaining a bright and cheery disposition, by following orders to a 'T,' and by always keeping yourself morally above reproach." We writers wear our work like clothes chosen for a first date each time we send out a query, a proposal, a submission—

"MUSTER NOW, NOT AN HOUR AGO," one of The Three Hellcats ordered at 0530 sharp each training day. Platoon 1A responded by tumbling out the double front hatch and onto the catwalk. When mustering from the front hatch—or anywhere else—women recruits were not allowed to shout and bark like dogs as we heard men doing in a parallel universe outside WRTC. The Marine Corps battle cry was denied us. No OOH-RAH for us! Half-whoop, half-scream, pure stress on automatic, OOH-RAH fired from the lungs like a shell from a barrel before exploding against the sheer chaos of the unknown-but-always-conquerable It. It being every mission a Marine is ordered to accomplish; "It" being every work a writer produces through shed blood, sweat, tears, and ink.

Each morning, we were expected to be eager to eat at 0530 because Marine Corps chow was a thing that mattered, a thing to be scarfed down before the twenty minutes eating time expired. Minutes were counted down from the time the last recruit sat down. Of the recruits who barely picked at their prison trays, most were weight recruits—a few pounds over their maximum allowable weight like those many stories a writer must cut down, revising a monster to reader size before an editor will claim it. Being a weight recruit meant constant harassment by The Three Hellcats and non-stop threats of transfer to PCP, the Physical Conditioning Platoon. For writers, revising is work haunted by threats of burning, abandonment, and failure—The Three Fates seem always to be breathing over the writer's shoulder: spin the yarn, unravel it, cut it—the essence lost, the work dismembered, as too often happens when writing is overworked.

PCP meant more than eight weeks of boot camp and possibly being lost forever in an administrative shuffle from one platoon to another. Writers sometimes quit after the revision process drags on for weeks, months, or years. Fred Leebron, Queens writing program director, often said, "Writing is a game of attrition; don't attrite." Many recruits give up after being assigned to PCP. Being assigned was a constant threat; an artificial stress that caused injured recruits to deny illness and weight recruits to become pickers, starving themselves no matter the level of hunger attained as the result of natural stressors of daily training. For a writer, losing the heart of a piece in revision is a constant threat. But sometimes in letting go, the heart is found beating and alive though hidden among lineouts and deletions. Revision fuels artful writing; starvation occurs when a writer refuses to feed a work with revision and creates an anorexic manuscript without substance.

Chow, like everything else in recruit training, was Government Issue. We were told we could talk quietly during chow, but we knew better. Every minute of chow time was required to shovel down pasty tasting grits, scrambled eggs, bacon dripping with grease, and burnt-dry toast. Like an ellipsis at sentence's end, Chow Hall leftovers were picked up daily by a farmer and used to slop his hogs. For writers, to revise is to spend time alone with the work, to feed the creative process. For recruits, to eat Government Issue food was to chew on a shelter half, to smell and to taste green canvas until the heart pumped Marine-green blood, to know that even we recruits were Government Issue. Like a writer eating, drinking, and breathing language, we recruits ate, drank, and breathed the Corps, alert to everything within sight and hearing. Slyly we would glance in the direction of the Hellcat-in-charge, watching for her to rise from her own chow-filled tray before heading for the hatch. When she did spring from her seat, our trays were put up, empty or not, and we mustered out yet another hatch. Writers have deadlines shadowing what the work might become with more time, and there is never time enough.

Outside the chow hall, we formed squads until we swelled into a platoon on the catwalk, each recruit standing at parade rest with her feet twelve inches apart, her hands perfectly clasped in the small of her back. I was careful to place my hands and feet just-so. By the end of my first official week of training, I had already found myself on many different occasions—none of which were held to celebrate my Honor Grad potential or leadership abilities—standing at the position of attention in the Hellcat Hut hatch for a dressing down, a standing-by to stand-by that always culminated in push-ups, mountain-climbers, and side-straddle-hops on my part, accompanied by a one-way screamfest conducted by one or the other of The Three Hellcats. Sergeant Crays most often instigated my dressing down, always for some new infraction of the code of conduct for recruits. Smiling at a male recruit or not pressing a crease just so resulted in an equal measure of DI ranting, the screamfest mastered by generations of DIs. Mustering all her starched, pressed, lipsticked, curled-blonde-hair glory, Sergeant Crays had already told me more than once, "You'll be lucky if you ever see private first class." A writer encounters many Sergeant Crays, but learns to believe in herself, in her work, despite the many bombs dropped on her most cherished turns of phrase—

"Aye, aye, Ma'am!" I shouted at Sergeant Cray's face each time she put me down, spit flying from my mouth, rebellion shooting from my eyes. What Sergeant Crays said was a thing that mattered not at all, no more than what the barflies back home had said about the certainty of failing boot camp, or what my mother said about me never finishing anything. Something had damned well turned up, and I wasn't about to let Wonder Woman stand in my way with her "You'll never make it in my Corps" attitude. Sergeant Crays seemed to sense who I really was, a far from patriotic mixed-up kid. I was certainly not like our platoon guide, a cute little dark-haired thing who wanted to be an Olympic-class gymnast but wound up carrying the platoon guide-on, a scrap of gold cloth embroidered with "1A," the guide-on our standard and she its bearer. Sergeant Crays and our All-American Girl guide had probably never even slept with a man—

"A-ten-Hut! Forwardddddd, Harch!" Sergeant Crays bellowed to the platoon. Chugging into forward motion, we recruits marched away from the chow hall, forward being a most important thing always undertaken by the left foot first, each step thirty inches deep and taken at one hundred twenty steps-per-minute into the unknown. Sergeant Crays called cadence, "Alignment, step, Alignment, step, Alignment-tothe-Right, step, step, Yeft-a-right, step, step," correcting as we marched along the catwalk, each of us aware that should we even be marched into a wall, we were to continue in the designated direction without ever, NOT EVER, adjusting our choreographed dance of pivots and steps unless we were commanded to do so. Conventions of writing are often just as stifling. The blind faith required to follow them is no less important than that recruits must exercise in following DI commands.

During drill, a hissy-fit recruit or two was always seething in my direction: "To the right, to the right"—as if I were any less expert at alignment than the others! Keeping specific head-to-chest and shoulder-to-shoulder distances between recruits required nothing less than perfect vigilance, just as writers too often demand perfection of themselves. The quest for perfection dulls the mind, squashes creativity, and blurs the work in the same way the square black-rimmed plastic glasses I'd been issued as a recruit distorted everything in range of sight. In recruit training, my body seemed in revolt against everything I willed of it, as if all of me were a numbed limb awakened from a long sleep. This is also how the need for perfection affects writers—numbing, stifling, denying the work what it wants to become—

"Alignment, step, Alignment, step, Alignment-tothe-Right, step, step, Yeft-a-right, step, step, Yeft-a-right-Left-right-Left-right—"

A sense of foreboding unsettled the chow hall grits in my belly—

"—Yeft-a-right, step, step, Yeft-a-right-Left RIGHT-LEFT—ALIGNMENT TO THE RIGHT RECRUITS—STOP-STOP-STOP...RECRUITS, STOP!"

My chin was tucked neatly against my throat, my back was perfectly straight, and my fingernails neatly brushed the seams of my blue trousers as I swung my arms six inches to the front and six to the rear of that seam—Wonder Woman couldn't be after me—

"Aye, Aye Ma'am," the giant blue caterpillar shouted, and came to a halt timed to the beat of ninety-eight black oxford-clad feet stopping on concrete.

"RECRUIT, WHAT'S WRONG WITH YOU?" Sergeant Crays blew up in *my* face, the red of her eyes intensifying the blue on their lids, the fury in her face dimming the blush on her cheeks, the spit flying from her lipstick-covered lips like hail from a fiery sky—her speed and agility in reaching my position proved she had been either a track star or a hurricane in another life. I never once stopped hoping someone else would be singled out for screwing up, that someone else would earn not only the wrath of the DI but of the platoon en masse, yet with every thirty-inch step I took my dream of wearing Dress Blues home moved further away from becoming reality. Writers sometimes believe editors are mean Sergeant Crays. Maybe; maybe not. But rejection letters always scream, "WRITER, WHAT'S WRONG WITH YOU?" Sergeant Crays' treatment helped prepare me for those rejections. I'll always be grateful for her and for rejections. I've learned much from both, particularly to respect all writing that comes across my desk no matter its difference from my own.

Following morning drill, we hurried back to the squad bay to change into PT (physical training) gear—a gray-blue flippy skort worn with blue utility blouse, white socks and white tennis shoes. Mustering out the back hatch, we marched through early morning light, crossed the parade deck, and lined up platoon by platoon in the PT Field with its ominous array of PT Tables: five-feet-high by five-feet-square dinner tables with red painted legs and sweat-soaked green canvas-covered tops. A DI leapt onto the PT table and warmed up the platoon with a heated one-way discussion of our many shortfalls as weakling recruits. While we were being side-straddle-hopped and run-in-place into submission, a brass bell sounded—

"Colors!"

Everyone on Parris Island faced the source of the music, snapped to the position of attention, and stood perfectly still and silent. The Stars and Stripes rose to the accompaniment of "To the Colors" piped through loudspeakers placed throughout the Island. After the flag was raised, the music stopped. A single second of silence enveloped the hundreds or thousands of recruits and trainers until—

"Carry On!" echoed across the Island followed by echoes of platoons, both male and female, resuming training exactly where they had left off: "1-2-3-7-1-2-3-8...."

For writers, distractions are legion. For me as a recruit the thought of men close as an echo was maddening. The other side of the island might well have been another planet, where male recruits were moving their arms and legs like a strangely huge, alien insect. Perhaps they were even wearing their chrome domes, steel helmets painted with chrome spray paint to reflect the sun. Maybe they were jumping around with rifles, wearing combat boots, and—

"Mountain climbers, Recruits, dig-dig-dig, Recruits, dig faster."

"1-2-3-1-1-2-3-2...."

"Dig, Recruits. NO PAIN NO GAIN," Sergeant Harkor screeched while she mountain-climbed atop the PT Table. Her feet moved like dashes splashing in puddles of ink—

REVISE, REVISE, REVISE—

Our DIs told us many times that they did everything we had to do. We were never left alone, not even for a minute, just as the muse never really leaves the writer. It is the writer who gives up, not the muse! We recruits were told that we could do It just as well as our DIs if we put our brain-housing groups to work accomplishing the mission. The stress of training was a matter of recruit perception, as is the stress writers experience while learning their craft. Sweat pools in the morning taught us recruits to be grateful for all we were receiving, just as a writer feels grateful for the finished work despite all that is sacrificed to achieve completion. For us recruits, the sweat dripping into our eyes proved we were giving, too. The thing we thought we couldn't do only served to make us stronger once we did It!

THE GLORY OF THE FINAL DRAFT—

"Face your fear or die, Recruits!"

Transformed from writers into authors, we might begin to fear success *more than failure.*

What awaits us in that world beyond the work?

Transformed from recruit into Marine, we would be proud to be green, proud to serve, proud to be women in a man's—

"Faster! Faster! Faster! NO PAIN, NO GAIN!"

—And then, REVISE again.

Overload, Regularity, Progression, Variety, and Balance: the PT strategy of recruit training was designed to ensure recruits passed the minimum requirements of the PFT, or Physical Fitness Test. Writers use much the same strategies to create publishable work. Writers often juggle more than one project at a time. They learn to cherish their workspace and to write each day. As they write, the work progresses from draft to finished piece. Then comes the time to move on to the next project, perhaps in a different genre. Throughout the writing process, balance in the work and in the writer's personal life is difficult. The work often overtakes life!

Women's PFT standards in 1978 called for running a mile and a half in fifteen minutes or less, performing at least twenty-two sit-ups in a minute or less, and hanging from a pull up bar during a flexed arm hang for at least 22 seconds. Each event had to be passed in order to achieve the minimum PFT score. No recruit who failed the PFT could graduate from boot camp. The flexed arm hang part of the PFT was performed on a pull-up bar. The bar was so high off the ground that we women recruits had to give each other a leg-up just to mount it. The bar, designed for the pull-up part of the men's PFT, was made of thick steel to fit a man's grasp. It was far too thick for most women to get a good grip. While hanging from the bar, fingertips faced the chin and the chin couldn't rest on the bar. When the event monitor shouted, "Drop," recruits stopped holding up the one being tested and the timer began ticking off seconds. Time accrued until the chin touched the bar or the elbows were no longer flexed.

When I dropped from the bar during trials, my head swam with the vertigo I'd experienced since my first crossing of the Mississippi River during my childhood. As a nineteen-year-old recruit, I was unable to hang from the bar longer than eight seconds.

"Do you want to end up in PCP, Recruit?"

Slush pile? Rejection letter? How does another revision sound?

Staff Sergeant Raines' words shot through me, straight into my heart. Others might fail or be sent to PCP, but not me. I couldn't fail. This was my last chance for a decent life. My bones shook. My gut dropped to my ankles. My head swam with thoughts of the great abyss. PCP! For the first time in my life, fear made itself perfectly understood.

At PCP, my Senior Drill Instructor informed me, I could join weight recruits and other non-PT-ing failures for an extended stay at WRTC. "Maybe you'll graduate by next March," Staff Sergeant Raines said. Then she dismissed me.

But there was nowhere to go!

Sergeant Harkor barreled over me, her hot breath hissing against my ear: "Strength comes from inside, Recruit. In my Corps that's called Intestinal Fortitude. You better get some, Recruit. You're gonna do push-ups every chance you get. That's an order and that's the only way you'll hang with this platoon. Hit the deck and gimme twenty—"

Find that intestinal fortitude, Writers! You can do It if you believe you can. No matter how hard you have to work, the work is worth it. Empty your desktop and pour your mind onto the blank page, but fill it. Shed tears for those beloved words that must be cut, but cut them. Search for the essence of your work in the shards of your life—you will find it.

From reveille to singing The Lord's Prayer, I did pushups during every second of free time until I could do push-ups all day long, until I could brush my teeth and read my mail while doing pushups. When my last chance to pass the arm hang arrived, I wrapped my hands around the steel pull-up bar as if to choke the life out of a lion. No weapon could have helped me fight that battle. That's a problem with writing, too—nothing but a firm belief in our work will bring our writing to life in the world.

Something inside me changed by more than degrees once I mustered the intestinal fortitude to pass the flexed arm hang. Growing up in a small town and not having much hope for a decent future had caused me to lose faith in the American Dream. Overcoming the obstacles of recruit training renewed my hope in the Dream by proving I could do It, whatever It might be. When *It* is writing, the obstacles are no less than those encountered in boot camp by recruits.

When writing memoir, seeing oneself as a character in action is far different from being the actor living the event. In a way, the stakes are higher because the outcome is known and honesty is required in the telling. There can be no plot adjustment, no invented crisis or climax, no titillating plot points added. Memoirists must create from experience, not imagination. But imagination does play a role through ordering and presentation of a true experience. Some might argue that this is revising the past. The narrator's truth, and rendering it into something universal, is what matters in memoir writing. Even the truth is in a constant state of revision in memory. Milspeak writers weren't simply revising the past by writing memoir; we were revising our emotional attachment and our emotional perception of the past. Milspeak writers weren't exactly cleansing the past in the traditional sense of catharsis that occurs when watching tragedy unfold on a stage or in a film. But catharsis—cleansing of emotions through identifying with a character's tragedy—was happening for the writers and me.

Translating experience into words cleanses perception of the past by restructuring emotional involvement with memory. Milspeak writers are taught to use timelines to separate actuality from the tricks memory plays when mixed with years of re-imagining. Timelines are a tool for *re-imaging* memory. Creating timelines of events replaces the fog of memory with the clarity of facts through researching the event and combining personal timelines with cultural and/or historical timelines. Something valuable is acquired no matter how difficult the experience. The truth of the matter beyond the shadow of imagination is revealed. Relationships to the wider world are discovered. The successes hidden by disappointment are uncovered. No matter how traumatic an event, learning something positive from something negative is more acceptable to the mind than living with the emotional hangover so often lurking beneath the surface in trauma survivors, whose imaginations have become a filter for trauma, overshadowing fact. Finding positive value in events that previously might have seemed to bring up only negative emotions is life changing, an act of meaning making that transforms personal experience into something with universal meaning. For Milspeak writers, the personal is rendered universal through timeline work and memoir writing. If the work resonates with a reader, the process is reversed, rendering the universal personal. In both cases, catharsis is the process at work. This process makes writing an act of self-healing and healing for readers. For Milspeak writers, this catharsis reaches its climax during Read Aloud. For me, the process is ongoing each time I visit MCAS Beaufort or MCRD Parris Island while leading a seminar. The place and the writers stir the past in me, and I, in them.

Writers had arrived to MCWS 1 and 2 with ideas and had left with a story or the start of one. They seemed to find the experience rewarding; so did I. Participants had found an outlet for their creative energy; so had I. Writing and sharing their experiences was cathartic for them and for me. I wasn't sure where the Milspeak experience was taking me professionally or emotionally; but, after several years of self-exile from the military, my renewed contact with the military began a process of homecoming for me.

Ten years after retirement you're a dead man—this was once a saying among Old Salts in the Corps. Perhaps this belief became legend as Old Salts watched their comrades drop one-by-one at that ten-year high water mark. Perhaps the high water mark is reached because many military retirees find nothing in civilian life equals the excitement, challenge, and purpose of active duty. Leaving the military means losing life purpose— military retirees, like many civilian retirees, often feel they are no longer needed, that their contribution to society has come to an end with the end of military service. What occurs following retirement is a pattern for what often happens to military people in general when leaving active duty, regardless of length of service. For every transformation a human being undergoes, an opposite and equal, lesser, or greater transformation will eventually transpire. Boot camp is a major transformer of human beings. At the completion of service, reentry to civilian life will generate an opposite and equal, lesser, or greater transformation. Civilians expect to be transformed by boot camp. They don't expect to experience as charged a transformation when leaving the service. But that transformation will transpire, with or without permission, regardless of length of service.

As I did, many military people set sail into the difficulties of beginning a second career without a military connection to serve as anchor. We sometimes drift into romanticizing our active duty pasts. A sedentary lifestyle and lack of military-lifestyle regulations brings increased drinking and smoking. Old habits get older and more difficult to live with but more unbearable to break. When I left active service, I was fortunate to have a foundation and anchor in 12-Step program philosophy. For others, the rigors of training, of having a daily training schedule and a mission to accomplish disappear amidst the flotsam and jetsam of disappointments. Professional disappointment increases personal disappointment. While trying to embark on a second career, I have found that civilian employers more often fear the baggage a military person might carry than do they recognize the potential of a military person to contribute to the office. At other times, I have experienced total indifference on the part of potential employers who do not respond with even a note to indicate they had received my application portfolios.

Lesser transformations following completion of service result in despondency, depression, illness, and homelessness. Sometimes, death follows heartbreak in the thwarted search for belonging that too frequently accompanies the transition from military to civilian life. After fighting ten years in the Trojan War, Odysseus required ten years to find home. In his book *Odysseus in America: Combat Trauma and the Trials of Homecoming*, Dr. Jonathan Shay points to Odysseus' journey as a metaphor for the combat warrior's journey from military life into civilian life.[1] That journey is more than a metaphor for combat veterans; it can be applied as template for understanding the journey all military people embark upon when leaving active duty.

Odysseus' journey can be studied as an archetype called into action in the psyche of every military person leaving the service, no matter duration of service or traumatic encounters. Military people, no matter rigor of duty, no matter the circumstances of departure or the length of service, require a lengthy period of time after leaving military service to find home. Maybe the length of Odysseus' journey holds the key to understanding the amount of time—time required to find home will equal length of service. Seldom do military people recognize this need for time in the chrysalis while the home-going process is unfolding, while a balance is struck between military life and civilian life through assimilation of military skills and disciplines with those required to live a successful life among civilians. In finding home, one's place in the civilian world, a blending of military disciplines into civilian virtues, aspects of self are assimilated into a unity of being. Something old dies so that something new can be born. Not everyone assimilates in a positive way. Some veterans encounter a broken bridge lined with many No Trespassing signs. Others encounter a Cyclops who thinks of them as "Nobody." Sirens wail—but only the service member hears them, while her family members' ears are filled with wax. There's a Lotus Eater waiting on every street corner with the latest drug to ease emotional pain. Not even Odysseus could resist Circe. Each of the challenges Odysseus met symbolizes one a transitioning service member will meet. Either the military member battles the monsters along the way and finds home (a greater positive transformation) or she dies a thousand deaths (a greater negative transformation).

Inability to find home results from refusal to change or from being unaware of the internal as well as external voyage required for entry into a new world following active service—what Aristotle might label errors of accident or ignorance. While military people might remember the length of time and training required to become militarized, they usually do not realize reincorporation with the civilian world will equal or exceed time required for militarization. Like Odysseus' men, military people sometimes simply do not possess the will to overcome the monsters encountered on the way to the new world that confronts them following retirement or departure from active service. They think the civilian world they are rejoining is the one they left when entering military service. Some do not even try to assimilate. These military people do not find home and family restored after an active duty career ends. There is no happy victory over the suitors populating the Palace of Necessity and Want when desire meets reality over the death of a dream in the veteran's mind. For those who do not recognize the magnitude of reentry to civilian life, it is the suitors who defeat the home-comers. The military stereotype undermines their efforts to assimilate; job applications go unanswered; the promised place in the defense industry doesn't pan out; the spouse resents having the retiree underfoot. The children, now grown, have lives of their own and no time for the retiree. The children one never had become shady if-onlys and what-ifs. The adjunct teaching position never becomes full time, while the abandoned thesis becomes a dream not deferred but denied. Hopes for a happy future are dashed on the rocks where Sirens sing.

I thought divorcing the military would save me from drowning at the high water mark. Years after my retirement from the Corps, Milspeak was gradually bringing me home to the military family I had left behind. Through leading Milspeak workshops, my perception of the past was being revised. In 2006, I didn't notice this change happening. My life was taking shape as a big "Y"; the Y's leg, the foundation of my teaching life, was my desire to write, and not only to write but also to be published. I saw my teaching career begin and move in two directions. In one direction, as a creative writing teacher, an evolving Milspeak was taking me down the road toward excellence. In the other direction, my career as a college adjunct instructor was a frustrating rut in my lane of the highway. Although I was finished as a teacher at USCB, a USCB professor had recommended me to Technical College of the Lowcountry (TCL). I was hired as an adjunct to teach two dual-credit survey of literature courses to high school juniors and seniors, not at the college but at the students' schools, one a private school and the other a public school. Both schools were located within two miles of each other, but were more than an hour's drive from home. The private school was small and neat, its faculty and student body 98% white. The public school was large. Police were stationed in the halls. The faculty and student body were 98% black. Later, when I discovered TCL hadn't been able to keep an instructor coming back to the public school, I figured that my military background must have made me seem perfect for the job.

Because I had not found fulltime employment, my hopes for my future were in writing. If I could write something worthy of a reader, I could continue to be a contributing member of society. The thesis I had been revising to achieve my goal was by this time a miserable memoir. Giving up on it after spending two years of my life writing it was inconceivable. I pulled sections from it, developed the sections into short memoir, and submitted those to literary journals, keeping always in mind Peter Stitt's (my primary thesis advisor in graduate school) adage: "Write for a reader, not to yourself." But that was a problem with writing—if I write for a reader, how can I not become a slave to convention, to the formulaic, to what sells books? There is one important fact to know about the effect of twenty years active duty upon my writing and teaching life. For two long decades,

I had to lead my life by someone else's rules. When I retired, my motto became "Never Again." Never again would I bend to convention simply to earn a buck. Never again would I be the Dragon Lady, or wear horns on my head. Never again would I allow quality control to overrule common sense. Never again would I allow myself to be stifled, suppressed, oppressed, or repressed. Abandoning my miserable memoir went against everything I had learned during twenty years in the Corps.

That my story might not be worth telling was my biggest fear in those days of reliving the past while revising my miserable memoir. When I began graduate school, I had no intention of writing about my life—I wanted to write essays about war and peace, poverty and terrorism. When I began graduate school, I had never heard of creative nonfiction. After my first residency at Queens, I realized a truth about my idea of writing and my fellow students' notions. We stood at either ends of the labyrinth that leads to the point where we each must face our fears at the end of the day. My writing was too dense, too full of ideas, too hard to read; theirs seemed simplistic to me.

"Your work reads like a foreign film," one of my first residency pod-members had said during our first workshop session.

"These are nice images," another said, "but what does it mean?"

I was thinking that I must be mentally screwed up. There wasn't enough time to learn all that I needed to become even a good writer. One thing I learned from my education is how little I know. But what is an essay if not a trial, an attempt to understand something or someone? Can that trial be truthful unless every falsification is examined? What is memoir if it does not contain the writer's beating heart?

After my first residency at Queens University, a piece I workshopped during the Internet submission period was chosen for publication in *Gargoyle* magazine. "Alphabet Story" was my first published work. I was ecstatic. At the beginning of my second residency, ecstasy was translated into humiliation when a fiction student I thought of as a friend greeted me: "I can't believe you came back," she said, without a hello.

I began working with Peter Stitt in January 2004 during my second residency. He cornered me in a classroom one afternoon before workshop.

"Why aren't you writing about your military career?" he asked.

"There's nothing to tell," I said.

"I don't believe that."

Peter, I soon learned, was always quick to point out a writer bullshitting the reader. I gave him the lowdown on my lowbrow military career and revealed the highlights of my high life.

"That's what you should be writing about," he said.

His words had hit their mark. During our Internet submission period, I tried to do as he asked. But during that period, my sister-in-law's final descent into alcoholism reached conclusion. After six-weeks comatose on life support, my sister-in-law died. I couldn't focus on writing. My last submission for the semester was due in two weeks. I had nothing. My tenure as a Queens' student couldn't be delayed. I had no time for delays. Problems I was encountering with the VA made asking for a delay out of the question. In fact, I mentioned nothing to Peter Stitt, Queens, or the VA about what was going on in my life. My problems were my own. A gunnery sergeant in the Corps takes care of others' problems without complaint, no matter the extent of hers. Not only that, but writing is either part or all of me, either hobby or profession. I am a writer because I am good at nothing else. Everything else I have done, from waitressing to serving twenty years in the military, was driven by the longest held hope: If I keep working, I will have time to write.

On Easter morning 2004, eighteen days after my sister-in-law's death, I was sitting on the deck of my pink house on Coosaw Island. I was finishing reading a book, *Mao II*, one of ten or so required titles for the upcoming May 2004 residency, my third of the five required for graduation. I still had nothing for my workshop submission. I began writing about that Easter in hopes that I could write myself out of the bad spot I was in. While it was unfolding, I recorded how that year's Easter morning was for me—a struggle with survivor's guilt and the alcoholic's desire to drink away guilt. That effort was neither the first nor the last time writing saved my sobriety, my sanity, and my life.

Later that week, I tried to revise the stub for a reader. Who that reader might be, I did not know. I had nothing else to give. Had I done a better job keeping to facts, giving descriptions, and making sense? I kept to the villanelle styling of the piece and made a diligent effort to avoid saying outright what I really wanted to say about consumerism, Easter, the health care and theological industries, the stigma associated with alcoholism, and the treatment of death in our times. All these subjects had been the focus of intense study during the writing of my undergraduate thesis, an inquiry into the transformation of secular symbols into sacred symbols. I did not try to give my entire drinking history in "Letting Go." I gave only what was necessary.

"Letting Go" appeared in *The Gettysburg Review* in January 2005. After my graduation from Queens in May 2005, Peter emailed to tell me that "Letting Go" had earned an honorable mention in *Best American Essays 2005*. This honor was completely over the top. Knowing something I had written was well received made revising my miserable memoir even more difficult. I hadn't been able to see my whole story and translate it into a longer work for a reader, as I had been able to translate a day in my life in "Letting Go." I still had not learned to read my life as text, something I was trying to teach Milspeak writers. My biggest question of the miserable memoir remained, Is this story worth telling?

In 2006, I was missing having readers for my work-in-progress and I needed expert advice in order to know how to proceed with my work. After asking Tristine Rainer to assist, I paid her more than a thousand dollars to read and critique my memoir-in-progress. The decision was one I rationalized by telling myself that letting the work rest while she read and critiqued it would be good for me. If the work was any good, she might help me find a publisher. I could shift gears and concentrate on teaching and writing shorter works. With Tristine reading my miserable memoir and guiding me in refining it, there would also be time to work on smaller pieces about things like stenciled calf-skin flats trimmed in red velvet and grocery stores, magnetic "Support our Troops" yellow ribbons and Selective Service.

After reading my miserable memoir, Tristine offered to publish it through a press she was founding. She also suggested I read James Frey's *A Million Little Pieces*. This account of alcoholism treatment had been written as autobiographical fiction but marketed as memoir. The book became a best seller before the truth was exposed. On its pages, I recognized a brilliant million lies about alcoholism treatment—but it was James Frey's narrator's truth. Frey showed me what kind of writer I did not want to be. Tristine showed me that, too. By March 2006, when the publishing contract was presented via email, I was hesitant to sign because I did not want contract pressures weighing on me during revision. Writing for a reader is one thing; writing for a publisher is another altogether.

One deadline or another had stifled me all of 2005 and most of 2006, not even accounting for my teaching responsibilities and being a new teacher. I was also reliving my sister-in-law's death through my aunt's, uncle's and longest friend's deaths. My aunt died of lung cancer January 5, 2006; her husband died January 7; my friend, the last from my hometown, died March 3, 2006. She was already dying when I last saw her, the summer before she died, when I had visited Highland after my aunt was diagnosed with cancer.

For my friend, a lifetime of addiction was ending in death by hepatitis C and cirrhosis. She was a shadow of the woman who had been my best friend in high school. She had never been able to change her drinking and drugging ways—enlisting in the Marine Corps had saved my life; my friend died on the anniversary of my boot camp graduation. I had tried to help her in earlier years—talking her out a marriage that was beating her senseless, and years later, offering my home to her to attempt recovery. She had never seen the ocean, she told me, and wanted to. That's a good reason to come to Beaufort, I told her; maybe some time away from what you're used to will help. After our summer visit, I had tried to reach her by phone and left messages, which were not returned. My friend's daughter called the day after her mother died and gave me what she knew of her mother's last days. Sometime during November, she had been beaten to bloody pulp on a St. Louis street corner, found by police, and remained unidentified until her daughter became worried and tracked her down in a hospital. My friend spent her last weeks semi-comatose in a hospital bed, just as my sister-in-law had—both women shared my disease; men had abused all three of us during our childhoods. Despite my own recovery as an alcoholic, I was unable to help either of these women I loved.

I was seriously questioning the validity of continuing Milspeak. What if I was hurting more than helping with Milspeak? Just who did I think I was?

David Ellard, my Marine Corps Community Services Liaison, and I weren't certain what MCWS was accomplishing, but MCWS 1 and 2 writers had enjoyed the experience. That was success enough for us to plan for MCWS 3 to be held in The Blackbird Zone at MCAS Beaufort immediately following MCWS 2. David sent out a revised flier via Marine Corps Community Services' email network. Although MCWS 3 was going to begin only a few weeks after MCWS 2 ended, we hoped the workshop would draw more participants than MCWS 2, even though we always worried that no one would sign up for the next MCWS.

As MCWS 3's start date grew closer, my life seemed to have become one long string of grief. Teaching commitments took up more and more time. I needed a little free space in my mind because I wanted to finish revising the miserable memoir for publication. Finishing it seemed more important than ever after my friend's death. Maybe my addiction and recovery story would do for strangers what I had been unable to do for the people I loved—help them find their way into recovery from addiction. In revision, the miserable memoir had already been taken from first person point of view to third person and back to first. I had cut it, chopped it, and rewritten the beast into mush. I was unsure if it could be saved. I seemed to be failing it as I had failed those I loved. Abandoning my miserable memoir was beginning to seem the only solution to its problems. Waging war with its scenes of disaster while I was grieving kept my mind going backward into the abyss of memory. There, something a writing instructor had said to me during my first residency at graduate school refused to die. I had cornered him in the Queens student union café on the morning after a brutal workshop session and asked his advice on becoming a writer.

"What do you have to offer?" my Aeolus asked in answer to my question.

"My life has been an experiment," I told the writing instructor, who wasn't my instructor and would never be. He was a faculty member, just sitting there, enjoying a cup of coffee before the ruckus began. That ruckus happened to be me, sitting down, crying, wondering how vast the ocean between Marine and teacher and writer, wondering if I possessed the proper gear to traverse that great sea, wondering if I'd made a huge mistake by not studying library science. How I wished that I had chosen library science instead of creative writing! I wanted him to tell me to go home and become a librarian—

"Everybody's life is an experiment," the Keeper of Winds said.

That made me feel better. Terminal uniqueness is a killer of the nth degree—or so I had learned attending 12-step meetings. But that sort of answer is still a lie: individuals are unique. Experience, and how we assimilate experience, makes us who we are.

From the abyss of black memories that haunted revisions of the miserable memoir, another ghost approached—those burning-at-the-stake words said to me by a writer at the beginning of my second residency: "I can't believe you came back."

Married to those remarks in memory were fresh comments made by people more aware of good writing than anyone else I knew: the New York agent who had read the miserable memoir at the request of one of my writing instructors. He said he wasn't interested—my writing was flat. Then came the Farrar, Straus, and Giroux editor who had asked to read a version of the miserable memoir when queried with a three-page proposal. His own verdict was, "...ultimately, it lacks a definite cohesion needed to move forward." This on the advice of his reader, who mistakenly read my miserable memoir as bad fiction and said of it: "elements are linked together almost entirely incohesively...organization provides for little character development, particularly with regards to secondary characters, or interest on the part of the reader...with little to no redeeming factors." Although results for Middlebury College's Bakeless Literary Prize, in which I had entered a version of the miserable memoir, had not yet been released, I knew my work would never make its way past first readers and into the judge's hands.

How could I sign a publishing contract? How could I ever manage to please readers with my vapid-moronic syntax and error-riddled prose? What sort of publisher would touch a story like mine? And who was my audience? Military readers, those who would most likely read a veteran's memoir, would no doubt hate me for the past that made me who I am today. Military readers would perceive my past as bringing discredit upon the Corps. I pushed on regardless of self-doubt, read through the miserable memoir again, made notes, and stalled as I recognized how poorly written it was, how the plot stalled into nonexistence and incoherency, and how stupidly literary and metaphoric I was trying to be. For once in my life, I was ready to agree with my mother: maybe It was too much for me. Just add the miserable memoir to Sally's Great List of Unfinished Undertakings.

Writers write—that's what we do, no matter what. No matter how good or bad.

Three writers signed up for MCWS 3 in the midst of the furball of chaos, insecurity, and grief that my life had become while teaching high school students college courses, revising my miserable memoir, and sorting through publishing contract clauses. Among them was Gary, the swat team detective who had to pass on MCWS 1 because of work and on MCWS

2 because of location. Three times he had signed up! It fired me up that anyone wanted what I was offering through leading Milspeak.

Instead of giving up on myself as a writer, I signed the publishing contract with Tristine, and I agreed to take a fulltime teaching position offered by a rural private school an hour's drive from home, where I had been teaching for Technical College of the Lowcountry. Two dreams were realized: adjunct teaching became a fulltime position and I had a publishing contract for the miserable memoir. Both decisions were difficult, as difficult as cancelling MCWS 3. Only three writers had signed up, I didn't want to take the chance they would drop out, and I wanted time to revise the miserable memoir for publication.

The trouble with revising my miserable memoir was becoming, for me, the trouble with honesty: both failure and success scared me shitless. There were so many people to protect. They shouldn't be blamed. I had created the twisted mess of my past. The figures in my life were players in my personal drama, not the Drama of "I," the narrator. Tristine suggested using composite characters. Using composite characters would mean creating composite events, which would lead to a long string of creations, including plot. As it was, creation of composite characters had been avoided in my miserable memoir. All events had actually happened as I described them. All conversations had occurred and were reconstituted as I remembered them, sometimes word for word, sometimes in shadowy relief, and sometimes in principle alone. I didn't want to turn my miserable memoir into an autobiographical novel.

Instead of using composite characters, I decided to change names, just as I had changed every mention of Alcoholics Anonymous meetings to 12-step meetings. I also removed all mention of my hometown's name, referring to it instead as Cowtown. I didn't want my experiences in Highland, Illinois to be representative of the town, just as my military experiences are not representative of the military in general. Nor is my experience in recovery representative of Alcoholics Anonymous. Being a writer does not make me a spokesperson for any people, place, or thing. As Milspeak workshop leader, I am hardly a spokesperson for military writers—I can only share my own experience as a military writer. The miserable memoir did not paint a pretty picture of my hometown in keeping with my mentality when I lived there, but vilifying the place was as inappropriate and pointless as vilifying the military, my ex-husbands, my mother, or my father. Still, nothing I could do was enough to completely disguise the real people that I write about. That's only part of the trouble with writing.

Writing about people, places, and things in my life is only worthwhile if, in learning about my life in the military, as an alcoholic, and as a person struggling with ambiguous memories, the reader comes out of the experience convinced that change is possible for anyone, that enlisting in the Marine Corps saved my life, that I am as flawed as anyone else, including my mother and father, that my heart loves long and never forgets, that amends can be made for past mistakes, that Life is for living, that experience is the teacher and mentor we all share, that missteps can be corrected, that forgiveness is possible and that writing is a healing art. This is why I share so much of my experience in this anthology. Another reason is that perhaps my story will reach those like me who were or are one of society's lost, like my father, like the Vietnam Veteran holding the sign, "Anything Helps," like me at nineteen-years-old when I lived in my 1964 Rambler American, like me when entering treatment for alcoholism in 1985, and like me in 1992 when I sobered up.

We memoirists worry about revealing ourselves and revealing others. We worry not only because we live in a litigious society, but also because we know that the people we once were and are, and the people we love or once loved, will be judged by a reader. Memoirists do not have the shield of fiction, but the narrator in memoir, like a protagonist in fiction, is a product of the writer, a persona—"N" the Narrator, who is used to create a work of art from memory, facts, and synthesis. The writer takes license in adjusting N's tone and managing what he remembers and reveals about himself, his experiences, his intimates and associates. By necessity, the memoirist must make war against self and associates before making peace with the past. One of my thesis advisors, Jane Alison, once described this as becoming violent with craft. Sometime a scalpel must be used as an ax when it comes to revision. But what of these associates, N's intimates, the society that lives in memory? What right does the writer have to manage the tone and experiences of human beings lassoed into serving as characters in memoir? Why not blend those living and dead into composite characters who can act and reveal power relationships with the narrator to better develop plot— what plot there might be in the actuality of a life? Should composites be made of major, minor, and scenic characters? How does one choose?

The real issue with composites rests in the rock-hard contract between memoirist and reader. Composites raise the question of integrity regarding other events. The reader might ask—did she really do all those things, wreck all those cars, win those awards? Ad infinitum. Like James Frey, did she make things up to build a good story? I am a writer, a human being who uses written language to share life experiences and lessons learned from the great experiment that is life. I'm going to make mistakes. I might hurt people I love no matter how hard I try not to, but I'm not going to call a work of fiction a work of nonfiction or vice versa. More important than the many questions about memoir writing raised by Freysian truth-warping is the contract binding three beings involved in the writing and reading process: the writer, the reader, and the indescribable power that brings writer and reader together—poetic faith.

My solution to the problem of writing memoir is to try to share my work with those mentioned in it before the work is published. The trouble with writing, in general, is more difficult to resolve. Maybe the reader will hate "I" without ever knowing me—that's the trouble with writing.

Above all, writing is a form of communication unique to human beings in its purpose to share with a reader the thoughts of the writer. Through writing, a writer finds a voice, one she might not know she possessed before trying to put her thoughts on paper. Empowerment lies in finding that voice and sharing that thought, not least of all because to write is to risk being known. For Milspeak writers that struggle is great. Military memoirists struggle with bringing discredit upon their service when writing about their military experiences. To take that risk is to exercise moral courage. The dilemma encountered in deciding to take that risk is real, as is the fear.

What follows in this chapter about a creative writing workshop that was cancelled are essays and memoir by writers who helped develop Milspeak. Here too, are works by mentors who took time away from busy schedules to sit down with Milspeak writers for an hour or two to discuss the trouble with writing. My own mentors are among these authors. Often without knowing they were doing so, they gave me hope to go on and helped me to develop as a writer, a teacher, and a workshop leader. These writers, like my boot camp drill instructors, showed me what is possible. Without them, there would not be a Milspeak. I would not have had the skill or courage to go on. Without them, I would not be writing. Without them, this book would not be in your hands.

Notes:
[1] Shay, Jonathan, M.D., Ph.D. *Odysseus in America: Combat Trauma and the Trials of Homecoming.* New York: Scribner, 2002.

RE-MEMBERING

By Shawne Steiger

Six years ago, I needed a reason to get up in the morning. I was plagued by relentless pain in my face and recurrent infections. It affected my ability to talk, to eat, to sleep, to wake up. I sought help from doctors, oral surgeons, the Mayo Clinic and the Internet. I contemplated suicide. I contemplated narcotic addiction. I contemplated locking myself in the house and watching soap operas all day.

I was working with Daena Giardella, an improvisation teacher and creativity coach, at the time and she talked often of the value of "saying yes" to the unexpected. In the book she wrote with Wren Ross, *Changing Patterns: Discovering the Fabric of Your Creativity,* she writes about her time living in Tel Aviv during the first Gulf War: "My creative process was merged with my day-to-day experiences living in the pressure cooker of potential danger while continuing ordinary chores and activities.... I learned the practical necessity of being in the moment...."[1] Being in the moment means "saying yes" to the impulse to engage in life, even when bombs are exploding around you.

I frequently wished I had pursued an MFA in addition to an MSW, but I had always lacked the courage to go ahead and do it. Until I got sick. I had begun to believe that whatever I had would kill me, and I was already bargaining with myself that if the pain and illness didn't improve by such and such a date, I had permission to kill myself. I just kept extending the deadline. My body was the danger zone.

I needed a reason to live. So I applied to MFA programs and I was accepted at Vermont College. Every day I had pain. Every day I had fatigue, joint pain, brain fog, infection. Every day I wrote. I stopped bargaining for suicide. I didn't write about my unsolved health problem, but I channeled everything I couldn't fix into my fiction. I wrote a chapter from the point of view of an elderly woman who has lost her family in the Holocaust. I wrote it sitting on the floor in a waiting room at Mayo. I didn't get answers at Mayo, but I got more than thirty pages of fiction.

Writing in therapy is not a new idea. Clinicians have researched and demonstrated the efficacy of free writing and journal writing in a variety of settings.[2] My original plan for this essay was to write a summary of some of that research. But a simple Google search turns up a CNN article called "Writing for Therapy Helps Erase Effects of Trauma."[3] Within that article, you will find information about Maxine Hong Kingston, who has been teaching creative writing to Veterans for years. You'll find a reference to James Pennebaker's study demonstrating that writing about stressful events increases T cell activity, meaning that it improves the immune system.[4]

Maxine Hong Kingston writes, "Singing, hugging, dancing, we were a community. But it is in words that each individual reveals a unique mind. The Veterans needed to write. They would write the unspeakable. Writing, they keep track of their thinking, they have a permanent record. Processing chaos through story and poem, the writer shapes and forms experience."[5]

In his anthology of writings by female prisoners, Wally Lamb describes the moment that moves his disjointed group of writers from the edge of hostility to community. A woman who had said she would never share her writing suddenly changed her mind: "In a barely audible voice, she read a disjointed, two-page summary of her horrific life story: incest, savage abuse, spousal homicide...When she stopped, there was silence, a communal intake of breath. Then, applause—a single pair of hands at first, joined by another pair and then by everyone."[6] This student had "sledgehammered the dam of distrust, and the women's writing began to flow."[7]

These were some of the books and articles I turned to when I was looking to prove that teaching Veterans creative writing would be helpful. These words supported what I already knew from my own experience; writing doesn't just produce something to read. It saves lives. The lives of the writer as well as many readers.

The majority of research in the mental health world focuses on expressive writing. Study participants are asked to write about a stressful event, being sure to include their emotions. They are not asked to think in terms of plot, character, structure or point of view. They're simply asked to journal. The studies uniformly document that expressive writing helps.

But what about taking it even further? My belief was and remains that teaching people with PTSD to write a structured, crafted story about their experiences offers benefits that expressive writing alone can't accomplish.

PTSD is, at its core, a disorder of fragmentation. The memories are experienced and stored in shattered bits of image, thought, sound, and sensation. They knock at the mind's door in the form of intrusive memories, flashbacks, nightmares, anxiety, anger problems, avoidance of triggers, emotional numbing, relationship problems, substance abuse. The pieces of one's story announce themselves, unwanted and frightening, but rarely in a coherent linear form with beginning, middle and end. Rarely with emotions, sensations and inner experience organized and linked together.

Edna Foa, who developed an evidence based practice for treating PTSD called Prolonged Exposure Therapy, uses a reading analogy to explain why traumatic memories continue to haunt people with PTSD. She suggests that dealing with unprocessed trauma memories is like opening a book. You read one upsetting chapter or paragraph, then slam the book closed. The book keeps opening, you keep reading a paragraph here, a chapter there, you get upset, you close the book. You never finish the book or recreate the coherent story. Exposure therapy is aimed at creating that story. It's interesting to note that the exposure therapist's job is to push a Veteran to move from a brief summarized version of his story to a lengthy scene, complete with sensory detail. When I began using exposure therapy, I was already doing that, because I'd been teaching Veterans the difference between summary and scene.

When a Veteran writes her trauma story, she is catching a fragmented experience in a net of words. The first draft is often as disjointed as the memory is in her mind. The tense may change, the point of view shift, and sensory detail may be absent. Teaching him the elements of craft, point by point, gives him a structure within which to organize his experience. Asking him to concentrate on tense brings separation between past and present: the trauma is not happening now. Even if she chooses to write in present tense, she is gaining distance through craft; she is practicing 're-membering,' reintegrating the pieces of herself. When the story is structured, with a beginning, middle and end, the Veteran organizes his trauma. When he transforms a six-sentence paragraph into a two-page scene, he engages in exposure therapy. When he reads that paragraph out loud to other Veterans, he gains more exposure therapy. When she goes home and revises she is exposing herself to the trauma yet again. Every exposure reduces the anxiety and makes the trauma more bearable. When the story is completed and shared, when it is no longer a memory but a piece of art, she has progressed beyond exposure. She has made meaning of what was chaotic and terrifying. Made the experience something bigger than himself alone in the world. There is a sound of a clapping hand. Then another. And another. He finds community and meaning and a reason to get up in the morning.

When I ask Veterans to revise and craft their work, I hope they gain the healing that comes through exposure. When I encourage them to publish, I hope their words transform not only the veterans who wrote them, but also at least one person who reads them. Maybe that person will share with another and another. When a reader's eyes are opened, when an audience is moved to greater understanding and perhaps healing, trauma is transformed into meaning. Making meaning of trauma allows the combat veteran an opportunity to step away from the conviction that nobody "who hasn't been there" can possibly understand or accept him. It's a way of putting a hand out and inviting others to take it. In taking the hand offered, the process of re-membering is fulfilled.

I was surprised to find myself opening this essay about teaching creative writing in a Veterans Administration PTSD clinic with such a personal story. I had planned to summarize a bunch of dry articles proving that teaching creative writing to Veterans with PTSD is helpful in reducing symptoms such as anxiety, intrusive memories, and avoidance of triggers. I certainly didn't plan to talk about *that*. But writing what you didn't plan to write is often where the healing is. Giardella reminds me to "Embrace the unexpected."[8] That advice once carried me home from despair—to engagement with the writing that saved my life.

In the middle of my MFA program, I found an answer to my health puzzle. Treatment improved my symptoms dramatically. Yet, sometimes I miss the feeling that I could die any day. Why? Because it drove me to say 'yes' to my creative impulse, every single day no matter how sick I felt.

When I came to the VA, I wanted to give Veterans a chance to find meaning through creative writing. My goal in teaching writing to Veterans is to help them say 'yes' in that same way, to empower them to embrace the tragedy of their losses and transform their memories into an artistic whole of re-membering. I frequently discuss radical acceptance with my clients at the VA. Instead of focusing all your energy on wishing things were different and struggling to control what you can't, you focus on creating a meaningful and engaged life while working to change what you can. Instead of wishing you had not been to war, wishing the war had not changed you, wishing you didn't have chronic pain, wishing you still had your marriage...

Instead of wishing, you accept.

You make meaning. You don't try to pretend the baggage isn't there. They're a part of you. But so is the rest—following the impulse and saying yes to life.

Notes:

[1] Giardella, Daena and Wren Ross, *Changing Patterns: Discovering the Fabric of Your Creativity* (California: Hay House, 2006), 6-7.

[2] Frattaroli, Joanne, *Experimental Disclosure and its Moderators: A Meta-Analysis* (Psychological Bulletin, Vol.132 No.6; 2006), 823-865.

[3] See note 2 above.

[4] Woolsten, Chris, "Writing for Therapy Helps Erase Effects of Trauma." *CNN.Com.* http://archives.cnn.com/2000/HEALTH/03/16/health.writing.wmd/index.html.

[5] Kingston, Maxine Hong, *Veterans of War, Veterans of Peace* (Hawaii: Koa Books, 2006),1-2.

[6] Lamb, Wally and the Women of York Correctional Institution, *Couldn't Keep it to Myself: Testimonies From our Imprisoned Sisters* (New York: HarperCollins Publishers, 2003), 4 -5.

[7] See note 6 above.

[8] Giardella, Daena and Wren Ross, *Changing Patterns: Discovering the Fabric of Your Creativity* (California: Hay House, 2006), 136.

THE CLEAR AND HONEST STORY: A RECONSIDERATION OF WRITING, TRAUMA, AND TRANSFORMATION

By Dinty W. Moore

To be honest, my first reaction to the phrase "writing as a healing art" is to say, "no, no, that's not it at all." As someone who has carved out a career centered on writing, editing, and most importantly, teaching the art and craft of writing, the idea that putting thoughts and scenes down on paper is focused on the healing of past wounds, that art is a form of therapy, seems antithetical to what I do.

Yet another part of what I do, as an essayist, is to examine my most firmly-held beliefs, always remaining (in theory, at least) open to discover that I am slightly off-base, a few inches wide of the mark, or—in some cases—just plain wrong. Goodness knows I've been wrong before.

And recognizing when one is wrong, being open to admitting it, and remaining willing to make changes, is one of the greatest strengths a writer can have.

Thus, here is my chance to examine why I am so immediately opposed to the idea that writing is "a healing art." Healing, after all, is unquestionably a <u>good</u> thing. And yes, I've had some harsh trauma in my own life that has taken years to make well. So, what's the problem?

My knee-jerk opposition, I'm sure, comes partly from my experience in the classroom.

People unfamiliar with the teaching of writing—and here I am talking about "literary" writing, not the more utilitarian forms like technical writing, business writing, or the newspaper article—immediately assume that writing teachers basically attempt to convey the craft of assembling sentences, or piling sentences together in such a way that they make a paragraph, and then stacking those paragraphs so that they make something whole.

Now, that is part of it, certainly, but not the most important part. The hardest—and most valuable—lesson I have to teach young poets, fiction writers, or literary nonfiction writers is to step outside of their own thoughts, to imagine an audience made up of real people on the other side of the page. This audience does not know the writer, they are not by default eager to read what the writer has written, and though thoughtful literate readers are by and large good people with large hearts, they have no intrinsic stake in whatever problems (or joys) the writer has in his or her life.

To put it another way, only by focusing on the readers, by acknowledging that you are creating something for them, something that has value to them, something that will enrich their lives and make them glad to have read what you have written, will you find a way to truly reach your audience. And that—truly reaching your audience and offering them something of value—is how I define good writing.

So maybe what I'm worried about is that the word "healing" makes it seems too much like we are writing just for ourselves, that the primary audience is the writer, and if the writer likes what he has written, understands the images and sees the texture, well then that's good enough.

Yet that's not good enough, in my eyes. Of course the writer feels the emotion in her words and of course the scenes seem life-like when she reads what she has written. The scenes and emotions are already fully alive in the writer's memory or imagination. But can the reader feel the emotion as well? Are the scenes alive in the reader's mind? That's the test.

So, as a teacher, all of my instincts tell me that a solipsistic, inward-looking writing for the self is—well, dare I say it?—the quickest path to bad writing.

My negative reaction to the phrase "writing as a healing art" is also, to a great extent, colored by my work as an editor. For the past fifteen years, I have been an advocate for the genre of literary writing commonly termed 'creative nonfiction' and have for more than a decade been running a magazine devoted to the form, and for about the same amount of time, the genre has been under attack.

One of the highest-profile assaults came in 1997, when James Wolcott, writing in *Vanity Fair*, asserted that "... creative and nonfiction are coming together to form a big, earnest blob of me-first sensibility."[1] Wolcott termed contemporary nonfiction a "pierced-navel-gazing orgy" and a "journalism of the self...reaching for a phantom nipple."

Those are some colorful (and cheap) shots taken by Wolcott, and maybe they should just be ignored, but at about the same time, *New York*

Times book reviewer Michiko Kakutani wrote that "The current memoir craze has fostered the belief that confession is therapeutic, that therapy is redemptive and that redemption equals art, and it has encouraged the delusion that candor, daring and shamelessness are substitutes for craft, that the exposed life is the same thing as an examined one."[2]

Wolcott and Kakutani are clearly of the opinion that contemporary nonfiction writers are too concerned with their own well-being and that this concern for the self is somehow poison on the page. They have used this claim as a bludgeon to denigrate the entire genre of creative nonfiction, and every six months or so, some new critic launches a fresh attack, often using the words of Wolcott or Kakutani as a launching pad.

So I am sensitive to such charges. Perhaps overly so.

I promised in opening this essay that I would remain alert to the possibility that I was wide of the mark or just plain wrong. And having listed my main objections to writing as healing, I think it is good that I left that option open.

Let me begin with the criticism from Wolcott and Kakutani. I read as much current nonfiction as anyone these days in my various roles of writer, teacher, and editor, and I don't see self-indulgent navel-gazing or shameless self-exposure replacing the hard work of open-minded examination. Quite the contrary. The more memoir that is written, the harder it becomes to stand out from the crowd, and the books and essays that do stand out from the crowd and achieve publication are the opposite of what Wolcott and others want to brand the genre. They are carefully-constructed, deeply considered, and sharp.

My other objection went like this: "Solipsistic, inward-looking writing for the self is ... the quickest path to bad writing."

"Bad," though, is an odd word once you look at it closely. Right now, my daughter's small black kitten is making a mess of our living room, and I have no hesitation calling the kitten bad. So much so that I think she imagines "bad kitten" may be her actual name.

But how is writing <u>bad</u>? Does it somehow scratch the sofa of truth, make a mess of the living room of ideas?

In a way the metaphor works, but the truth is, that scratching and messiness is where all writing starts out. First drafts are supposed to be muddled. Early thoughts and sentences are mere attempts, not statements.

Writing is a process of moving ideas and images from a state of hesitancy and tentativeness to a state of firmness and clarity. Or to put it succinctly: writing that self-indulgently attempts to reach only the person doing the writing may be bad writing, but only if that's where the writer stops his efforts.

But here I may be wrong again, or at least half-wrong.

Writing aimed at the self—at the writer—is bad in the sense that it often isn't "good" for the reader, but that doesn't mean it is harmful. It doesn't actually destroy cushions and furniture. People are not injured. Lives are not diminished.

As I mentioned above, healing is a positive step, and one for which I am personally grateful, so if writing brings about positive therapeutic benefits, how can it be anything but good?

Finally, it turns out that I am wrong in one more way, most relevant to those reading this essay now. I was invited to contribute my thoughts to this anthology because various brief essays from my magazine, *Brevity*, are used as models in the Milspeak writing workshops, and when I learned that this anthology was in fact devoted in part to an exploration of writing as healing, I jumped to rapid conclusions. I let my long-standing reservations about "therapeutic writing" leap to the foreground, and I began my argument ill-informed.

There is no faster way to make a fool of oneself in print.

Had I merely read the writing available from the Milspeak workshops, the brief essays posted on the website, the voices of Korean War veterans, Gulf War marines, and military spouses, I would have seen that I had no need for worry. These stories are strong, carefully rendered, vivid, and alive. Perhaps it made the writers feel some sense of release to put these thoughts down on paper, but that is not where the writing, and crafting, stopped. All of my concerns stated above—and the charges of folks like Wolcott—are belied by simply spending some time with the clear and honest stories that have come out of the Milspeak workshops.

Can one be healed of one's own misconceptions? If so, the therapeutic effect of the essays produced by Milspeak writers is that I am no longer suffering under my previous delusions.

Write on.

Notes:
[1] James Wolcott. "Me, Myself, and I." *Vanity Fair* (Oct. 1997).
[2] Michiko Kakutani. "Woe Is Me: Rewards And Perils of Memoirs." *New York Times* (21 Oct. 1997): 8.

IS IT ART, THIS MENTORING, OR ALL IMAGERY?

By Tom Sheehan

Mentoring may all be a matter of reflections, the mirror, the images you see and hear and love, the aromas of a place and time as you listen to a voice that does not go away...ever. My grandfather, Johnny Igoe, read W. B. Yeats to me when I was a youngster, rocking in his porch chair, smoking his pipe, making music and rhythm in his life, and in mine. Johnny Igoe, the little Irish Spellbinder I swore was going to guide me forever.

Then came a high biting, cold spring day in 1955 that I knew would be memorial. The sun but snippets, ice still hiding out in shadow, winter remnants piled up in great gatherings with me bound to a shovel for the tenth day in a row. That's when I heard of Johnny Igoe's death in his 97th year.

Grass, buds, shoots and sprigs of all kinds were aimless as April. All vast morning I'd hunted the sun, tried to place it square on my back. But the breeze taunted, left a taste in my mouth, a word in my ear, an aromatic briar cutting beacon-like through darkness.

"Your grandfather's dead," someone said and the visions came immediately, all of them. I saw Johnny Igoe at ten at turf cutting, just before he came this way with the great multitude. I saw how he moved the ponderous earth at his odd jobs, the young Irish scorching the ground he walked. He had come here and I came, and I went there, later, to where he'd come from: Roscommon's sweet vale, slow rush of land shouldering up into sky, clouds shifting selves like pieces at chess, his earth ripening to fire.

This little man, of the great porch voice or the warm kitchen voice, poled his star-lit way down the Erie Canal, swung a sledge in Illinois, a hammer north of Boston, and died in bed. The tobacco smell still lives in his room. His books still live, his chair, his cane, the misery he knew, the pain, and somewhere, he is. For all this, he might be housed in this computer. For now he visits or never leaves, Yeats' voice on a record. But the voice is my grandfather's voice, the perky treble, the deft reach inside me, the ever lifting out. In the dark asides before a faint light glimmers, it is his perky pipe's glow I see, weaker than a small struck match, but illuminating all the same. I smell the old Edgeworth tobacco faint as a blown cloud, the way a hobo might know a windowsill apple pie from afar. I hear his rocking chair giving rhythm to my mind, saying over and again the words he left with hard handles on them for my grasping.

The images never leave. They grasp like words grasp. Like a mentor's grasp.

So Johnny Igoe was gone. I looked for a secondary image to touch, another mentor in place to get the new kick in the pants, the mind still screeching for words not seen together before, the drive at perfecting a craft yet hanging at odds. It came from an old teacher as we closed down the years. John Burns was in his 63rd year in the Saugus High School English Department. He brought all the other connections with him. In one of his classrooms, I sat in the chair that poet Elizabeth Bishop sat in during her freshman year at Saugus High School in 1925. I saw her report card. I heard the words again rising on the air. Via images, I was newfound.

John, now 93, a rugged individual with controls, inspires stories: his art of language, his humor, his vast reading practice, his near death as a Japanese Kamikaze exploded on the deck of his ship in the now-quiet South Pacific, his unflappability, his tutoring. Came the day that I visited his office at school and the discussion that said: *In time much of what we know fades away, continually moves around us, blinking and scattering, but with a waft of air touches back. It's a face, a name, a childhood haunt in momentary dispose, each waiting to be identified or merely given the solace of place. Though we cannot name it at first, cannot frame it visually clean or bring it to contoured image, we yet strike for it.*

Our hometown of Saugus kept touching back at John and me in that manner. We wanted to hold tight to all that came our way, had come our way. It had already found breath in one of my poems...*because we have all been where we are going, into selves, shadows, odd shining, all those places the mind occupies, or the heart....*

A book to fill the void was in the offing, we agreed. The word went out nationwide: we were looking for articles, vignettes, pictures, graphics, anything that would lend both resonance and nostalgia to a book we had dreamed up, a book about *Things Saugus in the 20th Century.* That day, coming off a six-mile walk around our town, I paid one of my numerous late-day social calls at his school office. It was here where we had generally discussed our past in this town we so dearly love, which has been so good to us. But for that matter, names of people and places often eluded our memories, slipping into some unconfined space of the mind where retrieval was hesitant, unsure.

John once mentioned Charlie's Pond. To me, it had been lost for more than fifty years. In turn, I cited Cinder Path as a place of endless winter excitement where we steered our old Flexible Flyer sleds down the long and twisting run from the site of the old Stand Pipe on top of Baker Hill. That ride, so clearly impressed on my mind to this day, the wind wild and cold on my face, the careening like electricity running the whole gamut of my body, went clear down to Cliftondale Square. It was an exhilarating and headless ride, now and then under a splash of weekend moonlight or brittle starlight.

He had forgotten Cinder Path, it seems, or had not been there. Perhaps those years so memorable to me he had spent in the South Pacific creating different memories. Other names and places came and then went flitting away in a number of our meetings, like meager and endangered moths caught up in late October. They were like air around us, barely touching, but being known, having names, a place to hold onto, a corner of the mind. The past we wanted to remember, to respect, was surely slipping away from us. Pieces came and went in the relentless tumble, some of them crying for recognition.

Muckles Brown, at length and only after some eventful prodding, came back to life as he was, enormous across the chest, shoulders like Atlas, but faint Anna Parker was just about gone forever, her and the first electric car in town. The Pigeon Plucker and Hoag's Castle had also danced their last. The names and faces of memorialized heroes were more surely cemented in place. The Kasabuski brothers (killed within two weeks of each other in the Italian Campaign), for whom our hockey rink is named, and where I had spent more than ten years with my sons, are linked forever in my mind. The VFW Post #2346 bears the name of a Baker Hill boy, Arthur DeFranzo, who was decorated posthumously with the Medal of Honor for his heroics not long after D-Day, Arthur, never forgotten.

Nor is Scott Procopio, all the way from Iraq, for whom the Legion Post #210 is named.

But other names too quickly failed at the tip of the tongue. A host of them from all corners of our town: Lick, Skink, Doggie, Big Syd, Paints

Brown, Beaver, MaryB, Simple Ellie, Ollie and Dolly, Sinagna, Tarzan Doyle, Crazy Albert, Leonard the Blind Man, The Indian.

For John and me, a face would come back mysteriously in a fleck of light and leap away on a silent ride into complete darkness. Sometimes to a place that *was,* a favorite place of youthful years...disrupted, dug out, filled in, carried off...that no longer exists. It wasn't a pleasant experience. Doubts, we knew, did exist. About ourselves. About our memories. About our ability to muster a true respect for the past. About duty and what it calls for.

John, his face as red as mine, his eyes like relays, looked up at me as I walked into his office that eventful day. He has a way of *smiling* an announcement; perhaps the teacher pleasantly at his work always smiles this way, the corners of his mouth like punctuation. For a moment I saw it, and then heard it. On the edge of his chair, as if he had been the long day waiting for me, he said, "Let's write a book." The blue eyes zapped electric again. They went into a further spectrum; his usual excitement and keenness for every day was hyper, and then some.

I nodded; my mentor had called.

"Before it's all gone," he added. "Before we forget what we're supposed to remember."

He was doing what I had so often done, measuring time. It had crept quite often into my poetry, like a Jersey barrier on the loose in my stream of thought. John, it was easy to see, was there. And if there's anything in this world that he can lay claim to, it's a sense of justice, a sense of honesty, a sense of duty. His spirit and energy are compelling. In mere moments, after a minor and unspoken assessment of where such a decision might take us, a kind of nostalgic Limbo possibly being our destination or assignment, we were off and running.*

So, in mentoring, it is payback time. It is my turn. I am 80 and just getting up to speed, hoping the run lasts, that I touch a soul, that two new words hang together for at least one person, one comrade, and that *that* someone finds direction, a proper kick in the pants, an image to lean on. If he reads this, I am thinking now of him, seeing his face I have not seen, crossing the phantom space between us, finding the reflection of a Viet Nam veteran, from a distance, looking for those words with handles on them.

A Gathering of Memories, Saugus 1900-2000, 2000 printed, 2000 sold, 500 more printed for the demand and 500 sold, people looking for them on eBay these days, three found to date and reported to us. This is the third report of a successful search on eBay for a copy of *A Gathering*, as copies were sold to 47 states, three territories, and eight foreign countries. One copy is online in the National Library in Paris, the gift of a French editor and his wife, Guillaume and Kim Destot. They stayed in Saugus on a lengthy visit to America a few years ago, spent part of their visit in Saugus with the Sheehan family and were featured in local newspapers.

All proceeds from our books on Saugus go to the John Burns Millennium Book Associates Scholarships for Saugus High graduates. Eight, so far, have gone on to college.

We had approached a local bank president, presented him with an 8-page proposal to borrow $60,000 to print a book that was not written...who was going to do what, when and how. It was loaded with promise and subtle excitement. A week later we walked into his office, six of us. He stood up, said, "You have your money."

Six of us signed on the dotted line, each responsible for a portion of the loan, each with deep belief in the project. 400 copies were sold the day of release, 452 pages of nostalgia and history, profiles and photos, poetry and panorama. The loan was paid off in five months.

So we did it again: *Of Time and the River, Saugus 1900-2005: A Continuation*. 2000 printed; just over 1000 sold to date, John Burns still in the mix of *Things Saugus*, hundreds and hundreds of Saugus High graduates still saying he was the best teacher they ever had at any level, John Burns, the mentor's mentor.

I'm one of them.

TRANSFORMATION

By Lisa Kahn Schnell

At funerals in northwestern Ghana, where I lived as a Peace Corps Volunteer, close relatives of the deceased receive strips of cloth to tie around their own wrists. Friends and distant relations contribute more and more strips, until finally, when the loved one is buried, the wad of cloth might have grown as big as a grapefruit. Even in the midst of grieving, mourners must remember who contributed which scraps of cloth; in the days and weeks after the funeral, they return the strips, a process which takes them out of their houses, back into the fresh air, and among friends who will cheer them in their darkest moments.

Fortunately I'm not in mourning, but I do collect bits and scraps—experiences, conversations, images. While I can't give these things back directly, writing allows me to convert them into something new, something I can return to the world. Writing helps me remember, understand, and appreciate life, and it keeps me from getting buried by the chaos of my days.

Still, I would not say that I write to heal myself, at least not intentionally. The idea of writing to heal makes me think of journal-style writing that remains emotionally raw and unshaped, its power inaccessible to most readers. I love my journals, but even though the untempered emotion found within their covers is critical to my writing, I don't consider it an end point for the work I share with others. After an initial, fervent burst of writing, I follow smaller, subtly compelling paths, collecting and combining bits of thought, experience, and sensory impressions along the way. When the process is going well, I never know what I will discover, or where the paths will ultimately lead me—I find it impossible to plan the journey to a finished essay ahead of time. My main goal is to explore details that expose a more universal truth, something larger than me or any single event, something that someone else could read and say, "Yes, yes, me too, exactly."

"Circling," a piece of mine that is used in the Milspeak program, emerged in a fury of writing during a moment of emotional pain and fear when I believed I was miscarrying my baby. I wrote because I was alone and distraught and didn't know what else to do. Through writing, my feelings about my own situation combined with memories of an event that occurred several years earlier in Ghana. A young woman had died late in her pregnancy, and the image of the baby still moving inside her haunted me; I had wanted to write about it for a long time, but wasn't sure how to approach it respectfully. Once I focused on the details of my own experience as a young, scared, pregnant woman, my unconscious mind leapt to connect the two scenes. Revision helped me blend my own emotional experience with a scrap of memory to create something more than just a description of either. Although the young woman's story and my own unite through sadness and loss, what I discovered through writing "Circling" is a sense of the continuity of life, in all its myriad forms.

Another of my essays, "The Things I Gave Her," is obviously influenced by Tim O'Brien's *The Things They Carried*, particularly the eponymous essay. When I returned from Ghana, feelings of inadequacy overwhelmed me—how could I not have done more? Couldn't I go back, given all that I had learned, and try again? In particular, I longed to make life better for my dear friend Genevieve, who kept me safe and sane while I was there. "The Things I Gave Her" is a result of those feelings, feelings that initially tumbled onto the page as a list of wishes and memories. By restructuring the original jumbled list into a more logical, coherent whole, the piece became a sort of letter to Genevieve, a note of sorrow and regret, admiration and respect. I hope the result conveys some of the urgency I felt, and sometimes still feel, to thank Genevieve in a way that would make a difference in her life. The piece hasn't changed anything tangibly—Genevieve still lives the same life she lived before. But writing the essay was a humbling experience for me.

I wrote both "Circling" and "The Things I Gave Her" soon after I returned from Ghana, when I was shedding stories easily. Writing compelled me, maybe because in addition to readjusting to life in the United States, I was also newly married. We were living in an unfamiliar, small town, and I didn't have a job or close friends nearby. Fresh memories helped my writing, and so did enrolling in a creative non-fiction writing class, where I learned not to wait around for the so-called Muse. In Ghana, every scrap of writing felt exotic, glorious, and inspired. How could I have imagined the muck I would produce in class? My writing teacher taught me the importance of showing up for work every day: each afternoon, for two hours, I kept my hand moving and wrote. Even though one corner of my head screeched that 99% of what I produced was awful and embarrassing, I loved the 1%, those moments when words flowed through me and revealed fresh insights. Even the days of awful writing took me out of my house, out of my head, and into the company of my peers again.

To keep myself on track now that I'm no longer an official student, I have created what I call my "Daily Work Plan." This plan—part meditation, part writing-related reminders—is a portal into the part of myself that can create strong, emotional writing. Sticking with my plan helps me to be patient with the inevitable diversions along my path, and with the process of shaping the finished piece. Each day I sit in the same place at the same time, and as I work through my plan I grow calmer, focused, and more centered. Relying on this structure creates a safe space for words and emotions to come out, and allows my writing to be freer and looser. It reminds me of the traditional baths in Japan, where I immersed myself in warm water and focused only on the sensory experience at hand. All my needs were taken care of, and since there were no distractions or questions about what I needed to be doing, everything else disappeared. This is how I try to write now. Ultimately, the discipline of staying on my path does bring a sort of comfort, despite the dark places it sometimes takes me, and despite the challenges of searching out truths and trusting what I find.

One of the stated goals of the Peace Corps is that returned volunteers share what we learned in our host country with the people of the United States. I think this goal applies in a much broader sense. If experience has led you to discover stories, big or small, then it is both a responsibility and a worthwhile goal to communicate those stories to others. I find writing a great way to do that. Writing makes me brave enough to walk into the emotional fray and focus on the details of a particular scene. Writing helps me lose my whining, uncertain, doubting self and find the part of me that can withstand any journey. Ultimately, my essays and stories are just so many scraps, with a bit of order imposed on them, that I choose to share with the world. Each piece of finished writing has transformed me in some way, and I hope each piece can provide some measure of insight or comfort to someone else, too. And that is healing in ways I never imagined.

THE PRISON OF OUR DAYS

By Bob Cowser, Jr.

In the deserts of the heart
Let the healing fountains start,
In the prison of his days
Teach the free man how to praise.
        W.H. Auden, "In Memory of William Butler Yeats."

When a colleague asked me to suggest writing teachers to staff a new program in a local prison, I thought of myself first—as usual. Prison teaching had crossed my mind many times since I'd moved to northern New York, where the prison-industrial complex is a kind of growth industry and prisons dot the landscape like Wal-Marts. I've discovered it's not an uncommon daydream among college professors everywhere, a daring twist to an otherwise mild profession. Extreme teaching.

But my interest had a personal dimension too. While I was growing up my father often taught extra university courses at the state prison in Lake County, Tennessee, which I'd toured with a civics class in high school. A quiet, gentle man, he was not often given to grand gestures of which a son might be proud, but the work in prison was something I had always admired. Now I wanted to understand. And I suspect I needed a way to feel proud of myself again too. I had recently been tenured at the toney liberal arts university where I'd been teaching, but not without a considerable fight. The experience had shaken my confidence as a teacher and I needed a temporary change of scenery. Prison would provide that, at least.

I was to do my teaching at Ray Brook, a medium security federal prison located between the picturesque Adirondack resort villages of Saranac Lake and Lake Placid. We contractors were told during our day-long orientation that among Ray Brooks' 1250 inmates were John Gotti, Jr. and an alleged Arab terrorist the staff seemed proud to host. A short timer in every respect, I looked forward to the 80-mile commute into the mountains from my home in the foothills, for the solitude and the break from routine, for the legendary mountain air and vistas. Plus I was curious.

But everyone else, those doing real time there, staff member and incarcerated man alike, seemed to be counting the days, like a grunt in a Vietnam flick hoping his number doesn't come up before he can rotate back to the world. The education staffer who escorted me from the front gate each time waxed rhapsodic about his new motorcycle and all the time he'd have to ride it when he retired in a year or two. At the control center where we were outfitted with walkie-talkies and body alarms, C.O.s counted the hours until the end of the shift. In class, the incarcerated men wrote essays about release and the resumption of life as they'd known and loved it on the outside. No great insight, I guess: nobody, but nobody, wants to be in prison.

The prison campus had served as the Olympic Village during the 1980 Lake Placid winter games, and they say the dorms date from that time, the feds adding only fences and barbed wire to the compound to achieve the makeover. It's an oddly beautiful spot—those dorm buildings nestled into hills and knolls above a mountain meadow—and nothing like the gothic castle of a state prison, just across the road, where I'd mistakenly pulled in on the morning of my orientation.

One former Alcatraz inmate claimed that it was "The Rock's" proximity to San Francisco—the prison island sits only a quarter mile away—which destroys a man. "Worse than hell," he claimed, were the night winds carrying the smells of San Francisco's North Beach red sauce eateries and the laughter of women and children all the way out to The Rock.

I began my visits to Ray Brook imagining that the worst part of prison life would be isolation and the tantalizing proximity to natural beauty and the life outside the walls that a prisoner is denied. I encountered some of that. During my first stint as "artist-in-residence," one of the best essays written by an incarcerated man described the great lengths he went to make in prison the traditional Christmas lasagna his Italian mother used to make. He hoarded commissary tomatoes in his cell for weeks, strained cottage cheese through a gym sock until it passed for ricotta, and stood in front of a microwave oven for four hours—all for that taste of home.

But most men thought the time they were doing was relatively easy, and called the place "Club Fed." Much worse to be across the road at the state pen, they told me, locked up with murderers and child molesters. The men I taught were predominantly drug offenders, doing 18 months to two years for possession with intent, with a bank robber or corporate criminal thrown in here and there; still, not boy scouts, I know. Perhaps they'd done nastier crimes than those for which they had been busted, but most had served time elsewhere and knew it could be worse.

My writing assignments were simple: explore a turning point in your life, an important relationship, and use the tools a fiction writer would use to tell the story. What their essays revealed amazed me. In his first essay, Chicago-land gang-banger Rob described thirty days in the hole and how he eventually learned to survive there. Then, in his second essay, Rob wrote about his semester at a state university (he had won a scholarship through a reform school essay contest). It was an institution he never learned to navigate. "I couldn't get used to all those white people smiling at me all the time," he wrote. Southy bank robber and first Gulf War Veteran Scott, who was listed on one of those stupid criminal web sites for the manner in which he'd bungled the heist and been caught, wrote beautifully about the neighbor lady's collie. The dog was his only friend in a lonesome Boston boyhood.

What ate away at these guys more than anything, I learned from their writing, was how they'd hurt the people who loved them and counted on them—children, especially, and mothers. They'd made promises they now couldn't honor. Lonnie, a Philly drug dealer, wrote about the day his older brother, his mentor in the business, was shot in the street in front of their mother's apartment. His mother wailed and wailed. In another piece, Lonnie explored his estrangement from his own young son, and imagined the boy out on the Pop Warner gridiron without his father's guidance. After the class's discussion of Lonnie's second essay, which he'd read to us in workshop, he had a kind of revelation: what he felt about his son, the regret, must be what his mother felt about Lonnie and his imprisonment.

Now does that kind of insight heal us in our broken places? Is writing a healing art? I don't know. I'll confess to leaning toward Pollyannaish optimism on this question. My younger sister, a psychological evaluator at a juvenile detention facility in the Midwest, considers most offenders already hopeless by the time they reach her. "They're writing what you want to read," she told me when I described my work at the prison. "They're so good at conning you, you'd be amazed," she told me.

In a recent interview with my university's student paper, I'm quoted as saying the most frustrating thing about prison teaching is that at the end of the day the students are all still in jail. I regretted saying that as soon as I saw it I print—of course the point of prison teaching can't be freedom for the incarcerated students. The point is to read to their stories and afford them the opportunity to write them. "Everything happens for a reason," or so the cliché goes, but the point of prison teaching is to move those men beyond such platitudes, to help them participate in the making of meaning, aid them in discerning what patterns and connections they could find in their experiences. Maybe, through writing, they might understand what those proverbial "reasons" are. To know what's eating at you, to put your finger on it, to see shape and meaning in your life—now that's something.

Perhaps not healing, but something.

For entire semesters or sometimes just for a weekend, I teach the memoir form to groups from all walks of life—college students, graduate students, high school students, prison inmates. My approach with every population is the same radically simple one outlined above. Tell me about people and events that have shaped and changed you. Tell me with as much candor as you can muster. The details will take care of themselves. You can do this, I tell them, because you've been telling stories all your lives.

I am grateful to the men in those first prison classes for reminding me how simple telling a story can be, for reminding me what the act and practice of writing can reveal *and* restore, for restoring to *me* my faith in myself as a teacher, for bringing me back to my dad and the roots of my urge to do it, for helping me to heal.

What can I say? —I think of those men all the time.

CHILDREN WRITING GRIEF

By Rebecca McClanahan

If it is true, as Edna St. Vincent Millay wrote, "Childhood is the kingdom where no one dies that matters," then for many of my students, the kingdom was vanquished early on. No matter where I traveled in fifteen years as writer-in-residence for a metropolitan school district—from tree-shaded classrooms in affluent neighborhoods to bullet-pocked trailers of the inner city—students wrote of loss. Sometimes grief broke classroom rules of decorum: once, it broke a window; once, a desk. But for most children, the act of writing seemed to order the chaos, to provide a place to house the raw emotion swirling in their heads and hearts.

When a poem struck me—by its language, rhythms, its surprising vision or depth of feeling—I asked the author if I could share it with others. No one ever said no. All seemed thrilled that I valued what they said and how they said it, and that I felt their work would be of interest to someone else. Occasionally a student asked that I not use her name: "I want to be that guy with the big A," one little girl told me. (Many students, I found, were impressed by Anonymous, both his name and his prolific output. They always assumed he was male.) Some of my students opted for pen names, one boy employing the middle name of his dead brother. For this essay, I've chosen to identify the student poets only by first name and grade level, in part because of the personal nature of the work, and in part because this shorthand reminds us of the universality of what is being expressed. *Jane* could be anyone—my niece, your daughter.

In fact, there were many Janes; that is, for every example I've included, I read many that echoed the sentiment. What emerged from my reading of hundreds, then thousands, of these poems were not only the facts of singular lives but also the patterns beneath the facts, the myriad yet universal ways grief weaves its path through the lives of the young. I offer the work of my former students for two reasons: first, as a way of demonstrating how children approach the losses that are thrown their way; second, as *poems*, or sections of poems, in which children are speaking the truths of their lives, sometimes fluently, sometimes haltingly, but often with astonishing honesty and beauty.

Dylan Thomas asserted that "After the first death, there is no other," but my students' poems suggest that in many cases, a series of small deaths precede the large ones. By deeming these losses "small" I am not suggesting that they are trivial. I use "small" here only to distinguish these losses from the death of a close family member—a loss that appeared, in most of my students' poems, to represent the zenith of grief. The "smaller" losses served as rehearsals, if you will. In waving goodbye to a friend, for instance, the children were practicing for the larger grief play.

Separated

Red car rolling off,
waving your hand
like wiggling rubber.
Fog shadows behind
the car. The engine
sound is fading away.
The sight of the car
floats forward. Your
shaking hand of
rubber swiftly floats
down.
    Penelope, 5th grade

You can't get a friend back. I had one but I moved... When we picked those berries I would say we can make a blackberry pie and we did but the crust was hard but it tasted good. It was good while it lasted.
    Shea, 3rd grade

Despite the sadness of separation, to some of the writers the memory of a lost friendship remained more sweet than bitter. After all, there are more friends where that one came from, as one boy told me, pointing beyond the classroom window to a playground crawling with possibilities. Replacing a parent, however, was another story. The losses engendered by divorce cut deeply, and the consequences were seldom bittersweet. Some children's expressions were powerfully direct, piercing in their brevity.

> *My parents got divorced and my dad got me.*
> *Anonymous, 3rd grade*

> *I am sad I am between Mom and Dad.*
> *Barry, 4th grade*

Other poems painted an entire world of loss, each "leaf" and "stump" echoing with an audible silence.

> *You hear silence when you are*
> *thinking of how it was when your*
> *father was home to love you.*
> *I think of an old stump sitting*
> *in a field with wild flowers*
> *prancing around and laughing*
> *at it mockingly.*
> *A silent gentle breeze*
> *ruffling leaves.*
> *It is a road leading to*
> *a place far off.*
> *Pamela, 6th grade*

Sometimes, reading a child's poem, I could almost feel the child struggling to speak what T. S. Eliot called "the word within a word...swaddled with darkness"—to break through the silence. "We knock upon silence," a Chinese poet once wrote, "for an answering music." Some of my students looked for solace in the music of rhyme or rhythm, as in this poem entitled "I am Sorry."

Today I cried.
My sister sighed.
For my mother tried
Sweetly to say my dogs died.
Matt, 3rd grade

Some tried to sing the dead one back:

I woke up in my grandfather's lap
And I heard his leg go tap, tap, tap.
He was singing a song to me,
It was such a cozy place to be.
Anitha, 4th grade

A few children were so tongue-tied that they remained unable to tell their stories without appropriating the words of others, in the form of rhymes, songs, or prayers. When invited to write about his grandmother, who had been dead six months, Jeff, a sixth grader with a learning disability, produced this:

God be in my hede
And in my understandyng
God be in my harte
And in my thinkyng
God be at myne end
And in my departyng.

In writing out a benediction he'd heard in church, Jeff was imitating adults who find comfort in the words of those we consider more eloquent than ourselves. Tombstones, for example, are carved with quotes by Shakespeare, Milton, or the biblical David: AIDS-quilt panels are stitched with contemporary poem fragments or song lyrics. For some survivors, even ad copy and singsong Hallmark clichés seem to offer relief, a safe holding pen for otherwise unrestrained emotion.

For others, the experience of grief is an opportunity for original expression, for giving voice to what had previously been mute. These are the natural poets in our midst, those who not only see the world in new ways, but translate these visions into words. In some students' poetry, grief broke out in startling music or in vivid images and colors. Crawford's poem seems to have been germinating within him, bursting forth at the first invitation to write about his loss.

Silent tears

Silent tears, silent tears,
Drink me up and swallow me down
And lick your lips
And rub your stomach
And ask your mom for more.
But not too long ago
Silent tears had petals in them.
And they will choke you
When you swallow them.
       Crawford, 4th grade

His images reveal the intermingling of sorrow and joy, the human hunger for the memory-petals found within tears. To remain silent—to be unable, as many of us are, to "ask your mom" for permission to consume the grief—is another kind of death, as the poem suggests. In all my reading, in all my firsthand experience with death and loss, I've yet to find a truer image for grief than Crawford's. Nor have I found an expression of loss more eloquent than the following poem, by another fourth-grade boy. Barry's simple lyric captures the helplessness of being small; he even hints that the sky is blue because it shares in his mourning.

The soft blue sky sounds sad. I wonder why I am small...So sad so
sad are you mad are you sad can I be soft because we is changing
we all ways change!

Children aren't the only ones who feel vulnerable in the face of loss. For adults, too, the changes that accompany loss are forces to be reckoned with. The death of a loved one breaks our accustomed world apart, knocks our inner hinges loose. If we are too brittle, we will break. If we are soft, malleable, open, we can shape-shift into new forms. Hollowed out, we are able to contain new worlds, but first we must be emptied. In many student poems, especially those of older students, sorrow found its expression in images of boundless skies, black holes, and voids.

This feeling inside me
Is like no hope,
Or the little hope in you
Is not feelible.
It's like being nowhere,
Empty inside
Like an empty house,
A heart with nothing in it.
    Jeremy, 6th grade

I see my heart so vacant
that the wind blows through it.
Then I see you holding hands
with the air.
Then I see you gone.
    Mario, 9th grade

Some authors attempted to fill this vacuum by creating a past they were left out of. In their poems, loss was measured not by what was once possessed or experienced, but by what was never known. Children are notoriously egocentric, and for some of my students it was nearly impossible to imagine a world independent of themselves. Let's say a child has heard stories about a relative who died before the child was born or before he got a chance to know her. This will not do; suddenly a big piece is missing, a connection lost, one that the child comes to see as vital. So the child writes the lost one into present life, imagining shared scenes or, in some cases, envisioning the relative's death. Often the child is portrayed as a caretaker or, in the very least, as personal historian. In the writing of such poems, the children seemed to be salvaging a past they never knew, reclaiming their lost place in history and emerging as the ones in power.

The Aunt I Never Knew

In my mind I imagine
me pushing her in a wheelchair
with her face blooming like her name.
Aunt Mary Lily
I would say.
yes Zach
she would answer
Please
don't ever go away.
        Zachary, 5th grade

Great Granddad

The last things are hard
Where gun fires like fire
I can feel on my hand.
We got his old army clothes
With red blood like apples.
He died on the day at Guam.
We think he got lost
In a Japan building.
        David, 4th grade

Perhaps this act of imagination, writing oneself into another's story, represents another type of rehearsal for children—a relatively painless, bloodless method of practicing for death by borrowing the grief of a parent or older friend. In one of my own poems, death is personified as a kind of Mafia boss. At first we know him "by reputation only." Later, he sends "messengers to do the small work: claws through the belly of the sparrow...colorless wings of dead moths." This progression is not unlike the way my students became acquainted with death. After the child had absorbed the loss of a best friend, a neighborhood or school, a divorced parent's companionship, death started sending in the hit men. The loss of a pet was the first encounter many students had with physical death, and it affected them deeply, perhaps because the death was often witnessed firsthand.

When I went to put his dropper to his lip,
He would not move his thumb to sip.
I tried to pet his curled body,
And he didn't lick my finger.
I ran inside and tears fell from my eyes.
I couldn't miss the bus,
But I really didn't care if I did.
    Sarah, 4th grade

Like adults, these grieving children responded with a wide range of anger, guilt, fascination, and sorrow. But unlike adults, who often deny the bodily details of the death, rushing quickly through the harsh memory to get to the other side, the children appeared unafraid to wade into the pain. "What other way is there?" their poems seemed to ask.

Separation is the purring
of my car in my ear
when he died.
The yellow autumn leaves
were the color of his fur
when they fall off the trees.
It feels like a big part of
you being taken out.
    Blair, 5th grade

In my mind
I see my dog
On the table,
With the veterinarian
Giving her a pill
That will put her to sleep,
With a smile on her face,
And she is dying.
    Jason, 3rd grade

And death kept drawing nearer, the distance dissolving little by little—from roadside park to veterinarian's office to the child's own house. For most of my students, the first family death was that of a grandparent or great-grandparent, and often the end had been preceded by a series of smaller deaths as the child witnessed the deterioration of an aging mind or body. It's as if the child lost the loved one in installments, and thus began mourning months, sometimes years, in advance.

> *Seeing my grandfather staggering with old age through the tall grassy field, seeing him walking wobbly without his cane, makes me want to cry knowing someday I'll never see him again.*
> *Cathy, 4th grade*

To hold onto the loved ones, the children often imagined them young again—wishing them back the way they were. Sometimes these wishes took the form of dreams.

> *In my dream my grandmaw could run very fast. We would feel the wind on our faces. She would be helthy, we would fly. We would soar with the egles!*
> *Ben, 4th grade*

Dreams

> *Grandma dreams of*
> *being soft and young*
> *Dancing in the nice warm winds*
> *over the trees and flowers again*
> *To sing aloud on a stage of soft hands*
> *To be her old age again...*
> *To wish away the tears of the past*
> *To tell her mother how much she loved her.*
> *That's what she would dream.*
> *Felicia, 5th grade*

When the end came, especially in the case of an elderly relative to whom the child was not strongly attached, the resulting poems often read like codas. Perhaps the scene had been rehearsed so many times, dreamed and imagined, written about, talked through, that the actual death was anti-climactic. Or perhaps the reportorial tone of some of these poems represented a defense against emotion. One third grader, Sophia, spent many lines of a long poem detailing how much she loved her aunt, listing the things they had done together—playing with Barbie dolls, frying chicken, singing. The death scene, however, was confined to two lines: *I rode in a lemo to her funarul. That's the end of my aunt.* Another child recalled the barest details and stated them matter-of-factly, like the narrator in a Dickinson poem who, at the instant of death, heard a fly buzz.

> *I was at the hospital visiting my great-grandmother.*
> *It smelled like alcohol.*
> *Her face was pale with big blue eyes.*
> *Then she said good-bye.*
>   *Shannon, 4th*

Other children dwelled a bit longer on the dead one, then quickly returned to the business of living.

> *When my cousin died, I felt as if I wasn't one of the family anymore. Like I was the wide reciever on a football team, and I had just dropped my 19 touchdown pass. Then, I knew my aunt was suffering more than myself. One year later my aunt is getting married, and we are all almost over it.*
>   *Josh, 3rd grade*

Dead is dead, life is now; aunts remarry, school starts up, we put one foot before the other. Like the survivors in one of Robert Frost's poems, since we are "not the one dead," we turn to our affairs. And what if the dead forget to be dead, try to stop our progress? Then, we, the living, set them straight:

> *In my dream my great-grandfather old and wrinkly comes to see me, he says he will never leave agin. I tell him great-grammy is getting married agin he says <u>no</u> she is not, she loves great-grandpa better.*
>   *Lindsey, 4th grade*

In many poems, however, the narrators did not move immediately back into their lives after the death of a loved one. Perhaps their attachments were stronger, or their grief timetable longer; children vary as much as adults in the depth and duration of their mourning. Only one kind of childhood loss seemed without exception to evoke intense, nearly inconsolable pain. When death stole a sibling, the wave of grief broke hard, and its ripples were felt long afterward. No longer was death a species or a generation removed, something that happened only to pets or to old people. Now, suddenly, death was personal.

Without my brother it's like a rain inside me that's flooding my eyes A desert with no one around A wave washing sand away swift and fast ...
   Amy, 7th grade

My Brother

I wish he didn't have to go he made my heart soor and poor. He made me crumble up into an dryed leaf. If he was to life today I would be an happy sun shine over the world. Why did you have to go.
   Kelly, 4th grade

In cases where the sibling who died was an infant, the expression of grief took on special poignancy, as if the loss had happened too quickly to be absorbed. Months, sometimes years afterwards, the child reached back into memory, searching for details to hold onto.

Her eyes glowing as she wiggled in her crib
In her pink and white dress, ready for sleep.
I miss her now.
A cold swept her away like dust on the floor.
   Vanessa, 9th grade

Natalie

*I hated to lose
A pretty little girl called
Natalie.
She perished at birth
Without any pain,
But she did leave a stain
In our family photograph.*
    Tony, 7th grade

This notion—of the loved one leaving a stain of memory—ran through many of the poems. The children seemed to want to salvage whatever they could of the lost friend or relative, even if it meant recalling the most painful moments—the death scene, the last time they saw the loved one, or the moment they received the news of the death. Some, like sixth-grader Loula, wrote several versions of the same event as if, with each telling, the memory might become more bearable. Here is the fourth revision of Loula's poem:

*One windy night, dad told me my uncle died.
My heart beat fast like wild horses thumping against the ground.
Outside was a smell like the daisies on my grandmother's table on
Easter day.
My throat felt dry and guilty.
In my ear I could hear the wind blowing.
I could hear the crackle of the leaves.
The sky was as black as the jacket I was wearing.
The moon shone so bright I could see a face in it.*

But in some cases, unfortunately—especially when the death was by suicide or homicide—the ending was not peaceful, or was missing entirely. Antoinette, a second grader, drew a picture of a valentine-heart floating over a river of blood (my younger students seldom distinguished between the heart as an organ and the heart as a doily cut-out, though when they wrote of pain, it was always the bodily heart that took the blows.) Below the picture Antoinette wrote these words, using one of the huge, thick pencils schools issue to children in the primary grades:

I love myself because
I am not dead.
The blood comes from my heart
because my dad got shot.

Often these children seemed angry not only because the loved one died and left them alone but also because of the way the death occurred. Here, a fourth grader named Omeka rails against the violent end of her uncle:

I am still mad at hem he did it for staying out lat...he was 24. he
was my grandmoms oldest son...he was kill I did not want that to
happen. But it did and I'm mad sometimes becuse I think of you..

Omeka's switch from third person to second, from "he" to "you,' is a switch that often occurred when my students wrote about death, as was the switch from past to present tense. These switches, which appeared to be unconscious, reveal as much about the nature of grief as do the images or details presented. More than mere grammatical lapses, the moves from "he" to "you," from "then" to "now," are moves toward intimacy and immediacy, and to correct them is to violate the truth of the children's stories. Once, while working in a fifth grade classroom, I overheard a well-meaning teacher pointing out what she perceived as an error in a child's paper. "Here," she said, "you've written 'My dog died on a rainy Sunday morning', but down here you say 'I love my dog.' You need to be consistent with your verb tense." "I am," the boy replied. "I still love my dog."

Omeka, near the end of her poem about her uncle, alternated swiftly between present and past, also employing another device often seen in the grief poems of children—repetition. In Omeka's case the repetition escalated into a kind of keening, a wailing not unlike that of mourners at a graveside:

He is my untal o yes he is
he was my best untol o yes he was
But he dead o that the true
o yes he dead

In writing "he was," Omeka acknowledged the reality of the death, but the phrase "he is" reminds us that the lamentation was not yet over for her. It continued in memory, and the poem was one way for Omeka to close the curtain on the event. One morning in class, a fourth grader named Sharon, expressing her anguish at never saying goodbye to her nineteen-year-old cousin, wrote an alternate ending to her death drama. After she had begun with *Oh No the day is gone I'm still all alone how could this be Otis not here with me never said good By*—she turned the page of her notebook and began writing furiously, nonstop, for the remainder of the class period. I watched, amazed, for Sharon was not a student known for what teachers call "staying on task." Finally she waved me to her desk. "Read this," she said. She had written several pages about a dream in which Otis had appeared. In the dream, her heart started beating fast. She smelled cologne; then she saw Otis. At this point, Sharon slipped into present tense, as most of my students did when recalling a dream, actual or invented. Otis turns up his music "like he youst to befor he died." She says, "I thout you wher dead," to which he answers, "I am and I am in colleg in heaven." He takes her to heaven, where they see everybody, even God, who tells her to hug Otis, "becase it's time for you to go." She embraces him, all the while crying, "no pleas no." But when she wakes up, she comes to school and (switching back to past tense) "got over it. It was the last time I will ever see him agin. The End."

In almost all the poems that contained a revision of the death scene, the vehicle was a dream, which, as one sixth grader told me, "is a place you find in your sleep." When this place was a traditional heaven, students seemed to take comfort in well-worn images.

Haven in the ski

I thingk abot my gradfarther evin if he is in haven the ski was brat with havenly blue the clods are white and pofy the aire is frash and evrybody is free with gold wigs and white robse as thay toch the clods softly and whin you thingk abot haven you will fill light and for aver sleep in piec.
     Shaughnacie, 5th grade

But in my experience, examples like Shaughnacie's were rare. The dream scene in most of the poems was, not heavenly, but earthly and homely. Almost always, the child himself was beside the loved one, both engaged in some mundane activity.

> *In my dream my grandmother is rocking me in her chair and she*
> *is happy to be alive and to be singing to me again.*
> *Thomas, 4th grade*

Unfortunately—or fortunately, depending on how one views the progress of recovery from grief—one requisite of a dream is that the dreamer eventually wakes. For some, this waking is a swift, clean transition, like the sensation of cold water being thrown in your face. For the fourth-grade girl who wrote the following poem, the boundary was less clear. I choose to name this crossing the transition between dream and *wakefulness* rather than between dream and *reality*, since the life of dreams can be as real as the life of waking.

> *When I woke up and turn to my left*
> *I saw you and I walked right up to you*
> *You didn't say anything I thought that you were a marige*
> *I stake my hand out to see if you were really there*
> *or if you were in thin air*
> *When I new that you were there I passed you*
> *while the breeze sweeps the sand and goes through the tree's*

Like the biblical doubter, Thomas, who demanded to feel the risen Christ's wounds in order to know that he was real, the child reached out her hand. We are not told what the hand discovered, only that after the child reached out, she knew "that you were there." With this knowledge, she was free to "pass" the loved one, to move beyond the nightmare of death and its harsh waking, into another space. What remained of the loved one was the breeze: a soft, invisible force with the power to reshape its earthbound neighbors, sand and trees. For the children whose poems I have read and loved, this unseen power—call it nature, God, truth, art, or simply tears with petals in them—is as indisputable as it is mysterious. It weaves through

140

their young lives, through their sufferings and joys, which turn out to be not so small after all. It is difficult to read these children's words and not celebrate the wisdom of the young in matters of the heart, their crazily sane methods of survival, and the imaginative ways they move from grief toward healing.

The Spirit of my Granmother

In my dream
I see my granmother
Standing by the door
Watching us play
As we ride our bikes
And she's singing a song
I hear beauful thunder booming
And lighning flashing
With her spirit upon us saying how beauful
Are the raindrops falling
    Chonte, 4th grade

SAVING US FROM OURSELVES

By Ian Pounds

In the autumn of 2007 I was a writing mentor for a captain in the Marine Corps. She had recently completed her second deployment in Iraq where, among other things she took a billet as mortician, the first to receive KIAs from the field. She'd been writing about her experience, but did not know how the essays should evolve. What struck me was the honesty in her work and the absence of self-indulgence. An officer in the Corps is not likely to boast. Placing emphasis on everything around her, writing memoir as if the "I" is another character, she had leaped the early lessons I normally drive into students. In this way writing inadvertently gave her opportunity to look at her experience objectively, to put it in perspective and create meaning. I was pleased just to be a conduit for her pursuit of a book, a sounding board and confidence builder.

Something I learned from the experience stuck with me as much as her writing. We had finished our session and had been chatting aimlessly over a cup of coffee. Then, after a moment of thoughtful silence, she confessed to me the pain of not receiving mail from her fiancé while deployed, and consequent to her depression, the effect it had on her own letter writing. We civilians tend to think of the military as a singular force. Behind the scenes, behind the "one for all" credo it is a group of individuals, each with his or her story to tell, a story rarely indulged but for letters. I fret about e-mail and blogs, so temporary and ill composed. Where would we be without the letters written across the ages, humanizing history? To put pen to paper and speak from across the continents is no ordinary task. Anyone who does knows the immortal nature of such an act. Compound this in the hands of a warrior; *she's writing her last words to the world, again and again.* Now more than ever it is vital we encourage veterans to write those letters they may not have had the wherewithal to write while deployed.

Why must we write? To make sense? Unquenchable curiosity? To put to rest? To stand out, give voice to the voiceless? Or is it something less practical yet more omnipotent, what Rilke described as the future entering into us so that it might change itself in us, long before it happens? Whatever it is, all writers must go through a dark night of the soul to get where they are going, that moment they kill the protagonist, unflinchingly, without remorse. Like the Purple Heart who goes back into battle, to survive is not enough, not until the story has been truly written, not until the mission is achieved and the comrades come home. Then, finally, there comes the completion of the act, for a singular history to become all history, the telling of the tale. In that spirit I offer a letter I wrote to the world the evening of the day my wife accepted her commission as a second lieutenant in the Marine Corps. I share this in solidarity with all warriors who cling to the notion that such an act has a place in the world of letters and, whether in the making or the sharing, has the power to heal, to save us from ourselves.

Virginia 10 August 2007
21:00—22:00
On this day in 1519, Ferdinand Magellan set out with five ships to circumnavigate the earth, something that had never been accomplished. He would not survive, but his voyage did.

Black and sultry and late. Suzi is passed out in bed. We just made it back to the bungalow. She didn't eat enough dinner. Too wound up. Too much letting go. I'm drunk too, but I'm upset and jazzed and happy and relieved and sorry. After everything, I let down my guard, my defense, my better sensibility. The youngest of five, I wanted to shine, too. No medals for me, a slap on the back. Before she closed her eyes, inside, I secretly wanted to steal her thunder, ruin her day. All this glory.

I'm scared she'll die. Rape. Body parts. They'll be there, the ones that know what it's like to be a Marine. Not me.

Walking home, arm in my arm, leaning, happy with me, thankful. Exclamations. How could I not simply embrace her? Let her shine. I did, oh I did, until the very end, the last minute, and then I cried. I watched her at dinner with the colonel soaking up her adulation and eagerness, stories stories. Ode to joy. I was sidekick. Talk to the wives, this is Marine business. Wine, bottles of it. Good stuff. Mirrors on the wall, artifacts of service everywhere. Purpose and reason and service and reward, everywhere.

Vodka.

Before that, champagne. I sang a song. How I wrote it. Thank you. In light of war, how thank you. Family, family look at me. I think of the Who. See me, feel me, touch me, heal me. Can't ask for any of that. Hold on, shut up. Let her shine. Sacrifice. Driving driving, dog walking, miles parting, angst. Alone. Home. Gone. See me.

Find the one, the Gunny that pulled her through. A tall black woman with vocal chords the size of a low E string on a guitar. First salute not gonna happen, or wasted on a lesser woman. But another last moment prevailed, and there she was, as we walked out from the commissioning, as she arrived. A different human being in front of her, not the fear of failure. Silver coins mean something here. Tradition means something. And what an oath, what a right hand up. Swear it. Service Alpha uniforms, greens that call to mind a story I read, a movie I saw, a dream I had. Tradition. Butter bars on the cover, the collar, the shoulders. Right hand, uphold the Constitution, of her own free will, so help her God. They all did. They all will. And it was over.

Fifteen cannon shots shook the bleachers, the pavement, the sky, and my body ached for her body. That would have to wait. The number of times already exists, the number of years a war lasts, the number of casualties, the number from Charlie that will die. There is a number of times, already fixed, Suzi and I will kiss, will face one another in bed, will say the three words.

Hot. Damned humid, damned hot. Sun diffused and so we swam in light and steam. My baby blue dress shirt, how did I get into it? Mottled with splotches of sweat, darker blue on the chest, under those arms, dripping down the back, ring around the neck. She looked so beautiful, so strong. Her forest cammies, her cover low over the eyes, her brown hair cut just so to the line of her jaw, her sleeves rolled high and tight. No rifle for her, she'd need to come forward, she'd need a free hand to shake, another one to accept the physical fitness award.

Grrrrrrr... said the commander to one tough Candidate, no longer a Candidate, with a new dream, one she will wake to and sleep to the rest of her life, an eagle for her country, an anchor for the high seas, and a globe for service all over the world. Marching forward from the rest, above and beyond, and who was there on those bright aluminum bleachers pumping a beating heart?

Charlie in tight formation, rifles at arms. Not any parade. The power of one. A greater enemy will fragment willy-nilly at the brunt of it. The Commander of the Troops at one end of the deck sounding the order, "Come on you bastards, you want to live forever?" It was November 10th, 1775. It was Fallujah, it was Hue. It was Chosin, Iwo Jima, Montezuma, Tripoli. Rushing forward, always forward, never back, to now. And she was there.

The band played the hymn, we all mouthed the words. From one place to the other, from everywhere to forever, always. I raised the camera, put it down for good. This one's going to be stored elsewhere. I believe in God. Now. Where is she? Please, please watch over her. Please, damn it, please. Don't you realize there is a platoon that doesn't even know life will change, out there waiting? Don't worry, she's on her way. She'll take care of you. Trust me. You've never seen a mother and her cubs? I have. I've seen it for real. I've seen her battle a male twice her size, a male that would eat those cubs, hungry, starved even, and she didn't back down, and she won't I tell you, she won't as long as you are there for her. Even when you aren't, she will be.

O Nine ten. Ninety degrees. Officer Candidate Class 195 waiting. Families waiting. The blacktop of the immense parade deck warping the air. Heat. I closed and opened my eyes and looked at my watch. Another twenty minutes. An hour. Two hours. Three. The sun rose hazily. No sleep. I thought of Suzi lying awake in her rack for the last time. A thundercloud that passed slowly in the night dumped everything it contained over Quantico and moved on. It wasn't much of a relief. I got out of bed and made coffee. Ate half an apple. Opened my computer, searched the blogs.

Charlie Company 1st Platoon, OCC 195 is graduating at the end of this week. I am full of happiness for all the graduates, but sadness for myself. I know I'm missing out on something and I don't know if I'll ever get it back. I'm not sure I ever want to get it back. In the abstract I want to be a Marine. Face to face, I'm not so sure. I don't think I want to be that hard. I don't want to fight every step of the way for the rest of my life. But it is a beautiful life, beautiful like driving through an empty desert. It's solitary and hard, sometimes exceptionally hot and then freezing cold within a matter of hours. Only the toughest learn to survive there, and there is honor in that. You get pride, the kind of pride that those who haven't experienced it don't understand and never will.

Who is this woman? She left in week four on crutches. She didn't last long enough to bond with Suzi, to see her lead, to see her shine. Yet she knows what Suzi knows and what I can never know. What, I ask, is so impossible to understand? Was I not there? Was I not behind her eyes?

I'll tell you the way it went.

It was fucking hot. The Obstacle Course ran west to east. All of them were there, Candidates, instructors, officers. Week nine. The final race. Suzi the fastest, but not now. Now two young Candidates; broader, taller, more athletic. You're thinly worn, so don't think, Suzi. Act. And she did. She tossed her body in. Hearing and seeing is precious stuff. Keep it for the directly in front of you. Go. Go hard. In the middle, the descending poles, dare to open your ears. A chorus of brutes screamed *oorah* and *kick some ass* and *don't let up*. Damn if she wasn't ahead of the other two. She glanced to the side. Arms waving her on. Kick it up a notch. Over the log hurdles, the parallel bars, one final sprint. And then the rope climb. Arms burn, ankles wrap, push, pull, up we go. She tapped out the top before the others had even arrived. A minute and forty seconds. You can descend the rope now, Suzi. Plant your boots firmly. Walk tall but not proud. Report your time straightaway to the SI. Salute. Join the other Candidates with humility. No fist pumping. No high fives. Inside of you, keep your confidence and your allotment of joy. Remember who you are.

WRITING IDENTITY IN THREE GENRES: TEACHING CREATIVE WRITING AT THE AMERICAN UNIVERSITY IN DUBAI

By Jillian Schedneck

"Miss, I'm Saudi," Sarah began, leaning forward in her desk as if explaining something essential about her role in this class. "So, you know, there's a lot to write about."

The class, seated in a circle, erupted in laughter while Sarah, her long, dark curls spilling around her face, chuckled in surprise. I had asked my creative writing students at the American University in Dubai to be prepared to share the topics for their personal essays, focusing on particular stories and scenes, but Sarah assumed the simple fact of her origin would be enough to impress the American teacher. I asked her to be more specific.

"Well," she considered, "I could write about women not being allowed to drive." Alia and Basil slumped in their seats. We had heard that before.

"The assignment is to write about *you*," I said. "Your relationship to Riyadh, how it shaped you."

"It's complicated...but I'll think of something."

I continued around the circle, hearing from Sabiha, a Tanzanian with Indian ancestry who never felt she truly belonged to North Africa like those who could trace their lineage for generations. Farah told the class that she left Azerbaijan for Dubai at nine and felt at home in neither place. Karla was comfortable anywhere but her native Philippines. Lama, who was Lebanese, grew up in a rural, conservative town in the western region of Abu Dhabi, neighboring emirate of Dubai, and felt completely alienated from her peers and surroundings. Basil, brought up in America, resented his parents and himself for their lack of involvement in the Palestinian cause.

With Dubai's nearly eighty five percent foreign-born population, I shouldn't have been surprised that almost all of my fifteen creative writing students had complicated relationships with their pasts, native countries and subsequent jumbled identities. While "Who am I?" is a question asked by most college students of any background, Dubai's unique position helped bring such concerns to the forefront, particularly in a creative writing class where one's idiosyncratic worldview inevitably rises to the surface. You can feel alienated anywhere, but in Dubai, the land of transient expatriates and guest workers, the odds increase. The small native population was often accused of closing itself off from the international foreign majority. Expatriates often complained that there was no dominant Dubai culture in which to assimilate. The city also lacked recognizable history—there was little besides ultra-modern shopping malls and shimmering towers to allow for any kind of cultural identification. Almost everyone I met outside of university seemed to exist in two places at once: Dubai, the city of money, comfort and superficial concerns, and Cairo, Beirut or Montreal, the cities of their daydreams and idyllic memories. All of this made it difficult for my students to feel rooted anywhere.

The rest of the class came from India, Pakistan, Finland and Nigeria; some had been born in Dubai, and others arrived recently to attend university. And while these were the privileged ones (the university parking lot resembled a car show, with Hummers, Range Rovers and Escalades) I had to remember that wealth didn't always mean finding an easy place in this world.

"This is great material," I told the class. "You've also brought up some really big and complicated issues. So the question is: how will you write about it all in just a few weeks?" I teased.

The students chuckled but no one ventured an answer. Farah and Marwa stared at me wide-eyed, pens poised, waiting to write down the magic answer. Sabiha folded her hands neatly, ready to hear my sage advice. Far from challenging me, a twenty-eight year old American only a year-and-a-half out of graduate school, they swiftly handed over total control of their essays.

"You have to figure out how to write your own stories. But I will give you some advice: write in scenes, zoom in on important details and images and try to show your emotions through actions and setting." This was not the answer they were hoping for.

I watched their frustrated faces brainstorming ideas for scenes that might highlight some of their complicated relationships to the places they called home. In my notebook, I wrote about my own national identity—fourth generation American with Old World roots from the Ukraine, Sweden, Russia and Austria. I had no ties to any of these countries, languages or histories, and I felt unbelievably plain and stable compared to these students. Growing up in New Jersey, I envied my first generation Indian, Korean, Filipino and Spanish girlfriends who easily floated between the vast, white world—the one of their accents and clothes and tastes—and that other world their faces called up. I wrote about dancing at my friend Sonya's sister's wedding, listening to Teresa's father tell the story of meeting her mother during the Korean War, eating tapas and learning Spanish words with Melissa and her mother. I saw it was a lovely thing to possess layers of belonging and identity, to hold two worlds at once. Yet America, with its welcoming dominant culture and strong ethnic communities, seemed to allow for a much easier blending of identities.

With each genre my students and I encountered, it was clear that, far from feeling at ease in two places and cultures, they worried about belonging nowhere. They constantly reminded me that their identities were terribly in flux and that their own places in this world, any sense of rootedness, teetered on the precarious.

Creative Nonfiction

During the first week of class, I handed out the introduction to Amin Maalouf's *In The Name of Identity*. An award winning novelist who lived half his life in Lebanon and half in France, Maalouf responded to the question of which identity he considered most authentic by writing: *What makes me myself rather than anyone else is the very fact that I am poised between two countries, two or three languages and several cultural traditions. It is precisely this that defines my identity. Would I exist more authentically if I cut off a part of myself?* He worried over humanity's default need to locate a fundamental truth or essential identity, a hardened core of allegiance presented at birth that cannot be altered by later experience. Yet only when we are welcomed to claim all pieces of our identity—national, regional, religious—can we begin to act as bridges between cultures rather than instigators of prejudice and exclusion.

When we discussed the short essay in relation to their own experiences, my students also expressed dissatisfaction as they recalled the many times they had been asked where their true allegiances lie. They too had trouble figuring out if they felt more affinity for Pakistan or Dubai, Gulf Arabs or Levantine Arabs, English or Hindi or Arabic.

Lama raised her hand and said, "Honestly, when I'm asked if I feel more Lebanese or Jordanian or UAE, I want to say, 'I'm from Mars!'"

Alia said, "I want to tell people that I feel a part of the multicultural community of Dubai, but I think they'll look at me funny. How is that any kind of real belonging?"

"Can it be?" I asked. They looked at me skeptically.

For Alia and other expatriates who've grown up in Dubai, it isn't possible to become a UAE citizen; only those of native local origin hold Emirati passports.

Surprisingly, Sharina—the only Emirati in the class—shared her classmate's confusion over who she was and how to answer the question of her primary allegiance: "There are two kinds of Emiratis, Miss, Arab Emiratis and Ajami Emiratis, who have Persian roots because their great grandfathers settled here from Iran hundreds of years ago. So there is a split there—are you more Persian or more Arab? The Persian Emiratis try to hide their Iranian roots because now it is seen as better, more authentic, to be Arab. I am Arab and people sometimes ask me if I feel more Bedouin or 'modern,' because I go to school here and speak English more easily than Arabic. You can never be both."

I asked the class if they thought creative writing could help people understand these issues, to see that no one should have to choose a single identity, but can claim every influence. Some nodded weakly, others more vigorously.

I made my final plea. "I think it's an important step. Readers need *your* essays, stories and poems. They need to see the world from your points of view."

Our time was up. I handed back their weekly assignments about an important friendship and asked to speak to Sharina after class. In her essay, she had written: *In an Emirati girl's life her priorities are already set for her: reputation, religion and family. And as it turned out, it is bad for my reputation to be seen with a guy, let alone be his friend.* Her essay tells the story of her relationship with Yusuf, another Emirati student. Their mutual friends wouldn't believe they weren't romantically involved. Her mother had even told Sharina that friendship between opposite sexes wasn't possible. In order to preserve her reputation, she had to stop meeting with him outside of class.

I had often spotted Sharina and Yusuf in the Starbucks next to my office. He had been in my composition course the previous semester and I knew him to be earnest and sweet. Slight with shaggy hair, he made you think of the word boy rather than man. Sharina, on the other hand, was forthright and spirited, unlike many local women I had taught. While a small distinction between her and many of the other local girls in Dubai, the way Sharina wore her sheyla, or headscarf, spoke volumes about her personality and influences. She covered her whole head and forehead so not a peek of hair was exposed. Almost all the other local girls on campus wore their sheylas tipped back several inches so that a black sweep of bangs crossed their foreheads. This small difference implied that Sharina was more conservative than the other girls, and it also suggested that she wasn't interested in following any trends. I could see why Yusuf was drawn to her.

As a former resident of the more conservative emirate of Abu Dhabi, where separate seating sections for women and families in restaurants was the norm, I was delighted to see Emirati men and women sitting together on the comfy couches in the university Starbucks, watching American music videos and sipping lattes. Because I had known young women in Abu Dhabi who suffered because of this strict separation of the sexes, I was always glad to see Sharina and Yusuf together.

A week before, I had spotted them sitting on a bench outside the Art Building. Their heads were bent in intimacy and I smiled once again at the pair they made. Yet in Sharina's essay I learned this had been the moment when she told Yusuf they could no longer be friends. She wrote: *I was angry at our society. But I have accepted and embraced who I am and where I come from, along with the baggage and issues that come with my identity.*

Somehow, I didn't quite believe it. Sharina's conservative culture was at odds with her modern identity, shaped by the western attitudes of Dubai and this American university. I handed Sharina her essay and told her that I knew Yusuf, and had often seen them together. I wanted her to know I was on her side, for whatever it was worth, and that she could explore this story further in her longer essay. She could highlight the pull and push between the traditional and more liberal cultures that Dubai was asking its youth to navigate. But she just shrugged, resigned to their failed friendship.

Then she turned to me, smiling at the thought of Yusuf, and said, "Yusuf's Ajami. You can tell by his nose."

The class wrote several drafts of their essays, but as always in an introductory course, there wasn't enough time to truly bring them through to a more satisfying completion of their stories, to tease out those themes in a more nuanced narrative. They had taken a huge step, though, in determining their particular split between cultures, landscapes, histories and languages, and how all of this had shaped them.

Their essays were filled with the strangeness of returning to the lands of their national origins for funerals or annual summer visits. They wrote of pungent spices and bright colors, of parents who asked them to understand their roots in a matter of weeks and cousins who felt at ease in the chaotic streets of Karachi or Beirut. Sarah wrote of being reprimanded by the *mutaween* religious police for laughing too loudly in a Riyadh Starbucks. She recalled her grade school friend who suddenly ended their friendship because they weren't from the same tribe. These were the things that kept Sarah at a distance from Riyadh, yet the resounding call to prayer, and the desert, wilder and vaster than in Dubai, pulled her back. Sabiha wrote of visiting India and feeling completely overwhelmed by the land of her ancestors. Many wrote of their relief upon returning to familiar Dubai, but it wasn't quite home either. Even Sharina wrote about feeling like a stranger in her own house. Pale and skinny as a child, her sisters thought she appeared translucent, a ghost, and her solitary behavior didn't help. My students' essays were so full of this alienation that I started to worry their only impetus for picking up a pen was to describe their state of isolation. Then I read Karla's essay on her latest visit to the Philippines. She concluded with: *And now there's a new side to me that's in Dubai. Since everyone is from different cultures here, there's more freedom to just be a mix of everything you've come across.*

Poetry

One of the first poems I gave my Dubai students was called "A Place With Promise." Through vivid images, poet Maggie Anderson describes her conflicted relationship to her home state, West Virginia. Anderson wished the landscape could start over, that she could *wash the slag dust from the leaves / of sycamore and make them green.* To ask this place, *shaped by hills / and rivers, by poverty and coal,* to begin again and become a place with promise once more. I asked my students to write about their place with promise. Which landscape or memory would they hold in their arms if they could? I wanted their writing to move beyond national boundaries and more deeply reflect a sense of place, evoking wind-swept dunes and brick houses, dim hallways and moonlight, shadows on coral stone houses.

Farah wrote about Dubai, and I immediately understood how the city could fit under the title "A Place With Promise." While we all felt the drag of it sometimes—the traffic, lack of cultural outlets, the people we had come to love always arriving and then leaving—we needed to be reminded of its promise, the good intentions of meritocracy and safety, a haven for the bruised Middle East. I suggested they use one of Anderson's lines as a starting point: *I keep trying to say what I notice here / that's beautiful.* Farah wrote about the dhow boats along the old Creek downtown, the now iconic buildings she had seen rising from the sand, the concrete stumps of the new subway systems, of oil and sheikhs, long flowing robes of authority and majesty. I encouraged her to write more on this theme for her poetry portfolio.

When Farah told me on the first day of class that she was from Azerbaijan, I mentally thanked my friend and colleague who had recently handed me the novel "Ali and Nino." This novel's setting is in Azerbaijan, a country at the crossroads of the East and West. I had never heard of the former Soviet Union country before the book entered my hands. If I had not serendipitously been given that novel, I might have asked Farah where she was *really* from, told her to stop imagining a country that didn't exist because we weren't writing fiction yet—that's how strange the name Azerbaijan sounded to me. Fortuitously prepared for our introduction, I mentioned "Ali and Nino," the national book of her homeland, and became Farah's instant hero, someone sympathetic to her country and identity plight. Whenever I saw Farah I entered the world of Ali and Nino, glimpsed the old walls of capital Baku. I pictured her as Nino, even though that character came from the neighboring country of Georgia. Farah's delicate face, big eyes and lithe body created the perfect female protagonist in my imagination.

But Farah's life had not been filled with the trials of loving the mischievous, noble, warrior Ali. Farah's mother had a severe nervous breakdown when her daughter was five, and they were estranged for three years. No one had told Farah where her mother had gone; she simply appeared again when Farah was nine, right after they moved to Dubai. Azerbaijan became the place of her mother's mysterious illness, and Dubai her cure. Farah had written her essay about visits to Baku, where she didn't speak the language or share the same values as the girls her age. Like Dubai, Baku had become an oil-rich city, but something was different between the two: in Baku she was expected to fit in, and in Dubai no one quite did.

After class, Farah asked, "Miss, where are you from?"

I must have blushed. Six weeks into the semester and I hadn't even told them I was American? Did I think it was written on my forehead? When I said I had grown up near New York, she nodded in approval.

"We thought you might be Canadian." She collected her Mark Jacobs purse and turned back to face me. "It's still exotic to us, you know, to be American."

This surprised me. I had assumed that America's collective cache was long over since 9/11. To me, exotic meant attraction to the unknown, yet my culture was all around them, especially in this American university.

"That's good to know," I said. Perhaps Farah thought it exotic that I had specifically chosen Dubai because of its great mix of cultures. Unlike so many of my students, who seemed adrift here, my residence was a matter of intention rather than circumstance.

Before they handed in their final drafts, I asked my students to bring in poems from their country's authors. I encouraged them to read aloud in their native languages, which received unanimously averse reactions. But once they got their tongues around speaking in a language not everyone understood, once they realized that the subjects their ancestors cared about were the same for all of us today—love, acceptance, mortality—their voices opened up and rang with syllables that were undecipherable to me. Somehow I understood.

Marwa read Khalil Gibran's "You Have Your Lebanon and I Have My Lebanon." As an American exile, Gibran had a distanced and sympathetic perspective on his homeland. This sentiment resonated with many students as Marwa read, *You have your Lebanon and its dilemma. I have my Lebanon and its beauty.* In Gibran's Lebanon, exiles *migrate with nothing but courage in their hearts and strength in their arms but who return with wealth in their hands and a wreath of glory upon their* heads. / *They are the victorious wherever they go and loved and respected wherever they settle.* The children of his Lebanon are *the lamps that cannot be snuffed by the wind and the salt which remains unspoiled through the ages.*

Since my students were reading from their country's literature, I read to them from mine. My choice? "Two Countries" by Naomi Shihab Nye: *Skin remembers how long the years grow / ...it remembers being alone and thanks something larger / that there are travelers, that people go places / larger than themselves.*

After reading works from their home countries, Sabiha and Rhonda read poems from the cultures they felt the most affinity for, places that had nothing to do with their native origins: Portugal and Italy. "I don't know why, Miss, but I felt so good in Lisbon," Sabiha said. "Sometimes places find you," I said.

In her final poems, Farah included a meditation on life in Dubai. When I read, *I remember when all you could see for miles were the rolling desert dunes,* I recognized her place with promise. She would scrub the city clean with piles of sand until it shimmered with new hope like the sparkle in her mother's eyes when she finally woke from her delirium and reunited with her daughter.

Fiction

All the local newspapers were following the case of Qasm and his onyx stone. An old man from Yemen, Qasm had come to Dubai to sell his precious stones at a booth in Global Village, a two month long fair showcasing elaborate pavilions with jewelry, textiles and sweets from twenty-two different countries. The centerpiece of Qasm's collection was his onyx, which he claimed made its wearer impervious to bullets. Back in Yemen, he claimed he had tied the onyx around his sheep and shot a bullet at her four times; she survived without a trace of injury. Potential buyers were treated to this story and shown the primitive shape of a gun etched into the stone as further proof of its reliability. The advertised price was over four hundred million dollars. The police soon arrested Qasm for attempted swindling.

At his trial, Qasm announced that he wanted the chance to prove his stone's magical powers, and asked to wear the onyx while standing before a firing squad. Qasm's lawyer argued that if his client wasn't able to prove his stone's power, then the case must be declared a mistrial.

Qasm pleaded, "I am willing to prove to the world that it's a bulletproof onyx stone. I am ready to face a death sentence if that's what it will take me to prove that the stone is doubtlessly bulletproof. I didn't con anybody's money, but the police tricked me and filed a malicious case against me." The court, of course, did not allow Qasm to test his stone. He was sentenced to six months in jail followed by deportation.

I handed my students copies of one of the several newspaper articles on Qasm's case and gave them their assignment: write a short story from Qasm's perspective. Did he really believe in his magical stone? They grumbled. I agreed the assignment would be challenging, but I wanted them to write from a totally different perspective, and Qasm was about as far from their own identities as they could get. The article and assignment would also allow them to see Dubai through a different lens, one where people believed in charms and amulets, spells and incantations—things my cosmopolitan students espoused as old world. I wanted to learn how they would grapple with this modern/pre-modern split within Dubai.

Forced to see Dubai with fresh eyes, as a place of scams and rubes rather than emptiness and longing, they wrote about sleepy villages and big city lights, cops and swindlers and shady lawyers, all within the carnival atmosphere of Global Village. Some gave Qasm sharp manipulation techniques and armed him with deliberate intent to scam gullible tourists. Others rendered him desperately in need of money, his ruse his only hope for survival. Only Lama wrote from the perspective of a Qasm who truly believed in his stone's power and was willing to risk his life to prove it. In Lama's version, Qasm did stand before the firing range. When shot his onyx slipped off his neck. Qasm floated high above the city, watching the people below, bound by gravity and circumstance and denied the pleasure of being uplifted by stones and magic.

For the final short story assignments, I asked my Dubai students to write from the perspective of a different gender, nationality or age group. Karla chose to write about Donald, a schizophrenic. By the end of the piece, her protagonist pities the nurse who berates him for living in two worlds at once. She wrote: *My dear Ms. Greta doesn't understand. That room where I live is not empty. It is filled with many things, things that only I can touch with my head. Poor, poor Ms. Greta. So unsatisfied, so lonely, so... normal.* Besides being incredibly funny, her story revealed something important to her classmates: it would be a shame to be "normal," to claim only one identity. Her story showed the great advantage of bouncing between two or three identities, welcomed in all rooms, countries and worlds.

On the last day of classes, Sharina brought the final draft of her story to my office with Yusuf in tow. I had sensed that their separation wouldn't last. Yusuf waved from the doorway as Sharina approached my desk, handed me her story, and whispered, "Does my sheyla look ok?" She wore a white headscarf instead of the standard black. Her skin looked softer, her brown eyes shone brighter. I told her she looked beautiful. She smiled and joined Yusuf in the hallway—they were probably on their way to Starbucks.

Sharina's story was about a young Emirati man named Zayed, who is on vacation with his mother and sister in the east coast of the country. At night, he ventures from their rustic resort complex and enters Chalet 19, a den of impropriety. Women, naked except for veils, dance luridly while men throw money at their feet. The next day, Zayed tries to rationalize his behavior by telling himself that he didn't really lose control or truly enjoy that scene. As he starts a fire to cook for his mother and sister, his white headdress, called a ghetra, falls into the flames. *I sat slight panicked and realized that I had no other choice but to watch helplessly as my ghetra became fuel for this growing flame, soon to be nothing more than just ashes by daytime, dragged away by that salty sea breeze my mother had so longed for.* Like the burning ghetra and her black sheyla, I saw that Sharina and all of my creative writing students that semester, had lifted off the old and, however painfully or unwittingly, opened up to something new.

MCWS 4

30 September – 28 October 2006

Participants:
Sondra
Charlotte
Kathryn
Yvonne
David
Jack
Vivian
"N" – The Narrator

I now know why men who have been to war yearn to reunite. Not to tell stories or look at old pictures. Not to laugh or weep. Comrades gather because they long to be with the men who once acted at their best, men who suffered and sacrificed, who were stripped of their humanity. I did not pick these men. They were delivered by fate and the military. But I know them in a way I know no other men. I have never given anyone such trust. They were willing to guard something more precious than my life. They would have carried my reputation, the memory of me. It was part of the bargain we all made, the reason we were so willing to die for one another. As long as I have my memory, I will think of them all, every day. I am sure that when I leave this world, my last thought will be of my family and my comrades. Ahh. Such good men.

—Anonymous quote provided by F.P Siedentopf, a Milspeak Writer

WE'LL NEVER FORGET

I drove to the grocery store the day after the terrorist attacks of September 11, 2001, something many New Yorkers were unable to do. "We'll Never Forget" bled in red letters across the rear window of a small car in the grocery store parking lot. How long does it take to forget what can never be forgotten? Soon yellow magnetic "Support our Troops" ribbons were appearing everywhere. They reminded me of another fad, the Smile buttons that were everywhere during the 1970s. Newscasts soon began focusing on lack of armor in Iraq and on service members' injuries: limbs, eyes, and faces lost to IEDs, lives lost in combat. People seemed hesitant to talk with or about the injured; the injured weren't talking. By the fifth anniversary of 9-11, messages in red paint on car windows were long gone. Some Americans called for an end to remembrances of 9-11. Many Americans were too busy trying to keep their own lives together to recognize the seriousness of the military family's situation: longer deployments, shorter time home between deployments, and, for many troops, loss of income when military duty means giving up the part-time jobs that so often provide a hedge fund for young military families. Civilians are led to believe that the military takes care of the military family. And it does. But that care goes only so far.

On the enlisted side in 2009, an E-1 with less than two years service earned $1399 per month plus allowances before taxes (state, federal, county, and property taxes in many cases). An E-3 over two years in service earned $1753.50 per month. On the officers' side of the pay scale, an O-1 with two years or less in service earned $2655.30.[1] For many young enlisted military members, duty usurps the necessity of carrying two or three part-time jobs in addition to fulltime military service; extra income falls away. Reservists called to active duty lose income and sometimes find their pre-deployment jobs gone upon returning home. Many young military families depend upon food stamps and food distribution programs to make ends meet. What about the situation of military children, who do not have the support of a hometown? But how can civilians know what military life is really like if we do not tell them? Fear of repercussion prevents many military members and their families from seeking available help. False pride keeps many from asking for assistance to handle bills or their memories of wartime experiences. Military people usually feel that to seek financial assistance and to tell of their need is to betray the military and their country. Telling is too often perceived as disloyal whining by those among military leaders who are somehow better equipped to handle the financial and personal stresses of military life. As a young enlisted woman, I wasn't one of those equipped to handle that stress, but pretended to be and dealt with it by burying it in binge drinking.

In 1980, when I was a young married Marine corporal/E4, my paycheck couldn't meet the cost of living in Hawaii while I was there with my first husband, a former Marine utilizing his GI Bill benefits to attend college. A trip to the Navy Relief Society's office each week provided us with a brown paper bag of supplies: a dozen eggs, a slab of cheese, a loaf of bread, a pound of frozen hamburger. My husband held a part-time job, as did I. For a while, I worked as a cook at the base bowling alley. Later, I took a job as a cashier at a gas station in Kailua. Still, we could not afford to feed ourselves because of my binge drinking and the cost of living.

When we married, my wedding ring was a twenty-five dollar gold band; his ring was fashioned from a silver spoon. Our honeymoon celebration was a trip to the drive-in movie. Our rented home, a tiny duplex apartment, was furnished with eighty dollars worth of used furniture purchased at a Salvation Army thrift store. Change saved in a sock bought beer. I drank what I could when others were buying. We didn't visit local attractions— we had no money for it. We seldom ate out. Visiting Waikiki was out of the question. The best we could manage were trips to beaches where no admission was charged. Keeping gas in the car was a chore. Most mornings, I ran to work so my husband could use our beat up car to get to school. After my first reenlistment in January 1981, our lives improved. I received a few thousand bonus-dollars and promotion to sergeant. Twenty percent of my bonus went to taxes. The rest was spent on furniture, linens, and a newer used car. Much of the bonus money was wasted, including the thousands spent on the car. Drunk at the wheel, I totaled the car by driving into a highway divider. My husband and a friend were sleeping in the car at the time of the wreck. The car was folded into a "V" by the impact. No one was injured. I spent the last $600 of my reenlistment bonus money buying a used 1968 Volkswagen station wagon. The financial strain during our three years in Hawaii was too much for my husband and me—I compensated by overdrinking, which only added to our problems; my husband responded by building a life of his own. When I left Hawaii, I left him.

Young military people today experience the same hardship, if not worse. Each time I go out to eat or to Wal-Mart, I see them working, waiting tables, cooking, standing behind registers. The men are easily recognized by their high and tight haircuts and polite manner. The women are more difficult to spot—our gender provides the perfect camouflage. When I see these hard-working military people, I know that their families will suffer when a part-time job is lost to war-time deployment, particularly junior ranking military people whose pay seldom meets the costs of living at home or abroad. Certainly, much is done to ensure military families are cared for. Daycares, schools, after-school programs, single-Marine programs, educational programs, counseling—programs abound within the Marine Corps Community Services network and in similar programs offered by the Corps' sister services. The Navy Relief Society remains a strong helper to military families, as does Red Cross, Chaplains Helping Hands Fund, and many other organizations. But the economic situation for the military family has yet to catch up with the reality of the American economy.

During 2006, many service members and their families were already experiencing the effects of multiple tours in support of Gulf War II, although this news did not reach civilians through the media until The Surge of 2007. The angst experienced each day a loved one is away is torturous. The family rebuilding that takes place upon return from war or deployment must be accomplished while facing survival in a struggling economy. For many families the financial, emotional, and physical strain is too heavy a burden to bear.

When civilians forget the purpose of maintaining a strong military even in peacetime (as demonstrated following the Vietnam War and the end of the Cold War), military funding diminishes leaving America with a flawed defense system and military members and their families in a bind. Despite the military's ongoing involvement in global conflicts during the 1980s and 1990s, many civilians decried what was believed to be an oversized and unnecessary military presence in America and the world after the Cold War ended. The military was downsized, along with the military budget. The economic future of the military family was destabilized and has yet to recover.

Will history repeat when Gulf War II ends?

By sharing the military experience, Milspeak writers are bridging the gap between the actuality of military life and the civilian community's understanding of it, a way of healing the divide between military and civilian cultures that was opened during the 1960s' civil strife and anti-war protests and continued to grow during the 1980s and 1990s. The sense of being disconnected from their military felt by and reacted to by civilians during those decades was reversed through the events of 9-11. For me, supporting our troops means giving what I can to make their lives a little easier to bear, but it also means achieving peace while not forgetting the necessity of maintaining a strong military during peacetime. The civilian community cannot understand what it does not have the opportunity to know, or knows only through media spectacle. Lack of understanding leads to lack of support in terms of the civilian community's support of the military. Milspeak writers share their experience to build understanding. This is only one reason Milspeak is an important tool. Milspeak writers' stories as a unity say, "We'll Never Forget and We Won't Let You."

The Milspeak program schedule had to be revised before MCWS 4 began. Our lunchtime workshop was changed to Saturday mornings because I was teaching fulltime at a school nearly an hour's drive from MCAS Beaufort. As usual, I ran the change by David Ellard, my Marine Corps Community Services liaison. David was willing to try the new plan, although both of us were uncertain if anyone would be willing to give up precious Saturday mornings to participate. Money is important to military families, time even more so. Time seems infinite, but seldom is and is never replaceable; money seems finite, but can always be replenished by hard work or assistance. Time is not money—time is invaluable.

Although I was still questioning whether Milspeak was doing more harm than good for its writers for many reasons, I decided to let participants decide if the program should continue. There is always a moment before each MCWS cycle begins when I wonder if anyone will sign up. I try not to predict outcomes, but wait out the uncertainty. As long as writers sign up, there will be a Milspeak. David sent out the MCWS 4 flier, and with publication in Marine Corps Community Services' newsletter, *Happenings*, requests to participate in MCWS 4 began coming my way.

Dear Sally,

I'm gonna go out on a limb here. I have spent years writing secretly, before it was just a hobby. Something to kill time and release frustration. I would like no love to be good at it. I have followed my husband to the east, west, north, south and three different countries. I want something in life that's my own. I want to write. My husband writes poetry but only if he thinks he's gonna get something out of it from me. For me it's how I breathe, it's how I exist. Its my heart's desire. Please let me in. I know that there will be those who will not show for the second or third class, but I will be there. If I have to sit on the floor that will be fine with me.

Sally,

I am interested in your class. I have always loved to write and am an avid reader. I have a love for the classics! My style of writing tends to be on the humors side. I love writing about my day and my family (lots of material there!). I would love to find a way to make my writing more developed and consistent in style. I've been doing some blogging online and have been told that my writing is encouraging and humorous. This has encouraged ME to become more dedicated about something that has come to mean so much to me. Thank you for offering this class!
*is this class open to retired dependants?

Hi Sally -

Please consider accepting me as a student to your creative writing seminar this fall. I have made several attempts at the beginnings of memoir and I enjoy writing about my life experiences. However, I believe any opportunity to learn more about the craft can only serve to improve my knowledge and skills. I know nothing about scriptwriting techniques. I'm not a veteran. I married into the Marine Corps. I sense that participating in a class with a new instructor and new students will be invaluable to me. Thank you for your consideration.

Ma'am:

I would very much like to participate in this seminar for several reasons. The last 10 years, I have been a stay-at-home mom to my three amazing children. They are all off to school during the day now and I find myself with actual time for me! It has been my plan all along to return to school when we reached these years and nurture my love of writing. Up to now, my outlet has been our annual Christmas Letter, and hours of journaling. My hope for this seminar would be to find a starting point and gain a better understanding of story structure so that my journals can become a story. I have never had the pleasure of a seminar or class such as this and would be so excited to have some guidance and direction with my writing.

Thank you for your time.

Sally,

I would like to participate in the CWR being held on MCAS beginning Sept 30. I cannot remember when I did not want to write. It has been something I have tried a couple of times and thought the articles were pretty good, but nothing like I would like for them to be. I just don't know how to transfer the feeling of what I want to say to words on paper. I would like to be considered for one of the slots in the class if there is room. I am an MCCS SC employee, but feel that I should only be considered after all of the military applicants. They are just so much more important and deserve all the goodness in life.

I appreciate this opportunity and will anticipate your reply.

Many other requests to participate in MCWS 4 arrived. Among those, Jack, a Korean War Veteran, sent lengthy memoirs written for his family. I read and commented on his manuscript. Sensing he wanted to do more than write for his family, I asked that he attend MCWS 4. Many more writers than I could handle as workshop leader requested to participate. All were accepted. I knew by this time that some writers would drop before we began or quit after Seminar Saturday, so I padded enrollment. Being able to improvise is a plus with a program like Milspeak, particularly when the workshop leader is facing a fulltime teaching load in addition to a packed workshop. But my armor of naïveté was becoming a liability. What would I do if everyone who signed up for MCWS 4 showed up? How could I possibly handle it all? Was I, like Icarus with wings crafted of wax and feathers, flying too high?

In accepting—all at the same time—Tristine Rainer's offer of a publishing contract, the fulltime teaching position, and continuing with an unfunded writing program for military people, was I setting myself up for failure? If I failed, would the death of my dreams lead to the next drunk as had happened in my past? This question of failure leading to drinking again had all along been foremost in mind when I considered the emotional toll of not realizing my dreams, particularly where Milspeak is concerned. For me, alcoholic drinking had always been preceded and accompanied by an emotional pattern—rejection, failure, and betrayal led to shame, remorse, and anger, which led to drinking to take the edge off emotional pain resulting in a perpetual, vicious cycle that had repeated throughout my life until January 27, 1992, when sobriety became priority number one. In 2006, everything but sobriety became priority. I had always been ambitious, but was ambition running my life?

With MCWS 4 set to begin September 30, 2006 on a collision course with the first month of my fulltime teaching schedule, I decided to dwell in Faith rather than upon my limitations and the amount of work just ahead on the road to excellence. Doing the next right thing included teaching two classes of eighth grade language arts students; teaching high school juniors and seniors enrolled in four dual-credit college courses; holding a seventh grade study hall, plus monitoring an eighth grade homeroom; revising the miserable memoir yet again; continuing to promote my writing by seeking publication in journals; and, working with a dozen Milspeak writers—all at the same time. *Once a Marine, Always a Marine*—Marines never give up and we never leave anyone behind. I decided to ignore the possibility for failure, to take whatever came my way and to take it as it came. That was before I had a clue about the mental gymnastics required to accomplish it all, and before the Pep Rally at the close of the first school day.

Before I reached the gym, I heard the thunder of hundreds of students screaming and pummeling the bleachers with their sneakers—the voice of the student body. The smell of teen spirit hit me when I walked into the gym. After edging through the doorway and peering around the corner of the bleachers, I noticed parents were there, too. My stomach flew to my feet. When the cheerleading began, I began sweating. The flashback to my high school past was inevitable, I suppose, but the fear I felt was a surprise. My mind raced as I searched for escape. I couldn't back out the door—parents were watching; every teacher had stared at me as I came through the door—there she is, the freak Marine. My fingernails dug into my palms as physical memory formed my hands into the position required when standing at attention.

My outcast years as a high school student, the after-years spent in alcoholic agony—many moments from my twisted past raced through my mind. The headmaster had hired me because he thought it best for the school—but none of these parents would want me teaching their children if they knew who I really was—a recovering alcoholic. None of these teachers would accept my low-residency MFA credentials as suitable—I had neither South Carolina K-12 teacher certification nor an education degree. If they knew who I really was, they wouldn't want me anywhere near their children. Hot tears were blinked away. My throat closed, panic working toward surface with each wave of sound from the cheering and the pummeled bleachers. The smile on my face felt eternal.

As quickly as it began, it was over. The Pep Rally came to an end, not my fear. I remember little of the rally, except the end. From out of the bleachers, the wife of my husband's construction partner climbed down and walked up to me, holding her arms out for a hug. Both of her children were enrolled in the private school's lower grades, and she would be working in the lunchroom during the school year. She put her arms around me, and said, "I'm so glad you're here." I couldn't have made it through that teaching year without knowing she was there.

The other English teachers offered no help before the school year began or during it, although I was honest with them about my limitations as a teacher and sought their help. Summer 2006 was spent preparing course syllabi and language arts instruction—without most of the required texts and supplemental materials for the eighth grade courses. I didn't even know supplemental materials existed. I developed my own by reading books about teaching eighth graders. Later, I learned the other teachers' resentment of me was due to my taking their best students into my dual credit college courses. Although these courses, which earn college and high school English credits, would be held at the private school, enrolled students left their longtime English teachers with those students who didn't qualify academically for my courses and those who just didn't care about school, the type of student I had been during high school.

The headmaster was no help, either. On the first day of class he introduced me to my new crop of dual credit students by saying something that went like this, "This is Professor Drumm. No matter what, you should challenge her. Challenge every liberal professor you meet in college. Make them prove their liberal philosophy to you." His introduction was stunning. I wasn't a professor—that title requires a position in a university—and I had no idea he thought I was a liberal. Maybe I am. Maybe I'm not. Just as I have no religious affiliation, I have no political affiliation—I have a long-term issue with loyalty to anything other than authenticity and the Four Freedoms. What was most baffling was that the headmaster was setting me up for failure by labeling me a liberal in an ultra-conservative school in the rural South. My students latched onto a perception of lack of support and ran with it. The 2006-07 school year kept me struggling with my students, struggling with my incompetence, and struggling with my colleagues' lack of acceptance. Once again, I was an outsider in a community I had chosen to join. At the school year's end, I received apologies from more than one student and teacher for being excluded, ignored, and defied, confirming that I had not imagined the ostracism.

By September 30, when MCWS 4 was to begin, I was already overwhelmed. I hung on at the school, not to prove the teachers or the headmaster wrong but because I was there to teach my students as best I could. I would not quit them, just as I would never quit a recruit or a writer attending Milspeak. Cancelling MCWS 4 before it began was an option. I was overcommitted and drowning in student writing. My schedule did not allow for extended work on my own writing. My days began at 4 a.m. and ended after 10 p.m. What little free time I had was eaten away revising the miserable memoir for publication. I slept little. Every weekend was spent evaluating student work and preparing for class. My husband was on his own most of the time. But if I cancelled MCWS 4 as I had MCWS 3, would there ever be another workshop? Quite a few military writers were depending on me to hold the workshop. How could I cancel after reading their emails, after promising them a workshop? Room was made in my schedule to work with MCWS 4 by letting household chores slip. Grocery shopping, laundry, cleaning, and cooking were out of the question. Fortunately, my husband is supportive of my writing, teaching, and Milspeak work, and takes over these chores when my schedule outruns the hours in a day.

Eight writers crossed the threshold into The Blackbird Zone, our classroom at MCAS Beaufort, for the MCWS 4 Seminar Saturday craft talk. Examples of narrative and descriptive writing strategies from short-short works of creative nonfiction published by the online literary journal *Brevity* were introduced. Selections were Rebecca McClanahan's "Orbit," Jillian Schedneck's "Teaching Errors," Lisa Kahn Schnell's "Circling," and Bob Cowser Jr.'s "Crime Scene Photo."[2] Each of these short creative nonfiction pieces was composed in 700 words or less and contained aspects of craft I wanted to emphasize: structure, narrative technique, character development, and strategies for using figurative language. Plus, the short pieces from *Brevity* are perfect models for Milspeak writers' use. Using short nonfiction to teach narrative and descriptive writing techniques is more effective than attempting to "tell" it by using handouts, the whiteboard, or by reading excerpts from longer works. The beauty of teaching from short memoir pieces lies in the form's compact structural nature and revealing of events. The chronological, logical, or thematic ordering of events in these short works creates energy through use of exquisite detailing and sensory language to get the point across in a minimum number of words.

MCWS 4 writers left workshop motivated to do their best with first drafts. I have no doubt that the quality of their work was influenced by exposure to the *Brevity* selections. Because we didn't have a guest writer (I couldn't find one), we didn't meet on Second Saturday. Writers emailed first drafts the Tuesday following the Columbus Day holiday, which coincided with Second Saturday. I forwarded drafts for pod member critique by using a mailing list, which kept participants' email addresses private. During MCWS, I encourage writers to share email addresses, but this is not required. I do my best to protect participants' privacy and do not share their personal information or writing without their explicit permission.

Manuscript exchange is always chaotic, particularly when work is late and the workshop leader also has 101 students. Although I had hoped to trim the MCWS editing process because of my teaching schedule, I wanted each Milspeak writer to produce his or her best possible work. Each draft was carefully read. Extensive marginal comments, a synopsis, and suggestions for revision were provided.

Critique procedure is briefed during Seminar Saturday and again in short form before each workshop begins. Workshop can be both rewarding and painful, but it must be honest. During discussions, I share my experiences having my own writing critiqued as a way of encouraging Milspeak writers to approach the process honestly. My writing-life failures and successes are shared, as are some aspects of my life experience that pertain to writers' subjects. MCWS is not a typical workshop experience. There is something more at work in what we do together. As workshop leader I invest myself physically, mentally, emotionally, and spiritually in the process.

To begin workshop critiques, pod members share their responses one at a time with the writer whose work is the focus of the moment. Writers are asked to stick to the story at hand and not drift into their own experiences—we have never failed to break this rule, one I learned in a traditional workshop setting. Breaking it is one of the most positive aspects of Milspeak. I am always amazed by similarities of experience among the participants, no matter differences of time, place, or occupation. Each writer's personal experience is validated by the understanding and compassion everyone brings to workshop. This interaction empowers the writer and is one of the healing elements of workshop.

Another MCWS rule is that we speak of "N," the Narrator, rather than Sally or David, the human beings, where story is concerned. Using N as a communication tool opens a safe haven for the writers. Unlike the writer, who is subject to judgment by others, N is a character in a story. N's experiences are easier and safer to discuss than Sally's. N is a persona, not a person. N's experience begins and ends in the story; Sally's life goes on. Most Milspeak writers are receptive to this workshop method. Writers will sometimes try to defend the work rather than ask what will improve it. Because of our being military people, I don't hesitate to point out defensive tactics and to emphasize that it is N and the clarity of N's story under discussion, not the writer's judgment at the time of the event.

Once all pod members have shared their comments on a particular piece, my assessment is shared. Pod members listen. Each critique is an opportunity to fit in craft talk. The writer then has an opportunity to respond. We have only three hours to work with during each workshop—

the primary reason for vigilant focus. The writers and I give our marginal notes and written summaries to each writer for use in revising the next draft. I always invite email questions on my comments and remind each writer that he or she is the final authority on what makes the page. I don't usually offer my phone number, although on occasion I have given it.

During MCWS 4 Workshop 1 (Third Saturday), writers met in two pods of four to exchange comments. Pods met in separate rooms—an interesting move, since there is only one of me. Fortunately, David Charles was attending his second MCWS and was able to keep his pod on track with the workshop critique process while I worked with the second pod. When I joined the group David was leading, the magic of workshop was underway. The writers had bonded and were discussing the group's last piece. David had done an outstanding job of guiding his group through the process without me. The seed was planted that Milspeak writers, if willing, might be able to begin their own groups.

Everyone in both pods was surprised by the depth of comments they received and by the sense of mutuality among the pieces within their groups. That day tears flowed all around. How could it not be so? Death had called in many ways and on many levels. We had boarded a ship, witnessed a battle, and discovered a body hidden amid stowed gear. We witnessed the string of grief in one narrator's life. We stepped into a mother's combat boots as September 11, 2001 unfolded, and we stepped into a military mortuary in Iraq where we met a gentle spirit who cares enough to treat the dead as human beings with histories of their own. We laughed that day, too, when Mogan David's heinous crime was revealed, and when we learned what happens when an adult's toys are checked at point of entry to a foreign country. When one narrator experienced sexual harassment, many heads nodded with familiarity. We learned through one narrator's experience that love at first sight can be true love, especially when death is ringing the doorbell. For many of the writers, the trauma experienced when death is encountered had emerged—be it physical death, the death of an ideal, or the death of love—but so had the joy of living.

During Celebration Saturday, David, a veteran of the Cold War and the War on Terror, read "Confession," a humorous snippet of experience from his days as a military criminal investigator featuring perp Mogan David:

I chose to write this, a true but tongue in cheek account, for a few reasons. First, I donated deeper emotions, and did so more publicly, than I had anticipated with "Always Faithful"; so, I wanted something much lighter my second time out. Second, I had mentioned in the first story that I was a Marine criminal investigator. It seemed logical to back that up with a law enforcement story. Third, the majority of my Marine Corps career had been spent as a criminal investigator; it played a big part in making me who I am. I really enjoyed writing "Confession"—can you tell sarcasm is a popular tool in my family? I was relieved to learn that writing could be fun. There are many things in life that are enjoyable: friends, co-workers, humor and interesting experiences, to name four. Writing about my experiences does not always have to be a gut-wrenching exercise.

Jack, a Korean War Veteran, wove past and present into a tribute to those forgotten in nearly every ground war, the Navy. When I first read "The Fez," I mentioned to Jack that the Korean Conflict is remembered as a ground war, and the Navy's role in winning that war often goes unmentioned, as does the Navy's part in the Vietnam War and the Gulf Wars. "The Fez" gives pause to reflect on how much we have forgotten about service members' sacrifices during wars that have faded from public view. Of his MCWS 4 experience, Jack reports:

> An old, retired sailor, I had begun writing a life history for my five grandkids, knowing how my forbearers had shied away from giving me any information. "Isn't he cute?" was the only reply I got from my family. "The Fez" was a first attempt at converting some of those hundreds of pages into something people might have an interest in. Sally put us all to work on one-another's works to produce readable copy.

Vivian wrote an account of her experience breaking through the glass ceiling of chemical sales two decades ago, and of the hard times and hard men she encountered. From Vivian:

> I'm now working to complete my MFA at Queens University of Charlotte. I met Sally at a poetry reading at the then Firehouse

Bookstore in Beaufort. I learned about Milspeak from information published in *The Boot*, the base newspaper serving the Marine Corps Recruit Training Depot and Marine Corps Air Station in Beaufort County. Although I have had some publishing success, the Milspeak experience, and in particular, Sally, encouraged me to explore new directions in my writing via the Milspeak seminar format, providing me with a structured approach to reading and critiquing my work along with fellow participants. I submitted "Swallowing Clay" during my first Milspeak seminar and as part of my body of work in my application to Queens.

On September 11, 2001, Sondra, an active duty Marine, was on a duty call away from her normal workplace. At the time, her youngest child was in daycare on a base near the Pentagon. Sondra presents the human heart in conflict with itself at a fundamental juncture in the dilemma of being both mother and warrior:

> I've often wondered if my piece, "Time" conveys the intensity of emotions that surrounded me in the months following the terrorist attacks. The event struck me in ways that I would never have expected. I literally saw my life through a different set of lenses. I set my mind to making a transition—instead of squeezing as much as possible into each waking moment, I urged myself to appreciate each one as if it were my last. That simple shift has made all of the difference for me.
>
> Sally's workshop helped me in ways that I had not anticipated. I enrolled in the workshop because I had previously been introduced to and struggled with creative non-fiction. I knew that the root of my problem was distaste for opening myself up to scrutiny. With fiction, the protagonist can be any kind of character, with little fear of criticism from the reader. However, in non-fiction, the author is out there for anyone to judge, as not just an author— but as a human being. Sally helped me to get beyond that. She saw that there was more to my story than I initially wanted to tell, and she encouraged me to reveal it.
>
> One of the wonderful things about writing is the cleansing process that it invokes. Writing "Time" was as much a soul

cleansing as the months after 9/11. The most difficult part of my transition was adjusting my priorities. Since enlistment in the Marine Corps, my number one priority had always been the Corps. Even after I was married to my active duty husband—the Corps always came first. The births of my children did not change that mental commitment. It was only after the attacks that I realized that their births *should have* changed my perspective. Admitting it out loud shamed me, and committing those realizations to paper pained me. Typing, backspacing, and retyping through tears was the process of "Time." To this day, I still cannot read it with a dry eye.

The balance of mother and Marine is delicate. Fear of failing either the Corps or my children is constant and that sense of failure precariously looms in the distance. At this time in my life, I am looking toward retirement from the Corps. I do so, while doing all that I can to appreciate the present. I collect my remembrances and hold them until they become stories to share. I hope sharing this one has benefited you as much as it did me.

Kathryn has written a profile of her marriage and a testament of love, the kind of love we learn too little of in our era:

Working with the Military on Parris Island and Marine Corps Air Station Beaufort for 32 years has been an incredible experience. I am so honored to be in the presence of these Military men and women, who somehow have been given the gift of unselfishness. The kind of mind and heart it takes to fight to protect the citizens of our great country is just amazing to me. Those of us who are privileged to be Americans should all stand proud of these men and women. Even after 32 years of seeing the young men and women going through recruit training, I still get goose bumps watching them cross the streets in formation while chanting. When I hear the Marine Corps band start to play at graduation ceremonies, the tears just come automatically. I thank them personally and individually every chance I get. God has truly blessed us with them.

This class was such an enlightening experience, that I am looking forward to taking another one. In the first draft of my true story, I wrote mainly about the main character, my husband. When it was critiqued, the comments were mostly, "Who is the other person in the story. There needs to be a connection between that person and the main character." When I started filling in the pieces about the other person, me, I was made to feel so special that I have been allowed to share the life of this person and that maybe I played some part in who he had become. It is something I had always known in my mind and heart, but seeing it in print created emotions that were exciting and welcoming.

Since I took the class, I have written several short stories. I find, that for some reason, all of my short stores are about funny real life situations. I have not yet tried to write a real life story about an emotional situation, but having been in the class with others who have very emotional stories to tell, I think I might not ever be able to do it on my own.

Sally Drumm, our instructor, is so patient and gracious with her time, that I think she could encourage anyone to write, so that story that is inside of me might come out after all. She makes one feel like they have her undivided attention when it comes to any part of the process, from discussing what to write about, to the first draft critique, all the way to the final product.

This is a class that more people should take. Writing your thoughts on paper as Sally taught us to do and then sharing them is a great way to help other people who might just need one word that you have written to answer a question in their mind. We don't know just how much or little it takes to help someone.

Yvonne and Charlotte revisit a time and place both painful and unforgettable—the world of death, a place no one wishes to know, but one we each will visit. How these women navigate this world holds a lesson for all. In "Life as Dream," Yvonne, a civil service employee, has written a moving lyric memoir of loss and hope. The comfort she gives her family is a comfort to all, her faith an example for all. Charlotte, too, wrote a lyric memoir, "Hymn," a moving account of her experience in a military mortuary in Iraq. There is great comfort in learning that our war dead are cared for in a foreign land, as we would care for them, our loved ones, if only we could be there with them. "Hymn" gives us hope that there is and has been a Charlotte in every moment of every war. Charlotte writes:

I had been meaning to write about Mortuary Affairs ever since my time with the MA unit in the summer of 2004, in Camp Taqqadum, Iraq. In my mind, I would narrate parts of the story, remind myself of details, reflect on the meaning of the experience, and think of ways to communicate it. Of course working as a caretaker for the bodies of combat casualties is not something that easily slips from memory. But I wanted to make sure I got it right, if I did write about it. At the same time, I was afraid of writing. Perhaps the memory would be best left intact and untouched, without the weight of written words holding it bound to the page. Putting fluid memories of life experiences into words and sentences freezes them into a form of some kind or another and I was scared that what was for me a source of solace and strength, as well as of tears and grief, would come out cheapened from the writing process.

When I signed up for MCWS-4, it was only because I knew (and had known since I was little) that I wanted to write. When it came time to think about something to write about, it quickly became clear to me that I could write about nothing unless and until I wrote about Mortuary Affairs. Sally made it possible for me to do this from the start by creating a supportive atmosphere and assuring all the writers that we were in a "safe zone." The format of Milspeak was perfect for me: it would force me to write a short piece, which would actually be read, but would not be judged or criticized. I don't know if I could have written the piece for a civilian course. I would have felt extremely conspicuous and "other." Knowing that my fellow writers had also been around the military for years made it possible for me to tell my story.

I had only a vague idea about how I would write about MA until I got the email from Sally reminding participants that submissions were due that day. Instead of going home after the workday was over, I sat in my office at the Recruit Training Regiment headquarters building and typed for about two hours. It was not particularly difficult to recall and relive those weeks in Iraq—I just steeled myself and jumped right in. In fact, writing the story was the easiest part. Dealing with what I had written was much harder.

When it came time to read our contributions in front of the class, I thought I was ready. I never thought I wouldn't be able to control my emotions. I was crying before it was even my turn to read. Reading the words out loud was one of the most intense and difficult experiences I've had! I could compare it to Day Three of "The War," the weeklong field exercise at The Basic School, when I was carrying ninety pounds of gear and hiking or running through the woods and seeing spots dance in front of my eyes for hours at a time. Just keep going. Get through it. One foot in front of the other. One word, then another. Eventually this will be over. You won't die. (You'll pass out before you die, Officer Candidate School instructors would often remind us.) So when the reading was over and I looked up to the smiles, applause, and hugs of my fellow writers, the relief was immense. I put "Hymn" aside and didn't pick it up for months.

That first Milspeak seminar was my entry into the world of writing creatively for an audience; but it was much more than that. It was when I started writing about my first deployment, a process I am still engaged in currently. It was the beginning of my transition from Marine officer to civilian, a transition much aided by the encouragement and advice of the other veterans in the class. It was also when I met Sally, who was always there not only as a writing mentor but also as a friend. One of the many ways Sally helped me was by encouraging me to try to get "Hymn" published. Eventually, I sent it some literary magazines. It was accepted by *The Gettysburg Review*, and published in the Fall 2008 issue. It was also published in the book *Powder: Writing by Women in the Ranks from Vietnam to Iraq* (Kore Press, 2008), and I was even interviewed on NPR about my contribution to *Powder*.

When members of the military family cross the threshold into The Blackbird Zone, neither they nor I know what the end result of our work will be. We embark on an adventure in writing, where travel for the writer is dangerous territory in the unexplored landscape of Self. Stepping into The Blackbird Zone, we step into a safe zone. Our classroom is made safe by shared experience of military life. We understand each other's experiences in a way that only comrades in arms are capable of, knowing that each day we serve in the military is a day we have made a choice to place our lives on the line, and often on hold, for the good of others. Our moments together in The Blackbird Zone slip quickly by, as if Time itself has lost the ability to control its own passage. Perhaps this is how birds in flight feel as they are swept by wind from one perch to the next.

Notes:
[1] Current Pay Scales are available at many Internet sites. Figures cited are from MilitaryFactory.com at http://www.militaryfactory.com/military_pay_scale.asp
[2] Selections from *Brevity* are available at http://www.creativenonfiction.org/brevity/

CONFESSION

By David Charles

After reviewing the new case just reassigned to me by the Chief Investigator, I just had to talk to the duty investigator.

"A Criminal Investigator like you had all this on the Marine and he waived his rights and actually talked to you and you still couldn't get him to come clean?" I asked, and smiled at my friend, Sergeant Pat Pierce, who was a damn good interviewer. The guys in the office often compared confessions, bragging which was best or the most creative or whatever. That was how we got better at it, and I had learned the most from Pat.

I had once seen Pat praying with a suspect in his office, both of them down on their knees on the stale, dingy-green carpet, their hands in prayer position.

"Go ahead," Pat was saying to the suspect, "tell God exactly what it is you are asking forgiveness for."

Sure enough, the young Marine kneeling in his office continued his prayer, "Lord, forgive me for taking my roommate's ATM card and taking his money. It doesn't matter how much I needed the money, or why, or that Joey was stupid enough to have his pin number with his card. It was wrong to steal and I'm asking for forgiveness."

"Good," Pat answered, only a cold trickle of sweat revealing the effort he was putting in, "but now tell God how much money you took and what you did with it."

"Lord," the suspect continued, "I took two hundred and twenty dollars from Joey's account. It was all the funds he had available. I thought the bank would give him his money back but that's not what's important. I used that money to go out and have a good time cause I've been sending all my money back home State-side to my wife and I needed a break from everything. Lord, even though I needed that break, there's no excuse and I'm sorry for what I did to Joey."

Pat was quite proud of that confession but had no luck with the previous Friday night's duty call, the case I'd just been assigned. A young Marine, I'll call him Mogan David, had hit another Marine over the top of his

180

head with a wine bottle at the enlisted club. The Victim in this case, who was dancing with Mogan David's newly ex-girlfriend at the time, had sustained a severe laceration of the scalp requiring some eighteen stitches to close up. The black, crusty, dried blood along the red, puckered scar in the crime scene photos spoke of the training days that the Vic would have to spend on limited duty.

"You won't get that guy to confess," Pat assured me. "I did a good job on him but he wouldn't give it up for nothing! He didn't come clean to me that night—he's not gonna come clean to you. That's for sure!"

I had done some background checking on the perpetrator. Mogan David, from an urban area in Mississippi, had a high school diploma and average intelligence, and was single. He also had a minor record for fighting and a questionable tattoo—possibly gang related—both had required an enlistment waiver two years before when Mogan joined the Marines. This grunt was from the mean city streets, but I knew I could loosen his tongue if I took off the kid gloves—no soft shoe and no prayer for Mogan and me. Timing was essential to success.

I quickly made arrangements to re-interview the suspect, Mogan David, who had waived his rights once. The longer I waited the more likely he would ask for a lawyer or just clam up altogether. I called his unit first sergeant and set the appointment time. I would pick him up from the company gunny's office and return him there when I was done with him. I also set things up in my office just the way I wanted them to be when Mogan David marched in. On my desk, Polaroid pictures of the dark-colored, broken bottle in the evidence locker were placed in an opened file with other photographs. Old, practice fingerprint lift cards were laid on my desk alongside the pictures. To the case file, which already had statements Pat had taken from witnesses, I added a pile of blank paper, making the file look even more impressive. Last, a photo line-up, minus one photo, was readied to add Mogan David's likeness.

When I arrived at the Charlie Company office, a sullen, tall, dark-skinned Marine sat in a chair in the hallway, waiting for me. Mogan David, detained in the company office, looked like he had been sleeping—guilty people often sleep while detained and awaiting the inevitable interrogation. He recognized me as a criminal investigator right away. With my suit jacket barely covering the basic issue .38 revolver in the holster at my side, and the tie I was wearing, I definitely stood out from the camouflage-utility clad Marines all around me. Ignoring the sulking Mogan David, I stepped silently into the Gunny's office and closed the door. There wasn't much the Gunny and I had to say at this point, but I took my time so Mogan David could stew in the hallway. After about ten minutes of small talk, I stepped back out into the hall.

"Get up Lance Corporal," I said gruffly, "you're coming with me." Not waiting for Mogan David to stand, I started for the door. To ensure he was in fact coming and for my own safety, I kept an eye on him, noticing his uniform was squared away, clean and pressed, except for the wrinkles from slouching while waiting for me. I walked to my unmarked, G.I.-issue sedan, opened a door for Mogan David and waited for him to approach.

"I've got to cuff you now," I said, pulling out stainless steel bracelets connected with a couple links of chain. "Them's the rules."

Turning Mogan David to face the side of the car, I cuffed and searched him with efficiency, put him into the back seat, and closed the door without another word. We drove across base to my office in silence.

"Are you going to give me any problems when I take those cuffs off?" I asked as we settled into the Investigations Office.

"No sir," Mogan David replied.

I took the cuffs off. He rubbed his wrist, released a deep sigh, and then slouched slightly, just the response I was waiting for. "Stand with your heels and back against that wall over there." I directed him to six feet of open, bare, flat-gray concrete wall. "Bring your feet together so you are at your full height," I ordered. He came to the position of attention and stood there like a wooden Indian while I snapped a couple Polaroid photographs, waited for them to develop, compared them, and finally added one to the last opening in my photo line-up of olive-drab clad, young black men with regulation hair cuts. Mogan David only moved his eyes, soberly watching me the entire time. I slipped the line-up back into the fattened case file.

Moving to the fingerprinting stand, I directed him in the dance that is fingerprinting: inking each finger, his hand held and directed by mine, rolling and pressing each individual fingerprint, then covering the palms of his hands with the harsh smelling ink, the ink as black as the crusted blood on the Victims head, before rolling Mogan David's palm prints onto regular, blank sheets of paper. Palm prints are rarely done, but I wanted him to experience full evidence gathering. I pointed out the special, greasy, hand cleaning cream and paper towels to Mogan David. While he cleaned the ink from his hands, I silently compared his prints to the developed ones laid out earlier in the photo lineup and glanced over the fat file awhile. He dragged out cleaning his hands for quite a long time. I saw the wheels turning in his Jarhead's brain as the greasy smell mingled with the foul ink odor.

"Okay," I said gruffly, "let's get you back to your unit." I headed for the exit. Turning I saw he followed with a perplexed look on his face.

Outside the sedan, Mogan David volunteered, "Aren't you going to talk to me?"

Repressing a smile and aiming my best scathing look at the target I saw in his face, I barked out my best drill instructor impersonation, "Why the hell would I do that? You've already lied to an investigator. I've got eyewitnesses to what happened. Plenty of people saw you at the club and can pick out your photo. I've even got pieces of your broken wine bottle and several good fingerprints that I'm sure are yours. Why the hell would I want to sit around and listen to your damn lying?"

Mogan David stared at me with a wide-eyed, amazed look on his face, the wheels turning behind those eyes. His face fell. "I won't lie to you. I promise. Just let me tell you what happened."

"Alright," I stated flatly, and then added a bit more edge to my voice, "but you better not be wasting my time."

We walked back into the building. Passing by Pat's office doorway, the investigator who had taken the duty call and interviewed the Perp without success, I couldn't resist a wink. Stepping into my office, I pointed out a chair to Mogan David, told him to sit, read him his rights, and had him sign the waiver of rights form.

"Go ahead," I said, "tell me what happened."

"That bitch said she was droppin' me. Just like that. No warnin'. Nothin'. We just sitting there at the club and, you know, she said she found somebody else and didn't want'a say nothin' else 'bout it. She just got-got up and walked over to that asshole and sucked face! Just like that! She went to this guy...must'a been havin' him on the side...and just ignored my ass! So I got that bottle of wine knowin' I was gonna crack his head wit' it. Watched' 'em dance, me drinkin' that wine—I ain't gonna waste good wine . . . I wanted the bottle to break when it hit, so I jus' sat there, drinkin' it while they wuz dancin'. Once it was empty, I up and headed for the dance flo'. He never even saw me comin'! Whack! I broke it ova' his head and laughed in that bitch's face when he hit the flo. They had it comin', treatin' me like that and all!"

"Damn," I replied when he finished telling the story. "No damn wonder you busted that jerk over the head! Now I understand. You know, if the commander hears this he'll understand what happened too. What you need to do is write what you just told me down on this paper, so everyone in the command who needs to can understand what happened!"

While Mogan David was busy writing out his statement, I stretched my legs, thinking about how this Marine's commander was going to throw the Uniform Code of Military Justice at him, regardless of why he injured the other Marine. As I stepped through the doorway to my office, Pat quickly pulled me out of Mogan David's earshot. I was happy to confirm that Pat had been listening in and learning from me this time.

"How the hell did you get him to talk like that?" Pat whispered. "You barely said anything to him!"

"First, you just gotta learn how to read and handle certain people," I started out with mock seriousness. Then I smiled and continued with a lighter tone, "Second, I knew your silky smooth approach didn't work for you this time. Wait until later when I've got the signed confession. Then I'll let you in on how I got him." I put away the smile, slipped on my stone-faced mask, and walked to my office to wrap up the confession.

THE FEZ

By Jack Hayes

I was watching the news on television that day in October 2000 when there was a report that the day before, the 12th, there had been an attack on one of our destroyers, *USS Cole,* in the Port Of Aden in Yemen—17 sailors killed and 39 injured by the action of two Muslim suicide bombers in a small boat; the rules of engagement had prevented *Cole* from firing first at the suspicious small boat. I had been in Aden years before and memories flooded my consciousness.

Aden was the last eastern hemisphere stop for our squadron before we were to move on through the Suez Canal for a final set of liberties in the Mediterranean and the crossing back to Norfolk, Virginia as we rotated out of the Korean War Zone. The stop in Aden had been one scheduled for our Destroyer Squadron Two as part of our circumnavigation of the globe when the four ships were deployed—we had traversed half the globe to the war and would travel the second half on our return. My ship was *USS Barton (DD722)* and the other three in the squadron were *John R. Pierce, Strong,* and *Soley*: all 2100-ton, Sumner Class Destroyers, each armed with six 5-inch, .38 caliber guns in three mounts of the main battery, plus six torpedo tubes, supporting 40 millimeter mounts, and depth-charge racks on the stern.

I was a reserve officer plucked from an embryonic business career and recent marriage to the love of my life, and I had been certain the Navy had lost all trace of me except my reserve pay record. I had graduated with a license in the Merchant Marine and a Navy commission from New York State Maritime Academy, one of six such schools established in 1875 to train mariners after the Civil War, during which five Confederate 'raiders' (built by the British for the South) had sailed the world and decimated the U.S. Merchant Fleet and its sailors.

Barton had received my orders aboard ship in the same mail as those discharging their chief engineer and Executive Officer, Lieutenant Commander Denniston, who assumed I was a seasoned mariner and was to be the chief's relief. So he kept the chief's cabin vacant for three months; he did not permit the Damage Control Officer, the chief's logical replacement, to move up. When I reported aboard to the Executive Officer, his first question to me was, "What ships have you served aboard, sir?" His face dropped when I reported *Barton* was my first—when I graduated there were few at-sea billets available since the merchant fleet was severely shrunken at the end of WWII.

Many of the reserves aboard resented being taken from new positions ashore to serve, but I figured I was to be aboard for a while and might as well dig in. Besides, when the damage control officer didn't move up as he should have, he had spent the entire quarterly allotment of the engineering department on the Shipfitters' Shop, the base of the Damage Control Department, and I inherited this well-equipped facility as my fiefdom. As it turned out, it was an important job, preparing the ship to be ready for repair in case of battle damage.

As I was getting acclimated with my new life, I met one of my classmates, Bob Hoffman, who had just returned from service in Korea on a tanker. He suggested that I "get as much shoring aboard as possible" and I had metal brackets mounted under all the weather deck over-hangs to hold it; shoring is 4 by 4 inch and larger boards which are used to brace damaged areas against collapse. This suggestion from Bob became life saving for us later in action overseas.

We left Norfolk in spring. Our theme was the then-popular "September Song" lyrics, "*Oh, it's a long, long time from May to December*"—the term of our overseas tour. We transited the Canal and refueled in Pearl Harbor and Midway while crossing the Pacific, landing in Yokusuka, Japan in June. On the way I was asked to look over the plant to find the source of lubricating oil that was showing up in the bilges. I localized the trouble to the main reduction gears and requested a repair ship inspection to find and repair the leak, and when we arrived in Japan, we moored alongside the tender, *USS Yellowstone*. A crew came aboard under the command of another of my classmates, Steve Long. Steve and I had a few good liberties together in Yokusuka, but *Barton* only had a few days to taste the wonders of Japan—the enemy only a few short years earlier.

The Navy, like all the military services, takes time to train, and we were first sent to sea with a small carrier and two submarines to practice action against submarine attack. After two days of this, we moved into the harbor of Hakodate in Hokkaido, the Japanese northern-most island. The complement of our ships was three times the population of this small town and, with men from many other ships, I spent the time on shore patrol to help keep the peace. We returned to Yokusuka, and after a few days during the next week topping off ammunition and provisions, the squadron was off to the "bomb line"—the war!

Barton and *Pierce* were assigned to spend 45 days inside Wonsan Harbor on the Eastern coast of North Korea. Since we were always within range of enemy units on the shore there, we never stopped moving in the harbor and only the covered general quarters stations—the main battery, bridge, engine rooms, etc.—were manned so the men would not provide easy targets. But we regularly provided bombardment for Marines somewhere ashore and I learned to sleep while the two 5-inch guns in the after mount, 30 feet from my bed, fired every night answering "call fire" missions from them.

As senior ship in the squadron, we had a commodore and staff aboard, displacing everyone from our captain down from their normal quarters. He was assigned as Commander, Eastern Coast Blockade, directing *Soley* and *Pierce* in offshore work, and operating spies sent out from Yodo, an island we owned in the harbor. The spies came aboard every afternoon at 5 p.m. from an LCM, dubbed the barroom express, to report to the commodore. This led to my meeting another school mate, John Intorcia, who had not finished at The Maritime Academy and went to Fordham University where he joined ROTC and received a commission in the Air Force—John had been on Yodo for a year, attending to spies and captured North Korean prisoners. I met him one afternoon as we slowed off the island as we did every day to take spies aboard. John had a handlebar mustache, but we somehow recognized one-another when he passed by on the way to report to the commodore. He lived in a tent on the island in primitive conditions, and he requested he be able to take a shower when he came aboard every day. I told him he was welcome to shower so long as I could hold the sidearm he carried with one in the chamber because of the prisoners on Yodo. We had a deal, and in repayment, some time later I went ashore to his quarters and enjoyed espresso laced with Rye whiskey, which wasn't available aboard ship.

The carriers of Task Force 77, operating off the coast, sent planes every day to bomb the city of Wonsan, and one afternoon the Battleship *Iowa* fired on the town from a position a few miles off the coast. Three-round sets of 16-inch projectiles from *Iowa's* main battery could be easily seen flying overhead—they were only a bit smaller than a Buick and reported to each cost as much.

Then one afternoon our action really began. I was on the way to use the head when the "gong-gong-gong" of general quarters sounded, and I was determined to "hold it" until the action was over so I could avoid the obvious thought my crew would have that I had panicked. Grabbing my helmet and life jacket I ran to convert the midships Purser's Office to Damage Control Central, and we set up the reporting stations around the ship.

The North Koreans had mounted some captured 105-millimeter howitzers in caves around the harbor, and had opened fire on Yodo Island. *USS Pierce* was deep in the harbor, unable to bring her guns to bear, and recognized that if she moved up she would be a hazard to us as we made figure eights at 27 knots, avoiding the splashes of rounds when the enemy shifted fire from Yodo to us!

Half an hour into the action the bridge reported seeing a hit aft on the 01 level and it was my turn to go into action—I had to inspect the damage and report to the captain. All I could see when I stepped out onto the weather deck were the splashes of enemy shells close aboard. I climbed the ladder to the 01 level and could hear the rattle of shrapnel as it skittered off the deckhouse. Reaching the deck, I saw that the blast had been against the base of the forward stack; it was made of thin sheet metal and the blast had dissipated itself in minor damage.

But there was a small hole in the deck where the shell had burst and, when I climbed back down and opened the hatch to the Torpedo Shack below, I found BM2 Gray, acting Torpedoman, dead from a piece of shrapnel which had hit him in the back of the neck as he slept on his bench during the action. His general quarters station, at the tubes on the open on the upper deck, was not to be manned in the harbor, so he went where he thought he would be safe. I notified the forward battle dressing station about the body and climbed to the bridge area. I reported to Captain Seim after finding him on the open bridge, seemingly nonchalant as he leaned his back against the pilothouse while calling out rudder changes at 27 knots. He was a great, natural ship handler.

We fired 600 rounds of 5-inch ammunition during the action and silenced the enemy guns in 3 hours. When it was over, I went to the wardroom to relax with a cup of coffee. Our South Korean translator, Che, was there and asked me, "Where is dead sailor?"

I told him the body had been prepared and was in the refrigerated compartment to send home to his family. I could have decked him when Che burst out laughing,

"What good dead sailor?" he asked. "In Korean Navy we throw overboard!"

And, indeed we had seen many bodies floating in the harbor; both North and South Korea felt the same way about death in the ranks.

We were relieved from Wonsan and returned to Japan, and after another short stay and refitting, the squadron was assigned to Task Force 77. This force, comprised of the Battleship *USS Iowa*, four carriers and some cruisers, was protected from submarine and surface attack by a screen of 32 destroyers. *Barton* was senior in this screen and our commodore was in charge of them.

I was now main propulsion assistant, in charge of the engines; we had two screws driven by engines in two separate engine rooms, each of which was fed steam from a separate fire room. Each space was separate and waterproof, except for the piping to each engine room from its boiler room. These were major compartments, extending from keel to main deck and the construction was to minimize flooding in case of battle damage.

We had joined the task force on September 16, 1952 at 1700 hrs. Movies were scheduled at 2000 hrs in the crew's mess (an oater) and wardroom (*Scandal Sheet* with Broderick Crawford). The first reel was over and we received word that the admiral had called for a course change into the wind to launch planes, and for an increase in speed to 25 knots. All department heads reported to stations to be certain the changes were properly carried out. I had my chief boilertender in the control fire room aft, and I reported to the forward fire room to oversee the conversion there to superheated steam and the opening of all burners to get maximum steam flow to make the increased speed. By the time I went back to the movie the circular screen of destroyers had shifted due to the fleet course change and we were now tail-end-Charlie in the formation of ships.

Five minutes into the second reel of the movie, Crawford had a bum in an alley, meaning to kill him. Just as he pulled back his fist to belt the guy, all hell broke loose—a floating mine had come through the entire fleet and struck us on the starboard side at frame 88, in the center of the forward fire room hull; I would have been there 30 minutes later on my way to bed after the movie.

It is not possible to adequately describe the chaos that followed—lights out, superheated steam, 650 pounds pressure and 750 degrees, screaming out of holes in the piping below, people stumbling and yelling. We headed for the doors; the passageway aft was full of steam, so everyone moved toward the bow. The commodore transferred to *Pierce* and the fleet left us, thinking we had been torpedoed by an enemy sub. I went down the port side weather deck to midships and entered the passage to the engine room hatch; it was scalding hot from steam impinging on the underside and I didn't open it! We connected a headset and made contact with the engine room talker to find that several of the engine room crew had been scalded and one, John Walton, had been badly injured, having been cut as by a knife by the superheated steam streaking from a gap in the pipe when he tried to climb the ladder out of the engine room hatch. My forward fire room crew, Graf, Savoie, Thierfelder and Sherry were all killed and now probably part of the boilers in the fire room, which was fully flooded.

There were no further problems with the engines since the valves on the steam lines in these spaces (now full of sea water) had been secured and my Chief Boiler Tender, on watch in the after fire room, had been sharp enough to close the main steam stop on his boilers; so we still had 350 pounds of steam available to get underway on the one operable engine, aft. We fired up the after generator for lighting and got underway again at five knots on one screw.

Now was when the extra shoring I had brought aboard in Norfolk came into play. The forward fire room was completely flooded and we had to brace the bulkhead between it and the engine room to the machinery to keep it from bucking. There was leakage into the compartments forward of the fire room, too, and an eductor had to be set up to dewater those spaces. In the morning, a salvage tug came alongside, her divers going down next to us to examine the hull. We had a twenty-by-thirty foot hole in the center of the fire-room compartment hull and it extended to within six inches of breaking the keel; they approved of our shoring job. It took us four days to steam slowly back to Sasebo, Japan where we were ushered into a dry-dock.

I was on the bow as we entered the dry-dock, and there was a chalked message on the concrete wall: "USS WALKE (DD723)." We were DD722 and I asked the "talker" to ask the bridge if it was possible to warn the DD721, whoever she was, to be careful!

I telephoned Fran, my new bride, from the town to let her know I was alive after the action and how much I missed being with her. The battle had been reported in the newspapers and we bawled together for most of the call; it was important relief for both of us, even at 5 dollars a minute.

Barton spent a month in dry-dock in Sasebo. The Japanese welded a hull over the mine damage, cleaned the double bottoms, steam lines and forward turbine of saltwater to make us good to go on what remained of the 'round the world trip planned to rotate the squadron out of action when relieved by another as the war continued. The other three destroyers in our squadron had seen no direct action and *Soley* was selected to stand by us in Sasebo until we were ready in all respects to join them on the trip; *Pierce and Strong* went on with the trip as originally planned, stopping in Hong Kong and Shanghai, Singapore and Bahrain while we were in for repairs.

We stopped with *USS Soley* in Singapore for a delightful two days. The Raffles Hotel on the hill was famous and served as our daily haunt—and we found out that miniscule British cucumber sandwiches didn't really go with a beer party. We rendezvoused with *Pierce* and *Strong* off the entrance to Aden harbor and when we had a chance to meet up with their crew, we learned of the fantastic stop-over we had missed in Bahrain.

When they told us their stories about that visit it made the mine hit even more of a problem to us—we had missed a wild experience! Their ship's officers had been invited to a gala affair in Bahrain where they sat around a feast in a tent with the Emir. The meal was roast lamb—the whole lamb, head, legs and all—and rice. They were instructed in the proper way to prepare: *Wash both hands but reserve the right hand for eating, the left for wiping your bottom after defecating*; and to eat: *Tear the lamb flesh off, then grasp a handful of rice with the thumb tucked under it, and pop the rice plug into the mouth.* One of the lamb's eyes was for the Emir, the other was offered to the commodore who, thinking fast, turned to

Commander Arbogast, his First Lieutenant and a reserve officer lawyer from Pittsburgh. As if Arbo were his taster, the commodore told him to eat it. And he did! I would love to have seen Arbo gagging down that mouthful.

Approaching Aden from the sea the landscape looked like one large cinder—no sand visible but no vegetation whatsoever either. As we moved into the harbor, the benefits of the oasis in which Aden stood were apparent—lush vegetation everywhere. The British were in charge here and they had a bash set up for our crews, and a party and a dance arranged for the officers; they loaned us their wives to dance with.

It was a gay evening, just like you see in the British movies: some officers in short-pants white uniforms, others in formal dress with medals; wives attired in ball gowns—frilly '50s vintage; waiters shuffling around with drinks and canapés. The band was military but managed everything from Lester Lanin to the oompapa waltzes. I never was much for dancing and so had wonderful conversations with participants ..."Jolly good, you know?"

I was invited to one home and was surprised by the simple structure and decorations, much like the bungalow community in which I had grown up in its summer appearance. I had imagined the Raj's lifestyle as sumptuous. You had to appreciate the lengths to which the Brits went to make us comfortable, though an ulterior motive might have been to take the opportunity of our arrival to relieve boredom, which surely settled over this kind of duty...stuck in an oasis in the desert for years. Next day, after the party with the Brits, I had taken a donkey cab ride with a guide who wore a fez.

While I sat in my office in South Carolina, I turned and glanced at the old fez that is a saved treasure from my excursion into the Korean War. Its black tassel and red felt material were much the worse for the fifty years since I had bought it, cooties and all, from the head of the donkey-cart driver.

SWALLOWING CLAY

By Vivian I. Bikulege

My water treatment career began in Savannah, Georgia in 1983. I knew nothing about the business. I was hired because I had spunk, and a chemistry degree. I was fairly attractive which helps in sales. I was athletic with straight brown hair that fell to the middle of my back, long black eyelashes, and a bright, white smile complimented by a dimple. Originally, I had aspired to be a doctor, went from pre-med to pre-law with the thought of becoming a lawyer. I left St. Andrews College with a double major in chemistry and politics, but no plan to enter either medical or law school. Instead, after a three-year stint as an inside sales and customer service rep for a laboratory, I became a technical sales representative.

I walked out on my first job. I moved to Savannah running away from Raleigh North Carolina, an affair with a married man, and a two-year relationship with a younger guy from college. I was running away from my self. I was a mess and I needed to dive into something constructive. My new district sales manager was Tom Lockhart, a nice enough guy. Tall, he was almost boyish looking with strawberry blonde hair, and open-minded enough to give me a chance in the very masculine world of chemical sales.

My first company car was a Buick Regal. It was pretty, kind of an opal emerald color and a helluva lot bigger than the Chevy Monza I bought after college graduation. I moved into a shotgun apartment on Reynolds Street with a lady living above me in her one-room apartment. My white, brick shanty was $185 per month, and had a living room, kitchen, bathroom and bedroom, all lined up in a row running back to front. I parked the Buick on the sidewalk in front of my small cement porch, more of a stoop really, with its black and white aluminum awning. My landlord's house was in front of the apartments and Sam, his white beagle with black spots, would pay me visits, sticking his nose through my bedroom window, level with the backyard.

I began my job learning to inspect boilers, run chemical tests, and drive back and forth to the clay fields in middle Georgia. Interstate 16 heading west from Savannah was a stretch of nothingness in 1984. It still is. I would set the car on cruise, brace my left foot against my right thigh, one hand on the wheel, one foot on the floor, read the newspaper with my free hand, and listen to Joni Mitchell sing about "A Free Man in Paris" from the tape deck. I made this trip at least twice a month. I did not stay in Macon. That was too ritzy. I would stay in Dublin, and head up to the kaolin mines before dawn or stay closer to the work site in Milledgeville at the Villa North Hotel.

When I first started working in clay, two hard-ass technical managers, knowledgeable in polymer chemistry, trained me. The application of emulsion polymer to vacuum filters for clay retention was new to Calgon Corporation, and we were on the cutting edge of the technology and big dollars. Kaolin, or white gold, is mined, refined and used in paint and kaopectate, and I guess you can never have enough of either consumer product. Cliff and Bruce were not impressed with this twenty-six year old female with no experience and a foul mouth, but that is what they got, and as time went on, I earned my place with them and in the organization as a persistent and successful salesperson.

Once we were competent with the chemistry, it was time to take it from Engelhard to other companies mining that pocket of white Georgia gold. There were Thiele, Anglo-American and Georgia Clay companies. I did not make great sales progress with them. Very little as a matter of fact, but they liked me coming around if for no other reason than to learn what was going on with their competitors.

Roy Walters was one of the good old boys I called on. He was a purchasing manager for Georgia Clay and although I would have bet that he knew nothing about the manufacture of kaolin, every salesman calling on the company had to touch base with him in order to talk to operations. He was overweight, and very southern. I was a forward, Yankee female trying to sell a product, make a buck, and move on to the next prospect. So I would visit him, make small talk, and try to sell him on cost savings available through the miracle of Calgon chemistry.

After two or three sales calls, he told me he had a potential application. Please understand; this was not the bath oil bead Calgon that most people are familiar with. I sold stuff that no one would ever bathe in—sulfites, bromines, and chelants just to name a few. Roy's opportunity was for a clay retention basin remote from the main plant. The turbidity in the holding pond was excessive, and they wanted to reduce the suspended solids to make the water acceptable for reuse, and the environment. Would I like to take a ride and see it? Sure, that would be great. So Roy and I hopped into his Chrysler, a big Beluga-white automobile. White cars made sense out here. The Georgia heat reflected off of the car, and the fine, chalky kaolin dust blended with the car's exterior.

We rode a little while on the backcountry roads dotted with abandoned houses and telephone poles. Roy talked about Georgia Tech football. I mostly listened. To get to the clay basin, you traveled along a road that was like riding atop a levee on the Mississippi River. Once we arrived, Roy stopped the car and asked if I wanted to get out. No, I can see the situation from here. I was not sure what we could do chemically. The pond was mammoth, and without much turbulence. You needed mixing energy to apply any polymer effectively, and the volume of the basin would take a lot of polymer to treat it. A large recirculation pump would be in order to create the mixing. This was all good from a revenue and commission standpoint. Large treatment applications equated to more chemical. More chemical sales equaled more money trickling down to commission dollars in my pocket.

As I looked out the passenger side window over the opal white water, Roy leaned back in his seat. He held the steering wheel with his right hand and leaned his head against his left fist cocked up by the elbow he rested on the driver side door. He had a kind of mellow look on his face under tufts of white hair, beads of perspiration sliding down the sides of his puffy, red face, falling onto the collar of his short-sleeved, white cotton, button down shirt.

Letting his eyes rest on my breasts with a half smile forming on his lips, he asked, "Are those things real? Can I touch them?"

Sure they are, and no you cannot, I thought.

I was so stunned by the question, I laughed. I was totally amazed by his audacity, and although I covered my surprise with my laugh, my brown eyes must have opened wide to the insult as my mind raced to appraise the situation. I sat back in the white, leather passenger seat and looked out of the windshield. No longer assessing the chemical opportunity, I retreated into myself. Roy straightened up in the driver's seat, put the car in drive and headed back to the main office, this time in silence. I believe I thanked him for his time when I got out of his car, climbed into my Buick, and headed home.

Interstate 16 is a long ride back to Savannah from Sandersville, maybe two and a half hours. The asphalt gives you a long time to think. As I drove past southern pine trees and exit signs, I reflected on the career path I was choosing. Everyday, I walked through industrial environments in my chlorine-stained jeans, tight golf shirts and steel-toed boots, my hair rolled tight into a bun and tucked underneath my hard hat. Eyes followed me, and men often talked to my tits, not to my face or my mind. Incidents of this nature were not always as blatant or direct, but the innuendos were an everyday occurrence and I was not innocent to that fact. I was playing the game. I knew that if I could not get an appointment based on the brand name of the corporation I represented, the fact that I was female would open doors closed to my male counterparts. Men are curious. I would make cold calls, wander in through the back door of a plant, talk to some laborer, learn the names of decision makers, and then try the front door.

I kept that incident inside for about a week or two. I was not sure I wanted to share it with my manager. I had been sexually harassed, verbally abused, was not entirely surprised, and knew I would not get that business. Hell, it probably was not even a legitimate application, just a ploy to get me alone, and test my reaction. What I did know was that I was never calling on Roy Walters again. Because Georgia Clay was on my prospect list, Tom would need to know that and why my sales activity dropped to zero. When I found the right time, I did discuss the incident with Tom. He understood and agreed with my conclusion to take Georgia Clay and Roy off of my list.

Tom and I never talked about pressing charges or taking Roy to task. It was not really something you did back then. I did not anyway. If I opened up that box, I would be running to human resources every month. *It was not going to happen.* I was maybe nine months into my new job. I was a woman in the industrial chemical business and I enjoyed working in a man's world—women bored me. There were not many of us. Five, maybe. Cindy, Karen, Linda and me. Phyllis was in the mix somewhere but not "out" in the field. She was in Information Technologies. There were a couple of older women selling commodity chemicals and personal care additives, but that work was non-hazardous. They were not slinging five-gallon pails of biocide, or priming pumps that sucked sulfuric acid out of fifty-five gallon drums.

I was young and pretty once. Anxious to do a good job, to sell based on sound chemistry and my growing expertise. I had to discount or capitalize on the concept of men thinking with their dicks. *It had to be that way,* to keep moving forward. I did not really know it back then but then again, I knew it very, very well.

There were two Roy's that worked in those clay fields. One was a reputable, business-like plant manager. The other was a purchasing pig. *Still, it should not have happened.* Not even back then, when women were just beginning to break through the glass ceiling, thumb their noses at double standards and confront lust and the abuse of power in the workplace.

Time and circumstance carve their initials into our psyche and now, as my breasts sag from the pull of gravity and the effects of middle age, I wonder what might have happened if I would have slapped Roy across his face instead of swallowing his perversion in laughter, out there, in the middle of nowhere Georgia.

It is funny what you do not want to know about yourself. You wonder why you cannot talk to anyone, have someone available to listen to your thoughts every minute of every hour. But then again, you could not stand that. There is always going to be the good and the bad, the right and the wrong in business. You meet each situation on its own merit, decide how to manage it, or take no action at all. There is always grey between the black and white, and even the teeniest things that you push down deep inside want out, want to be heard. And so you write: "Roy was a pig."

TIME

By Sondra Meek

Mornings Before

"Let's get a move on!"

Sitting on the edge of her bed, with legs dangling and shoulders slumped, my six-year-old stares at the wall in a trance. She does not share my sense of urgency to tackle the day ahead. She does not understand the importance of every minute. I look at the clock and shake my head. I have lost all sense of pity for her.

"Amanda! You're wasting time. Go brush your teeth, brush your hair, and get dressed—now. I don't have time for this!"

She moves to the beat of her own drum, but once in the car, I settle into the morning routine. Amanda's before and after school care is local to our neighborhood, and my year old baby attends the day care on base. Looking at my watch, I realize that the few minutes that I have been delayed will cost me many more.

Dropping Amanda off, I am sure to remind her that she has stolen from me. Now I don't even have time for the drive-through.

"Thieves!"

As the overburdened stretch of I-95 south of the Capitol extends before me, with cars packed in every lane as we creep toward our northbound destinations, I cannot stop the seething anger and indignation that boils within me. Calculating the hours, I am certain the Virginia state legislature steals an hour and a half from me every workday. With my simple math skills, I conclude that including weekends, they rob me of at least ten hours a week.

"Ridiculous!"

To my left, I glare at the waste of space known as the HOV lane. Even the lure of minimal traffic isn't enough to get many strangers to ride together. The sometimes northbound, sometimes southbound lane is never used to full capacity. Adding lanes in both directions just wouldn't have been right—all that grass dividing the highway looks so much better!

I finally allow myself to smile as I imagine the opportunity to place a full handed slap across the face of the Neanderthal that came up with that brilliant idea.

"Jerk!"

Look at this guy. Some people are so rude. Traffic is finally moving, and this idiot thinks the left lane is for pacing instead of passing. No one goes the speed limit in the fast lane! Wonderful - the two cars in the left lanes are riding beside each other. What is wrong with people? There is no driving etiquette around here. If you're not in a hurry, then get the hell out of my way—'cause I am! I'm a Marine on a mission, and I have a job to do!

"For heavens sake!"

I'm finally off that cursed highway, and now I'm stopped at a Green Light! I hate the Beltway! When are they going to realize they need more ROAD around here?

"I'm sorry I'm late. Traffic was hell this morning."

Moments During

My boss reminds us of our 0900 meeting in Woodbridge. At least the three of us will be riding there together. Score one up for the HOV lane. We'll only be a little bit late.

This is an important meeting. We are working with the Marine Corps program manager to set the timeline and milestones for the new Department of Defense messaging software. We have obstacles to overcome, mandates to meet, and policies to publish. We are not happy that the secretary has interrupted this meeting.

"I'm sorry, but this is important."

She says this as she turns on the TV mounted on the wall of the briefing room. The pictures of the burning towers come into full view as she says, "...and also the Pentagon."

We are silent, stunned.

My thoughts race...Pentagon...military...war. My husband—my baby is on base. She is not safe. I realize I'm no longer at the table. I am pacing.

My boss calls her boss.

"We are in ThreatCon Delta. You must return to base immediately."

Our passage onto the base is slowed at the gate by the forklift placing barriers in front of the guard shack. The Marine that I am returns to the forefront of my being. I am on autopilot. My thoughts are focused on security, contingency operations, alternate network operations, and the myriad requirements necessary to overcome the obstacles presented by this occurrence.

I am numb. I am a robot doing what must be done.

I realize the time. I must pick up my children—I'm late.

The beeping answering machine is the only "Welcome Home" my children and I receive. My husband has been activated and will not be returning home for a few days. I will take him fresh clothes in the morning.

Beep. "Guys, it's mom. I know you're probably busy, but please call me when you can."

Beep. "Hey, it's Nito. You guys ok? Call me."

Beep.... Beep... Beep... Beep... Beep.... I'm grateful we are so loved.

I must watch the TV now. I hold Breanna as Amanda sits next to me. She knows something terrible has happened today, and I don't know how to explain it to her.

"Is that why you were so late, momma?"

I look at her, and though I answer, "Yes," I realize that I was late because I forgot to leave. I was doing "important" things, I want to explain. Being a Marine is not something I do; it is who I am, who I have been, and who I will always be. I want to tell her that I had to be there, because they needed me.

"Yes," I say again, while watching the sadness unfold before me on the television screen. Thousands are dead. They just went to work. And the Pentagon—I am a target even at home, now. I look at her again. My children are not safe.

"Why did they do that?"

I tell her that I don't really know why; there are just some bad people in the world.

"I love you momma." As she hugs me, I find emotions I sometimes forget I possess. As the cleansing begins, understanding comes slowly.

Being a mother is not just something I do; it is who I am, who I should have been, and who I always want to be. They need me.

Mornings After

Yesterday, the great eagle screamed and the clock stopped. I didn't know it could—but it did. The hands of time are moving again, but now I hear the slow, steady tick tock of each moment.

I hear my children sleeping. I listen to them for several minutes before I wake them. I see them through changed eyes in the morning light. Where are my children in "God, Country, Corps?"

On the way to work, I listen to the news, but then I turn it off and just listen to the sound of my breathing. I see the burnt orange, yellow, and red leaves in the trees. I see the way the sun shimmers through them. I think of the fire, of people falling from the sky. I taste the salt of my tears. I roll down the windows and listen to the birds. With red eyes, I try to smile at the driver next to me. I think she's trying, too.

I look in the rear view mirror. New eyes stare back at me.

Traffic is stopped for two miles off base. It will take more than an hour to get to the gate. I really don't care.

I have time.

GIANT

By Kathryn Parker

During the first week in November of 1964, as a senior at Columbia Commercial College in Columbia, SC, majoring in Accounting and IBM Automation, I walked with my best friend, Judy, from our dormitory to a local drug store. Judy and I lived in a dormitory just for women (this was before coed dorms existed). Two blocks down from my dorm on the same street was a boarding house just for men. Some of the male students living there attended the same college I did. Actually, I thought I knew all of the men staying there, and that they were all college students from my college. Just as Judy and I were approaching the boarding house, I noticed, parked against the curb was a car with a man in a police uniform with the sleeves of his shirt rolled up, looking under the hood. Admittedly, part of me was a flirt and just as I saw him, my flirting personally came popping out and without slowing my pace or stopping, I said "I'll bet I can do that better than you can."

Although I didn't know it at the time, I found out later that the man under the hood of the car lived there and, because he was a policeman, the boarding house landlady agreed for him to stay there even though he did not go to the same college as her other boarders. She let him stay because she felt safer with him there, and he could keep the college boys in line.

I don't remember if he responded to my interruption; if fact, I don't remember if he even looked up. About a half block later, I stopped dead in my tracks. To the total surprise of both Judy and myself, I said to her, "Oh, no—that is the man I'm going to marry." I wasn't looking for a husband. My goal was to graduate from college and work on my own for a few years, to practice being an adult. I tried desperately to put this man out of my mind.

A few days later, he came to my dormitory, and asked to speak to me. I opened the door, but did not come out and he was not invited in. He said, "My name in Barney Fife. I go to law enforcement school from 8 a.m. til 4 p.m., and then walk a cop's beat until midnight. My day off is

Thursday. Will you go out with me?" My first question was, "How did you find me?" He replied, "One of the guys in the boarding house was sitting on the porch when you came by and because I knew I had to find you and assumed you were a college student, I asked him if he happened to know who you were. He did know you and told me where you lived and here I am." I was silently amazed that he had gone to the trouble to find me, but still answered his question, "No, I have a date Thursday night."

With a flirty little grin, he said, "Well, you have two choices, you can break it or break it."

I was a little stunned and flattered by this response and turned without speaking, gently closed the door and went back inside. I could not quit thinking about his response; I just knew it meant that we had to see each other. Needless to say, when he arrived on Thursday, I was waiting. During our first date, I realized I had no choice but to be with him for the rest of my life. I could fight it if I wanted to, but it would not change the reality of our future.

A month and a half later, on December 17, we were married in a church wedding in Columbia with family and friends in attendance, all of us still quite stunned. There were so many questions and comments coming at us from all sides and most of them were basically the same: "How do you know you love each other?"; "You just haven't known each other long enough"; "It is just infatuation"; "You're making a big mistake"; "Are you pregnant?" He was 24 and I was 19, so one would think these questions would make us wonder or at least check ourselves for doubt; neither of us picked up on that.

We would have married sooner, but it took too long to have the invitations engraved, addressed and mailed, and I had a long, white, formal wedding gown to make. The dress was beautiful, a simple floor length white satin dress, with long sleeves and 12 covered buttons on each sleeve closing the openings. It had a round neckline and fell softly with two pleats facing the middle on each side of the front and back of the skirt. The train was 6 feet long, made from the same satin, tied with a soft bow in the front, and matched the dress's pleating. I made my veil from a piece of cardboard that came from a friend's shirt that had just come back from the laundry. I cut a piece of cardboard one and a half inches wide and twelve inches long, and covered it with white satin. To the inner side of the satin crown was attached three yards of illusion, which fell softly over my face and just below my shoulders. I often wondered why I chose to use that cardboard instead of using a real crown, it was kind of a silly thing to do. I know now that it happened because what appears to be one thing is often something entirely different—it reminds me of that fact.

Luckily for me, he helped select the wording for the invitations because that is when I learned his name was not Barney Fife. Barney Fife was a nickname given to him by the guys he lived with, because he was a policeman. Little did I know who this man was or who he would become. How could I know? I had never stopped to think about that, I only knew we loved each other.

I have been treated for chronic depression since I was 18, and because of that illness I have deep issues with own my self worth, and still wonder what I did to deserve having him in my life. He has been a tremendous blessing. Maybe I had amnesia and don't remember the very special deed I did to deserve this blessing, but I have learned to accept it and continue to hope that if a mistake was made, nobody will find out and have it reversed. Even after 42 years of marriage, I am still in awe of him.

His calm, even temperament, and spontaneity are surpassed only by his sincerity and warmth and his continuous ability to stay happy and keep others that way. Focusing on the positive is one of his greatest assets. I truly cannot remember him having ever expressed a negative thought. He has taught me to display positive responses to negative situations. I know now that a half-eaten candy bar is not a sad thing because half of it is gone, but to find joy in knowing there is still a half of a candy bar left to enjoy. I will never be as good at it as he is, but I will spend my life practicing. All through our marriage, people have asked me if he is always as happy as he seems. My reply to them has always been, "Yes, he wakes up happy and goes to sleep happy. He always has a pleasant and cheerful disposition. What you see in public is what I see at home."

He has a great love of people and community. Because of his association with different organizations, he is known throughout the community, the state, the country, and even in several foreign countries as a very people and community-oriented man. He is a charter member and a past president of the Port Royal Rotary Club (now known as the Rotary Club of the Lowcountry). You might have seen him picking up trash along the highway, serving at the Lowcountry Supper during the

Beaufort Water Festival, working in the Rotary fundraising booth, bagging groceries for less fortunate families during the holidays, or any number of other generous acts of kindness.

One thing he is most proud of is that he appointed the first woman to his Rotary club's board. She eventually became the first woman president of the Port Royal Rotary Club. This also resulted in her becoming the first woman president in any of the three local Rotary clubs. He served under the leadership of the first female District Governor of Rotary District 7770 as the Assistant Governor for area 5.

Beaufort High School Interact Club is another special organization to him. This group of young people can be relied upon to accomplish the best possible results from any project it undertakes. He is always amazed at their dedication to community service and supports them by attending meetings and participating in their fund-raising projects. Once he even paid them $20 not to have to buy something they were selling for $1. They call him "the coolest guy."

He is a member of the Port Royal Masonic Lodge, Omar Shrine Temple in Charleston, SC, Scottish Rite, The Billkin's Club and the Royal Order of the Jesters. For ten years he clowned as Jelly Belly, raising funds for the Shriner's Crippled Children's Hospital. His clown outfit was a full tux, a red pizza-shaped polka-dot hat, red and yellow striped shoes and he had a tongue painted on his chin as if it were hanging out. The hours he spent making balloon animals and doing his magic tricks, to him, seemed like minutes. All of the money he raised was donated to support crippled children.

He has, at times, said, "I feel like I should be paying someone to do this, because it is so rewarding and makes me feel so good." He also said, "The more you give, the more you receive." What greater gift than that of time can you give? It just comes naturally to him. I should interject here that he did have one small situation that required a lot of work when he was clowning. He always had trouble finding shoe polish for his red and yellow striped shoes. That really bothered him.

Most of his insurance career was been spent in the "debit" insurance business. This is the type of insurance business where agents to go to a person's home to sell policies, then services them by going back to the person's home weekly or monthly to collect premiums, file claims and address the policyholder's concerns on the spot. This has been a perfect job for him because it is completely in line with his constant need to protect his flawless ethics and do what is right for people. For example, he read an obituary in the paper one day of someone who had once had a policy with his company, stopped by the home of the deceased to give his condolences, and asked if he could help file the insurance claim. The family told him the policy had been dropped and no one was paying on it any more. He had the policy researched and found that it was still in effect, filed the claim, and delivered a check for $5,000 to the widow. Without his caring and considerate ways, no one would ever have known to file that claim.

He served as president of the Beaufort Association of Life Underwriters, and later served as president of the S.C. State Association of Life Underwriters. While participating in national conventions, helping candidates run for office and holding places on boards, with his unforgettable comical personality, many people around the country know him. I have received phone calls and notes all through our marriage thanking me for "sharing him." I am proud that he is so dedicated to his fellow man and woman and his community. Anytime anything needs to be done, a meeting needs to be attended, just call and he's there.

The biggest argument we have had in our 42 years together is about which one of us loves the other the most. Special personal moments are hard to pick from because there are so many, but a few memories come to mind about his character. A few years ago, I broke my left ankle, and, as a result, suffered from RSD (Reflex Sympatric Dystrophy), a painful sensitive nerve condition in my lower leg. He would rub "witch hazel" on my leg, but before he did he would warm it in the palm of his hands. How sweet is that?

On another occasion, I had been on a business trip to Washington, DC for a week. On the night I arrived home, he picked me up from the airport and as he drove us home I thought how happy I was to see him. I had missed him terribly. When we arrived home, he had dinner prepared and served it on Christmas plates. After enjoying the dinner, it dawned on me that it was June, and if we were eating off Christmas plates, everything else in the kitchen must be dirty. When I asked him if that was the case, he said, "No, having you home is like celebrating Christmas." Ahhhh!

To share my thoughts on how this man is as a husband, being married to him has been one long adventure: clowns, travels, hedgehogs, squirrels, cats, dogs, and even baby flounders and flat mailboxes. Our marriage has truly been a treat. He still makes me laugh. Recently, as he explained the way squirrels think while they are being fed, his comment was "Squirrels are really very smart. To them, I am just a big pecan, just a big walking, talking feeding station." He has made my life very interesting and I would not change any part of it.

In my opinion, the main reason that our marriage has worked so well for us is that we truly respect each other and accept each other for who we are. Maybe each of us needs numerous changes, but we have not taken on the challenge of each other's faults. We have left that for each of us to conquer on our own. All marriages take a lot of work and we have worked on ours. It has not been hard work, but work we both enjoy.

One of the goals on a list that I created for myself, is to do everything possible to make sure when we meet in Heaven; I will not overhear him telling his friends that I nagged him to death. I have found that nagging, in the common sense of the word, is not necessary. I have created my own form of getting things done by writing him love notes. They always begin the same and end up something like this: "Your mission today, should you decide to accept it, is either take a nap or take out the trash, whichever sounds better to you." I am careful not to write too many of these and always sign them with ILYTM (I Love You The Most).

We are the perfect example of opposites attracting each other. I like a place for everything and everything in its place. His idea about surfaces is that they were made to have something put on them. We don't argue about this—I just remember that instead of his being at home with cluttered surfaces, he could be in a bar drinking. Compromise is so easy. For the past 42 years, I have been living in anticipation of our next adventure. When I go to sleep at night, the anticipation of his whereabouts by the time I wake up the following morning has always been very real. I am always happy in the morning when I realize that he is still with me and accept his presence as a gift. I have enjoyed and treasured each of these 15,330 gifts.

In February of 1999, he became ill and by March was diagnosed with Non-Ischemic Cardiomyopathy, a severe heart condition. His cardiologist told him for his own welfare, he must retire. This was devastating news to us. My mind ran like a speeding train with no brakes—I just could not get away from this news fast enough and the train kept running. I begged,

"Please, God, help my husband." Suddenly the brakes started to slow the train down as the initial shock wore off and I was able to think clearly. I couldn't decide if I was more upset about the possibility of losing my husband or losing this wonderful community servant. He is so great in both roles. He went to a class reunion recently and one of his old classmates said she had heard he was not well. She said, "Don't worry, we're all going to a better place." His response: "I can't even imagine a place any better that where I've been all my life."

I could go on and on about this man, who, if you haven't seen him in any of the places I've mentioned, could be seen picking up mail at the Beaufort Post Office downtown, and then picking up trash from the parking lot—"Just because it's my town and I'm proud of it."

His doctor told him that if Diabetes does any more damage to his kidneys, he would have to have a transplant. When I got home and heard this news, he was telling me the details of the doctor's visit when the phone rang. A fellow Rotarian was calling and said he was trying to find someone to follow him to Warner Robins Air Force base in Georgia to deliver his daughter's car. She had been in Afghanistan for 6 months and was coming home in a few days. Without hesitation, my husband said, "Of course, what time do you want to leave?" On the way back home, the man thanked my husband and said he was surprised that he answered so quickly. My husband's response was, "After what she is doing for me and our country, I had no choice, even if you had asked me to drive to Washington." One day he is told that a kidney transplant might be in his near future and the next day he spends five hours traveling to support a person fighting the war. Always, doing good for others outweighs any bad news he is given.

This person, outside of our own community, might not be recognized by this description or his appearance. You might have expected someone everyone knows, but this man lives in my world and is the reigning giant. This man is my husband, Bertis Reed Parker, Jr.

That's my story and I'm sticking to it—"Bert, I do love you the most."

LIFE BY DREAM

By Yvonne R. Green

"I will never leave you nor forsake you."
Death where is thy sting, oh grave where is thy victory?

Blue-gray waves dash against the waterfront's walls. I look out toward the horizon early mid-morning. No, no sunlight. From a distance along the cold concrete slabs, two figures come closer, one dragging the other. A feeling of fear, a feeling of concern mixed with curiosity arises, comes closer and closer to a state of recognition. A large grayish-brown, wolfish dog pulls and tugs a mangled body into my space and suddenly I awake out of an oh so surreal dream on that cold January morning 1988. Lord, what does this mean? A feeling of trouble lingers. A prior conversation with my cousin in-law Brenda springs to life: "When you dream of blue water it signifies death."

Early Saturday morning, 22 May 1988. I love gazing at my two babies, eight and five years of age, and remembering my Terrieca six years before when her daddy had set her up for a bribe—"If you will stop wetting the bed I will buy you a new bed." The sassy two and a half year old, daddy's girl—he always wanted his first child named after him, Terry; I loved the name Erica, so we named her Terrieca—replied, "Okay." A dry bed every night after since and since a promise is a promise, a spanking brand new oak bunk bed with a ladder was set up in her little bedroom. "This is my bed," she proudly claimed.

Okay, I have to get going with my Saturday morning regular chores, cleaning and washing, and I have to prepare for the upcoming Memorial Day weekend trip to Disney World only a week a way. A planned surprise for the children. The day gradually ticks way. As I work, the children play.

Right after midday, Ronnie a neighbor and family friend who lives about two miles away, rushes into the house—my daddy's on the front porch; my momma's outside peddling around.

"Yvonne, Yvonne, I just heard Terry was in a motorcycle accident in Poppyhill!"

"What?—" I think they must be sending him to Savannah. "—What happened?"

"I don't know how bad it is."

"Oh my Lord. Daddy," I fearfully called, and he called momma, "Bertha keep the kids, we will be right back."

We jumped into his yellow Ford Thunderbird, my body shivering...cry can't cry.

Talk, can't talk.

"Honey, try to stay calm. We will be there soon."

Crossing over Whale Branch Bridge—*blue water oh so still.* Oh so careful driver, go the speed limit. My feet press against the floor, try to make the car go faster. The car turns off Highway 21 onto Poppyhill Road. Been a year and a half since I lived down here. Less than a quarter of a mile to go. A straight black paved road. Houses on left, trailer on right, house on right, trailers on left.

Car stops. We're at the spot. The spot in the road. The spot.

The news.

Wailing coming from all around, his sisters, his cousins, his mother, friends and foe.

"Yvonne," someone's grieving voice cries out my name, "Terry just died. They helicop him to Savannah memorial, but he didn't make it."

Daddy, my Daddy and my Pastor, Daddy's comforting arm comes around my numb body. Lord, how am I going to tell Terrieca and Terry?

"He was test driving his motorcycle and his cousin Tommy truck pull in a driveway ahead of him and they just hit. Threw him off the bike. All the way in front of his mail box."

My eyes travel that direction. Looks the same. Old oversize-big mailbox next to three smaller regular-size small gray mailboxes with three digit addresses. I can see him now, taking a break from work, Terry, leaning on the mailbox, cutting jokes with the boys, waiting for the mailman to come—

"He didn't have his helmet on..." someone says from the crowd.

Terry an avid motorcycle rider, racer, and auto mechanic could pull anything with wheels apart and put it back together again better and faster. No schooling—just a dog-gone good backyard mechanic.

Just that quick he is gone....

How did I get back in the car?

We're back at the house like a blink of a genie's eye. Composed myself. My children, Lord Terrieca, Daddy's girl.

I slowly walk down the short hallway. Turn left. Baby girl sitting on the bed.

"Junior, come here. I got some bad news to tell you two about your daddy."

Terrieca's big brown eyes, olive brown in an oval square face look up at me.

"Momma," she says, tears welling in her eyes, "I know."

"What?"

"I had a dream night before last. I was afraid to tell you because I didn't want it to come true. I dream daddy got killed. Oh God, Mommy tell me that's not what you want to tell me, please Mommy tell me the dream not true."

"Honey, that why I had to leave in a hurry. I'm sorry I have to tell you this, but ya'll daddy just died an hour ago—"

"No mommy, no mommy—" echoes blue-gray through the cinder-block house as I hold my two young'uns against my breast. No, no sunlight.

One tragedy after another, we buried Terry Green, Sr., Saturday, 27 May 1988, and Poppa, whom my children lovingly called Daddy cling to him, especially Terry, Jr. Terrieca became my momma's pet.

Daddy started having more frequent doctor visits. I started working two jobs to make ends meet. My sister takes him back and forth. I realize how sick dad is during an early morning scheduled surgery when the doctor briefs the family. My head in a fog when the doctor looks at me and says, "You know, your father has Cancer."

No, I didn't know. I was shocked, angry at my sister.

How come she did not tell me the extent of daddy's illness?

I feel like a fool, stupid, left out.

Knowing how much I loved my dad and mom, knowing they were always there for me and I always wanted to be there for them, from that moment, I knew I would have to stay by my parents' side, no matter what.

The healthy strong man, his body shape began to change. One leg became real large as the fluid builds up and his pants tighten around his thigh while the other pants leg remains lose fitting. His neck becomes swollen as my heartache to take away his discomfort as he has done over and over for me. Reassuring me that what ever happens in life, "I can do all things through Christ who strengthens me," Phil 4:13, scripture that remains in my heart today.

I pray for my father healing like I never prayed before...until God answers my prayer one night. I dream I asked God to heal daddy and in the dream the voice said, "No, your father will die." I wake up crying because the voice was spoken by one of Authority with complete blessed assurance.

My life felt like I was constantly running on roller blades, between running to the hospital, working, sleepless night, running home when momma call frantic to help get daddy up when in his weakness he fell, and I vow not to give up even to the end. I thank God for Mr. Buster, Cousin Lula Green and Rev. Hamilton who really went beyond the call of duty by helping my mother, sister and me take Dad to his early morning treatment to Savannah for radiation treatment and other medical appointments. Dad must have saw the helplessness I felt. And Daddy, looking up at me from his chair, said, "Honey, you done all you could do and don't worry, God will bless you." Then Daddy finally gave in to momma's request to go to the VA hospital. After being there for about two weeks, he was scheduled for minor surgery.

Mourning Monday morning, 31 January 1989. I sat at my desk. A warm feeling engulfed me like a hug at 9 a.m. I smell daddy's masculine scent, and I break down and cry. My co-worker Earlene came and embraced me with a hug, and said, "Yvonne, go to your daddy."

About twenty minutes later, my sister called and said the hospital called and said to get there right away. Hurriedly picked the kids up from school; hurriedly drove to Charleston VA hospital. Every day we went, the parking lot was so full we usually had to drive around in circles or sit in our car while it idled and wait for a spot.

Today we got there and a spot was waiting for us.

I looked at my sister and said, "This is very unusual."

We hurriedly ran through the door. A nurse was waiting and asked me if she could take the kids.

Then I knew dad was gone.

I don't remember the elevator or how I got in the room, but Dad lay there so peaceful, so handsome, like he was ready for the Master to come for him. Now I knew why he always sang, "When peace like a river attended my ways, when sorrow like sea billow rolls, what ever my lot, thou has taught me to say it is well, it is well with my soul."

My sister and I rode home too choked up to talk in long conversation. We listened to the radio. The song, "In the Living Years," ministered to us about a young man whose father has died and he is remembering his dad and wishes he had spent more valuable time with him and now he realizes that it is toooo late. Then I thank God I have a good relationship with my parents, if it wasn't for them it would be "no" me. My conscience is clear.

We arrange for the funeral for Saturday to give my sisters and brothers who live away from home time to make arrangements to get here. Strange to see Dad's obituary, *Rev Ernest Rivers of Big Estate,* in the paper. As Momma reads this section as she does daily, she says with a reassuring voice, "One day I will see my obituary in the paper."

I laughingly tell Momma, "No, I don't think so; probably we will, but you won't be able to."

She looks at me and grins, "I think you are right, Eve."

Momma endured through the years with God's grace and mercy.

06 Feb 2004. My sister and I stayed with her until I finished building a house next door. We went every place together the four of us, Momma and Me, Terrieca and Terry, Jr. Even after the children grew up and left home it was Momma and Me. Don't seem like Daddy been gone fifteen years. Terry sixteen years. After all this time tragedy crept in again.

Momma's an avid senior citizen participant. She lives for the daily trips, Bingo at McDonald's, lunch every fourth Thursday at Tabernacle Baptist Church in Beaufort, and get togethers with her friends. Momma's health was failing gradually, so I gave Janet, the Senior Center Director and Momma's friend, my work number and cell phone just in case she needed to reach me, or if Momma needed something. Lord, I never thought it would be so soon.

My cell phone rings. Janet: "Yvonne, Ms. Bertha—" she lovingly calls Momma, Ms. Bertha "—have a terrible headache, she want me to just take her home but I think I better see if you want me to bring her to Beaufort and we can meet at the Doctor office."

"Okay," I say. "Just tell her you are coming to Beaufort and she can ride along to meet me."

The hospital is full. The Doctor office is full to the max. The Doctor says to get a cat scan. One thing leads to the next, until the lab x-ray shows "bleeding on the brain." I call my sister at work and my daughter and give the bad news, "Momma was rushed to MUSC Charleston."

Within the hour, tests show she had a stroke.

Momma is still alert, adamantly stating she did not have a stroke, that she is fine. And as the hour ticks away things turn worse for worse. Surgery is completed and Momma stays in Charleston for a week. My daughter and I stay with her every night, keeping my sibling informed of her condition, until they send her back to Beaufort. Rehab.

Momma is improving, looks like she will be going home. Then comes a blockage in her intestine. Emergency surgery. Doctor has to perform a life and death surgery. God is right there. Another two weeks she is tremendously improving, we start making arrangements for home care and look forward to her being discharged from the hospital. Saturday afternoon, my sister and other family members sat in Mom's room joking around. Momma asked my sister if she had already cooked for her husband. We laugh knowing she is from the old school, when the wife's job was to take care of your husband. Then in the next sentence, Momma says she has to go home and cook for her husband. We looked at mom and at each other and I asked her, what is your husband's name? She looked at me like I was crazy, like you don't know? and said in a matter of fact voice, very proud voice, "Ernest."

Silence.

Mournful Monday morning around 2 a.m., 15 March 2004. Death Angel come and take my dear momma while I sleep next to her on a small sleeping cart. I slowly awake to check on her and she lay motionless. No, no pulse. Skin cold as I hold her fragile arm. The lab tech come through the door to draw blood as I cry out for my *Momma, momma, momma.* No, no answer, just *"CODE BLUE, CODE BLUE............"*

After that, Doctor gave the final word. Momma was gone. One by one, I called my eleven siblings, four live here, the others live in different states. I thought I could protect one of my last jewels from leaving, but then The Lord revealed to me again the vision that came to me about seven years earlier when my son Terry was hospitalized with an asthma attack.

I stayed right by his side, didn't want to leave. The pastor had invited the Citadel Gospel Choir to perform at our church. I wanted to go to church, but I didn't want to leave Terry. As I slept by him on a cart, I dreamt he had died, and I couldn't even get up. My hands were crossed tight against my chest, and the Spirit said, "Although you are here you cannot keep him from dying." Then peace, peace that passes all understanding, came into my soul and I could hear momma singing, "Any way you fix it LORD it will be ALRIGHT with me."

Home going service for Mother Albertha Rivers, Saturday 1:00 p.m. First African Baptist Church.

We buried momma right next to daddy, on the left near his heart.

HYMN

By Charlotte M. Brock

I sat outside the hangar on a wood board and sang and prayed. I didn't believe in God but I opened my mind, my heart, my soul to the universe and asked for guidance and tried to prepare myself for what I was about to do. I sat, knees pressed on my chest, and sang what I could remember of three songs over and over.

They were my favorite from Mass, which I hadn't been to in years until I decided to attend the Catholic service, out of boredom, when I arrived in Camp Victory, Kuwait, in February 2004. By chance, three of the songs sung in the makeshift chapel that Sunday were my three favorite hymns: "Be Not Afraid," "On Eagle's Wings," and "Here I Am, Lord."

A few days later, as I sat in an unarmored HMMWV, facing outboard, ready to take my M-16 off "Safe" and fire at any moment, I watched the Iraqi countryside flashing by... *Be Not Afraid. I go before you always. Come, follow me! And I will give you strength.* I couldn't remember the rest of the words... something about arrows flying... and not getting hit by the arrows.

Our convoy made it through all of Southern Iraq, up to the Tigris Valley, and West to the Anbar Province without getting hit, although the convoy that followed us was attacked. When we stopped for the night at U.S. camps, we could hear the call of the Imam from a Mosque a few hundred feet away. Getting ready to go to sleep, laying on top of my vehicle, I looked at the stars and felt alive and happy and ready for anything.

Sitting outside the hangar a few weeks later, in Camp Taqaddum, Iraq, on that wood board, I hugged my knees and rocked back and forth for a long time and sang out loud. I was about to do something that I was sure would change me forever. I was about to do something that scared me and fascinated me. I was in awe at the task at hand. I wanted to be ready. I wanted to know that I was making a conscious choice to do this. I wanted to know that Charlotte, the Charlotte inside the Lieutenant, inside the Marine, inside the grown woman, inside the world traveler and the college graduate and the well-lived teen was ready. Beyond experience in the ways of the world and knowledge of heartache and all-knowing cynicism, there was still a Charlotte who was innocent and hopeful and full of love and wonder. The me I imagined I was as a little girl. I had to find her and make sure she would make it through the next few hours.

I sat with my back to the hangar, looking out at the desert. *Here I am, Lord. It is I, Lord.* In the distance, bunkers, hangars, tents. It was late afternoon and I watched it get darker. *I have heard you calling in the night!* I tried to remember the rest of the song. I felt the hot air and the board and the sand. I watched the sun and the horizon approach. *I will go, Lord, if you lead me.* There was something magical about that song. About how it seemed to have been written for this moment, for me. *I will hold Your people in my heart.*

I came to feel peace. I was calm; time didn't flow like it usually did. The present moment and the future times when I knew I would look back on this hour were merged. Everything in my past led up to now and nothing in my future would be the same after tonight.

Time passed nonetheless and I got up and went back into the hangar. It was dusk and getting cooler. I had left my blouse inside. I put on a pair of hospital pants and waited with the other Marines. Any minute, a plane would be flying into the AACG/DAACG (Arrival Air Control Group/ Departure Air Control Group). Finally we got the call. A team of Marines went to meet the airplane. They came back after about 15 minutes and parked the truck at the back entrance of the hangar. When I heard them open the door, I turned around and busied myself with putting on rubber gloves, then a facemask. I stared at the equipment on the table in front of me: scissors, pads and ink for fingerprinting, various forms to fill out, pens, plenty of bottles of disinfectant, towels and cleaning gear. I could hear steps behind me, slow, hesitant steps from people carrying a heavy, awkward package. I heard them as they talked themselves through lifting it to the height of the table, and putting it down. My back still to them, I heard them unzip the bag. I took a breath, made a final decision—*be not afraid*—and turned around. I was looking at dirty combat boots; then cammie pants, a blouse. I forced myself to look at his face. He was dead.

So this was death. So this was a dead body. Simple. Here was a man who was no longer alive. Here was a soldier whose family did not yet know how he would be coming home. Here was a person with a life, a story, thoughts and a consciousness like mine, but no more. Here was what everyone I knew—mother, father, sisters—would one day become. Here is how I would end up one day. A body. Gone. Simple.

One Marine was in charge of taking notes and filling out paperwork while another cut off boots, socks, trousers and shirt as needed to find wounds, tattoos or other distinguishing marks. It took two of us to take fingerprints of each hand, each finger dipped into ink, pressed onto little boxes on a paper form. We went through the clothes, emptying and inventorying the contents of pockets. We looked at dog tags; the main job of the MA (Mortuary Affairs) unit at Camp Taqaddum was to get tentative I.D. on all U.S. casualties—whom we called "Fallen Angels"—and to prepare the remains for shipment to Kuwait, and then to Dover Air Force Base, where they would be positively identified, using DNA samples.

This soldier was not in too bad a state. He had died a few hours before, from gunshot wounds, and rigor mortis had already set in. His body, although dirty, stiff and pale, was intact. His face was set in a rictus, which made it difficult to look at him for too long. The smell was wet and sweet and thick. He was THERE. My position in the huge room was relative to him. He was the zero around which we moved, quietly but quickly. Even as I was there, and fully engaged in the work at hand, I could see myself looking back and regarding the scene from above. As he was seeing it?

You who dwell in His shadow for life...

As I worked more and more bodies over the next weeks and months, I came to sense, or imagine, or imagine I was sensing, them looking at us, at me.

And He will raise you up, on Eagle's wings...

Floating somewhere among the rafters of the hangar, they took note of what we were doing. They observed as we carried in the body bags from the back door, set them on the "operating" tables, and pulled on the zippers. They saw what they looked like dead, and looked to see how we, the live ones, reacted. I could not grimace or turn my head in disgust. They might see it and feel sorry for themselves, or for me.

...Bear you on the breath of dawn.

Here were bodies of men whom their loved ones would cry over, would want to hold and cherish and love. The mothers and wives of these Fallen Angels were present in some way to me, in addition to the men themselves, the souls of the dead and their survivors looking down and observing us. They couldn't act or touch or talk, but I could. I could take care of them as if they were babies. I could look at their faces and see that they were individuals, and unique, and beautiful. *Make you to shine like the sun!* I could find something to love about them. *And hold you in the palm of His hand.*

In the weeks that followed my first MA experience, an image kept flashing in my mind, a memory or a symbol that I couldn't quite identify. It had to do with me at the table, with the Angel. Seeing myself there reminded me of something but I couldn't say what it was. Had I seen this in a dream? Read it in a book? It was something more universal, something timeless yet deeply tied to me and my memories.

When a call came in that we had Angels incoming, I would feel dread— but also adrenaline and anticipation. *Here I am, Lord. Is it I, Lord?* I wanted to be there when they came. *I have heard you calling in the dark.* I wanted to take care of them. I had to, nobody could do it as well I could. *I will go, Lord, if you lead me.* Nobody was as conscious of them as someone's baby as I was. No one would touch them as gently and look at them as lovingly as I would. *I will hold your people in my heart.* I was never as conscious of life and of my soul as when I was waiting for their arrival.

There were times when I wanted to kiss them. My hands lingered on them longer than was necessary. I didn't want to be the note-taker; I handled the bodies themselves. I reached across the table, grabbed a shoulder or a hip and pulled it in to my body, to allow the Marine on the other side to get a look at the back. I pulled IVs out of their veins, as gently as I could— I knew it was crazy but I didn't want to "hurt" them. I cut off socks and looked at dead feet and toes. I saw holes in every part of their bodies. I saw bones sticking out of flesh. I saw brains leaking out from heads and eyes that had been popped out of sockets. Bodily fluids dripped on my boots. I gagged at horrid smells. I jumped back when the swollen, bright red body of a drowned man belched up water and weeds.

I opened a bag that had no semblance of the shape of a man. We found a head. An arm with a hand. And a hand. The rest was torn rags of a uniform, gore and intestines and slabs of skin covered in shit and blood. The head was perfect, serene. I closed his gray eyes. He had a beautiful face with fine, perfect features and a small, distinctive moustache. He was a Gunnery Sergeant and he had a ring on the fourth finger of each hand. We spread him out over three tables to try to figure him out. I put his hand in mine and took it over to a table, then got his arm, torn off above the elbow. I fingerprinted him. It was much easier to get each finger at the right angle since there was no body attached. We identified what we could and tried to put him back in the bag in some kind of order, but all we could do was put his head where his head should be and his hands on either side. We put the rest in the middle.

Half a dozen sailors were killed at once by indirect fire. They had been playing soccer at their camp on a Sunday morning. They came to us, and occupied all the tables in the hangar. Another time, soldiers were hit by an IED hidden in a tree. They were Civil Affairs soldiers and they had been going to a village to distribute supplies to a school. Their lieutenant was not hurt. He came to see them at MA. Here was a young man in his early twenties, like me, who had just lost four of his soldiers. Here was someone who would have to talk to their parents and live the rest of his life with this burden. And here I was, me, Charlotte, who had to talk to him. And say what? What can be said? How do you offer comfort to a stranger? How do you avoid banalities and platitudes but still say something you mean? He asked if he could have his soldiers' dog tags. We couldn't give them to him. But I got a piece of paper and a pencil and got the imprint of his soldiers' tags for him. I was so happy to give him something. I was proud of myself for thinking of doing this.

The time spent in MA was time spent in a world apart. Nothing mattered like taking care of the people who came to us. MA was the center, the core, of my existence. It was what had meaning, significance in my life. I was a caretaker, a love-giver, the mother of the dead. I was Mary bringing Jesus down from the cross and washing her son's body before laying it in the grave. That was the image that kept coming to me but had been just out of reach in my subconscious—the three Marys washing Jesus' body. I was the eternal feminine holding the body of the fallen warrior, who in death is just a little boy.

But I was not in a painting. I was not the stoic, beautiful heroine in a Greek tragedy; I was not the Virgin Mary, or even the reformed Mary Magdalene. This was Charlotte, with weaknesses and passions and a past, and despite my exceptional ability to dramatize my situation and my life,

MA was significant in a way that goes beyond the horror and desolation of death. But part of me is still there. Part of me wishes I was still with them. Part of me feels MA is where I should be, wiping away the blood and grime from a young man's face so that his fellow soldier can come tell us that yes, it's really him.

MCWS 5

14 April–12 May 2007

Participants:
Debra
David
Charlotte
Vivian
"N"—The Narrator

What tends to emerge from the great novels of the twentieth century is the idea of an *open* encyclopedia, an adjective that certainly contradicts the noun *encyclopedia*, which etymologically implies an attempt to exhaust knowledge of the world by enclosing it in a circle. But today we can no longer think in terms of a totality that is not potential, conjectural, manifold.

—Italo Calvino. *Six Memos for the Next Millennium: The Charles Eliot Norton Lectures 1985-86.* New York: Vintage International, 1993 (116).

Literature does not exist in a vacuum.

—Ezra Pound. *ABC of Reading.* New York: New Directions, 27th printing (32).

METROPOLIS RISING

On Easter morning 1992 in Okinawa, Japan, I sat behind my barracks near a stream that ran beside a sunny hillside blossoming with orange-gold gladiolas. The sun had risen once again and wholeness felt possible for the first time in my life—I was nearly three months sober in my second attempt to achieve lasting sobriety. As the sun rose that morning, I made a vow, the first meaningful vow I have ever made. To the sky, the earth, the water, and the air—whatever Spirit is or is not—I promised to try at every intersection of my life to follow that power's guidance, to do right by others, to help when I could and to get out of the way when I couldn't. Then, as Cat Stevens' "Morning has Broken" played into my cassette player headset, and I sang along, happier than I had been in years, a bagpiper in full Scottish dress walked into view. Amazed by the sight, I removed my headset and listened to him play. I had never before seen a bagpiper perform live. His appearing seemed like a gift, or an answer to my committed vow. I had no idea what sobriety or my vow would bring.

On that morning, there was no way of knowing that before I retired from the Corps I would become partially disabled during a deployment to South America, that my dreams for a landscape design career would be crushed by my injury, that my fear of winding up a greeter at Wal-Mart would drive me into college, that I would complete a six-year college degree in four years, that I would be divorced for the second time and married for the third time to a man whose mother as a child had emigrated from Scotland to this country, or that my lifelong dream of becoming a writer would translate into an MFA degree, a teaching position, and being published. I didn't know that I would spend Easter Sunday 2004 writing an essay that earned a mention in *Best American Essays 2005,* or that I would be leading a writing workshop for military people during Easter Weekend 2007. Traveling the road toward excellence while keeping my vow has been difficult, but each step I've taken has given me strength, uncovered ability and given me a sense of empathy that would have otherwise been drowned in the next drink. Had I not survived alcoholism and failure on so many levels, I would not have started Milspeak in September 2005. I wouldn't have been equipped to understand or work with writers who enter The Blackbird Zone.

I try my best to practice a spiritual way of life, but often fall short. Never have I fallen farther than when I was teaching at the private school in an ultra-conservative Christian community during the 2006-07 academic year. Each day, so many thoughts crowded my mind as I drove Snake Road on my way to my cave-like classroom at the private school, so many thoughts that one day following Christmas break, when a low-flying turkey buzzard nearly smacked my windshield, its spade-shaped head and red-gobbled neck extended toward the marsh, my mind jumped onto the road and my hands clenched the wheel, but I didn't pull off the road. Despite the jolt of awareness and the adrenaline pumping through my body, I traveled on. Having traveled so many miles in my lifetime, I didn't even bother to pull off the road to settle my mind. Instead, I turned up the stereo and thought about the students I would soon have to face. The high school-college students, who, misunderstanding the power of the pen and not realizing that I would see their comments, had written falsehoods about me in teacher evaluations collected by Technical College of the Lowcountry.

Although I was employed fulltime by the private school, TCL administered dual credit courses for the private school, and the college paid $5000 of the $30,000 salary I was paid for my teaching year at the private school. The College uses instructor evaluations for retention validation and delivers these reports, minus student names, to instructors to help improve teaching skills. This method of evaluating instructors is upside down and backwards, and would be equivalent to having troops write officer performance evaluations if such a practice were followed. Having my sixteen- and seventeen-year-old students write my teacher evaluations was a demeaning, ridiculous practice, one that is practiced by many educational institutions. I had received student evaluations of the first half of the academic year during Christmas break. After reading them, I wanted to quit the private school, but those evaluations only added fuel to the fire beneath the stake that was my teaching year.

In their evaluations, my students had ranked my performance during first semester at 1.6 percent against a 4.5 percent national average and my past 4.6 percent average. Maybe their comments are what stopped me from asking Milspeak writers to evaluate their workshop experience. My students' comments devastated me. I had been burning my life to present my students with meaningful coursework on writing and literature, the two loves of my life. I was certain their evaluations meant the end of my teaching career, that the technical college would never ask me to teach another course, and the evaluations would become a permanent part of my teaching record. The worst of my students' thirty-six written comments:

I once described myself as a lover of literature. I was once unhappy if I did not have a book. Mrs. Drumm has single handedly ruined this for me...she has zero personal skills. She comes across completely incompetent. This course felt like it was made up the night before. This teacher evaluation is the most effort I've put forth all year and I have an "A" in this class.

Other comments were similar (I've corrected spelling errors): Please hire a new teacher; She is way too abrasive and neurotic; This course has not been fun; This is the worst class I've ever taken; She hates us gays and lesbians; She is very demanding; She expects a lot out of freshmen; The teacher needs to focus on the essay itself rather than the format; She is very mean.

The first time I read them, shortly before Christmas, my students' comments flew into my mind like a great sea of birds crashing through a windshield, storming my mind, battering my cave, causing me to question my competence, humiliating me, making me want to quit because of shame—I had failed my students. I decided to discuss the evaluations and quitting with the private school's student guidance counselor, whose office was the social hub for teachers.

"Herd mentality," the high school guidance counselor labeled the comments, and offered no solutions to the problem. They learn from old cows, I thought, and kept my mouth shut about quitting. In previous discussions about student performance, the guidance counselor and headmaster has frequently told me my students were just "country kids" and I shouldn't expect much from them. That's not my style.

Instead of quitting, I faced the students and explained the power of the pen—that thing that launches rockets and bombs; that signer of peace treaties, declarations of war and declarations of independence: the pen guided by a mind, always guided by a mind in opposition to or in alliance with other minds. Substituting pen for rifle in The Rifleman's Creed was effective in helping my students understand the power of the pen: This is my pen; there are many like it, but this one is mine—I must master it as I must master my life...I will....

My teaching year was one of my toughest years ever, a constant exercise in mental, physical, emotional, and spiritual gymnastics. I'm not sure how, during that difficult and busy time, I managed to write a play, *Jick's Journey*, the story of a little girl's first encounter with death and her adventures in a dreamland. University of South Carolina Beaufort's drama professor, John Blair, invited me to write the play with his student theater group. John, a mentor during my undergraduate studies, has continued to play that role in my life. The opportunity and the offer were a statement of John's belief in my potential. He was the first person to call me a writer, by awarding the title on graduation day, before presenting me with the Honor Society's award for proficiency in the Humanities. The problem with accepting the opportunity to write the play was that John contacted me about a month before the play was to be performed. I write long and take my time doing it, but I decided to try.

During February 2007, I wrote the play with Dennis Adams, a Beaufort County librarian, Romance language scholar, and columnist. Dennis is a constant in John's theater troupe, Rogues and Vacaboundes, which joins theater students and members of the community to rattle the boards. Theater students helped me develop their characters. Dennis wrote many of his character's lines in Romanian. His character, Vlad, a depressed Romanian flea, represents one of the phases of grief, as do each of the other characters Jick encounters in a dreamland on the night of the day her puppy died. Dennis also found appropriate Romanian Gypsy music to accompany the play. Together we wrote the lyrics of the play's theme song, which was based on an ancient Romanian folk song and sung to a melody adapted from Georges Enesco's "Romanian Rhapsody Number 1."

I designed the set, sewed costumes for the cast, and acted as "Mom" in the play. William Orem, an artist and student actor, created masks for the animal characters. Dennis created his Vlad costume and mask. My husband Pete built the set with help from the cast. Pete's mother, Margaret, offered an old mink stole for use in Nerus the Otter's costume, and helped me craft dead birds of white socks fitted with paper wings, then filled with beans and covered with white feathers. John Blair's wife, Jane, painted depictions of the characters on set pieces. Jick, the play's heroine, was based on one of my seventh grade study hall girls, Little Eads. She and her friends helped with Jick's dialog. The strongman pose Jick often strikes is Little Eads' own. Two of my world literature students from the private school helped backstage during the play's three-night run at USCB's Performing Arts Center. Stagehands, most of them junior enlisted Marines, friends of our leading lady, J.C. Day and her Marine husband, moved set pieces between acts. We left the curtain up between acts because these young Marines and my two students made themselves part of the play as shades, ghostly presences moving trees, rocks, and water from place to place. They threw our mortar barrages of dead birds, symbols of broken peace.

The most unusual day of my teaching year came on April 16. At the end of that day, my name crackled through the intercom. I was to report to the headmaster's office. Unsurprised by the summons—they were equal in frequency and intensity to those I experienced during boot camp summons to The Hellcat Hut—but unsure what I had done wrong, I was certain I was about to be blamed for something my middle school students or my college students had reported.

After knocking on the headmaster's office door, I stepped across the threshold into his cave, and said good afternoon.

"Something has to be done about that class," the headmaster demanded, with his usual one-dimensional attitude.

"The seventh graders?" I asked my Cyclops—to him I was Nobody from Nowhere doing Nothing. I was a mistaken judgment on his part, a teacher he wished he had never hired. To me, his one-dimensional opinion of his "country kids" was insulting to them and to me. The headmaster's favorite teacher, a sheepish man who taught in the cave next door to mine, leaned against a doorframe in the office, his girth that of a boulder's. Both men firmly believed in the power of paddling students to instill in them discipline in study and life.

"I hate seeing them walk all over her," he said to the headmaster, without looking at me.

"They're disrupting other classes, bothering other teachers. We'll have a talk with them," the headmaster said, his tone implying that the woman standing before him with a twenty-year military career behind her could not handle 20 seventh graders.

The headmaster droned on, complaining of my students and me. His big frame, white hair, and gender reviving many ghosts from my past. This same performance had occurred all too often in the military, this two against one, this male against female having-the-last-word duel. Oh, those were scenes—my battles to earn the right to the title of Marine, battles waged from the time I enlisted in 1977 until I retired in 1998. Those scenes were nothing compared to this day at the private school. In the military, being called to the carpet is as expected as rounds fired downrange, but minimalization, repression, and oppression in an academic environment is stultifying.

The title I had aimed for, Teacher, seemed as out of reach as Marine had been.

The Cyclops muttered on while my eyes glazed over. I thought about recent events at the school and of madwomen in attics. A week prior to the dressing-down at hand, the headmaster had seemed relieved when informed of my intentions not to return for the next academic year. When he had asked my intentions, I knew from students that he had already announced plans—to the students and not to me—for his high school's college courses to be held on the TCL campus. Without asking me, the guidance counselor had told TCL that I would teach those courses only his students would attend on the TCL campus, or so I learned from TCL. Learning of this, I had made clear—to the college and not to the headmaster—that I never again wanted to teach the private school's students. All this before asking my intentions for the next academic year! I suppose once he learned that I had no intention of teaching college courses to his students at TCL's campus, the gloves came off.

So, while that gray shade-of-a-Cyclops continued grasping at seventh grader behavioral problems in his attempt to put me in my place. I recalled the lower school administrator who made a point of warning me at the beginning of my teaching year about my seventh graders, a class she had dealt with in preceding years: "They're the worst class this school's ever had." I thought about how much I like my seventh graders, how brave they are and hard to tame, and how much progress they had made by learning study strategies other than copying paragraphs from textbooks, and of how they began to see themselves as human beings instead of statistics during our time together. How needy they were! I didn't know the source of that neediness, but these children were like my public school students the previous spring. Despite the age difference, they too had an edge that would help them survive in an insensitive world.

And, while the Cyclops' spear-of-words was missing its target, I thought about that school day, April 16, 2007. During first period, I had taught my survey of literature students Billy Collins' poem, "The Names," about 9-11 loss, grief, and moving on—"So many names, there is barely room on the walls of the heart." Two of 27 students raised their hands when I asked who among them had read the assigned poem. Despite extensive footnotes in the text, the two students who claimed to have read the poem neither understood nor recognized that the poem was about September 11, 2001. During second period, my six world literature students had discussed Kafka's *The Metamorphosis*. Each of the six shared his or her reading of the story; all six focused on the dysfunction between Gregor, the vermin, and his family, his keepers. During third and fourth periods, I led two classes of eighth graders through the wonderful grammatical world of complements. During fifth period, my free period, I read war poems written by my world literature students following a week spent studying *The Waste Land*. Four of the six students in world literature really cared about their work. They are the four I returned for after Christmas break, when I had wanted to quit the private school. From one of those four, in a poem written from the point of view of an Iraqi student in the war zone, comes this stanza:

> The constant murmur of shouts and shots,
> The rumble of explosions in the distance,
> The death of my countrymen in the streets;
> It is all something one becomes accustomed to.
> The earth shudders; the pictures fall again.
> Why bother picking them up just to let them fall once more?

But the seventh graders? I recalled one of the seventh grade study hall boys bleeding into study hall, the last period of the school day. Another study hall boy had thrown a plastic Gatorade bottle against the bleeding boy's head during the twenty-minute break before study hall met. I sent the wounded boy to the school nurse. The bottle thrower was sent to the headmaster. The boy's head wound required several stitches. The perpetrator—what had he received? A chuckle behind closed doors for hitting an unpopular boy? On another day, the bottle thrower came to study hall and held his finger out to me, his finger obviously broken. Once again, the violence occurred during the break before study hall. The boy who had received the head wound earlier in the year followed the broken-fingered boy into the classroom, his arm dangling uselessly, his shoulder broken during the incident in which the other boy's finger was broken. The same two boys, at it again—one popular, one not; both, intent on getting even. Both boys were sent to the nurse. When I reported these and many other incidents, the headmaster's response was always an extended variation of "Boys will be boys"—to him all problems in the classroom were teacher management issues. And what of students' complaints about attention deficit medication? Medication they complained made them sleepy, sad, barfy; medication that made them feel different from those who didn't have to take it. I knew all about feeling different. But what of the parents I had spoken with who admittedly changed their children's medications at will—too much, too little, never a balance? And what about Spirit Week at the school year's start? Boys wore Rebel flags as capes around their necks and roared like wild animals shoving, kicking, and hitting through the halls, while the headmaster and others chuckled, and remarked the activity was to honor their heritage—

"The end of the school year?" I interrupted the headmaster. "It's the end of the school year and you're *finally* going to do something about those boys?"

"Have you heard about Virginia Tech?" he asked as nonchalantly as a Cyclops asking for another bowl of wine. "Have you heard about the shootings?"

"What? What shootings?" Tears burned my eyes—I'd been in my cave of a classroom all day without a phone, a radio, the Internet, a television, or a friend. "That's...that's pathetic—"

"That's one of the best schools in the nation," the headmaster began.

I turned away and left his office without asking permission—I was no longer in the military and didn't have to pretend not to be outraged by way the news was delivered or that no one had told me sooner what was going on. And what was the purpose of his lead-in to this news of another school shooting? What did how I managed my classroom have to do with a school shooting? What did my seventh graders have to do with any of it?

In my classroom, I took my keys from my desk, grabbed my bag of books, my lunchbox, and my purse, and walked to the parking lot, to leaving, to driving home through the small town and past the people locked behind their doors, to making my way down Snake Road through a countryside shriveled by drought. I wanted my island home, my dogs, and my loving man, all of them waiting for my return. Home.

Making my way toward the five rivers to be crossed before reaching home, I tuned the radio channel by channel, listening to every source I could find. I listened and imagined that young man opening fire, students scattering like a bird-sea parting. I listened to reports he was a creative writing student. Later reports implied his being a "bad" writer was an indication of instability, maybe even a cause for the attack!

Where do they come from, these devastated students who kill each other? Why do they bully each other to death? Do these killer children arise from our culture of violence? From an educational system that no longer functions by no longer teaching values, that teaches to tests instead of to human beings? Do children bully each other because they learn bullying from us, the adults in their lives? What did my students learn from teachers' and the headmaster's treatment of me? How we adults treat each other matters. What is said around the supper table matters—children are the greatest and most open-minded observers of life. Hate mongering among adults is perhaps the worst and most frequent form of education for children—this is what I learned from my year of teaching.

Perhaps my colleagues ostracized me because of my Marine Corps past. Who knows what was said about me over supper? Most of the teachers at the private school were women. To them, I must have seemed an aberration of womanhood: a childless, godless Amazon. To most men, I will never truly be a Marine. To women, I will never be anything else. I am caught in a paradox; their vision of me is not how I see myself. They threw upon me what they thought I was like a sheepskin—I was a living, breathing stereotype in the midst of their conservative fears: a liberal and a female Marine. Maybe I was being oversensitive or overly critical. Nevertheless, on the last day of the school year, having failed my first chance at a fresh start in a new career, I once again became officially unemployed. On that day, I drove home knowing that I would never again have to travel Snake Road, that in life some things cannot be mended, that the bird sea will part and I will move on—

I will.

The second blow of the year soon followed the horrific events of April 16, 2007. The fulltime teaching position and publishing contract were dreams realized at the same time; both shattered at the same time. In a classic case of artistic differences, the mentoring relationship I had enjoyed with Tristine Rainer ended when I withdrew from our publishing contract. Working with my miserable memoir made me a better writer. Working with Tristine readied me to let go of the miserable memoir, to abandon it, to move on. Sadly, Milspeak writers lost their home on the web when my relationship with Tristine ended.

Physical and mental exhaustion had descended on me by the time MCWS 5 began in April 2007. The old limp from my back injury had returned. I came down with a terrible cold that hung on for months. Sleep time was reading and writing time. My weight fell below 115 pounds. Adding even more to my schedule, I signed up for my first writer's conference, slated to begin the first week in June. For the conference, I wrote an essay about my school year. Several manuscripts appeared in my inbox for critique during the conference, and military writers were filling my inbox with requests to participate in MCWS 5. Ignoring the signs of physical breakdown that hint at forthcoming emotional breakdown, I forced myself to trudge on. Down the savage path or the road toward excellence—take your pick. I seemed to be going nowhere, but I still didn't believe that the dice I threw in 2003 had landed. Whatever the outcome of my journey, the good in my life has always outweighed the bad. I held onto my hope that by transforming my writing I could still achieve my dream of becoming a published author. I hoped the nine writers signed up for MCWS 5 would find, as I had, that what once seemed weakness could be translated into strength. I hoped they would learn that the series of coincidences and uncertainties that make up a life are the very mysteries from which all beginnings find origin, that Life's many mysteries make living beautiful and bearable.

Four writers attended MCWS 5 Seminar Saturday. Three—Vivian, Charlotte, and David—were returning for another go at the Milspeak process. Debra was the new writer among us. Basic tenets of good memoir were the theme of the craft talk. When first drafts arrived, I read each work carefully, then read it again while commenting in the margins. As usual, I searched for the nugget of truth—the universal in each piece. I did my best to bring that essence to a full shine by providing each writer with a typed summary of the piece and my suggestions for revision.

My writing and publishing struggles are always shared with the workshop in session. MCWS 5 learned of the end of my publishing contract with Tristine and of my sense of gaining a new beginning from that ending. For the first time, I shared with writers a piece of my own for critique, a meditation essay I've been working with for several years. Sharing my work was an unusual step. Subconsciously, I suppose, the need to get feedback from other writers overrode my longstanding and sensible rule to exclude my works-in-progress from a workshop I am leading. In retrospect, I know I was seeking solace. The workshop was my anchor, my place of refuge among like-minded people when I was roiling in negative experiences with the private school and publishing. Sharing my work with the writers was a way of revealing more of myself through showing, rather than telling. In a way, it was like telling a war story around a campfire during a deployment. And I wanted the writers to know that I am a student, too. Sharing my work was a small experiment in the context of the larger project that is Milspeak, and one I doubt I'll repeat, mainly because Milspeak's focus should always be on the writers' efforts to produce their best work, and not on my efforts to produce my best work.

For MCWS 5, Debra chose the difficult subject of molestation by a parent. Her first draft was well constructed, the writing crisp and image-filled. For revision, I suggested Debra try condensing some of the descriptive passages at the beginning. The reader needed a better understanding of Dad, and this is where the adult narrator should step in, analyze the situation, and reflect. I shared with Debra that I had experienced reader disbelief when I had workshopped a section of my memoir that reveals what I feel is the worst experience I've had, the Christmas my father molested me when I was a child. My readers didn't believe me that things had happened exactly as I described. I believed things had happened as Debra described and told her so, but asked if her narrator was hiding the facts of her molestation behind her veteran father's speech on the history of the Vietnam War. Was N trying to protect her molester?

Vivian wrote about time spent alone in the desert town of Yucca Valley while her Marine officer husband was deployed in support of Operation Desert Storm. "Marine Wife" will appeal to a large audience, the many people who are unaware what it means to be a military wife during war.

There are many other reasons for this memoir's appeal to readers: vivid descriptions of camaraderie among women, of a working woman developing a career in an isolated location, and of women drinking together as salve on emotional wounds. There was enough material in Vivian's first draft for a book-length memoir, one that would be welcomed among military spouses struggling to find their place in the military family. For revision, I asked Vivian to try reordering the presentation of events by beginning the piece with what was the first draft's last paragraph, an encounter with a roadrunner. I asked her to keep in mind that the roadrunner is a trickster appearing throughout the piece in the guise of the universe playing a major trick on N: giving her a lover, then taking him away, before bringing them together again with both of them changed. Vivian is working this piece into her graduate thesis, a wonderful and rewarding reason to continue revising a memoir that wants and deserves to be a compelling and healing book, a story that will prove a great help to military spouses. Vivian recalls her MCWS 5 experience:

In this workshop, Sally specifically requested that participants focus on some aspect of their military experience. I decided to explore a relocation I made from New Orleans Louisiana to Yucca Valley California, following my husband and changing the course of my career only to be faced with his deployment to Desert Storm. Left behind in a desert of my own, I faced the challenges of my new environment in the company of fellow military spouses who met the uncertainty of war and loneliness together.

This workshop emboldened me to face my mistakes and myself as a military spouse. My nonfiction writing provided a means of revealing my deepest disappointments in my role as wife to a company commander. One of my hopes is that by sharing my battle with loneliness, despair and alcoholism, other military wives might find solace in their journey through the unknown territory of war. They may even recognize some of their mistakes in my voice. Milspeak provided me a forum to gain the courage to seek forgiveness from my spouse and offer my story to the military community.

Charlotte decided to write another chapter of her experience in Iraq.

"Orion" holds reader interest on several levels. Not many outsiders know what it's like to be employed as a Marine, to have a Marine as a boss, to have Uncle Sam as your CEO, and they certainly don't know what it's like to be fired by such a chain of command. Charlotte best explains her intentions in writing this memoir:

> With "Orion," I wanted to keep writing about my deployment to Iraq in 2004, in part because I wanted to tell the others in the class more about the circumstances surrounding my first piece. I think "Orion" gives the reader a better idea of who the narrator is; the who-what-when-where-why; in fact, "Hymn" belongs within "Orion" chronologically. By now, I had some idea that eventually I'd write a book-length piece—a work still in progress today.
>
> I felt lucky not only that there was a group like MCWS that I could join, but that I had the time to attend. Most Marines on Parris Island work on Saturdays, and in fact I had had to switch some duties around in order to be able to come. It was also difficult to find time to write. If it hadn't been for Sally and the others expecting something from me, I would have never written anything.
>
> What further encouraged me was that Ian Pounds, from Middlebury College's Breadloaf Writer's Conference, took an interest in my work. Sally emailed me to tell me about it and I was delighted of course, but when Ian and I started corresponding, I was even more amazed to learn that his wife was a student at the Basic School—she was a newly minted Marine officer at the very beginning of her Marine Corps adventure. I couldn't believe my luck—not only did I have a writer-mentor, but I had a new friend who had a genuine interest in the female Marine experience. Ian and I exchanged many emails on writing, editing, publishing, and women in the Marine Corps. Ian helped me by providing motivation and encouragement to keep writing even when I didn't have any MCWS sessions to go to; his confidence in me as well as his practical advice were instrumental in my developing a plan for, and starting to write, a book.

David, returning for his third seminar, wrote about investigating the death of an infant. David's minimalist writing perfectly fits his subject. His descriptions are vivid, his scenes clear, and the moments he chose to include are powerful. The experience from David's perspective:

> By the time I chose to participate in MCWS 5, I understood that Sally wanted participants to be able to write about and examine powerful moments in their military career. She really wanted those who experienced combat to be able to examine and heal from their intense combat experiences. I had not experienced combat in the true sense of the word; however, law enforcement provides some intense moments as well. It surprised me that when I thought of intense events as a young Marine criminal investigator, I thought of this experience. Few people in this day and age reach adulthood as innocents and I certainly did not either. Still, this experience reduced what innocence I had left. Looking back, I know it was to be expected in my field of choice but that made it no less intense an experience.

Following Second Saturday's workshop, we decided that writers' next drafts would be the final drafts for MCWS 5, cutting the regular schedule short by two weeks. This decision was made because I was exhausted from my teaching year. Debra, the only new writer, did not submit a final draft, maybe because the workshop was cut short. But perhaps I asked too much in guiding her to contemplate through writing the facts of the abuse she suffered at the hands of her father. Although I share my writing and publishing experience during MCWS, I try not to share too much of my life experience. I don't remember how much of my childhood memories of my father I might have shared with Debra, who, like Dusty Pack, had disappeared off my radar—her email addresses had ceased to exist. But the memoir piece I shared with writers was about my own experience being abused by my father and our relationship. Fortunately, unlike Dusty Pack, I found Debra. She had this to say about her workshop experience:

> My father was enlisted in the Army and retired after 22 years of service. I enrolled in the 2007 Milspeak Class and was thrilled to learn of my acceptance. Not having any formal writing experience, I was anxious and just a little afraid of what everyone would think of my writing techniques. Sally set my fears to rest during our first

class by stating that everything you write is worth the world and published or not it is still your creation. Sally encouraged me to write freely with color and description. My Milspeak classmates gave me the courage to unravel the ball of disillusionment that was held inside my soul, to let the poison of hurt pour out onto the paper thus releasing it from my heart. Thanks to Sally I continue to write as a form of therapy and self-healing and I strongly encourage others to do the same. The road is long but with every word another inch is knocked off of the wall that enclosed me for so many years. Kudos to Sally for teaching me that we all have battles to face and that with the power of writing we are strong.

To revise a devastating experience again and again is to slay the past, revive it, and slay it again, over and over. Writing out my experience with my father helped me to heal and to forgive, but his betrayal of my trust continues to affect many aspects of my life. Not a day goes by that I don't remember his abuse and what I cannot remember of it. I am always questioning the truth of the matter—his version of the truth, my mother's version, and mine. I experienced dissociative amnesia during that time and didn't recall it until I was undergoing alcoholism treatment in 1985. Years later, while revising my miserable memoir, my mother and I were finally able to discuss that experience. My mother acknowledged some of what I could recall. To have the uncertainties of memory verified is a gift of peace of mind. To write about devastating experience requires great courage, even more so to publish that work. As in all crisis writing, there must be a purpose in writing about the experience and sharing the story. The writer must know that purpose in order to safely navigate the territory of the spirit. Debra's story tells the little girl inside each abused woman who might feel she is alone that she is not. Hers is a story only she can tell.

THE GRAY

By David Charles

The beeper on my hip started vibrating while my wife and I were sitting in a well lit, white-walled church service in which the preacher was talking about some dark issue; it was likely about the dangers that black sin can bring to our immortal souls. The well-intentioned sermon was forgotten when the pager on my hip went off. I was a military policeman with a new assignment as an on-the-job-training criminal investigator (OJT) and when the duty investigator called, the OJT went to work. At first all I knew was an address and that someone was dead. I thought I was ready for what could have been my first chance to be personally involved in bringing a murderer to justice.

A quick stop by the Provost Marshal's Office (PMO) for a duty weapon, notebook and vehicle and then I was at the crime scene. A standard, lower-middle-class house served as the assigned quarters for some young military family. Inside the house was dark and messy but not the worst I had seen by far. Actually, it seemed tame for a crime scene. Medical personnel had been there and there was medical waste, wrappings, and such, here and there.

The duty agent called me into a bedroom. "What do you see?" he asked. It was common practice for an OJT like me to be questioned by the seasoned agent in charge of the crime scene.

"It's a baby's room. Disheveled but probably not to the point of neglect," was my initial impression. It was standard for the OJT to reply as if reading his crime scene notes. "There is a slight odor to the room, probably a dirty diaper pail somewhere nearby." I stepped up to the crib. "The sheets are wound up and there's . . .wait, that's blood on the sheets and the crib right?" The agent's answer was a blank expression that simply required me to go on. "There are dark fluids on the crib and sheets, possibly blood, possibly feces. It should be photographed before being tampered with and then the sheets should be taken as evidence. Swabbings should also be taken from the wooden parts of the crib that appear to have some of the dark substance on

240

them. The location of blood or whatever the material is could be important."

I turned my attention away from the colorful, cartoon-laden sheets with the ominous smears and looked around the rest of the room. Stepping near a rocking chair I said, "Possibly more fluids here. More swabbings should be done ... after photos of course." There was nothing else of interest noted in the infant's bedroom. "The small dresser and rest of the room is reasonably neat and there are clean clothes and diapers, which will go under the heading of negative evidence." This was noted because what was not at a crime scene could be just as important as what was there.

I did not get a chance to explore the other rooms in the house before being given my next assignment. I expected what was coming but did not want it to come.

"Go to the hospital, stay with the baby victim and find out what the doctors can tell us," the duty investigator directed.

Again, when the agent directs, the OJT goes.

About a month before, I had been sent to the hospital to wait for the medical results when a pilot had gone down during a training accident. The cause of the Harrier accident was still a mystery; the pilot had been ejected almost directly into the asphalt runway and had almost no chance of survival. Adult deaths are no problem. We grow up and then we die. I was okay with that idea as I waited for the doctors to do their job, even though the pilot had been a young adult. It wasn't even that bad that the other pilots were so rude. You see, Harrier pilots have a very dangerous, difficult plane to fly and it is evidently of paramount importance to them to believe that they are too good to "mess up" and anyone who did crash was beneath them. It was almost humorous the way the "brother pilots" were saying the recently killed pilot was too cocky, and was never as good as he thought he was. It was a cruel mental crutch they used; but like them, I did not have any real problem with the reality that death had come to the young officer. Too bad I couldn't use the adult crutch this time.

At the hospital I hesitate to go in. Why did the victim have to be a baby? This seems especially heinous. I take a deep breath. Two. What the heck is all the waiting for? I get out of the car and walk into the medical complex

241

with its bright lights gleaming off the well-buffed floors. The corpsman working the desk in the emergency room is the next brief obstacle. "I am here for the investigation into the Burgess infant death," I say to him.

He directs me to a waiting room because there simply is no space in the trauma room for a person to stand and watch.

"I'll come get you soon," he tells me.

I wait for an eternity that ends all too soon.

"You can photograph the body now. The doctor is waiting for you."

The infant corpse lies on the stained, white sheets. The skin is white and light blue, mottled all over with dark blue and black streaks. Here and there are brown and red marks, bruises, and abrasions. There are also needle tracks and there is a white, rubber tube extending from the small mouth. I stare deadpan. Somewhere inside I am glad the other investigators and I will be a part of the retribution coming to whoever has perpetrated this crime.

"Was the death due to the evident blunt trauma?" I ask the doctor.

"No. What you see as trauma is the result of medical personnel attempting to save the child."

"Then what is the cause of death, sir?" I remain outwardly professional even as I am seething inside like a boiling stew of rage and retribution inside the iron cauldron that is my tense body.

"Sudden Infant Death Syndrome. SIDS," the doctor states matter-of-factly, as if his pronouncement answered all my questions.

"What was the cause of the sudden infant death?" I challenge in reply.

"Well, er," the doctor is a little less smug, "you see, there is no specific medical explanation but this actually occurs fairly often. The infant in these cases seems to stop breathing, to choke, with no apparent reason. It used to be called crib death because that was the most common place for it to occur. Before anyone knows what is happening, the baby is just lying there, dead."

"So the parents—or a baby sitter—didn't..."

"No. The marks and coloring you see are from the medical attempts to revive the child. Before that, there was just some blood from the nose. Babies' bodies are so delicate that they often become very bruised during the rough handling of the treatment. The death certificate will say SIDS—Sudden Infant Death Syndrome. No doubt about it."

Finished, the doctor turned and walked away.

I was dumb-founded. All the rage that was boiling inside me was suddenly frozen into a solid block. There was nothing to be done about the senseless death of the helpless infant.

I called in the details to the duty investigator. "Okay, we'll wrap things up here. You can go. You're done for tonight," he said.

Evidently I went back to military police headquarters through the gray fog, walking through the earlier process in reverse. My notes went onto the desk in the investigations office, the keys for the vehicle went back to the desk sergeant, and the weapon went back to the armory. I know this because that is where they are supposed to go and I didn't have them with me when I pulled into my driveway and sat staring at my house. What I didn't know was what to do with the shock and the anger and the desire for righteous retribution and the image of the baby whose colors were all wrong lying in a hospital room.

Inside the house, I am quiet. I don't talk about the details. Marty is usually my rock; she shares the burdens of the day. It is just as well that she is at a Sunday evening meeting at the church. I can't talk anyway. Her mother Beverly is here to watch the children. We get along well but she senses my mood and leaves me alone. Tonight, I can't get the solid frozen mass out from inside me.

I walk into my daughter's room. Only a few months old, she is barely larger than the lifeless child I left moments before. I take her into my arms and rock her. I sit in the chair, look at her, and rock her for hours.

I won't let go. I won't ever let her slip into the gray world around us.

MARINE WIFE

By Vivian I. Bikulege

To me, Desert Storm was like a firecracker that fizzled. A long awaited confrontation that lasted maybe the span of three days, sputtered out in an impotent surrender by amateur Iraqi forces. That is how I saw it anyway. If the United States went into Kuwait to defend freedom, and secure our supply of oil through warfare, why not bloody it up real good and assassinate the instigator? I felt bloodied and part of me had died in the "Storm." I have the hidden scars to prove it.

I never hung a yellow ribbon on my door or fencepost like my next-door, model Marine wife neighbor. I did not plant a flagpole in my front yard. I was not a patriot but I was doing my part. I sacrificed time with my husband and experienced the stress of the unknown. I watched for Death's Angel. Jack and I prepared perfunctory wills when he left, and forgot about them when he returned. I was bitter, even hateful of the wartime experience, and had come close to compromising my fidelity. I drank my way through Desert Storm. I never wore my husband's rank, pretending to be a Captain or Major in status, and I had no respect for women that did. Frankly, I had no respect for authority in general.

In our first four disconnected years of marriage, I never really had to be a military wife. I was a thirty-something professional with a brand new MBA, a career in front of me, and all of a sudden, I was stranded in the High Desert of California. I was a chemical salesman for god's sake. I met Jack in a bar in Savannah six years earlier. Following my move from Raleigh North Carolina, and after having gone into a self-imposed moratorium on any social activity, I decided to venture out one evening in February 1984. Dressed in thick gray corduroys and a yellow, hooded surfer sweatshirt, I was not presentable for the downtown bar scene, so I headed down Abercorn Street, and landed at Doubles, some sad Army Ranger hangout in the local Holiday Inn. There he was, standing beside the only open barstool in the place. I needed a seat, and I guess he was looking for conversation or something else. After a brief exchange, he asked for my phone number. I challenged him to find my number in the local phone

244

book by successfully spelling my Lithuanian last name. With that smart-ass challenge in place, I left the bar and headed to my car. On the way, I stopped dead in the parking lot, and asked myself why I had gone out that night. I was looking. Jack was not bad in his tan Polo jacket and blazing green eyes, so I turned around to go back into Doubles and retrieve him. We left the bar, jumped into our cars and he followed me as I picked up a pizza and a bottle of vodka. We danced in the street outside my apartment, went to bed, and a week later he sent me a dozen roses for Valentine's Day.

After two years of being together in Savannah and three years of Jack being stationed at Parris Island, he was due for new orders. I was offered a job in New Orleans. He accepted an assignment there as a publicity officer. Living together did not seem like an option. The right thing to do was to get married. Begin to grow up at twenty-eight. Settle down. Settle. And so we did. Get married anyway.

I was a Marine wife by association only. I married a Marine but I had isolated myself from that world, and now I needed it to keep tabs on where my husband was. There was no Internet access then, no cell phones connecting us through the miles of cyberspace. The role of Marine wife did not define me, and I failed to emulate whatever model may have existed. I drank. I shot pool and got pretty good at it. I flirted. I disappointed my parents and siblings or so I thought. I disappointed myself in how I handled my lot. I was not around when phone calls came in from overseas.

But I looked up at the stars at night, and thought about him thinking of me, looking at the same sky. I wrote letters out of love and anger. I read and saved war articles from the Los Angeles Times. I watched CNN for minute-to-minute reports of foreign and American troops lining up on a desert chessboard, and then, I quit watching. I stayed in contact with Jack's family. I hosted a dinner or two for company wives. I raked the dirt. I had two of the only trees in the desert, and I watered them, refreshed by the sound of deciduous leaves catching a breeze in a hundred degrees of heat. On Sunday mornings, I drove to Joshua Tree National Monument just up the road and read the newspaper, drinking my personal bottle of Sunday brunch champagne, alone. My loneliness was rewarded by the companionship of the howling winds, as they siphoned through mountain passes, encapsulated in desert grit. Wind and dirt filtered through my window frame crevices at night, rattling the aluminum mini-blinds.

The boxes in the garage from the New Orleans move stayed packed and I would ransack them every once in awhile in a desperate attempt to find something only temporarily lost. My company car, a charcoal gray Buick, never saw the inside of that garage. It never saw much of any garage as I did a poor job of routine automotive maintenance.

Yucca Valley California is wedged between Twenty-Nine Palms and Palm Springs just above the Morongo Valley. I was lucky. I had a job. I could escape the High Desert with a real purpose. I went to Brawley and Calipatria selling chemicals to geothermal plants. I traveled to Orange County and San Jose introducing my company and myself to independent power producers. I stayed active in my faith and collected money for the pledge drive to build a new church, walking up and down the desert streets introducing myself to total strangers like some missionary in a foreign land.

Desert culture and the surrounding environment sent me into a state of shock for about one month after my arrival. People went barefoot at Vons' Supermarket. I quickly learned of the local Big Lots store where I could buy one-dollar bottles of wine. I found a gynecologist. I took golf lessons at the Blue Skies Country Club in Yucca but never practiced in between. I just drank at the club bar.

Two weeks after Jack left for Kuwait, our anniversary rolled around. He had left behind the gift of a Movado Museum watch. Now as I think back, time was what stood between him and me. Time to pass, time to worry, and time wasted.

I fell into the companionship of three women also living in Yucca Valley and off base—Jess, Marti and Jacqueline. Jess was the most hard core of the four of us in her attitude concerning our circumstances. She wanted to be tough on the outside but pulled out her eyelashes in some sort of anxiety-ridden response to our plight. Her house was decorated in an Indian desert motif of dream catchers and western depictions of coyote and Native American symbols.

Marty was single and was living with her Marine at the time of his deployment. To this day, I do not know why she did not pack it up, and get the hell out of Yucca Valley. She was the smartest of any of us and probably the prettiest too. She was definitely the youngest. When I was in town, Marty and I would spend weeknights watching Wheel of Fortune, eating macaroni and cheese, and drinking wine, trying to outguess each other as Vanna spun letters for middle-class morons trying to win a car, a trip, or some lump sum of cash.

And then there was Jacqueline. While Jess picked out her eyelashes, Jacqueline offered soliloquies on privilege, décor and proper behavior, all the while sinking into booze and depression. She was beautiful but big, tasteful but sloppy. I loved each of these women for who they were, and what they offered to me. I wonder if they ever really loved me back. I believe they did.

My brother and I coined a phrase for this foursome. We were the Yucca Sluts, and not because we were all that promiscuous or loose, but more of a slang term of endearment for four women alone on a man-less raft, shipwrecked against the rounded boulders of the Monument.

It was as close as I ever got to war and as close as I ever want to get. On a sun-drenched and lonely day in August 1990, I sat on a wooden porch swing built for two, surrounded by a landscape of stark blue skies and sandy, brown dirt. There was no grass. Prickly fingers of sprawling cacti scraped the earthen floor scratching the crusty ground in a search for water. A bottle of cheap André champagne was nestled between me and the armrest of the swing, and I held tight to a fluted crystal champagne glass, a wedding present from my college roommate four years ago this month.

On a wooden fence post in the front yard, a black and grey roadrunner stood like a desert sentinel alternating his view between the mountainous horizon and me. He was an alien to me just like my surroundings, and he shared no resemblance to the robins or cardinals I had been used to seeing back east. He was not ugly but he was not the cartoon character I had grown up with on Saturday mornings either, beep beeping as he outwitted the conniving coyote, and sped through an animated desert leaving behind a puff of comic strip smoke. He was quiet with terse spiky feathers and wild black eyes. The black quill plume on his head rose and sank as he surveyed the landscape that included me. I think we stared at one another, or at least I had fixed my gaze on him between rolling tears and gulps of alcoholic effervescence; half out of wonder, the other half in disbelief.

I wanted my husband and it slowly dawned on me that another, faraway desert, and this conflict or war or whatever the hell it was, separated us after we had just completed a nine-month separation, Jack in Okinawa, me in New Orleans. I wanted what I had not had for almost a year, him, his body and intimacy. I wanted to be made love to, and even something as commonplace as companionship—what I thought was common—those were the things I wanted, the ingredients of a spicy marriage rue.

I had sacrificed time with Jack, given away a year of our marriage to finish my MBA from Tulane. I had begun my degree the day after our honeymoon and confirmed with Jack that I would finish school no matter where the Marines took him. I would not follow him until I was done. Maybe I had made selfish choices. My decisions separated us for the last nine months of my schooling and now the call of a government, to a part of the world I did not recognize, made choices for us that I had not anticipated when I chose to marry a Marine. We had sacrificed our union to each other in response to promises we had made, and oaths taken but not fully understood. It seemed as though tragedy loomed, and at night when desert winds threw sand against the bedroom window, I had only the darkness and cold metal of our brass bed available to my touch.

When Desert Storm ended, my husband returned home skinny and dried out. Tears for time lost found a home on his cheeks. I was filled with anger. Saddam was still alive but Kuwait was liberated. Give me a break. Eventually, the troupe of Yucca Sluts disbanded moving to places like Camp Pendleton, St. Louis, Charlotte and Massachusetts. Our men returned home in a disjointed order, and our camaraderie disappeared as we retreated into marital bedrooms of safety, reacquainting ourselves with intimacy and touch, and the strangers that were our spouses.

The roadrunner returned the day I picked my husband up from base. I had not seen him but once or twice during the time Jack was in Kuwait. But the sentinel returned to the very same fence post with the same black eyes. He was like God's messenger. I believed he had secretly watched my exploits and now, he heralded Jack's return. He was a mute that had seen everything but did not judge, and I trusted him.

ORION

By Charlotte Brock

I started off my time in Camp Taqqadum, 12 miles from Fallujah, in high spirits, ready to do this thing, fight this war, set up communications in the camp, go out on convoys, DO STUFF. I volunteered for the night shift, from 3 p.m. to 3 a.m. early on because it would allow me to do more during the day. I would walk the mile or so from the communications compound to the female tent alone, in the early hours of the morning, with my right hand at my hip, fingers grazing my pistol, my eyes searching both the night sky for stars and the sand at my feet for holes, steps, or barbed wire. Every night I tried to remember the names of the stars and constellations from the stargazing handbook I had brought with me. Ursa Major was easy to find earlier in the evening, and Orion kept me company on my walk home. He was my favorite, and I came to look upon him as my friend.

Although exhausted by the early hours of the morning, I was exhilarated, excited, and full of hope. I was happy to be where I was, serving my country, and leading Marines in a combat zone. I was where I was supposed to be, and anything could happen.

I slept only a few hours a night, between 4 AM and about 8 AM, when the sun would light up the inside of the orange tent like a pumpkin. Waking up, already in PT gear, I'd swing my legs over the side of the cot, slip my feet into shower shoes, throw my towel around my shoulders, grab my toilet kit (a gift from my mother, it looked more like a tool box), and head towards the flap of blinding whiteness at the opening of the tent. No matter how light it seemed inside the tent, it was always painfully bright outside; you could hardly make it to the next tent over without your sunglasses. I wore mine on a string around my neck, whether I was in PT gear or desert digitals. The walk to the head was a couple hundred feet, but seemed much longer because you were walking in sand as fine as powdered sugar the whole time.

My first couple months in Iraq were relatively uneventful—I do say relatively. The camp was hit by indirect fire (IDF) the first night we got to

TQ and the rockets and mortars didn't stop for more than a few weeks at a time while I was there. We didn't have it nearly as bad as some camps, like Camp Fallujah, which got hit every day, but we received IDF often enough to make you go to bed at night wondering if you'd wake up in the morning—or if that rocket or mortar might just, randomly, land on you. One morning about three weeks into the deployment, I was about to fall asleep after staying up even later than usual—till ten A.M. A "BOOM" yanked me back into consciousness, into my sweaty, suddenly rigid body, into the hot tent. It seemed pretty far off but I knew what it was. I had learned to differentiate incoming fire from outgoing. Outgoing was "boom." Incoming was a rounder, fuller sound, "BOOM!"

I got up and poked my head out of the tent. Others were doing the same. Yep, it was incoming. Oh well, not much to do but try and get some sleep. Sit your butt back on the cot, rub your feet together to get the sand off, lay down, close your eyes, say a quick prayer just in case God does exist, think of going to sleep, of dreaming strange dreams, of floating off into your subconscious... BOOM!! This time louder, closer. You feel it in your whole body, the ground vibrates, and the tent shakes. Your heart pounds in your chest, in your ears, adrenaline flows, painfully, through your veins. Deep breath, repeat maneuvers from first mortar attack. Attempt to go to sleep once again: you really are exhausted, your eyes are burning, and you just want to escape from this damn BOOM! world. No such luck. A third BOOM, this one deafening, angry, implacable, it makes the ground shake and turns your body to silly putty. Good thing you were lying down.

There was no sleeping after that. I couldn't go back to the rack and lie there waiting for the fourth and final round to zero in on my tent. Weary, scared, weak, but determined not to show it, I strolled over to the Communications Compound and made sure my guys were all accounted for.

After the triple-mortar-attack day, I had a very difficult time getting to sleep. I put off going to bed, dreaded falling asleep; the sound of the mortars resonated louder than ever as I tried to turn my mind off and relax into slumber. It's funny how you get used to it though. Although normally I am an eight-hour a night kind of gal, I went for weeks sleeping two, three, four hours a day. I didn't really want to sleep at all. I wanted to live every moment of my life, to be aware of every sight and every sound, every person I talked with, and every breath that I took.

Things really started getting eventful about a month later. I started going to the Mortuary Affairs (MA) bunker after meeting the MA Officer-in-Charge, Mike Connelly, in the Dining Facility. He was very witty, making everybody laugh with his dry, wry, un-politically correct humor. But there was something dark and sad beneath the stand-up-comedian act. His smile was bitter and never reached his eyes. As I got to know him, he started sharing his worries with me; MA was not easy work. He struggled with the horror of it, the daily encounters with death, the tragedy of sending men home to their mothers and wives. I listened to Mike talk. I offered him my friendship and my sympathy. I opened my heart and my arms to this lonely, weary, haunted man. Soon, I offered to help him in his work. I honestly didn't expect he would take me up on that offer, but he did. I started working at MA in my "off" time, the twelve hours a day I wasn't on duty as a Communications Officer.

The other MA Marines and I received the bodies of U.S. Service members, as well as those of our Iraqi enemies. The MA Marines had coined the name "Fallen Angels" for the dead Americans. We tried to get ID on them, made notes on wounds and tattoos, and filled out paperwork, then sent them to Kuwait, their last stop before arriving to the U.S.

I only worked in Mortuary Affairs for a couple months. About 35 Angels. One day, out of the blue, my Company Commander, Major Danale, asked me to go for a "ride around the camp" with him. While I was trapped next to him in the pick-up truck, he announced: "Charlotte, I don't want you going to M.A. anymore."

"Going to the MA building?"

"Working there. I don't want you there when they have to work."

"For how long?"

"Let's say a month."

Silence. I blinked back tears. A month was forever. There could be Angels coming in tonight. I needed to be there. "Why, Sir?" I had to ask.

"I'm worried about you. Other people are. Chief Warrant Officer Connelly told me he was worried about you too."

I swallowed my tears and my impulse to keep arguing, to protest, to tell him he was being unfair and giving me an unnecessary and inappropriate order. Staring at the dusty brown road ahead, he muttered, "I want you to go the Mental Health guys too. Just to get checked out."

So now I was crazy. I was a weak officer, a woman who had cried in front of him and therefore must be having problems coping with deployment, with the war, with Mortuary Affairs. I fixed my gaze on the bleak, flat, treeless landscape and seethed in silence.

As soon as I could get away from the Communications site, I headed straight to the MA bunker, where Mike not only worked but lived. In a rage, I walked into his living quarters and glared at him. I could hardly get the words out.

"How could you tell Major Danale you're worried about me? How could you do that to me? What is he talking about, what is he worried about, are you worried? Or do you just want me out because I'm taking attention off of you, because I'm better at it than you, because you couldn't have written the MA SOP without me and you know it!" I was crying by now. "Why didn't you tell me, why didn't you talk to me, why did you go to my boss? How could you do that to me?"

Mike, a shade whiter than his usual pallor, put his face in his hands and in a shaky, whispery voice told me: "I am worried about you. Look at you." I was a mess now, to be sure. But an hour ago? I had shed some pounds, but wasn't that from all the walking in the 120-degree heat? I probably looked tired, but wasn't I supposed to, being a Marine in a combat zone and all? I had started smoking again, after five years, but don't many Marines smoke on deployments? Look at me? What about me?

"This is because of you!" I wiped tears and snot from my face. "I'm not upset about MA, I mean yeah, it's hard, but I was dealing with it fine, I was doing fine, I was fine. But now I guess I wasn't fine, since other people are worried about me. What is that supposed to mean? What have I been doing? Have I been acting crazy without even knowing about it? Why couldn't you have just talked to me? I would have stopped coming if you wanted me to. This is your place, I am here because you want me to be, if you tell me to go, I have to go. Why didn't you just talk to me?" Tears were streaming down my face again, my nose was running, I was blubbering.

Mike explained that he hadn't gone to my boss; Major Danale had come to him and asked how I was doing. He had answered frankly that he was worried about how I was holding up. The conversation with Mike was over.

I stumbled out into the hellish heat and blinding light, not knowing where to turn. I was lost. I had no idea how much MA had meant to me until it was taken away. I was devastated. I had kept a pretty good handle on things until then, I thought. I had been "dealing." MA was the direction my life had taken; it made me feel like I was doing something right, something good, something worthy. I wasn't bad at my regular job as a Communications Officer, standing a 12-hour watch, seven days a week, in the Systems Control center, but I wasn't great at it either, and I sure didn't have any passion for it. Sitting in the Systems Control Center, waiting for a phone call or an email telling me communications had gone down, I felt so static, so far from the fight. If I didn't show up for work, nothing would happen, except that I'd get in trouble. The Staff NCOs could stand the watch just as well without me there. MA though... MA was different.

MA was a world in which nothing mattered but the body lying on the table. In MA, the constant anxiety of dealing with the tangle of relationships I was in—Mike wasn't the only man I had grown close to—the pressure coming down on me from all sides as a woman in this 95% male camp—none of this mattered. I wasn't important, the Angels were. I was there only for them.

And now this duty was being taken away. What would my life mean anymore? And why? Because they were "worried" about me? My male chauvinist of a boss, who never set a foot in the MA bunker himself, didn't want me in there anymore? What right did he have to tell me what to do in my off-duty time, as long as I wasn't doing anything illegal? And Mike, who had cried in my arms numerous times, who had lost so much weight and become so pale that he looked half dead himself, how could he turn around and accuse me of not coping well? Mike, whose hands I had held and shoulders I had massaged, whom I had listened to for hours talk about his nightmares and his feelings of depression and helplessness, whom I had watched moaning, fighting, and crying in his sleep as I sat by his bed, who was he to tell me he was worried about me? I was doing a whole lot better than him! It was a bad joke that I should be the one pulled out of MA. I knew why though: I was a woman. I couldn't be expected to deal with this kind of thing. I wasn't strong enough. The incontrovertible proof of it was that I had cried: once when trying to talk to my CO about being treated unfairly by Marines in the company; once at a church service, the first I had attended in months; and now, here, in Mike's room.

From that day until the end of my first OIF deployment I no longer lived; I simply survived. I hung onto every shred of hope I could find, because my life seemed to get worse every day. When I walked my lonely walk through the desert at night I barely looked at the ground anymore. I was already low; tripping and falling meant nothing. I kept my eyes on Orion, and begged him not to leave me alone.

SWEAT

By Debra A. Pochie

The last day of my childhood innocence started with gently filtered early morning sunlight and the smell of yellow jasmine carried in by a river wind. Any room at my Grandma's house on Bay Street could have been mine but the enclosed back porch that faced the Beaufort River, was my private heaven. Awaking slowly, the familiar sounds of bluebirds and Grandma's soft singing voice competed to lift the dream fog surrounding me. Trying to hold onto that incredibly comfortable feeling you get just before going to sleep or before waking, I burrowed further down under the light cotton quilt and covered my head with my feather pillow. The sound of the sliding glass door told me that my time in bed was over.

"Time to get up girl and shake a tail feather," Grandma said in a lilting Southern accent.

Groaning, I rose from the antique fold up bed. I didn't have to wonder what breakfast would be. Breakfast at Grandma's was always whole milk mixed with two tablespoons of powdered chocolate flavored Nestlé's Quik, cheese toast on white bread toasted and slathered with butter and cheddar cheese slices. Plopping myself into the kitchen chair, watching her reach into the fridge for a one liter glass bottle of Coca Cola, the realization hit me that she never actually ate breakfast. She just had that one glass of caffeine laden carbonated syrup to get her body kick started in order to face the day. I think that glass of Coke was the best way to cool off during the dog days of summer. The heat was hitting the Low Country with a vengeance and even in the early morning hours the air was sticky and humid, lying over the town like a wet blanket.

"So what are your plans for today?" Grandma asked.

Pulling my hair back into a ponytail, I said, "The chain on my bike is broken so Dad agreed to pick me up."

With a nod she finished pouring her Coke and walked down the hall towards her room at the back of the house. Saturdays for my Grandma consisted of hanging laundry in the morning and penny bridge with lots of

Peach Brandy in the afternoon at the Garden Club, with what she called her "Lady friends."

I vaguely heard her say as she walked away, "Don't forget your key."

Picking at the lukewarm cheese and drinking my equally warm milk, I closed my eyes and tried to hear and smell the sounds of the beach where I would have much rather been going that day. With less than an hour left to get ready, I pushed the daydream away. With a sigh, I scraped my dishes and put them in the dishwasher. I lived part time with my Grandma and part time with my folks so I kept clothes for any occasion at Grandma's. I decided on a my white "Keep On Truckin" t-shirt—I had begged for it when our family lived out West—and my favorite pair of beaten up jean-shorts with all the fraying strings on the edges. I couldn't help but smile knowing what my grandmother's reaction would be when she saw me. For some reason those strings drove my Grandmother nuts. Time and time again I would have to stop her from cutting them off. "It's cool," I always said. She always responded with the "Look." Sitting on the edge of the bed I pulled on my white canvas Kid's sneakers.

Grandma's voice drifted down the hallway "Wash your face," she said.

Why she insisted on constant face washing was beyond me. If you were upset you washed your face, if you were hot you washed your face, in any crises you had better wash your face, and no matter what was wrong with you it was because you hadn't gone to the bathroom. Ignoring the whole wash-your-face bit, I walked out to the carport and sat on a milk crate in the shade.

A stack of newspapers and inserts had to be rolled and I was running out of time fast. Forty times to insert, roll, and add a rubber band with a final snap. When I was finally done I stacked all the newspapers tightly together in my canvas newspaper tote. I closed the top and sat back against my Grandmother's blue Mercury Cougar, being careful to avoid the film of yellow pollen that enveloped everything each spring. I watched as a steady stream of Beaufortonians passed by. Where people found anything fun to do in this town on a Saturday was beyond me. Beaufort was not a big town, and in 1983 and for a thirteen-year-old girl it was void of anything to do when school was out.

My father's white Chrysler pulled into the driveway. I pulled the large canvas bag up and onto my shoulder, wishing it wasn't so hot and thanking God I didn't have to use my bike today. I walked out to the car already feeling the beads of sweat forming between my shoulder blades, plastering the white cotton t-shirt to my back. I opened the passenger door and placed my canvas tote in the middle of the front seat to ensure easy access as I tossed newspapers from the window.

Dad looked over and said, "Ready to go?"

I nodded yes and rolled down my window preparing for our first stop. My father was a rather large man with reddish blond hair. Both are linked to German ancestry. His family was a part of the first German immigration to Beaufort County and my Grandmother, his mother, constantly reminded her family about their heritage. "If you don't know who you are, then how do you know where you are going?" she would chant.

Dad had recently retired after serving twenty-two years and two Vietnam tours with the Army. My father had been stationed at Fort Huachuca for four years before he retired six months before our morning paper delivery drive. The move from Fort Huachuca, Arizona to Dad's hometown, Beaufort, South Carolina had been a huge conversion for all of us. Culture shock does not even begin to describe moving from Western browns to East Coast greens, from military base to civilian neighborhood. My sense of balance was so rocked I felt at times like I'd been transported to another planet.

As we pulled up to the first house I readied myself for the moment I would lean out and throw the newspaper. If I threw the paper correctly it would land on the stairs of the house and not in a bush. With a flick of the wrist, the neatly rolled paper was flying over the well-manicured lawn and landing on the front steps. Easy enough to do when the steps are almost twelve feet wide with columns on either side. My neighborhood newspaper route was located in the Historic Downtown district, where my Grandma lived. The houses were large and close together. Giant oak trees provided plenty of shelter from the hot southern sun and the river almost always provided a cool breeze.

The route usually took thirty to forty five minutes by ten-speed bike so it only took twenty minutes in my dad's Chrysler before I was grabbing the last paper and throwing it out.

Sitting back I let the wind from the open car window caress my face and dry the dampness away.

My father eased the Chrysler onto Ribaut road. We passed the junior high school and I thought about the essay I had yet to complete for the

English Makeup class I had flunked my way into last school year and had to go to this summer for three horrific weeks. Ms. Adams the English teacher loved to find new and improved ways to teach. This year's summer school experiment in teaching was a Goldfish bowl with two inch white strips of paper. Written on these slips of paper was a year. A student was chosen weekly to draw a date from the Goldfish bowl. The class would research that year and over the weekend we had to complete an essay on what we had learned. This week the date had been 1967, two years before I was even born. Procrastinator that I am, page one hadn't even been started. Reaching into the canvas bag I pulled out a three-subject notebook and a pen, and reached over to turn down the Jazz station my father always blared.

"Dad I have one day to finish an essay about the year 1967, do ya think you could you help me with it?" I said.

Dad looked over at me and smiled. After a moment he said, "That was one crazy year for me, Deb. The Vietnam War was still going strong and for all we knew people over in the States were going crazy. I heard stories of women burnin' bras and men burnin' flags. Drugs hadn't really been a big deal before I left, but it seemed to catch on pretty damn quick in other places, and the type of Rock-n-roll my friends and I had grown up with was all but disappearin' on the radio stations. My life overseas was kind'a sheltered so all we got were bits and pieces of what went on over in the States. I guess you could say it all boiled down to a time of free love and personal independence for most people. Me, I was too busy fighting a war to get caught up in much."

He stopped talking while I wrote in my English notebook. We were almost home when he asked me the question that would change my whole life. He had been glancing over at me when he finally spoke up and said, "Deb, have you ever seen a man suck a woman's breast?"

I froze, my brain trying to wrap itself around the words he had just said and rejecting those same words as incredible nonsense. Just when I thought maybe I had heard him wrong he said, "Have you ever seen a man with a woman?"

I looked over and into the face of a stranger. I broke out in a cold sweat that had nothing to do with the mid-day heat. It seemed as if every inch of my skin was crawling. I reached for the door handle to open the car door not caring that the car was traveling at forty-five miles an hour down a busy main street. Desperate to escape from the sick feeling lodged like a heavy sharp stone in the bottom of my stomach, I suddenly began to wish I had skipped breakfast. Dad noticed my hand on the car door handle and pulled over to the side of the road.

In mere moments I had yanked open the door and was running without any sense of direction, not caring as long as it was far away from the picture permanently burned into my brain of the cold, leering smile pasted on his lips. Aside from the words he had said, that image continued to echo through my mind. Less than ten words laid my world and, yes, the last of my childhood to waste. As I blindly ran away from my father's voice, I cried for the death of that innocence and knew nothing in life would ever be the same.

Slowing down after a block or two I found a stump hidden behind a wooden shed so I sat down and let the torrent of tears fall. My heart was dying, with that death came sobs that seemed to pull out a part of my soul. The sobs shook my small frame each time they passed my lips and the air seemed to thin as if the darkness of my situation were taking even the oxygen from the air.

Breathe, breathe, I repeated like a mantra in my mind. I recited the word over and over until I had control again. When my breathing finally became normal and the tears slowed, a numbness that seemed to cover my entire body set in leaving me feeling hollow and, for a moment, blissfully devoid of any emotion. I lankly stared ahead when I realized I was only a few blocks from our apartment complex. One thought kept going through my head, "Home." Attached to that one word were a million questions. How do I go home now? What do I do when I get home? What will it be like at home now? How do I explain to my Mom what happened when I didn't understand it myself? With my heart and mind now racing once again I decided to hide out until my Mom got home from work. Now that I had a plan, I looked at the watch my dad had given me last Christmas. A part of me wanted to tear that watch off and feel it crush beneath the rubber sole of my Ked's, but I loved that silver watch with the diamond chip set in its onyx face.

Two o'clock in the afternoon and Mom wouldn't be home until four. I crossed through neighboring backyards avoiding the streets until I reached the paved bike path leading to the new wooden playground structures the apartment complex had recently built. I walked up the ramp and into the fort-like structure. The closed in quietness and cool atmosphere felt like a balm covering my stripped and quivering nerves.

I sat in the corner furthest away from the opening and pulled my legs up so my chin could rest on my knees. Slowly my mind drifted and my muscles relaxed, adrenalin slowed. An irresistible urge to fall asleep wrapped itself around me. Slowly my eyes closed. The crunch of leaves and snapping twigs jerked me awake. I looked at my watch. Fifteen minutes and Mom would be home. I stood and brushed the pine needles and dust from the back of my legs. I decided to slide down the green slide attached on the opposite end of the wooden fort. As I slid down I couldn't help but remember the times when Dad had caught me at the end of one slide or another. My heart gave a little squeeze and a new batch of tears began to cascade down my cheeks once again.

MCWS 6

25 August – 22 September 2007

Participants:
David
Shana
Jerry
Vivian
Charlotte
Jack
"N" – The Narrator

I don't know what can become of this story, but I wrote this after listening to a sermon. I would like to parallel the life of this girl with the falling of the Twin Towers. The falling of the towers shows how we are blinded by the sun of our own success and desires, that we believe we are safe, until on the rise of our sunny day comes a storm we were not anticipating and it leaves us unprepared, exposed, and vulnerable. The song comes from the sorrow that we experience and it is sung to encourage. But who gives us the song and who is the song? After being laid exposed and vulnerable through the ashes of pain and broken dreams comes a song...a new song.

—Shana, MCWS 6, commenting on her story idea

For Guido Farinaro USMC These are yours—not mine! With love and respect, your platoon leader, Pete Pace.

—From one of seven handwritten notes, with a set of his four star rank insignia attached to each note, left by General Peter Pace at the Vietnam Memorial Wall on the day he retired, October 1, 2007; "Peter Pace," http://en.wikipedia.org/wiki/Peter_Pace

BROKEN BRIDGES

By spring of 2007, I felt as though I was crawling from under a rock—a heavy Marine-green rock with a small town balanced on top. Two years had vanished in my apprenticeship writing, teaching, and developing Milspeak since earning my creative writing degree. The outcome was hardly what I had expected. I left my teaching job at the small town private school and was again unemployed. I had lost a publishing contract, and I was no closer to having a finished book than I had been when first beginning my miserable memoir in 2004. While I hadn't expected great things from Milspeak for myself, the writers were producing remarkable memoir, filled with the everyday of military life. I didn't want their work to go unnoticed, but I wasn't sure what to do. Milspeak didn't even have a website to showcase their work. The Milspeak project filled me with uncertainty. I still felt inadequate as a workshop leader and I wasn't sure what Milspeak was accomplishing. I had no time to apply for grants. Had there been time, I wouldn't have known where to begin. My self-confidence had taken a major hit during my teaching year. I was disoriented by failure to establish a second career and by my fears of doing more harm than good through Milspeak. Like Sisyphus, doomed to forever roll a rock uphill, I kept moving forward on the road toward excellence by doing what I thought was the next right thing, over and over, but at a severe price. I had become a stranger to myself. Step-by-step, I was learning how little I really knew and understood about the world.

The 2006-07 school year had ended unhappily. The experience worsened when one of two bridges between my island home and the mainland were rendered unusable. A barge captain drove a crane attached to his vessel into the bridge. Repairs lasted until fall 2007, adding half an hour each way to my hour-long drive to and from the school. The wait to cross onto Lady's Island from Port Royal Island sometimes lasted hours. On other days, the bridge was closed to traffic, which meant driving an extra thirty minutes to our second bridge over the Beaufort River, a drawbridge. On those days, the wait was interminable.

To reward myself for making it through the school year, I had signed up for a writers' conference. The stresses of the past year's teaching fiasco melted away with each mile of the several hundred I drove away from Beaufort, the South, and my teaching and publishing failures. The conference would be my first, and I hoped it would help me resolve some of my writing problems. I expected it to be an immersion in writing with other writers. It was, but the critique of my manuscript during the conference workshop was a trying experience that only added to my insecurities as a writer. Still, I did learn from the experience.

Out of four meeting days, my group spent only a few minutes discussing my work. That was not the case for the others in my workshop group. My synopses of their work and their manuscripts with my marginal notes were given to each writer. In return, the scribbling returned to me on my critique day was barely legible or could not be read at all. One member of my workshop group returned a copy of my manuscript covered with red ink. Another gave me nothing—no notes, no returned manuscript. The notes I did receive were useless because they either couldn't be read or said nothing of value, like Nice Work. It was obvious to me that no one in my workshop had spent time with my work as I had with his or hers. Not even the workshop group leader provided written comments on my manuscript. To me, this was a statement of value—my writing hadn't been worth spending time with.

I came away from my critique without any meaningful comments on writing I had struggled to bring to life despite the exhaustion and burn out that I was experiencing following a horrible school year. I had made time to treat others' manuscripts with respect; my own was shoved aside like wet newspaper. Was I so blind to my own flaws as a writer that I was simply wasting readers' time and my own by trying to write? I had struggled with the writing of others in my workshop, writing that was often difficult and sometimes academic, not only so that I could bring meaningful comments to workshop for those who had paid the same fee to attend, but also because I believe that everyone's work deserves respect, no matter how poor/dull or brilliant the manuscript or writer might be. Why wasn't that respect returned? Some of the workshop readers assumed I had abused the children in my charge. Had I? Was I so blind to my defects that I had abused those children?

Looking back, no matter how unintentional the damping of my spirit had been during the critique of my writing, being ignored by my workshop hurt. A judgment had been made—my writing was worthless. The Tarot cards had been laid on the table, but no one was willing to read the story they told. Was this because a stereotype had found flesh: I was a Marine—how could I have a brain; how could I be a writer; how could I be a teacher? Or was I being overly sensitive?

The written word is a bridge, a commute, a communication between the writer's and the reader's internal worlds. My writing was apparently as broken as the bridge in Beaufort. Based upon the response of my workshop and our leader, my prospects of ever writing something a reader might want to read were nil. Writing was proving to be as much a waste of time as sitting at the wrong end of a broken bridge. No one wanted to read my work and no one cared about my perspective on the great experiment that is life. Who was I to be leading Milspeak? I was the ultimate Fool, the Hanged Man dangling before the public, all of them misreading my part in the experiment; I, like Sisyphus, long refusing to let go the rock that for me is writing, was made ready to let go.

But there was another problem at the conference, a more personal, deeper problem. The emotional breakdown foretold by my physical breakdown during the school year had finally arrived. I spent most of my time at the conference crying uncontrollably, a symptom of PTSD. I couldn't stop the tears. The more I cried, the more of a freak I became—to myself. I didn't know what the others were thinking. I didn't ask them what they thought and they didn't ask why I was emotional—the other writers steered clear of me. No wonder! All the hurt, anguish, and ostracism of the past teaching year, all the rejections of my working life and my writing life took over my emotions. I was subconsciously reliving the pain of a life filled with rejection, of not fitting in, of being misunderstood, of being misread. My body was letting me know what was happening by leaking pain through my eyes.

I was witnessing the destruction of my dream for the writing life that I had pursued since I was a child, and I had let down a mentor—I was too damned dumb to write for a reader. I was also coming closer to accepting that I have PTSD, professionally diagnosed or not. I was in the process of diagnosing myself while the syndrome unfolded. Why did my life choices so often lead to failure and to emotional pain? In every community I had chosen to participate as a contributing member, I always won the role of outcast. I didn't want the starring role in the disastrous life story of a misfit. I was tired of living a melodramatic fandango. I wanted to know where and with whom I belonged.

On the evening of my critique day, I did the unthinkable and threw away the copies of my manuscript returned to me by workshop members. I made plans to leave the conference early, before the last workshop meeting and the farewell celebration scheduled to take place the next day. Enough of my own intellectual posturing and of trying to fit among people out of my league! I called John Blair and wailed. He and his wife, Jane, calmed me down. Thank God for friends. After packing my gear, I spent the rest of the night in a diner watching characters of the night come and go: the Empress serving my pie and engaging me in quiet conversation, the Page of Swords with his tattooed and pierced retinue clambering about a booth, the Magician perusing his newspaper, and me, the Queen of Cups, drinking coffee and forgetting her troubles in a scene from the past, the workers and customers in a diner so familiar to one who once had been a waitress.

There, in the diner, my staying so long unquestioned, I felt I belonged. In the same manner, I would later recognize my place among my students in the young men and women pursuing their futures and fulfilling their educational goals at Technical College of the Lowcountry, and I would find my place among military people stepping across the threshold of The Blackbird Zone. In the diner that night, I realized that leading Milspeak wasn't wrong. Milspeak is where I belong as a writer and mentor. And never, not ever, would Milspeak writers experience in our workshops what I had experienced in the writers' conference workshop. Teachers come in many forms. Their lessons are sometimes hard. My many teachers—books, people, experience—have taught me what sort of teacher, writer, workshop leader, and human being I want to become, and what I never want to become.

What of Sisyphus, broken bridges, and Tarot? What were these signs trying to tell me? The myth of Sisyphus, who was forced to roll his rock uphill because he had revealed one of Zeus's secrets, does not include a broken bridge. What would Sisyphus have done had he encountered a broken bridge on his way up the mountain? He would have found a way around or over the abyss. Both the Hanged Man and the Fool represent beginnings, the turmoil that precedes them, and the call to action. I answered the call. Re-see the work. Revise. Regroup. Retain what is working and discard the rest. Leave the past behind. Roll your rock, your pen, until you can roll no more. Take a deep breath, shake it out, begin anew the task before you. It is the task of your life, your contribution to society, your calling. Abandon yourself to your calling; nurture yourself, believe in your work, especially when no one else does. Move on.

On my return from the writer's conference, I stopped revising my miserable memoir and decided to try growing Milspeak. Maybe a civilian workshop would pay enough to fund Milspeak. Then, I could rent space off base to hold workshops, while keeping the workshop for military people free of charge and providing funds to pay MCWS guest writers. I'm grateful that Marine Corps Community Services continues to support Milspeak, but holding the workshop on base presents problems. Unless they are retired or disabled, once a service member leaves active duty he or she no longer has base privileges, including access to bases. Because Milspeak has no income, is unfunded and has no overhead, I was unable to rent a workshop facility off base. The local library informed me their building couldn't be used for my purpose. If I could make Milspeak self-supporting by holding a paying civilian workshop, I would be able to rent space for a military workshop even a homeless person could attend. Volunteers are hard to find, and I didn't have funding to bring guest writers to Milspeak seminars. Holding a civilian creative writing workshop might provide funds to do so.

In an attempt to create income for Milspeak, to make it self-supporting, I developed a memoir workshop program for civilians during the summer of 2007. Several interested writers contacted me about the Memoir and Personal Essay Seminar (MPES) for civilians, but no one wanted to pay the small fee ($160) for the five-week course. Those who responded to my ads—$400 paid for four ads in *The Beaufort Gazette*—wanted me to work with them for no fee at all. Instead of creating funding for Milspeak, I was creating more work for myself. I couldn't say no—I read the manuscripts people sent to me, provided suggestions for revision, and then I cancelled the workshop. Not long afterwards, an ad appeared in another local paper announcing a more established author would hold a creative writing workshop. The clinch line from my ad in *The Gazette* announced the new workshop by a more experienced and successful writer: "Do You Have A Story To Tell, But Don't Know Where To Begin?"

That a more accomplished writer would plagiarize my advertising idea was terrifically funny and baffling, an ironic ending to an honest effort.

The civilian workshop's failure to launch was disappointing, but doing the work to build it was rewarding. I needed to find a way to distinguish between the civilian workshop and the military workshop. I decided to use Milspeak as an umbrella title for the programs, with CWS (Creative Writing Seminar) representing the military program, and MPES (Memoir and Personal Essay Seminar) representing the civilian program. I don't know where or when *milspeak* was first used (it's not in my dictionaries), but my first use of it was during the 1980s when we troops discussed the new military language we were learning. Milspeak seemed a word perfectly suited for describing a writing program developed by and for military people. Fred Siedentopf, a thirty-year Marine Corps Veteran who attended MCWS 6, and has a great sense of humor, provides an explanation:

> For some reason, milspeak, mil speak, or mil-speak never appears anywhere on the Internet with an explanation and also never appears in any DOD publication of acronyms, abbreviations, or military terms. It only appears as a title for a list of terms that are considered 'Milspeak.' It therefore isn't an accepted word even in English slang terms. I would be reluctant to provide my explanation as 'fact' and give it only as speculation from an old warhorse's beer ravaged brain.

My teaching life continued to grow that summer. Although I was hesitant to teach following the previous year's disastrous results, Technical College of the Lowcountry's Dean of Arts and Sciences invited me to return. With her encouragement and support, I agreed to teach two courses during the fall semester. Although adjunct work wasn't fulltime, at least teaching those courses would pay my car payment during the four-month semester. I also began pursuing a fulltime teaching position. I had never wanted to move again following military service, particularly not from my home on Coosaw Island. Failure readied acceptance that I would not find a fulltime teaching position without moving. After opening a career services account with Association of Writing Professionals and requesting letters of recommendation from writing instructors and professional acquaintances, I began sending applications to universities advertising for a creative nonfiction professor in AWP's online employment listings and in *Chronicle of Higher Education*. My applications to universities went as far as Beirut and Saudi Arabia. Each application required a resume revision. During this application period, I discovered I was unqualified to teach at foreign embassy schools because I didn't have state teaching certification. I didn't apply only for teaching positions. The journalism and defense industries heard from me, as well as Embry-Riddle Aeronautical University's Beaufort location.

By end of year, the only interview request I received was with Embry-Riddle. A woman half my age interviewed me for the position as an administrative assistant in the Beaufort campus's office. Embry-Riddle didn't offer me the job and didn't say why, but the situational analogy didn't escape my notice—thirty years before, in 1977, when I was nineteen years old, my employment path had led from job to job to a fruitless search for employment in St. Louis. "Something will turn up," Mom had said at the end of that summer. It had. I enlisted in the Corps in 1977, an accident of chance. In 2007, I believed something would turn up if I kept doing the next right thing.

Also that summer, a newsletter informed me that MoveOn, a political-left activist organization, was planning candlelight vigils for peace across the nation. I wanted to be part of that. As a child, I had yearned for a role in the 1960s peace movement. I volunteered to organize a vigil in Beaufort at the Lady's Island boat ramp. A New York MoveOn organizer called me to orchestrate the event. I invited Milspeak writers to attend. They must have had a clearer picture of what the event might become because none of them participated. One Milspeak writer began sending me warnings and forwarded emails written by conservative pundits. I began to wonder if anyone would sign up for MCWS 6, or any future MCWS, if I participated in MoveOn's National Candlelight Vigil to end the war in Iraq, but I had given my word to lead the event. Working for peace is an important mission for veterans and not a betrayal of their service or their country, or a traitorous act. Peace is the Old Warrior's reward. Working for peace is also a means of exercising the Four Freedoms: freedom from fear, freedom from want, freedom of speech, and freedom of religion. To me, participating in the vigil was a pro-peace action, not an anti-war action. Participation was a way of honoring, not dishonoring, the war dead. Others thought differently.

The evening of the vigil was clear and bright. About thirty of us gathered at the boat ramp, including my husband and my friends, John Blair and Dennis Adams. Some of us carried posters. Everyone carried a candle. We formed a circle and read the Calendar of the Dead, a month by month listing of those killed in the Iraq War. Each person in the circle was given a chance to say something about how they felt. One mother shared losing her son to war and another shared her fear of losing her son to the war at hand. Longtime Democrats spoke about their long-term commitment to peace. Young people spoke of peace rallies they had attended. We formed a single line and walked from the boat ramp toward the Woods Memorial Bridge, the drawbridge crossing the Beaufort River. Without crossing the bridge, we turned and walked back to the boat ramp. A truckload of hecklers twice passed by our quiet march.

Old stereotypes die hard.

The next morning, a picture of us walking toward the bridge appeared on the front page of *The Beaufort Gazette* under the headline, "Anti-War Demonstrators March for Peace." I was quoted above the picture: "We might be quiet. We might not show our faces too often. But we do care, and we want a resolution to this war." The headline came despite a long discussion with the reporter the night before to make clear that we were not anti-war but pro-peace, that I personally wanted the government to provide a timeline for ending the war, and that while I was on active duty Colin Powell had promised all troops that we'd never be taken again into a battle without an exit strategy. I believed him then, and I believed when he appeared before the United Nations to inform the world of Iraq's cache of weapons of mass destruction. I believe now that General Powell left the Bush Administration because his trust in the administration was betrayed.

Recovery from betrayal is difficult.

Leaving MoveOn was a personal decision connected neither to hateful letters to the editor printed after the candlelight vigil story appeared nor to MoveOn's misguided campaign to discredit General Petraus, which occurred after I left MoveOn. But my reasons for removing my name from MoveOn's membership roles were legion. When I signed on, I thought the vigil was going to be a simple process of getting it together, holding it, and then moving on. All the preparation—media contact, people contact, and briefing/debriefing by computer calls—was complex, stifling, and stole the spirit from the event. The first phone call from the New

York MoveOn organizer surprised me, but not the second or the last, or the many emails that traveled between us; MoveOn had romanced me with phone calls, emails, and a personal representative because they thought they had found a military pawn in the conservative South. But the earth thrown on the casket carrying my membership in MoveOn was a mass email letter I received from a combat veteran representing a group associated with MoveOn. That this organization had my email address indicated MoveOn was sharing private information without asking. MoveOn's tactics demonstrated that the political far left is as inept as the political far right at solving our country's problems. Neither seems to understand balance or tolerance.

That year the frying pan was full of far bigger fish than me being exploited by many different institutions. Both sides of the political argument over the war in Iraq were making pawns of military people and members of the military family, an abhorrent practice: wounded warriors posed in posters for political gain by the ruling parties; Cindy Sheehan, grief-stricken mother, labeled a crackpot and tied to the political stake by the conservative media, bowed out of the picture; the group of seven generals who had opposed the war and President's Bush's policies—all of them lambasted from every direction for having their say; the many warriors who became media spectacles while being brought to court-martial in a misguided attempt to assuage fears of repeating in Iraq and Afghanistan the horrors of My Lai in Vietnam; and President Bush himself, our Decision Maker in Chief, tortured by both right and left by his Catch-22 decision to go to war in Iraq, a decision willed by the American people, many of whom now deny complicity. Every political action group seemed to be trying to lay claim to what goods they could to promote their agendas and strengthen their brand. Scapegoatism was alive and well in America—Terrorist had replaced Communist in American lingo. No less exploited than others of his stature, General Peter Pace watched his rock roll downhill on a path that led from his position as Chairman of the Joint Chiefs of Staff to a place on the United States Marine Corps' retiree roles. He, like President Bush, found a broken bridge where Sisyphus had found no bridge at all. Did General Pace retire because of marginal chances for reinstatement by a democratic congress? Was it because of his widely reported comments against homosexuality? Or was it because of his courageous stand against Donald Rumsfeld on the issue of torture? For me, the answer is clear—General Pace would not endorse torture.

According to the philosopher Kierkegaard, to exist as an individual is the most terrible thing. General Pace defines that thing, as does President Bush. This situation of leaders being punished for having their say contains part of the answer to the question David Ellard and I debate after each MCWS: Why do so few young active duty military people sign up for the workshop? Where in this country can young military people safely speak their truth about the military experience when even generals are pulled from the plinth for having their say? Our young military men and women sacrifice their all to keep the Four Freedoms alive, and yet they have so little freedom to enjoy. They sacrifice their freedom to secure ours. This silencing of human thought leads to humanity being silenced. If the strong cannot speak their minds in the city on the hill, then how can the weak be expected to? Witnessing their Commander in Chief vilified, their generals unseated, and their fellow warriors accused of war crimes, military people are often too frightened of repercussions to speak or to write about their military experience. They need a safe zone. They need to know they have a say. They need their voices. They need to know they can exercise the Four Freedoms. The Romans understood the importance, the depth, of the warrior's say. Why can't we? An incident that occurred not long after the MoveOn candlelight vigil sheds a bit of light on the answer.

My college composition class works through a research-based course, with each student keeping a research journal about his or her topic of choice. They don't shy away from controversial issues like homosexual marriage, war, abortion, choosing a candidate for the presidential election, or media violence. My students had chosen controversial issues to write about, so I opened class discussions by connecting their topics to local news and connecting that to national news. Not long after the MoveOn candlelight vigil, I spoke with my students about the experience and the resulting newspaper headlines. I mentioned to the class that as we pro-peace marchers were returning to the boat ramp, a truckload of hecklers drove by, turned around, and drove by again. One of my students suddenly turned flag-stripe red. Her mouth began working, but nothing came out.

"Are you choking?" I asked.

"No...no. I'm going to fail this class."

"What? You have an A right now. All you have to do is keep it."

"It was me, Mrs. Drumm. I was in that truck yelling at you."

What could I do but smile, assure her she wouldn't fail for exercising freedom of speech, and go on to use the experience as a teaching example? Never has a student of mine chosen to write about peace. The idea does not seem to be on their radar. Why? My classroom is always filled with teaching examples and reasons why young people do not study peace keeping, peace making, or the nature of peace. The biggest reason is fear of peace, of fearing even to say the word after the 1960s civil war our nation endured, which resulted in a cultural wound that has yet to heal. Americans in general are fearful of being labeled unpatriotic or a terrorist for working for peace. In our culture, peace is sometimes treated as the boogieman under the bed or a decade's worth of unpaid taxes—we have learned to fear talking about peace. In a culture ravaged by terrorism, supporters of peace are too often labeled anti-war rather than pro-peace, as I was by participating in MoveOn's Peace Vigil. This labeling frightens those (particularly young students gathering critical thinking skills) who might want to explore peacemaking and options other than war to find solutions to social and global problems with living. We forget that war is considered just when waging it restores rather than breaks peace. We too often miss the point that peace is the warrior's reward.

In another of my Fall 2007 classes, eleven students, all women, were enrolled in my survey of literature course. They were bright, eager to learn, and to explore correlatives in our daily lives and themes presented in literature. One day, Tara told the class she was campaigning for Barack Obama to win the Democratic Party nomination for president. Not only was she campaigning for Senator Obama, she and her mother were on the ground floor support team for Obama South Carolina. I asked her to bring me a campaign button. She did, along with a pamphlet and a bumper sticker.

The symbol on the bumper sticker, a white sun emerging in a blue sky from beneath the red and white rows of a plowed field, struck me as simple and profound. A white circle surrounded the whole, creating an egg of the symbol, or a stone; a pebble, perhaps, like the one carried by Lieutenant Jimmy Cross in Tim O'Brien's short story "The Things They Carried." A strange pebble, that of Jimmy Cross's, carried in his mouth, tasting of the sea and the girl he'd left behind, a gift from her he thought he loved. That tiny pebble carried more physical weight than the immense survivor's guilt experienced by Cross, a warrior-leader who had lost a man. The burden of the guilt he carried because of that loss drove him to cast away the girl, the love, the world he'd left behind. He was transformed, the tangibles and intangibles of life becoming one in the pebble Jimmy Cross carried in his mouth. Anti-hero becomes hero when he trades fantasies of home for realities of the world he finds himself in.

I began listening carefully to Senator Obama after Tara introduced me to his campaign. For me, the red, white and blue Obama Campaign logo became a symbol of the future, a future that everyone could participate in building, a future we could all share, one built from the dream of an individual who was ready and willing to roll the rock uphill again. Here was a man made ready to honor truth, to speak it, to hear it, no matter from which direction it might come; his, the voice of reason I had been waiting all of my life to hear emerge from American politics.

Life is an energy process, according to psychiatrist Carl Gustav Jung, its goal to achieve a state of rest. In the world of the sublime, the individual clinging to her own world meets the wrathful; the resulting destruction of her ethics opens her world—this happened to me during 2007, through my failure at the private school, failure to secure fulltime employment, failure to revise the miserable memoir, through loss of faith in myself, and loss of faith in the Bush Administration and the Republican Party's capacity to lead. What does any of this have to do with a creative writing program for military people? By the time MCWS 6 met, I was tired and wasn't even sure I wanted to continue with Milspeak. I was fed up with trying to understand the world and its truths. I wanted to transcend the negativity around me and the long ago past that wouldn't stop haunting me. I wanted peace. I began to believe that to achieve that peace, I would have to stop writing for a reader and return to writing to myself. I wasn't even sure I wanted to continue writing creative nonfiction in a world that prefers fantasy to reality. But David Ellard, my MCCS liaison, once again had given his valuable time to coordinate the workshop with me and to market the workshop. MCWS 6 had already been scheduled, and writers had been sending sign-up emails. I had given my word. Before quitting it all and crawling back into my shell, I would hold this one, last, workshop.

Two military wives wanted to participate in MCWS 6, but both wanted to write children's literature. My focus in MCWS has always been on nonfiction narrative and the empowering force of truth telling. Both Lara and Tamika were disappointed when I suggested MCWS might not be right for them. But Lara indicated she had recently rejoined the Society of Children's Book Writers and Illustrators and offered a web address, including the Southeast Regional contact person's information. Despite the many times I've been ignored when querying organizations for assistance with Milspeak, I contacted the Society by email, explaining the Milspeak program and inquiring if a published author might be willing to work with Lara and Tamika. Because of previous failures to involve other organizations and established authors in Milspeak, I was surprised to be contacted by Stephanie Green and Leslie Staub, both accomplished authors willing to work with Lara and Tamika. While I didn't hear from Tamika, nothing unusual after someone says they want to participate, I knew from reading Lara's emails that she was overjoyed to be working in her genre with an author. This experience gave me the idea to further pursue a Milspeak writer-mentoring program and planted the seed for a creative writing workshop for children of deployed military members, which I later developed as Make-A-Book.

Four of eight participating MCWS 6 writers were returning to workshop a new piece. Returning writers add experience to the seminar and assist new writers develop their work. Friendships made during past seminars are renewed and new friendships are made. With their long history of passing the torch and valuing experience, this element of Milspeak is one of the most important factors that make it work for military people. Among MCWS 6 writers were two active duty enlisted Marines, one active duty Marine officer, one spouse of a retired officer, two Civil Service employees, and two retired officers. The Corps, the Merchant Marine, the Army, the Navy, the Civil Service, and the military family were represented in MCWS 6. Five writers attended the second workshop of MCWS 6. Four writers met during our third workshop; four writers completed final drafts. When we met for Celebration Saturday, three writers attended, all retreads.

David returned to write "Drudgery." This memoir possesses movement and energy that perfectly relates the day-to-day work of a military investigator. N's work seems routine, but behind every door he knocks on lurks a surprise, and the ultimate truth behind a crime. David explains:

"The Gray," written during MCWS 5, had once again been a fairly emotional account for me to give; so, I chose to go in another direction with "Drudgery." People often think of law enforcement work as the television or movie depictions. I wanted to draw a picture of how mundane actual, successful law enforcement work could be, while still writing a story that could entertain. Like "Confession," "Drudgery" is laced with a dry humor that may not be for everyone, but some readers will appreciate it. Who hasn't had that experience where you continue to whittle away at a goal at work or otherwise where you don't expect to get anything more than a pile of shavings? Then when you least expect it, as long as you haven't given up already, you get the perfect result you were hoping for at the beginning. What most people don't realize is that 95% of law enforcement successes come after whittling down an ugly case.

Jack wrote a reflective, informative essay "Leaving the Service," an account of his reentry into the civilian working world following active duty during the Korean War. Jack's essay is peppered with advice for military people finding their way back into a civilian job following active service. Jack sums up his second Milspeak experience:

> In 1945 the word was that an employer was <u>required</u> to keep your job open until your return if you were called to active duty in service. This piece was intended to guide the service person to the reality that such promises were hot air and that their future was in their own hands and could be positive if approached with conviction.

Jerry, a Vietnam Veteran who served in the Army, gives a heart-rending account of his work in a Vietnamese orphanage during the war. His story is one that many veterans share. Our service members are often beloved by children living in war zones, but service members' contributions to the welfare of these children are seldom shared through the media.

Vivian returned for a third Milspeak workshop to write "Yucca Sluts." Vivian's continued willingness to share her story is courageous. Her experience will resonate with anyone who has experienced a brush with adultery and stepped back before crossing the line. Her story builds understanding about the difficulty of living the military life, particularly during wartime when situation intensity results in an overwhelming sense of aloneness in the world. Of her experience, Vivian writes:

I continued to develop my memoir related to my experiences as a military spouse in "Yucca Sluts." This was my toughest and most courageous work in the Milspeak forum. In this essay, I continued to confront the effects of alcohol on my behavior as a military wife and companion to other wives. I attempted to paint a picture of my environment, and the diverse personalities of my friends, the Yucca Sluts. To date, my encounter with adultery while my husband was deployed in Desert Storm has been my greatest writing challenge because my writing is an exposure of self that is hurtful to loved ones. The art of memoir forces the writer to face hurdles and make choices that may be best left dormant.

Two years after it began, Milspeak refused to die, rising instead from ashes of disappointment to become a growing and changing writing seminar that was moving on, going with the flow of expectation, realization, disappointment, and joy that is a writing life. The MCWS 6 writers saved the program by signing up, showing up, and working hard. How could any fledgling workshop leader give up when writers such as these kept coming back and brilliant new voices kept signing up? When Seminar Saturday rolled around, they were there, waiting to receive what I had to give no matter how imperfect that might be. The writing produced during MCWS 6 was proof enough for me that Milspeak was working for these writers. But I also began to better understand that their work could be of value to military people struggling with military life and seeking answers and solutions. I believed in the power of Milspeak writers' memoirs to heal wounds and to help repair the bridge of understanding between military and civilian communities, but we needed a way to reach those readers.

Knowing how difficult publishing can be, I decided to create a Milspeak website so that writers could continue to share their work. Server cost isn't high, about $7 a month, but paying out of pocket for the website is more than crazy. I had made only $354 from my writing since making the decision in 2003 to pursue a master's degree in writing rather than library science. From Fall 2005 through Fall 2007, my teaching earnings had totaled less than $35,000. But paying out of pocket for the website is worthwhile considering the return. Old friends and even family members have been brought together through memoir posted on the website. Through website exposure, a publisher might find the work of Milspeak writers and consider their stories worthy for publication in longer form. Any one of these writers could write a book-length memoir. The Milspeak website might attract authors willing to be guest writers, writers willing to start a program of their own near military bases, or writers willing to mentor Milspeak writers. The website represented potential for growth, something I hadn't planned for and hadn't expected. Building the website seemed the next right thing to do. At some point, I will learn to use more of the website features. Discussion boards could be used for craft discussions between workshops—there are many similar features available though the server, IX Web Hosting. The problem with using these features is that I, the Webmaster, have no training. My searches for a volunteer to develop the website always fall through—I haven't found anyone who wants to work without pay.

On September 27, 2007, with the Milspeak Writers Gallery posted to the website for the first time, I sent a newsletter to nearly everyone in my address book to introduce the voices and memoir emerging from MCWS 6 and previous seminars. Maybe the newsletter or the website link would be passed along; maybe someone in that chain would be a publisher interested in these writers' works. In the newsletter, I gave myself a title, Developer and Leader of Milspeak Creative Writing Seminars. Having a title might give our work a sense of legitimacy should that publisher find one of us. Did I mention Don Quixote is my patron saint?

DRUDGERY

By David Charles

Knock-Knock.

This is the fifth room I've stopped at on the first floor and I have a ton of screening interviews to go in this forty-year old, stucco-covered, concrete, three-story barracks that houses hundreds of Marines from the 7th Communications Battalion of the 3rd Marine Division in Okinawa, Japan. My job this afternoon is to interview anyone I make contact with.

The drab-gray door is opened by a young man wearing an olive green T-shirt, camouflage trousers and black combat boots. He is sporting a haircut that is short on top and shaved to the skin on the sides of his head, a style Marines affectionately call high-and-tight.

"Good afternoon," I say holding up my credentials. "I am Investigator Charles of the Criminal Investigation Division and I'd like to ask you a couple quick questions."

"Me? Why's CID looking for me?"

"Don't worry," I go on. "We're not looking for you personally. There was a report of some property stolen from Room 209 upstairs and I am checking with everyone living in this barracks to see if they know anything about it. Sometime earlier this week someone took a laptop computer that belonged to Lance Corporal Spillers. Do you know anything about where that laptop might be?"

"Not really. Lots of laptops around here."

"This one is silver with black trim and has 'Tim Spillers' etched into the back of it."

"Na, sorry."

"That's alright. What's your full name, rank and unit? I've got to document the people I talk to about this."

"Okay. Lance Corporal James J. Goss, Headquarters Company."

"Do you live in this barracks room?"

"Yeah."

"Thanks. Have a great day. If you do think of anything, please give us a call."

"Sure," Goss says, and begins to close the door.

"Oh by the way, does anyone living in this room have a laptop?" I ask.
"Yeah, I do."
"Can I see it?"
"Sure."
Goss heads into the room, and I follow to where a black laptop lays on a desk beneath a wall mirror.

The man in the mirror is twenty-five years old. His face already is grim with experience in law enforcement. His brown hair is cut to Marine regulations—the short hair on top of his head fades to nothing at the ears. The eyes are blue, alert, like lights on a police cruiser. Attire is casual civilian, appropriate to the heat of Okinawa, an island south of Japan. The detective's big shirt nicely hides the weapon on his hip. All of a perp's attention is drawn to the CID badge hanging off the pocket. I look myself in the eye, already regretting that I will follow standard operating procedures spending several hours to speak with dozens of people in an effort to retrieve a laptop computer that may well have been left unsecured and unattended by its owner, only to have the case remain unresolved. But this is how it must be done. This is how I must spend my time. So what if I have better things to do—what better things? Hell, Marines shouldn't have to put up with crime in the barracks they call home.

Goss turns around with the laptop, obviously not the laptop I'm looking for.

"Alright," I say. Glancing around, I see only the black laptop in Goss's grease-stained hands. No sign of the stolen laptop. "Just remember to call if you do hear anything."

The door closes behind me as I cross the hallway in two steps and knock on the next drab-gray door.

Knock-Knock.
"Who's there?" comes the muffled reply from within the room.
"Investigator Charles, CID. Open up."
Behind the door, the room comes to life with the rustled hustle of shove-it-under-the-bed, put-it-in-the-wall-locker, throw-it-out-the-window. It's Saturday and only Chesty Puller whispering in God's right ear knows what is going on behind closed barracks doors on a Saturday morning. The drab-gray door is opened by a young man in an olive green T-shirt, green running shorts and white socks.

"Good afternoon. I am Investigator Charles of CID and I'd like to ask you a couple quick questions."

"Why?"

"There was a report of some property stolen from Room 209 upstairs and I am checking with everyone in this barracks to see if they know anything about it."

"There's always junk goin' missing 'round here."

"Really? Well sometime earlier this week someone took a laptop computer that belonged to Lance Corporal Spillers. Do you know anything about where that laptop might be?"

"Uh-uh."

"This one is silver with black trim and has 'Tim Spillers' etched into the back of it."

His answer is a right-to-left shake of his head. I note he has a Horseshoe haircut: flat-top, high-and-tight cut so short that the crown of his head rises above the hair and the little hair remaining around Mount Baldy forms the shape of a horseshoe with the opening to the back. Ought to be called the Mule cut or the Friar. Wannabe Tough Nuts wear a Horseshoe.

"You mentioned other items 'going missing around here.' What else has been taken?"

"My stuffs were taken from the dryer last week." He said.

"Did you file a report?"

"Nah—but I heard of Gameboys and other stuff disappearin' too. I don't know nothin' else 'bout it.

"Sounds like you've got a thief in the barracks," I say shaking my head in sympathy. "Tell everyone to keep their eyes open; he'll probably get himself caught. What's your full name, rank and unit? I've got to document the people I talk to about this."

"Okay. Lance Corporal Robert Benson, Headquarters Company."

"Do you live in this barracks room?"

"Yeah."

"Thanks. Have a great day. If you do think of anything else, please give me a call."

"Sure," Lance Corporal Benson says and begins to close the door.

"Oh by the way, does anyone living in this room have a laptop?"

"Nah."

"Alright. Just remember to call if you hear anything."

I step back into the hallway and the door closes. I take the same ten steps down the hall to the next set of doors and pick one. . .

Knock-Knock-Knock.

Now at the twenty-seventh room, this door is marked with a two-foot gouge that reveals many layers of paint, each one a different drab shade of Battleship gray.

The drab-gray door is opened by a young man in an olive green T-shirt, camouflage trousers, black combat boots and an unbuttoned camouflage blouse with "WYZNOWSKI" over one pocket.

"Good afternoon. I am Investigator Charles of CID and I'd like to ask you a couple quick questions."

"Huh?"

"There was a report of some stolen property from Room 209 upstairs and I am checking with everyone living in this barracks to see if they know anything about it. Know anything about a laptop computer that belonged to Lance Corporal Spillers?"

"Don't know him."

"How about the laptop? It is silver with black trim and has 'Tim Spillers' etched into the back of it."

"No, man. Don't know him."

"That's alright. What's your full name, rank and unit? I've got to document the people I talk to about this."

"Ya' need my stuff?"

"Yep. It's how we prove we actually did our job."

"Geez," he says. "Lance Corporal Benjamin J. Wyznowski, Support Company."

"Do you live in this barracks room?"

"I stay here, Yeah. But it don't feel much like home."

"Thanks. Have a great day. If you do think of anything, please give us a call."

"Okay." Lance Corporal Wyznowski starts to close the door.

"Oh by the way, does anyone living in this room have a laptop?"

"Jones. My roommate."

"Can I see it?"

Wyznowski steps back and I walk into the room noting the posters all over the walls. I see everything from Playboy bunnies to Bugs Bunny with

Michael Jordan. Wyznowski points at a wall locker with posters of people I don't recognize and I think of how quickly generation gaps open up these days. I tug on the combination lock and look back at the Marine.

Wyznowski shrugs, "He's on float. I dunno how to open it."

"Alright. Just remember to call if you hear anything."

The door closes as I leave the room. I cross the hallway in two steps and knock on the next door.

Knock-Knock-Knock.

The twenty-eighth room . . .

Knock-Knock-Knock.

The forty-third room I've stopped at. I'm part way through the second deck and betting I could say the answers before they come out of the next Marine's mouth.

A young man in an olive green T-shirt, camouflage trousers and black combat boots, opens the drab-gray door. His skin is as dark as his boots and his hair floats like a shadow on top of his head.

"Good afternoon. I am Investigator Charles of CID and I'd like to ask you a couple quick questions."

"Me? You say CID's lookin' for me?"

"Calm down, please. There was a report of some property stolen from Room 209 and I'm checking with everyone to see if they know anything about it. Sometime earlier this week someone took a laptop computer that belonged to Lance Corporal Spillers. Do you know anything about where that laptop is?"

"Lance Corporal Spillers? Isn't he Lance Corporal Harris's roommate just down the hall?"

"Yes, that's right. Why?"

"When Harris left for Thailand a couple days back, he asked me to hold onto his laptop for him. Harris said he was afraid Spillers would steal it. If it was stolen, why would Harris want me to secure it for him?"

"If it wasn't stolen, why would he need you to lock it up down here when he has a locker in his own room?"

"Good point. Do ya' want to see Harris' laptop he left?"

"Definitely."

"It's in here in my wall locker."

Private First Class Fernandez leads me into his room where another young male with a high-and-tight haircut is lying in his bunk, looking up from his paperback book to watch us, the shape of what appears to be a partial six-pack under his pillow. PFC Fernandez spins the dial on a combination lock until it opens. Opening the locker, he pulls out a silver colored laptop with black trim and hands it to me. Turning it over we both see 'Tim Spillers' etched into the back.

"Son-of-a-bitch," Fernandez exhales, "it is Spillers' laptop!"

LEAVING THE SERVICE?

By Jack Hayes

So, you're thinking of leaving active duty?

Thank you for your service. Our country needs and appreciates people like you who uproot their civilian lives to put themselves in harm's way to defend our liberties.

Whether you left civilian employment or enlisted right out of high school, there are many decisions for you to make now in preparing yourself to get back in the action of business and family. Above all, you should start your planning as early as possible after you've made the decision to leave to prepare yourself mentally and to design tools which will get you back into the swing of civilian life.

If you enlisted after school and never really had a civilian job, the in-service experience you have had will be most beneficial. There won't be many businesses that will use your experience in arms and armaments. But, properly presented, experience you gained in your years in the service may be the road to finding a civilian job. Facility you may have gained with computers, skills developed in operating and maintaining autos and machinery, in maintaining records for your unit, or as military policeman all count. If you attained rank and had positive experience in planning for and directing the activities of a group, this kind of background may be especially interesting to a prospective employer looking for a budding manager.

Key to success in this, after your positive attitude, will be a well-prepared resume putting these skills before a prospective employer. Once you have made your decision to leave, search out the office in your military organization, which will help you to make a meaningful one, or get help on the Internet.

As an example of how this can work for you, I give you the experience of my son, just out of school, who was sent by an employment agency with six other applicants to stuff envelopes at a major firm in New York City—a menial job designed to make them a little money in the short term while waiting for a real opportunity. Most of his confreres went to this activity in jeans and tee shirts; he went in a suit and tie with his resume in his pocket. When they broke for lunch he asked for the human resources department and presented his resume. He was hired on the spot and is still with the firm in a management position.

Many of you will have had civilian employment that was terminated when you enlisted or served in a reserve unit and were called up for duty. The law requires your employer to take you back in the same job. Sounds good?

It may not be as easy as it sounds. Think of it in the eyes of the employer: if you had been any good in your job and made the position important, the boss certainly has had to hire and train someone to replace you. If it is a small firm, it may pose a real hardship to add you back without firing the new hire he has just trained and worked with. Even in a larger firm, you yourself may find that the old job doesn't have the zing for you as it did before you left. Certainly there will be some strain in the relationship between you and the boss to make it different working there now. If it works out for you, fine. It may not, however, so I suggest you take all the preparatory steps I've given above in preparing yourself mentally and with a good resume before you leave your outfit.

Here follows another example, this from personal experience, of the difficulty of resuming civilian employment following military service.

I left for active duty in the Navy in 1951 expecting to find my old job waiting for me when I returned. Before being called up, I was working as estimator for a structural steel company with a small office on 42nd Street in Manhattan. I had been hired when I turned up looking for a job with a sister company in the shipbuilding industry listed at the same address with a yard in Pascagoula, Mississippi. I had a license in the Merchant Marine from my school but the merchant fleet in 1948 was a shadow of its WWII strength and there were few seagoing billets to be had, and lots of guys like me on the beach. Shipbuilding was an option for me, but the shipbuilding division in New York had only one representative and was not hiring.

So, even though the structural steel industry was not one I would have chosen given the chance, I had knuckled down to find out what it was about. I had been with them for three years and was working toward a position that would allow me to show my strengths—direct work with customers and prospects. When I was called up after three years they said the job would be there when I returned. The law called specifically for that and I was not worried about my future when my Korean War service ended.

But what met me on my return to civilian life was a complete surprise.

The company had saved a slot for me all right, but someone else was doing the work I had been before leaving for the war. As I said, I had recognized that my strength was in direct sales and had been working toward a job with direct customer contact. But the job they offered when I returned was in the office writing letters to prospects in other cities—not at all what I had been working toward. I was being paid though, so I started answering want ads in the *New York Times*.

I saw an ad that promised training on starting my own business as a manufacturer's representative. I wasn't sure my wife would go along with a move to the Midwest or somewhere else. But I would be paid during training and there would be lots of time to shift gears if it didn't work out with this company.

It was in the heating, ventilating and air conditioning industry (HVAC), a technology I was familiar with from my training as a marine engineer. The plant and offices were in New Jersey, a two-hour trip each way every day, but jobs were scarce.

I took the training and waited for an assignment. Then it was announced that the company had been sold! I held my breath, waiting for the information on the buyer. If the buyer were an industry company, there would be no need for tyros like me. But it turned out that the buyers knew little about the industry; their interest was in the company's profit margin and the purchase price had been right for the buyers.

Now, fully trained in the industry, young and looking for a challenge, I was primed to move up. I remained with the company for twenty years, moving from trainee to managing the New York Office, to becoming the first field sales manager traveling to train sales agents throughout the country, and eventually becoming Vice President of the company. When an opportunity came to turn around a bankrupt for another company in the industry, I took on the task of becoming company President and successfully re-established the company as a public company on the American Exchange.

This by no means was the end of my business adventures and misadventures, but I learned that the very personal driving forces that had brought me through a gun duel and mine hit on a destroyer in the Korean War could be used to keep an even keel in civilian life as well.

You, too, can be successful in finding employment if you keep a positive attitude and plan in advance.

Best wishes and, again, thank you for your service.

REMEMBERING MING

By Gerard Boe

Prologue

Dear Ming:

I was cleaning up some old paperwork this morning and found a picture of you and me at the Cam Ranh Orphanage in 1970. The memories of my many visits to the orphanage to be with you and to comfort you came cascading back. I wrote a poem trying to express my thoughts about you and the many others at the orphanage.

Orphans of War
The innocent children of a terrible war
Are a sight and sound sent from God.
As you look at their faces,
They are still full of hope and love.
They cling to your arms as you hold them,
The look in their eyes is not what you see.
What you see and what you hear is "Love me"!
They are so shattered by war that they forget how to play.
Yet even with this as you look on each face,
You can see God at work in this wonderful place.
You hold them, you rock them, you watch as they sleep,
You pray you can ensure their safe keep.
You bathe them, you clothe them, you feed them a meal,
Hoping against hope that some happiness they steal.
Yet when it is all over and done, you look and you see,
Their loving expression saying, "Please love me!"

Chapter 1
The innocent children of a terrible war....
Getting There

As an Army Officer during the Vietnam War it was a sure bet that I would get a tour in Vietnam. And sure enough I received orders to the 9th Medical Laboratory at Long Binh. It was early December 1969 when I received my orders with a departure date in March 1970. My actual duty assignment was to be Officer-in-Charge of the US Army, Vietnam, Central Blood Bank, located as a tenant unit on the 6th Convalescent Center Compound at Cam Ranh Bay.

I began my preparations for leaving. First came immunizations for yellow fever, cholera, malaria and tetanus. Then all the work began, a power of attorney, and an updated will and of course the typical mass of Army papers.

My family appeared to take my departure in stride. They were somewhat prepared. We had discussed the possibility of my leaving some time back. Being a 35-year-old career officer required being competitive and this meant a tour in Vietnam.

Finally the day for me to leave came and I said good-bye to my family. Tears filled my eyes as I hugged my 9-year-old daughter and told her to continue to do well in school. My son was trying to be strong as we hugged and said our "see you later" and my wife doesn't want to let go until the last minute when I had to board the plane.

I left not knowing what life altering experiences waited in that small country on the other side of world.

After about 18 hours we landed in Saigon. The heat was excruciating and was compounded by the fact that we were shuffled into a large Quonset hut with no air conditioning, only a few fans to push the air around. Finally a Major showed up and gave us our "in-country'" briefing with the main emphasis on the importance of taking our anti-malaria pills each week. He failed to emphasize the side effects could be debilitating. Many of us had severe stomach cramps and diarrhea. The side effects were bad enough to put some soldiers in bed for a day.

Once the paperwork was completed I was given the OK to travel to Long Binh to my parent unit, the 9th Med Lab. There were military buses leaving at varying intervals so I waited for the next one to come along. I waited and I looked around. It hit me.

This is a war zone!

The windows on the bus were covered with heavy mesh wire to keep out hand grenades if they are thrown at the bus. Two guards, armed with M-14s stand at the front of the bus. But the wire mesh and the two guards could not keep out the heat and the smells. The odor of humanity was all around. Urine, feces, human sweat and animal odors are all mixed with the overwhelming smell of gasoline engine exhaust in this city of nine million.

Looking out the window I was surprised at the numbers of motorcycles, weaving in and out of traffic almost hitting the slower bicycle rickshaws and just missing the hundreds of people on bikes. How they keep from crashing into each other I cannot understand. I probably will never get used to the mass of humanity, the noise and the odors that hang in the air.

After arriving at the 9th Med Lab, I met the Commander and was given a clean room and enough time to take a nice cool shower. I was surprised at the facilities, I was expecting something out of "MASH" but they were very modern and up-to-date. After a short rest, I went out to meet Lieutenant John Murphy, a Parasitologist and Captain Arron Davis, a microbiologist; both of them were assigned to the 9th Med Lab and had been in country for a few months. We walked across the compound to the 95th EVAC Hospital mess hall and had dinner. I know I was hungry, but this was the best meat loaf and mashed potatoes I had tasted in a long time.

I spent two days at the 9th Med Lab getting briefed and becoming a little more acclimated. Then it's off to my assignment up country. Before my departure, I checked out my .45 cal pistol, a carbine and some extra magazines. I was ready to go.

Apprehensive but ready!

I was able to catch a ride out of Ton San Nuet Air Force Base on an Army aircraft going to Cam Ranh and then a quick jeep ride to the 6th CC compound, The flight was uneventful and I arrived safely. I stopped in to meet the Hospital Commander, Colonel Joseph Kmieck, and then headed for my unit.

My unit the USARV Central Blood Bank is located in a new building and is just a large open area building. All the space is utilized each night when we get the blood shipments ready. My responsibility is the packing and shipment of all the whole blood used throughout the country. This meant we handled hundreds of units of blood each night for shipment and use the next day. Each day we would receive utilization rate information from the various medical units throughout South Vietnam, we would then order the blood from the states (actually the Armed Services Whole Blood Processing Laboratory in Hawaii, ASWBL) to replace what we had shipped out. The rest of my unit was a jeep, a ¾ ton truck, 4 enlisted soldiers, some large blood storage refrigerators and three fresh frozen plasma freezers.

After a short time I begin to settle into the job and I found I had plenty of time to get involved with some of the hospital programs. The two programs I got involved with were the Medical Civic Action Programs (MEDCAPS) and visitations to a local orphanage.

Chapter Two
Winning over the hearts and minds—US military slogan
My First MEDCAP Visit

Even though the slogan of winning the hearts and minds was something started in the 1960s with President Kennedy's pacification program, the medical units in Vietnam continued to provide humanitarian help to the people of South Vietnam in the 1970s.

The medical personnel of the 6th Convalescent Center worked out a schedule to visit a number of small local Vietnamese clinics. The visits of course were done randomly, never on schedule for obvious reasons.

It was a Wednesday morning and I had been told that there was a MEDCAP group leaving for one of the clinics. I was welcome to go along. As I walked to the Headquarters building I could see a dozen people loading up a jeep and a ¾ ton truck with various medical equipment and supplies. I can see that my first trip out of the compound will be an educational experience.

As we pulled away, I noticed a jeep with two armed guards in front of us and another jeep following ours with another two guards. The nurses rode in the back of the truck with the corpsmen and I am riding in a jeep with our dentist Captain Tom Osborne.

After a 30-minute ride we came to a small village and I could see the people all standing in line in front of one of the buildings. There must have been 60 - 70 waiting for treatment or medicines. It took us about 15 minutes to get set up and then the doctor and nurses began to see patients. I went with Tom as he started on those needing dental treatment.

I was amazed! The elderly were there for extractions. Their habit of chewing "bettle nuts" for years had rotted their teeth. They showed up with bleeding gums, teeth loose enough to reach in and pull out, and foul smelling breath. The whole inside of their mouths were black from the "nuts." Tom was running behind, so he then began to examine the patients and those with very loose teeth he directed to me. So I donned rubber gloves picked up the extractor and began pulling teeth. He would identify the tooth, I would pull it, give the patient some antibiotics and stick a couple of gauze pads into the space where the tooth was and move to the next one.

This was certainly a productive and interesting visit. I felt good about the people we had helped and could only guess at the joy I would get when we visited the orphanage. Little was I to know that the visit to the orphanage would turn my world upside down.

Chapter Three
What you see and what you hear is "Love me...."
Meeting Ming

It was Thursday and we were scheduled to visit the orphanage. There was some concern because there had been some VC action last night in the vicinity of the orphanage.

I got up early and began to gather my blood utilization data so I could communicate it to ASWBPL in Hawaii. I had no way of knowing how this day was going to change my life. The trips to the orphanage were a different approach to "winning the minds and hearts." This was a different group of people. Most of them were nurses or female medics, although a few males did go, mostly to act as security.

Lieutenant Helen Holden was the nurse in charge on this particular visit. Although I was senior in rank to her, I deferred to her experience in these visits. She briefed me on the way. "Most of these children have lost one or both of their parents. Some of their parents are still alive but are seriously wounded and in the hospital with no way to take care of their children. So, they have been sent to the orphanage with the hope that someday they can get back together as a family." As we passed through the gates to the orphanage, she continued, "Don't be surprised at anything you see or hear, remember these kids have been traumatized to a far greater extent than you or I can possibly imagine."

Two nuns are waiting for us and help us take the things we have brought to the kitchen. I was immediately aware of the lack of laughter and playfulness. The children seem to be playing but there is no real laughter.

I look around and see children of all ages from infants to teenagers. I am confused "What do I do now," I ask Lieutenant Holden. She replies, "Just walk around and find someone to talk with and play with." I walk around the yard and then into a room in the building that appears to be a nursery. Sitting in a crib all alone and playing with her doll is a sweet little girl. I am immediately drawn to her. She is cautious and shy. A nun tells me she has lost both parents, is about two years old and her name is Ming. My heart goes out to her and I know I will visit here again.

Chapter 4
They are so shattered by war they forget how to play....
Ming Revisited

On my second visit to the orphanage I asked the nuns how Ming was doing. They said she was physically healthy but still very quiet and introspective. I immediately decided I would make her my "project" and try to get her out of her shell.

I had been warned that she didn't like to be held by strangers so I kept my distance and just spoke quietly to her. When lunch came I was elated because she let me feed her. I felt I had pierced her armor. Even the Nuns were surprised.

I always felt she could see the love in my eyes and she knew I was not going to hurt her. This helped her come around more quickly. Before the visit was over, I was talking with her and she had let me hold her doll for a while. But still not physical contact. I decided I would leave that to her.

I couldn't help but to love her. She was like a little doll. On this visit

Ming was wearing a red jumper outfit and with her dark skin, her dark hair and eyes she was beautiful. I wanted to pick her up and hug her and let her know everything was going to work out, but I couldn't do that. It was still too early. She was still standoffish and shy.

So, I just sat beside her crib and talked to her. She couldn't understand me but I think she understood the love and soothing in my voice. She became a little more animated just before we had to return to the 6th CC. I could see I was making headway and it gave me a warm glow to know I was somehow hopefully making her world a little less stressful.

Chapter 5
What you see and what you hear is "Love me"
Birthday at the Orphanage

We arrived at the orphanage for our regular visit, but the nuns had told us they were going to celebrate birthdays on this visit, so we had a variety of small gifts. I picked up a new doll for Ming and began looking for her as soon as we entered the compound. I had missed the last visit and missed that sweet baby. I found that more and more she was acting as a source of love for me in the absence of my own family, a situation I noted seemed to be the case with the staff in many instances. But, it seemed more than that for me. I felt I actually loved this small person who could break my heart with a frown, or send it singing with a smile.

I began to think of adoption! I had heard of many of the soldiers adopting children and even was aware of two children from the orphanage who were heading to the states for adoption.

After we stopped the jeep I jumped out and ran into the nursery. Her crib was empty. I panicked! I was at a loss. Then I noticed there were some additional cribs. The orphanage had received more children and things had been rearranged. I finally spotted Ming in the corner and walked over to see her.

To my amazement she stood up and held her arms out to me. I literally cried as I hugged her tiny body to me. That did it. I was determined to take Ming back to the United States where she could be safe and secure for the rest of her life.

Still carrying Ming I walked over to one of the nuns and asked what the process was to adopt. She told me it would be long and tedious but she would help me if I desired. I gathered some initial papers and took them back to discuss with the legal officer of the 6th CC to begin the process.

My first hurdle was to alert and then convince my family of the adoption. I felt it would not be a real problem because she was such a wonderful baby. I had forgotten that they did not know Ming as I did. They had the love of each other to rely on while I had only Ming over the past months.

So I called home the next night and casually mentioned the fact that many soldiers were adopting. I had spoken of Ming before and my wife began to see the direction I was headed. I could hear her voice stiffen up. I let the subject slide for the rest of the conversation. I decided to open the subject again in a letter home. I felt I could expound on the positives better in writing. I composed my thoughts and then wrote and mailed the letter.

Chapter 6
Time marches on....
Vietnamization

The concept of Vietnamization seemed to be failing and as the war drew down, the "Silent Majority" began to turn against the troops. There was national and international outrage as to some of the actions of American troops. This mentality also set itself in my family. While they were certainly supportive of the troops, they certainly were not supportive of my idea concerning the adoption of Ming, They made that clear. My wife had gathered the kids for support. They both expressed basically the same sentiment. They had been without me for a long year and they did not want to share me when I got home. I could see their mother's influence, but there was nothing I could do. While I loved this little girl and wanted to give her a home and a good future, I also did not want to lose my family. So I conceded the fact that I would not adopt her, but I would do all I could for her as long as I was in country.

Chapter 7
Yet when it is all over and done, you look and you see,
Their loving expression saying, "Please Love Me!"
Saying Good-bye

I went to visit Ming as many times as I could for the rest of my tour. Finally toward the end, she began to loosen up and smile. Then one day I heard a sound that was greater than music to my ears...she laughed. She broke out of her shell. I like to think it was because of me and the love I shared with her, and who knows, maybe it was. But the important thing was, she laughed. She had turned the corner and I knew she would be OK, soon to be playing with the other children, soon to make that long psychological adjustment toward a normal childhood. At least as normal as one could expect given the environment. Finally the day came. I knew it would be the last time I would look into that sweet face and those loving dark eyes; it would be the last time I held her, helped her eat or washed her face and hands. It was all I could do to keep from crying when we drove out of the compound and headed for our base.

It was not long after that that I received my orders to return to Fort Sam Houston where I was assigned to the faculty of the U.S. Army Academy of Health Sciences. I was thrown into a hectic position and did not have too much time to remember Ming. But, then as now, when I do think of Ming, it is to wonder what kind of a woman she became—I still miss her.

YUCCA SLUTS

By Vivian I. Bikulege

The Absolut Bloody Mary, a liquid red pepper with invisible fingers, strokes and then grips my throat in the after bite of potato alcohol. I rotate the cocktail glass in my right hand, cooling my fingertips, contemplating the heavy beads of condensation rolling down the sides of my drink, reincarnating as a wet spot on the white linen tablecloth. I watch the glass drain unaware of my drinking. I look up. The line across my face, my grin, acknowledges the women in the booth who had become my constant companions for the last six months. I look down. My mind, soothed by gentle intoxication, drifts to the disappointment of the previous night.

During a long distance phone call between Ohio and California, my brother and I created a crass term of endearment for the women I met and shared time with in the California High Desert. Yucca Sluts. It was a way of tagging something indescribable with perverted wit. We were not all that promiscuous or loose. We did not harbor any great affection for Yucca Valley, the town we lived in, and we were not experts on the local vegetation, strange contortions of cacti that included yucca plants. We were just lively, young women stunted in our growth by conflicts beyond our control. We had the latent potential of becoming sluts. Every once in awhile we would act out in slutty demonstrations, but the humor in the nickname of Yucca Sluts was more palatable than Yucca Bitches and after all, most bitchiness resulted from the void left by unanswered love. The name stuck.

Jacque, Jesse, Marti and I met in August 1990 shortly after our other halves left for Operation Desert Shield. We lived in Yucca Valley, a high desert suburb of Palm Springs, and a neighboring town of Twenty-Nine Palms, the Marine Corps base specializing in desert warfare. Jacque, Jesse and I were married to Marine captains. Marti lived with Bric, a first lieutenant assigned to Jim's platoon, Jesse's husband. In the queer way that Marine wives end up wearing their husband's rank, you could say Marti reported to Jesse, and in the months we were together, both women would tell tales on the wartime conduct of the other man.

Jacque and I had no such affiliations except through the mutual acquaintance of Colonel Jewel's wife, Maureen. Now there was a woman who was over zealous in assuming the privileges of unearned rank. She oozed Officer's Wife whenever she was present. Whoever she was, and whatever set of circumstances brought us to this place, one thing you could not deny, her power resided in her access to military information. She was the closest thing we had to knowing where our husbands were, what they were doing, and when they might come home.

Of the four women, Jess was the most hard core in her attitude toward our plight. She wanted to be tough on the outside, but pulled out her eyelashes in some sort of anxiety-ridden response to our predicament. Her house was decorated in a nouveaux Indian desert motif with dream catchers, Native American symbols and cheap clay sculptures of howling coyotes. Medicine men danced on her bookshelves playing songs that could not be heard, and would not be followed.

While Jess privately picked away eyelashes from their lids, Jacqueline would launch into rants at our get-togethers, rambling into random soliloquies on privilege, décor, and proper behavior, all the while sinking into booze and depression. She was soft and plump in a beauty reminiscent of the voluptuous women in Renaissance paintings, carefully clumsy in her youthful elegance.

To this day, I do not know why Marti did not pack it up and get the hell out of Yucca Valley. She was the smartest of any of us and probably the prettiest too. She was the youngest. Maybe she was running away from something, and Bric was her ticket to a different life. Maybe she really loved him, although she would end up marrying someone else; having two boys and moving back to her childhood home in Massachusetts. When I was in town, Marti and I would spend weeknights watching Wheel of Fortune, eating macaroni and cheese, and drinking wine, trying to outguess one another as Vanna turned letters for hopeful contestants trying to win a car, a trip or a lump sum of cash.

Why not just drive to Los Angeles and try to get on the Wheel, Jeopardy or The Price is Right? Did we sit glued to couches in our small rented houses because we might miss that phone call from the Middle East? There were no cell phones, and the guys had to wait in long lines to phone home. We were married to commando E.T.'s, aliens in foreign lands. We shared heartbeats through invisible airwaves that ceased beating when telephones were hung up. In fact, we had little in common with these faraway creatures, our husbands, our lovers, and our friends.

I could not find beauty in Yucca Valley. I could visualize insanity but no redeeming qualities for my circumstances seemed apparent. I could do this with someone, with a desert partner, but it was too much to ask of me to have him leave for a Gulf War, for oil, for Saddam, to save a small country called Kuwait. Where the hell was Kuwait? What was Kuwait? What is a Kuwaiti? Are they third world people hidden away in some corner of the world needing to be saved? What about me? Where was my Marine savior? And what does he need?

Desert culture and the surrounding environment sent me into a state of shock for about one month after my arrival. There was only one strip mall at the base of town where people went barefoot at Vons' Supermarket. I became a regular at a local bar called the Winner's Circle, and I quickly learned that Big Lots had a continual special on one-dollar bottles of wine. I found a gynecologist and a dentist. Not sure what the gynecologist was for but I love a great smile. I took golf lessons at the Blue Skies Country Club but never practiced in between. I just drank at the golf club bar.

The Winner's Circle, a faded yellow bar in a strip of buildings, sat beside a Mexican restaurant with a wagon wheel over the doorway. The Circle became the official headquarters of the Yucca Sluts. Fred, a tall, friendly man with a pepper gray beard, tended bar. There was a pool table and a juke box, and my song of choice time and time again was Neil Young's *Rockin' in the Free World,* with it's cynical lyrics about George Sr.'s "thousand points of light" and kindlier, gentler machine gun hands.

I went to bed with a man I met at The Winner's Circle while my husband was in the First Gulf War. I went to bed with him but did not have sex with him. I have always wondered about that. How do you go to bed with someone and not have sex? I had friends in college who swore to me that they had participated in these bizarre escapades, but I doubted them. Going to bed with a man without consummating the shared space was ridiculous to me. It still is, but I have learned that absurdity and truth can mingle.

The night I brought Ric home from the bar was the eve of my thirty-third birthday. At some point, between a joint and more wine, I changed into the old robe I had worn for centuries. An exaggeration maybe, but the robe was at least twelve years old, and had made its introductions to a variety of bedroom guests. It was floor length, brown velour, J. C. Penney special with cream, red and yellow stripes on the sleeves, and a strip of cream-colored velour outlining the neck and opening. It cinched together at my waist with a matching brown belt, covering my breasts and legs.

I had been drinking most of that Saturday. I was always drinking. Tempting trouble. Pushing the envelope as far as I could. Thirty-three was an ominous age to me because it was Christ's age was when he died. I am not comparing myself to Jesus, but I always thought that when I turned thirty-three, important things would happen to me. As a child, I imagined dying at a young age like Christ. Instead, in the dark morning hours of my birthday, I stood at the edge of adultery, like Christ in His Last Temptation, pushing that envelope, straining to keep from jumping off my personal desert mountain.

I could not lie in my marital bed with my head on the pillows because this was all wrong. We lay in that bed upside down, heads inches from the brass rails at the foot of the bed, swaddled mummies waiting to be thrown overboard, desirous for a wave that would push us toward one another. My denial is such that I could not tell you what state of dress Ric was in. Maybe I have blacked it out. I knew this was so very wrong, and I could not defile things any further than I already had. I was making myself sick. Eventually, when it was clear nothing was going to happen, Ric went home, showing himself to the door, knowing I could not live up to any invitation I may have suggested, drunk or sober.

I woke up later that morning, dressed, and made my way to church, intent on handing off my guilt in confession. I met Fr. Eddie in the rectory between Sunday Masses, and made my confession in his kitchen. The guilt did not wash away with my sins. I asked him if he had ever broken his vow of celibacy. He replied that this was my confession not his. I was seeking solace in the hope of a cleric's failure, expecting redemption through the shared corruption of vows.

I did not shower that morning. It seemed impossible to wash away the smell of sweat and drink, my subconscious sackcloth. I wore paisley leggings with gold and black colors intertwined in purple scrolls of printed fabric, a loose purple shirt and a brown suede hunting jacket. My hair was shoulder length and messy, oily even and I covered my head with a green felt hat, masculine, and a bit like a Fifties gangster. I drove down to Palm

Desert with the Yucca Sluts for brunch, paying for everyone's meal on my birthday. I drank Bloody Marys. I had to keep drinking to move forward.

The Palm Desert Marriott on my thirty-third birthday—hung over, twirling a Bloody Mary in a hand dance with guilt, looking and smelling like a desert rat come down from the high mountains, smiling, even laughing with these women, my friends who I nicknamed sluts. I wondered what they could see behind my brown eyes. They knew I left that bar with Ric to smoke weed but they did not ask about my evening, not a one of them, not one, asked anything, not a thing, nothing. I was damaged by then, truly exhausted by the threats of war, the uncharted course of death, booze, drugs, and the desert—I would finally see this when I had the courage to look into my own brown eyes.

MCWS 7

15 March – 12 April 2008

Guest Writer: Lisa Annelouise Rentz
Guest Contributor: Major General Matthew Caulfield

Participants:
Nancy
Stacy
Moe
David
Fred
Charlotte
Vivian
Jack

Now the wonderful is pleasing, as may be inferred from the fact that everyone tells a story with some addition of his own, knowing that his hearers like it.... But the poet should prefer probable impossibilities to improbable possibilities. The tragic plot must not be composed of improbable parts. Everything improbable should, if possible, be excluded; or, at all events, it should lie outside the action of the play itself.... But once the improbable has been introduced and an air of likelihood imparted to it, we must accept it in spite of the absurdity. Take even the incidents of Odysseus in the *Odyssey* where Odysseus is left upon the shore of Ithaca. How intolerable even these might have been would be apparent if an inferior poet were to treat the subject! As it is, absurdity is veiled by the poetic charm with which the poet invests it.

—Aristotle, "Poetics" in *Aristotle: On Man In The Universe*, published in 1943 by Walter J. Black, Inc. for the Classics Club®, edited by Louise Ropes Loomis; translator unnamed.

THIRTY YEARS GONE....

What role has higher law in human affairs? If Life truly is the great test tube and the individual life an exquisite lab slide, whose eye, then, is it above? Who is looking down the throat of the microscope, peering into the slide, watching the sea monkey swim? I suppose that would be one's fellow and/or female travelers, or The Other, as Levinas, et al. would put it. All along, the Great Eye might have belonged to the Great Pumpkin or Dr. Seuss. Or God. But at times that eye is mine, and there she is, still running, the little sea monkey doing the same thing and expecting different results. Thirty years after graduating boot camp and ten years after retiring from the Corps, my life seemed to be going in the same direction as in 1977—nowhere—when my fruitless search for civilian employment had led to enlistment in the Corps. In 2007 and 2008, one-way rejection letters streamed in from the many universities and employers that received my applications. This time there was no Corps to join, but something had turned up.

Starletta Henderson and Tara Crooks contacted me in October 2007 about doing a Milspeak interview on Army Wife Talk Radio, a program for military wives sponsored by Military.com. The amount of paperwork required by the hosts was enormous: credentials, program overview, etc. The interview was held March 10, 2008, shortly before the start of MCWS 7. With any luck, the interview would earn an invitation to carry Milspeak to the Army's Fort Stewart in Georgia. I emailed the interview mp3 file to my Milspeak News list.

Thirteen writers signed up for MCWS 7. I tightened up the Welcome Email and sent it. Some Milspeak returnees were a bit shocked by the Welcome Email. Maybe I was being a bit tough by asking everyone who signed up to make a commitment to see the process through to completion, but losing a few writers each Saturday was much harder on the remaining writers and me than insisting that each writer make a firm commitment to attend. After nearly giving up on finding a Second Saturday guest writer, I realized one might be across town at the Arts Council of Beaufort County: Lisa Annelouise Rentz. In late 2007, I had queried Lisa about guest writers for Milspeak's Second Saturday. Lisa, editor of *ArtNews* (the Arts Council's journal), offered to publish a piece about Milspeak. Maybe "Artifacts" would inspire some of Beaufort's local authors to participate as guest writers or maybe an anthology publisher would drop out of the sky, pluck us up, and carry our work into the world. Neither authors nor publishers appeared as a result of my writing the piece.

Press 53's publisher, Kevin Watson, had been on my email newsletter list along with every publisher and agent whose email addresses I could find. Kevin sent me an email on March 14, 2008, after he listened to the Army Wife Talk Radio interview. He asked me to edit an anthology of military writing, including fiction, poetry and memoir by Milspeak writers. Kevin asked that I prepare a proposal. Opportunity had arrived. The day after receiving Kevin's request for a book proposal, MCWS 7 met for Seminar Saturday. Eight writers were present. To say we were excited is a pale statement of the mood in The Blackbird Zone.

Because guest writers are difficult to find, MCWS did not usually meet during the holiday weekend between Seminar Saturday and third Saturday. The time between first and third Saturdays was used to develop the first draft. In fact, Second Saturday, when writers are still developing first drafts and need all the encouragement they can get, is the logical time to hold the guest writer's talk on the writing life. Because Second Saturday falls on a holiday weekend, attendance is optional but highly encouraged. Seven of eight MCWS 7 participants sacrificed two hours of their Easter weekend to welcome guest writer Lisa Annelouise Rentz, editor of *ArtNews*. Lisa provided handouts, including example articles. She discussed editing techniques, how to become a teaching artist, and how to create a character. Lisa said achieving creativity is like weightlifting: the artist builds the writing muscle, the brain. She asked writers to visualize their work to achieve clarity, and told us that thinking about composing isn't composing—Get Started Writing!

MCWS 7 first drafts were so good they were difficult to critique, but it wouldn't be workshop without challenging the writers. As I read them, I watched for creative opportunity: where scenes could replace summaries; where something might be added or deleted to tighten the story. Sometimes the real story is hidden in a mass of details. I share my suggestions with the writers, while always reminding them that the author has the final say in deciding how the material is presented, what is added, deleted, or refined. Three new writers completed final drafts, Moe, Fred, and Stacy.

Moe's work shined once he caught on to formatting his work and writing nonfiction instead of poetry. He tackled a difficult subject, his Vietnam War past and how it affects his present. Moe had this to say about his Milspeak experience:

> Writing somehow came to me as a gift. Then I met Sally Drumm. I was writing because it had, somehow, given solace and truth to my befuddled life. When Sally's creative military writing workshop confronted me, I dared to try it! I had nothing to lose! I had been dead for thirty-five years and still got to work everyday. I dared her to enter my dead zone and she did with the tenacity of an Australian hyena! Sally taught me that my ability to prose might have a reason.

Fred, a thirty-year Marine Corps Veteran, Vietnam Veteran, and veteran of a lifetime of escapades and adventures, was the biggest surprise of MCWS 7. Fred is the first writer to walk into The Blackbird Zone who has been a member of the Marine Air Control Squadron community, as I once was. I never thought I'd find a member of the MACS Pack crossing the threshold into The Blackbird Zone, but I have to admit I had been waiting. "Let Me Take You on a Sea Cruise," the memoir Fred wrote during MCWS 7, provides an inside view of Vietnam-era troop ships, pass-along paperbacks, and so much more. Fred explains:

> I've been writing a column for a few years now and it has been well received I think, at least I haven't been fired. When I heard about a creative writing class being given for the military past and present, and for military dependents, I decided to give it a try. What could I lose? It was free and the possibility of learning a few tricks to improve what I was doing was tantalizing. I signed up.
> The story I picked, my first trip to Viet Nam, could have been a tale filled with angst and anxiety. I chose instead to write, at least I hope I wrote, an uplifting and fairly humorous tale of how I got from point A to point E, while backtracking through points B, C, and D.

I deliberately did not write about my time in Viet Nam—I hadn't thought of it in a long time, and I was not ready for the catharsis of putting that experience on paper, let alone sharing it with anyone. Finally facing those memories after forty years was enough to put my soul at rest. For that alone I'm grateful for the CWS experience.

MCWS 7 was Charlotte's third workshop. "Hey Ya" is a trip into Tent City, Iraq, rendered in a voice both humorous and heartbreaking. Working again with this talented writer was bittersweet. Charlotte would soon leave active service and Beaufort to begin her transition to civilian life. From Charlotte:

MCWS-7 was my last workshop. It ended less than a month before my final days as an active-duty Marine, a tumultuous time full of decisions and job searches and moving plans and chaos. I was glad to have a few hours every Saturday to just sit and think and talk about writing with a group of friends. "Hey Ya" for me is mostly about Teresa, my "battle buddy" and fellow lieutenant, and the bond we formed during our deployment. I wrote about some of the lighter aspects of my deployment because I didn't feel I had the energy to write about the darker sides again. Doing so had drained me emotionally the first two times, and I was too tired to go through that again with everything else I had going on.

I was of course very enthusiastic about MCWS growth and was especially glad to see Stacy, a bright and motivated young Marine, join us. For me, she completed a circle. There was Sally, a retired woman Marine, who had gone through many of the types of experiences I had in the Marine Corps, and had come out on the other side as a teacher and mentor. There was me: I felt like I had seen and done my share as a Marine and was sufficiently wise and weary to begin my journey out of the Corps. Then there was Stacy; she was a newcomer to the Marine club, and I saw so much in her of my old enthusiasm and earnest desire to do well and embody Marine Corps ideals. Stacy was like looking in a mirror that shows you the best of what you used to be. In Sally I had long seen the best of what I could become.

It was only at the final MCWS-7 session that I realized what a circle we formed indeed. When Stacy read her piece on becoming a Marine, I could practically hear the clicks in my head as timelines and events fell into order; she had been in the Series I had commanded at Parris Island—she had been one of my recruits. I had not done well as a Series Commander; having to inspect the young women's bodies (including Stacy's) when they first arrived to Boot Camp for scars and tattoos had brought back unwelcome memories of inspecting the bodies of dead Marines. Distressed and mortified at my failure to cope with the demands of the job, I floundered and was eventually reassigned. A few months later, I had gone to my first MCWS and had met Sally, who had served as a drill instructor at the same all-woman battalion. Sally had helped me as I dealt with the emotions of writing about the bodies of fallen warriors. And here, over a year later, was Stacy, bringing it back full circle: back to my Marine Corps beginnings and Sally's, back to the time before I had started attending MCWS, back to the topic of my first piece, *Hymn*.

Listening to Stacy read her piece, the uniqueness of MCWS became very clear: it had brought us together, Sally, Stacy and me, and the whole was greater than the sum of parts.

David reached into his heart for the story of a billiard-hall conversation with his son. Given David's own status as a retired Marine, his account of his son's return from a combat tour with the Corps in Iraq is an especially poignant piece. From David:

Talk about emotional; this account was terrifically difficult to read on Celebration Saturday. I hope this story does some justice to those who send loved ones into combat areas and have to worry quietly and wait for their safe return. Being a Marine did not make it any easier. I had a particularly good idea of the situations my son was getting into. I appreciate my son sharing this account with me and allowing me to share it with others. This story should reach an extremely broad audience and my hope is that it inspires many conversations between military members and their families.

Jack returned for MCWS 7 and revealed his struggle as a young officer defending a serviceman accused of playing the system during the Korean War. Of his experience, Jack reports:

When you're up to your neck in work aboard ship, don't think the skipper can't think of a beauty to send you into left field. The ship was in dry dock. As chief engineer, I was into all the contractors' repairs of the major hull damage from a mine with TF77 in Korea. The Captain decided he needed a defense for a sailor, possibly wrongly accused.

Stacy, a two-and-a-half year enlisted Marine, brought MCWS 7 to life with her energetic writing. It was such a pleasure to be able to connect with this young enlisted Marine who is so eager to succeed in life. What a reward for an old warrior like me to know a Marine such as her!

Nancy made a good start on her piece, a revealing look at a young bride's life in Guam during the Vietnam War. She was unable to complete her work during MCWS 7 because a long awaited employment opportunity arose.

Leading the selections in this chapter, Lisa Annelouise Rentz reflects upon her Milspeak experience, Milspeak's connection to Beaufort, and the action of writing. Major General Matthew P. Caulfield, USMC, Retired, is also a guest contributor to this chapter with his speech written for the reunion of the 3d Battalion, 26th Marines (3/26), at Quantico, Virginia. The speech was delivered on 19 July 2008, four days after my fiftieth birthday. It came my way via my family attorney, George O'Kelley, also a retired Marine officer. Major General Caulfield's speech speaks profoundly of the Vietnam experience, all that our Vietnam Veterans have given and continue to give to their country and a new generation of veterans.

Celebration Saturday was more meaningful than ever, held for the first time at the MCAS Beaufort Officer's Club Santini Bar. The bar was made famous in the film *The Great Santini*. The film is based on the novel by the same title written by Pat Conroy, a Beaufort County resident. I met Mr. Conroy in the grocery store in the bread aisle not long before MCWS 7 met.

"You're Pat Conroy, aren't you?" I stupidly asked.

"Yes, I am," he answered.

While he leaned on his cart beside loaves of white bread and cartons of bottled water, and I on mine beside packs of hot dogs and cold cuts, we had a nice conversation about his military childhood, Quonset huts, and disabled veterans. I quickly explained the Milspeak program and asked him to join us as a guest writer. At first he said no. I said I understood. Then he said yes, gave me his address, and told me to write him a letter. He came over to me at the check out, gave me his address again, and said to not forget to write him a letter. I did write to him, but never heard back from him—maybe because I included an invitation to a campfire dinner of dogs-and-beans, or maybe because I didn't memorize his address correctly. Then again, he's probably never met anything like me before— what sort of person would invite Pat Conroy over for beans and weenies?

For the first time, family members attended Celebration Saturday. Everyone brought something to eat, and a tradition began: Celebration Saturday Read and Chow. Fred brought S.O.S. or Shit on a Shingle, take your pick. No matter the title, the dish has remained unchanged for a hundred years: fried ground beef (sometimes shredded beef is used, but not in Fred's recipe) slathered in milk gravy and served over biscuits. It was the first time Stacy heard of S.O.S, and the first time I had encountered the dish since leaving the Corps.

While I didn't mention it, except briefly to David, the brutal truth on Celebration Saturday morning was that my husband Pete's mother, Margaret, had been admitted to the hospital on the Thursday before Celebration Saturday. She called early that morning to say she needed help. I didn't have far to go to reach her, Margaret lives next door. After blazing into her house, I discovered she was dressed in her best for a trip to the hospital. She had already called for an ambulance. When I burst through her front door, my 86-year-old mother-in-law calmly looked up at me, and said, "I think I'm falling apart." The preciousness of life was never more apparent.

THE WEIGHT OF THE PEN

By Lisa Annelouise Rentz

As an editor and teaching artist, I do not give much advice or assign systematic techniques. Instead, I concentrate on giving encouragement to writers and work-in-progress: *Learning to write is like weight lifting, every repetition makes you stronger.* I find classroom-style writing sessions, where writers gather to share the adrenaline of their stories in exchange for responses, so intense and brief that each one is only a single curl of an arm holding a dumbbell. *Only* a single curl, but still vital: Life is physical and so should writing be. When I attended a Milspeak session as a guest writer, I hoped that my homemade maxim would be valuable, because—despite my eye for typos and syntax—the burden of writing is on the weightlifter.

Pain is weakness leaving your body is the slogan of a t-shirt that I see around town on Marines. That's a dramatic message, but the more I think about it, and the more backaches I try to stretch beyond, the more true it seems for someone who wants to grow. As a couch potato-bookworm-C-average student, even I comprehend why a warrior-poet literary tradition has manifested from the military experience: the warrior experience creates—though not exclusively—*voice*. Voice is a loud-and-clearness of narration on a page that any writer of any subject is lucky to have—*must* have to be successful ("success" in writing is just as varied as "the best" seems to be in Marine speak, based on the Milspeak stories I've read: "They were the best, whatever that meant..."[1]) Voice is not the pretentious tone of blog scripts, it is a trumpet of authenticity from someone who, like Harriet Beecher Stowe writing at night while her seven children slept, stole a break from the action, focused, and wrote original words for hours.

When people take the time to write as children or spouses or warriors, readers get to hear the call and to *be there*: in a deciding moment of a twelve-year-old watching a ROTC performance, or there where a soldier and an insurgent are tossed together, most alive and kicking, avoiding a grenade blast. A trained voice is the result of the eternal boot camp that is life: through practiced and heartfelt word choice (and plenty of acronyms and lingo too, in this genre), we get great stories to read about distant camps and protected homelands, and everything in between.

Beaufort, South Carolina, where a large but undisclosed number of military personnel and I live, is a small, Southern, military town. But this place is arisen from a geo-history of pirates and Spanish explorers, and hurricanes and islands that extinguishes stereotypes. The lack of cliché here is important for residents, and it also makes this town a writer's place. There's a reason Milspeak is happening here, under the specter of Pat Conroy and his Citadel and his Boos, with views of dolphins and kayakers splashing in salt marshes filled with invasive but yummy one-pound tiger shrimps, and with the many resident characters who populate Beaufort, including the best-selling novelist who answered my knock on her door wearing no pants at all. A slowed-down Lowcountry place like this gestates stories.

The Civil War is still visible here. My husband, from this State, classifies Beaufort as the Barney Fife of the South because locals fired their one bullet and surrendered to Federal troops in 1861. The twenty or so grand homes in historic downtown Beaufort were commandeered for generals, such as Sherman, for visits from Clara Barton and Harriet Tubman (considered by some to be the only American woman to lead a military attack), and for hospitals for soldiers. A few private walls in town have been preserved to show off the soldiers' healing-time graffiti, which is a lovely visual patois of old-timey script and pornography. *He's a pork belly thief and a son of a bitch.* I am a reader first; studying these details with all five senses: old houses are musty no matter how well preserved. Details answer my questions about the world and time, which helps me build sentences on paper.

Beaufort is surrounded by river water and salt marshes and improved by two long-standing factors. The big, sprawling oak trees, even considering all the heavy limbs they drop, and the warriors, who train, settle, and heal here and are so clean cut in appearance. My father was in the Navy, so that particular scrubbed confidence catches my eye. My neighborhood is across the river from the Marine Corp Air Station, and immediately behind the twenty-acre National Cemetery. The jets often blast overhead, flying parallel to the long-oared egrets slicing lower in the sky. Occasionally, I'll see a Marine in Dress Blues walking toward the cemetery gates, carrying a bugle. My favorite frame shop-gallery is always working on an intricately matted display of a squadron's autographs and insignia. A retired Marine neighbor lives around the corner with two giant, beautiful stag horn ferns hanging in baskets around his front door. Rifles crackle in the distance from the range on Parris Island. Another neighbor once told me about the groomsmen pictured in her wedding photo; they all died in helicopters in Vietnam.

Writing and reading about the warrior way makes sense of daily life here; *place* is in service of the events that bring people together. We have read our way to Thermopoli with Herodotus, Egypt with Caesar, and to Edo with the Samurai. That was then. Now we walk with a spouse to the departure hangar and experience *hurry up and wait*.[2] Life is meaningful, and so should writing be. When the writer works, calories burn on the synapses level, the lumbar takes the pressures of sitting, and the healing process—making sense of love or separation or force—must take at least as much strength as shaping clay on a potter's wheel or lifting a weighted bar during a strenuous workout. The exertion of getting words to flow together can lead to losing track of time, to the betterment of the writer's health. If time was tangible in my personal writing process, it would be like the mineral-rich, pore-cleansing, silver pluff mud of the marshes here, tempering my metabolism while I write and re-write. Minutes and degrees count in plot.

As I work with people and their writing, I see their reasons for writing in their grip on the yellow pencil or in the way they hold a certain notebook. Writing is unloading a truck full of much-needed supplies. Editing is sorting and shelving and signing in triplicate. There is exhaustion at the end. *The body is the outermost layer of the mind*, which is why the terms *warrior* and *poet* go so well together: keep it buff, keep it ready, because *something* is going to happen, something that has so much impact on all five senses that it will demand to be put into a most sincere and private art form—the simple, classical *peace* of putting ink on paper.

Notes:

[1] Atkinson, Stacy. "Bright and Pressed." MCWS 7.
[2] Greer, Monica. "Good-Bye." MCWS 8.

A BATTALION REMEMBERS

Comments by Major General Matthew P. Caulfield, USMC (Ret),
at the reunion of the 3d Battalion, 26th Marines (3/26),
at Quantico, Virginia, 19 July 2008.

What a beautiful setting here at the entrance to the National Museum of the Marine Corps, gazing across the fields as the sun sets on to our country's and Corps' colors. I was prepared to reflect on the leadership of one of our commanders, LtCol John Studt, as many of you know, a truly great combat commander. He preferred that I not talk about him, which I was going to do anyway until yesterday.

I visited three Marines in the Bethesda hospital yesterday. I received a call one week ago from the father of one Marine seriously wounded in Afghanistan. We had met a few years ago when I encouraged him and his wife to support their youngest son in joining the Marine Corps.

He informed me that his son was en route from Afghanistan to a hospital in Germany with two of his buddies. The family had hoped that he would recuperate in a hospital close to Boston; instead they learned that he had just received the word that after treatment in Germany, he would be transferred to San Diego Naval Hospital.

I passed on the information to the duty officer at I Marine Expeditionary Force and within hours was told that the Marines would go to Bethesda. By the way, the family was notified of his injuries by a cell phone call as their son was awaiting treatment in a field hospital. One hour later the father was called by the casualty assistance section from Quantico.

Among other assistance, the family was provided with an 800 number to contact their son during the evacuation and treatment in Germany. Later the family was provided an escort who arranged transportation from Boston to Bethesda and lodging at the hospital. As you know that is not the way your families were treated some 41 years ago. I learned that firsthand when my brother was wounded.

The Marine Corps has made a lot of changes in the past 41 years but none as impressive to me as the way the wounded and their families are treated. Our Corps deserves a lot of credit for that. One thing that has not changed is the age of the Marines who do the fighting. The Marine I visited, LCpl Ryan Walsh, is 21 years old; the squad leader Cpl Austin Crockett is 22, and the machine gunner, wounded most severely, PFC Richard Weinmaster, is 19 years old.

By the way, the Assistant Commandant was also visiting that day. It was good to witness how easily the Marines related to the Assistant Commandant. None of that "yes Sir, no Sir" rote. Instead, it was an articulate, two-way, respectful conversation in which the Marines mostly questioned the Assistant Commandant on future plans for their battalion.

Just before departing the hospital I mentioned that I was on my way to a reunion of Vietnam War Marines. Cpl Crockett asked what battalion, and I responded 3/26. Their interest shifted immediately, particularly when I mentioned Khe Sanh.

Many of you often wonder how what you did in Vietnam fits into a larger context than the view from a fighting hole. I know your guests tonight—wives, friends, children, and grandchildren—want to know what it is about you and your experiences in Vietnam that runs so deep. They wonder why, some 41 years later, you still got misty-eyed when you walked up to that wall yesterday and traced the names of your friends. I would like to tell them about you.

You visited your memorial, as well as the memorials to World War II (WWII) and the Korean War. The WWII memorial contains quotes and refers to great campaigns; the Korean memorial pictures great men. Your memorial is about every single one of your brothers and, like you, remains mute. Scroll from the first name through the 58,195 single names and there is only silence. A single name, silence, and yet some say it is the most powerful war memorial in the world. You know it is.

The WWII veterans have been named "the greatest generation." Now we hear the men and women serving in Iraq and Afghanistan are the "new greatest generation." What we have in our memorial are 58,195 single, silent names who know better. They respect and are inspired by those who went before and take pride in the achievements of those who follow, but they know—every single one knows—that no generation since the founding of our country is more deserving of the word "greatest" than your generation.

Let's look at the record. The archives in the museum behind you attest to the greatness of those who served in all of our Nation's wars. You toured the WWI, Korean War, and WWII exhibits. Compared to Marine casualties in other wars, your dead in Vietnam were five times—five times—the dead in WWI, three times the dead in Korea and, in terms of total dead and wounded, about the same as WWII.

The infantry soldier in WWII served 40 days in combat. Tarawa was over in 72 hours, Iwo in 30 days. You served in Con Thien for over 30 days, followed by a 77-day siege in Khe Sanh. Given we didn't have a rear area, a good case could be made that you served over 300 days in combat.

As for the enemy, Marines never faced a tougher enemy than the North Vietnamese [NVA] soldier. How did you do? You never lost a battlefield engagement. Your 58,195 dead accounted for 1.2 million enemy dead. Those figures are unprecedented in any of our country's wars. As a division commander in Desert Storm confided to me, "If the NVA were in those trenches, we would still be over there."

When we celebrated our 192d Marine Corps birthday in Vietnam, we stood in awe when the names of the Argonne, Belleau Wood, Iwo Jima, and Chosin were read. Today on our 233d anniversary, Marines around the world stand in respect when the names Con Thien, Khe Sanh, and Hue are read. Two out of three.

You fought with WWII 782 gear, fought with a rifle that malfunctioned frequently, lived on rations from Korea, and paid for decent rain gear when a courier was able to find some while on Okinawa. The battalion arrived as a unit, but afterwards replacements arrived individually—no buddies, all alone until friendships were forged in battle. There was no rear, no place to train and to hone skills.

We had to jury rig construction material from barbed wire stakes. Our battalion went to war without a parent division, was treated like orphans, and was assigned to whatever place was the hottest. We didn't have a "rear area" like many other battalions. We were activated, did the war, and got deactivated. Just like our predecessors in WWII—they did Iwo and were deactivated.

Let me describe one battle—Khe Sanh. Your battalion started the battle on 20 January with India Company engaging the forward elements of a division-sized force on the way to attack the main combat base and ended it on 14 April, Easter Sunday, when your battalion routed the enemy in a night attack on Hill 881 North. For 81 long days and nights you were totally isolated and cut off from other friendly forces.

Enemy artillery outranged the 155s at the combat base and the 175s in Camp Carroll. They fired at you from virtually impregnable positions in Laos that we could not attack. A fog frequently enshrouded your positions. On occasions the fog lifted from 1000 to 1200 hours; on other occasions it didn't. What that did to the defender is extend disadvantageous nighttime conditions to three-quarters of 24-hour period. The ability to sense the approach of an enemy force was severely limited, as was resupply, which was totally dependent on air support.

You lived below ground in hand dug holes. Dug with entrenching tools for the most part because you had precious few engineering tools or equipment. Construction materials for reinforcing positions never got down to you. Daylight provided no reprieve as movement above ground resulted in sniper fire and often mortar and/or artillery fires. Life in a hole in the ground with movement restricted had a toll.

Skin rashes were common. Bathing or even brushing teeth was prohibited by the shortage of water. On the hill positions all but the youngest Marines grew beards, as shaving was impossible. Clothes rotted and fresh uniforms were not a high enough priority. Rudimentary sanitation became a major effort.

Limited resources and the situation allowed only for the delivery of ammunition, food, and water, and even those items were in short supply. C-rations were often rationed to one-half a meal a day and water to one large C-ration cup per day. Rats were a constant irritant. Attracted to buried corpses and garbage from earlier battles on Hill 881S, the rats grew to enormous size and traveled in packs. Several of you were bitten and most experienced disruption to sleep by rats scampering across your bodies.

Your daily routine every day for 81 days was to live in a hole in the ground and emerge at night to a fighting position or listening post. More often than not you would spend the entire period of darkness on full alert, waiting for the enemy that intelligence indicated was certain to arrive on any given night. In all of this was the sure knowledge that the hill positions were untenable, and the combat base was indefensible. A determined assault, and the NVA always attacked with fierce determination, by a fraction of the enemy force disposed against you would be difficult if not impossible to repel.

But you did repel them, again and again and again—day after day, night after night. In the end you went on to attack at night, viewed the enemy running from the objective at first light followed by a lone Marine shimmying up a burned out tree to fasten our Nation's colors.

After Khe Sanh you deployed to the 1st Division's area of operations where you engaged in another kind of battle—on the night of your arrival when some of you tore apart the division's Enlisted Club. We never even tried to determine who was responsible, but if you are here tonight, thank you. What you don't know is that at the same time, your officers similarly were engaged in an altercation with several Australians and assorted others in the Da Nang Officers' Club.

The following morning the general summoned LtCol Studt, told him to pack up "his mob," and move back into the field. The general's sole concern, thank God, was the enlisted club. Anyway, that was the origin of your 57-day foray into the triple canopy.

You jumped off for what you thought would be a 1- to 2-week operation. A battalion that jumped off with you returned to their rear after 2 weeks due to non-battle casualties. The triple canopy, leaches, rancid water, mosquitoes, body rashes, and a lot more went on for 57 days. I guess the general was really pissed over what you did to his club. By the way, not once in those 57 days did the enemy initiate contact. You fired first in every encounter.

And how did you come home? Alone, without your buddies, nothing but memories of the greatest friends you ever had or ever will have. And something else. Let me read from what the Commanding General, 1st Marine Division, General James N. Mattis, wrote to his Marines on the eve of battle in Iraq in March 2003:

> When I give you the word together we will cross the Line of Departure, close with those forces that choose to fight and destroy them....
>
> We will move swiftly and aggressively against those who resist; we will treat all others with decency, demonstrating chivalry and soldierly compassion for people who have endured a lifetime under Saddam's oppression. You are part of the world's most feared and trusted force. Engage your brain before you engage your weapon. Save your courage with each other as we enter the uncertain terrain north of the Line of Departure.

Keep faith with your comrades on your left and right and Marine Air overhead. Fight with a happy heart and strong spirit. For the mission's sake, our country's sake and the sake of the men who carried the Division's colors in past battles, who fought for life and never lost their nerve, carry out your mission and keep your honor clean .... Demonstrate to the world that there is 'No Better Friend, No Worse Enemy' than a U.S Marine.

Let me repeat, for 'the sake of the men who carried the Division's colors in past battles, who fought for life and never lost their nerve, carry out your mission and keep your honor clean.'

General Mattis was thinking about you. His Marines went to Baghdad and beyond knowing of your deeds. The Marines I visited yesterday in Bethesda wanted to know more about you. Marines fight in Iraq, Afghanistan, and wherever the Nation calls because they know about you and can't let you down. If that doesn't define "greatness" I don't know what the hell does.

It is only fitting that a memorial for your battalion will be located in Semper Fi Park, so as long as our Nation endures, future generations, inspired by your deeds, will aspire to greatness. The inscription reads:

MEMORIES OF BATTLES DIM WITH TIME
MEMORY OF OUR BROTHERS WHO GAVE THEIR
LAST FULL MEASURE OF DEVOTION BRIGHTENS
WITH TIME. THEIR MEMORY ENHANCES OUR
LIVES. WE REMEMBER, KEEP FAITH AND HONOR
THEM WHEN SAFEGUARDING THE NATION
ENTRUSTED TO US AND LIVING OUR LIVES
IN THE SERVICE OF OUR COUNTRYMEN,
OUR CORPS AND EACH OTHER.

JUST BREATHE

By Bernard "Moe" Haagensen

I.

Outside of the window, a person could see a northern section of Charleston's south side. Up on the fourth floor, our vantage point held a spectacular view of an area most tourists would never get to see, or have reason to go to.

Inside that same window, a doctor was calmly finger-combing his straw-colored hair. His shoes were well worn and appeared to be very comfortable. During our sessions, he often wore striped long sleeve shirts, cuff links, and a tack on his tie. There was never any jewelry around his neck or on his hands.

Across the room's perimeter sat a large, handsome black man. A faded military hat was settled tightly over his brow, allowing the brim to shadow his eyes and nose. Loose and broken threads appeared on most of the hat's seams. Staff Sergeant chevrons were pinned over a '60s peace sign medallion. White sweat stains surrounded the hat's hemline. Both of his hands clutched a clear plastic bag filled with pill bottles. He would often shake the bag, as if to make sure there was something still in it. When confronted, he would describe a new hallucination or an old, but vivid, dream sequence.

This man's bearing indicated he was unable to enjoy the spectacular panorama visible through the hospital's huge Plexiglas window. While the other two of us were trading comments, about the skyline, he just slumped in his chair.

II.

At bi-weekly intervals, our very small group would gather in one of two different rooms. This room had windows; the other one did not. Every now and then, seeming stragglers—always wearing new shoes—would attend these sessions. They all had the ability to nod and smile, and we would never see them again.

I often wondered why my attendance was required here. Did it have anything to do my recent loss of a civil service position? Could it be my talent for getting thrown out of major chain stores? I always had enough money in my pocket! Could it be my drinking? Everybody drank!

III.

Before every session the doctor, who always dressed so neatly, would find his tiny band of former heroes roaming an interior hallway or standing in a nearby corner space. As he approached, his eyes always got there first. His glance was hazel green and piercing.

Once corralled, our small troupe would form a very loose knit pecking order and the good doctor would provide a direction. The two of us would tag along behind him like ducks paddling after their mother. What a sight we were: "Follow me! I'm the infantry!"

Observing this motley trio, a lesser fool might comment that the use of a cattle prod could be of some merit. A more learned fool would remind himself that these men were proven combat soldiers during their youth. To use any kind of force against them might turn their dream sequences into sudden and fateful reality.

IV.

The good doctor was acutely aware of this. His chosen field dealt with the many awkward situations these types of personalities could find themselves in, especially Viet-Nam-era veterans who had been 'out to pasture' for more than 30 years! The Iraq-era soldier was just entering the Veteran Administration system, but for any veteran, anxiety is equal in principle.

Anxiety was at the core of our many dysfunctions. Anxiety would actually rule our behavior without informing the brain's "better sense" region. The Iraq-era soldiers were probably experiencing the same, despite the 30-year gap between wars. For us, cases of "severe" anxiety develop, which in turn, lead to depressions of enormous proportion.

The doctor knew this, we didn't; the Iraq-era vets might not, either. We just wondered why it was so hard to keep a job! Maybe they will, too.

V.

As for the doctor, this was his chosen field, his place in society where he thought he could do the most good. This was his chosen arena, a place

322

where he could be himself, inside his own area of discovery and expertise.

His ultimate purpose was to counsel the psyche of human beings who had once been thoroughly trained, to act without "thinking," those believing their way of "thinking" to be the norm. Yet these circumstances were not outside the good doctor's realm as a behavior psychologist. His genuine caring and deep interest as practitioner to us "thinkers" was truly evidenced by his accepting the paltry government salary the Veterans Administration relinquished to such educated professionals.

VI.

During the 1960s and 70s these "thinkers" were unleashed upon the general public by the thousands. One could find these types of people in prisons, jails, halfway houses, or pushing shopping carts down sidewalks in any city of the U.S.A. The Department of Defense had disowned these "thinkers" when time limitations on veterans' benefits demanded.

Some "thinkers" actually tried to fit into their past environs, only to become nomadic and eventually desperate, succumbing to life's natural and manmade catastrophes. Others found themselves in hospital wards, such as this, many years after a homecoming that did not go so well.

VII.

Surveying the room again, I begin to hic-up. The situation is the same. There are still three of us, the good doctor at the helm, a wall directly behind me, (hic-up) and the pill-bottle-bag-shaker between us (hic-up). Such attentive students we are (hic-up): one with his head (hic-up) in the clouds, and the other with clouds (hic-up) in his head!

Suddenly the spectacular view vanished! Everything I see out of the window is turning darker! I close my eyes. When my eyes open, I realize I am leaning, both hands grasping the window's interior sill. My eyes are swelling and wet. All I see are poles, wires, antennas, and cement buildings, all stacked in front of a brackish gray sky. The beauty has disappeared!

Firm hands rhythmically pat my upper back.

"Take a deep breath," a man's voice gently whispers. "Breathe, just breathe...it'll be alright...welcome home."

LET ME TAKE YOU ON A SEA CRUISE

By F. P. Siedentopf

During my career in the Marine Corps I experienced some good times and some bad times, as I'm sure everyone has. How my "times" may compare to those experienced by other folks I have no idea, but I do know some of those good times may have been too good, legally and morally speaking. Whether it's due to the patina of time or the onset of old age clouding my memory, as I reflect back on some of my less than enjoyable experiences they now seem to be filled with tiny bright spots. If that sounds like fool's gold instead of the real thing to you, you're probably not too far off the mark. Some of those bad times have thankfully been lost from memory without some sort of recall trigger while others have softened to the point they can be used as amusing anecdotes. One of those nuggets of fool's gold is the tale of my first trip to the Far East, aboard one of the last operational troop transports. That story begins at the end of my sixth year of service in the Marine Corps. Up to that point, I was like a puppy dog eagerly experiencing everything that came along, even the occasional swat on the behind, or the military equivalent, a stern lecture from a disgruntled officer or senior enlisted man. To get to that story and so you can understand that story better; I have to begin much, much earlier than my sixth year of service. I won't start with the swat on my behind by the doctor as I came squalling into this world, but I will begin with some of my adventures after I officially became a MARINE!

After boot training I was sent for aviation electronics training at NAS Memphis, TN. I became a member of the Marine Corps Detachment band, which was one of the best times of my life, and all it cost was time. We had to practice after school for two hours a day and four hours on Saturdays. Thankfully I played the tenor drum and never had to worry about chapped or split lips like those French Horn guys, although I will admit to a bit of jealousy. They attracted a lot more ladies by spitting into a maze of brass piping then I did by pounding on a drumhead. Practice time and traveling to events left us with a limited amount of personal time, but we were glad to give of our time and talent, such as it was. Sounds altruistic I admit, but there's more to the story.

We were authorized to wear white duty belts, which indicated we had head of the line privileges at the Mess Hall, which is the only true and fitting name for the now politically correct "Dining Facility." Those duty belts were also our permission to straggle to and from classes rather than marching in formation. In the dictionary, "to straggle" means to move singly or in a small group separate from those who went earlier. To us it meant, sleep late and run like hell to make it to class on time. Because of band practice, we were also excused from the onerous chore of Thursday night Field Day. To the uninitiated that phrase means time set aside for an athletic event, but to Marines it means sweep, swab, and scrub the toilets.

Then it was on to Sea Duty when school was over. Although I had loved the Victory at Sea documentaries and had been enthralled at the scenes of destroyers plowing through mountainous seas, the mere thought of being aboard a ship scared the hell out of me. I couldn't swim! Part of our Sea School curriculum was "drown-proofing," making sure we all knew how to remain afloat even when exhausted. I interpreted that as "drowning" in my case and just knew I'd be washed out (bad pun) when they found out I couldn't swim. To my chagrin, I was granted a waiver, graduated Sea School and was immediately given orders to the USS Boxer (LPH-4).

The work involved aboard ship I really didn't care for. I maintained the Aviation Electronics Shop that was utilized by embarked helicopter crews. I spent three years aboard the Boxer and had only one occasion to work on the ship's assigned aircraft. The primary radio failed during a flight to pickup mail, and it took me longer to climb to the flight deck than to trouble shoot and replace a blown fuse. The best part of that shop was that it was one of the few areas of the ship with air conditioning. I also had a coffee pot and a small refrigerator, which was for battery storage, but would also hold soda and the occasional beer smuggled aboard.

Since the shop was lockable, I was able to engage in a game of chance now and then, secure in the knowledge that the Masters-at-Arms couldn't break up the game and put the participants on report. A Master-at-Arms is sort of a Navy deputy sheriff that performs police duties at sea, not unlike the Shore Patrol, or Military Police ashore. In truth, they were a cross between the Keystone Kops and the Gestapo, depending who was on duty. This is where I first learned that sailors liked to bluff with a four-card flush, raise with a low pair to try and buy a pot, and sometimes giggle when they had a sure-fire winning hand.

Although the tour of duty was two years, I stayed aboard the Boxer for three. I actually reenlisted for a one-year retention on station. If that doesn't make much sense considering I didn't like the work, I must have forgotten to mention the great liberty!

We'd normally spend about two months in our homeport of Norfolk, VA, preparing for a deployment. We'd load up a battalion landing team (BLT) of Marines and helicopter squadron personnel in Norfolk then set sail for North Carolina. The ship would circle off Onslow Beach while the helicopters flew aboard, and we'd then steam south to the Caribbean Sea. This was the start of a normal three-month cruise. The BLT would make a vertical assault on the Puerto Rican Island of Vieques, the squadrons would go ashore to the provisional airfield, and the Boxer would steam to St. Thomas to anchor off the port of Charlotte Amalie for two weeks or so. We'd then go back and pick up the BLT and squadrons before steaming around the Caribbean showing off "The Flag." We'd go back for another exercise off Vieques and spend two more weeks in St. Thomas before picking up those bedraggled Marines and worn out helicopters. Then we'd steam around showing "The Flag" some more.

In three years, we visited every major Caribbean Island Nation at least three times, and also made stops in Venezuela and Mexico. In a way, it was like being on a three year Love Boat cruise, without fancy staterooms and without ladies to engage in a game of shuffleboard. We also managed to have a little excitement during the Cuban Missile Crisis, and ship's company Marines formed up shore parties when we had to evacuate or protect the evacuation of American personnel from an occasional hot spot. I was finally transferred to MCAS Cherry Point, NC, at the end of my third year of sea duty in 1964, both happy and sad to go. I was going to miss the great liberty.

It was the summer of 1965. I was bored with my tour of duty at Cherry Point after having been stationed aboard the Boxer, having served aboard ship during the Cuban Missile Crisis, and the unrest in Haiti, where we had been evacuating Americans from the Dominican Republic. I was accustomed to a little more action than a seven to four-thirty stint in a support squadron. The off-base recreation also left a bit to be desired compared to more exotic ports of call like Barbados or Martinique.

I knew that helicopter squadron personnel were routinely rotating in and out of Viet Nam, so I volunteered for a transfer to a helicopter squadron. Instead of getting orders to a unit at MCAS New River, NC, I received orders overseas as part of a rotational draft, destination Viet Nam. I was finally headed for Viet Nam, but my most miserable adventure so far in life was about to begin, a month long trip overseas on a troop carrier. Rather than going to Viet Nam as a designated replacement to an advisory group, I was going as another body in a rotational draft.

In those days there were no unit deployments and rotations. Units were permanently based overseas and personnel were transferred to a major command and dealt out to subordinate units like playing cards in a game of Gin Rummy. This was also before we needed to save time by flying replacements overseas and we went en masse on a ship, not a few hundred at a time but a few thousand. All service personnel, with the exception of a few Air Force personnel, went to the western Pacific in the same way, as a mob. Some sailors were lucky to go over on their assigned ship and come back on the same ship if it was relieved on station. When the War in Viet Nam heated up in 1966, the military needed to get the most time on the ground for each man going over for a thirteen-month tour, so the idea of wasting a month of travel over and a month of travel back by ship was scrapped in favor of sending troops on leased commercial airliners. I personally think that someone in the Pentagon had a large block of Continental Airlines stock.

We were embarked aboard a troop ship that was used in WW2 and the Korean Conflict to move troops, and had been in service taking troops over and back to the Far East continuously since 1951. It probably had survived the intervening fourteen years without a major interior cleaning, just an occasional slap-dash coat of paint. Tied up to the pier she was an imposing sight, glistening Navy gray, bright white lettering on the hull, and bright white railings. There were no telltale signs to warn us of the less than pristine conditions of the troops compartments below decks. Had we known we might all still be in exile in Canada.

The ship, the USS General William Mitchell (AP-114), carried—in addition to a mob of troops—married personnel with families and officers who were part of the draft in staterooms. They had both a promenade deck to relax on and a dining area just like a cruise ship. Senior enlisted personnel were berthed in fairly spacious troop compartments but shared the mess deck with the troops though they had a separate seating area. The sergeants and below were jammed into compartments like sardines, although I think the sardines might have been better off, at least packed in oil they could move more easily than we could. For the first time in six years, each time I entered my assigned troop space, I questioned my sanity for ever enlisting.

Our bunks had very thin mattresses and were twelve inches apart vertically in tiers of 5 to 6. Tiers not attached to a bulkhead were attached to poles so that bunks were three inches apart horizontally. The room between tiers was barely more than shoulder wide, requiring us to shuffle sideways to move about.

There was no air conditioning. There was fresh air piped in, but it was warm, outside air and the circulation within the compartments was very poor. The temperature was always in the mid to high 80s (F), and the compartments were stifling both day and night. The compartments also smelled like gym lockers filled with a year's worth of unwashed sweat gear and socks.

Since we were passengers and had no assigned duties except to clean up our living quarters, we had a major problem with boredom. Most of us spent as little time as possible in our compartments, opting to go above decks and stake out a spot under a lifeboat or along side a crane or davit. There was very little space above decks and we always seemed to be in the way of some working party. To this day, I think those sailors invented reasons to get us to move.

Above decks it was too windy to play cards and too cramped to exercise, so our major amusements were singing with an acoustic guitar, telling sea stories (lies and bigger lies), and reading if you could find a book. We loved paperback books because three or four people could read them simultaneously. Simply tear the book down its spine at a break between chapters and you ended up with three or four sections. To start, the original owner would read the first section and pass it on. While he's reading the second section someone else is reading the first. Finish those and pass them on and now you have three people reading the same book. We were always very critical of someone who lost a section of the book, although the loss of a page or two was both inevitable and accepted.

Fresh water was at a premium, so showers for the troops were allowed only every other day for two hours the Navy way: Water on—get wet—water off; Soap down (or up)—water on—rinse—water off; your basic five minute Navy shower. At the start of the two hours the water was cold and got progressively hotter until most of it was gone. At the end of the two hours the water was tepid at best, the shower space was as steamed up as a sauna, and drying off was impossible since you were sweating so much. Some of the more pungent troops often relinquished their shower time and water allocations, which didn't help the aroma of the compartment. They were usually dealt with more critically than someone who lost a section of a book.

There was always a long line for meals. Many of the troops would simply finish eating, go back on deck, and get in line for the next meal. In most cases the wait was not worth it, so I would eat breakfast, skip lunch and sometimes supper. I often went down to the mess deck after supper to beg for a sandwich and was always sure of at least a bowl of soup. The biggest hardship was no coffee during the day, no soda machines, and the Kool-Aid dispenser on the mess deck always seemed to be empty or they were out of paper cups. The water from the scuttlebutts was barely palatable and as warm as the water during the last few minutes of our shower time. It made us wonder where the water for the Kool-Aid came from.

I have fond memories of that trip, the sparkles in that lump of fool's gold. Our ships destination was Da Nang, Viet Nam, but we were able to stop in Honolulu for a day and a half of really fun liberty while dropping off a few replacement personnel. I can attest to the fact that all the major stateside breweries have products that travel well. We also stopped in Yokahama for two and a half days, and I teamed up with a friend who had been there before. We grabbed a cab and headed for the Seaman's Club, a full service stop for Merchant Marine crews. The Old Hands always carried a Y1000 note for that cab ride to a Seaman's Club.

The Seaman's Clubs offer showers, a gym, a barbershop, a restaurant, a bar, a reading room, a game room, and telephones. They also have a money exchange that offers bank rates to keep you from being "ripped off" by taxi drivers and bartenders. After a shower, a meal, and a money exchange we embarked on a tour of the cultural highlights of this major port city.

When we left Yokahama, I realized that though I was halfway around the world and had just spent two and a half days immersed in the Japanese culture, there were many things similar to the culture of the United States. Beer is beer; a jukebox is a jukebox; strippers strip; bar snacks are expensive; and hangovers hurt just as bad. I also realized that I was just as incapable of finding museums and art galleries overseas as I was at home.

We headed for Okinawa, the ship's last stop before Viet Nam, but we were delayed a bit due to a typhoon. We had to change course to skirt the northern edge of the storm and then swing around behind it and ride the rough trailing seas into Naha. For two days the seas kept building until it seemed the ship would capsize any moment. It stayed that rough for nearly a day until the typhoon moved on and calmer waters returned. Having become inured to rough seas while on sea duty, I was able to enjoy meal times. With all the rail hangers and commode huggers, chow lines were very short.

Perhaps the brightest and most treasured memory of that trip was my interaction with the ship's crew. Having spent three years on sea duty, I learned one certainty about sailors at sea: they love to gamble. I also learned that most of them were very poor poker players, and I was a little better than average. I'll never be able to play Texas Hold 'Em in a World Series of Poker event, but I was good enough to put more than a few dollars in my pocket. The ship's crew on that troop transport ran true to form, and I found a game or two to sit in on the second night out from the States.

The poker games I sat in on served several purposes for me: they were a distraction from the miserable living conditions, places to relax in comfort since the games were held in office spaces at night, and provided access to a coffee pot. Playing cards all night also allowed me to get to the head of the line for breakfast, plus I was able to accumulate a lot of lovely green backs.

Accumulating that cash was most fortuitous, since my trip to Viet Nam ended in Okinawa. I was pulled from the ship to fill a billet at MCAF, Futenma when someone with my occupation specialty (MOS) was medically evacuated for a broken back. My sea bag and I went to Futenma and my service and pay records went to Viet Nam. I lived for five months on $15.00 "Health and Comfort" pay twice a month, my poker "savings," and gauging when the slot machines at the Enlisted Club were due to pay off. It helped to be dating the slot room cashier who kept track of payoffs for me. Luckily I was reunited with my service and pay records in Viet Nam later on.

I was the Aviation Electronics Technician on board Futenma Air Station. My job was to maintain the station's assigned aircraft. My place of duty was an alcove in the station tower next to the ground communications maintenance office. I was there with my folding field desk, a small toolbox, a three and a half legged chair (actually there were four but I could never get the short one equalized), and a phone. I waited for "the call" to work on the aircraft radios. It was insane.

The aircraft was a WW2 Navy/Marine Corps SNB (some called it a secret navy bomber) that had been used as a short haul, personnel and cargo mover throughout the Pacific Theater. I knew I would never get a call to work on this two engine aircraft. It only had one engine. The other had been sent out for repairs in 1963 (two years before), and the Naval Aviation Rework Facility in the Philippines estimated that repairs would take two or three months, if they could find the parts. The electrical system had been cannibalized for parts to support an aircraft in Hawaii some Admiral used for weekend golf excursions. It was all legal; his aide was a pilot and needed to log flight time anyway.

To fill my days I worked on ancient facsimile machines the tower used to get weather maps, serviced the emergency tower generator, and performed preventative maintenance checks on the tower radios. The two Okinawa technicians who were hired to do those jobs, plus all the repairs, paid me off in fried rice and yaka soba for lunch.

To get to Viet Nam, I kept bringing up the inanity of having a technician on hand to work on an empty aluminum box that resembled an aircraft. I suppose my logic or my persistence paid off, or possibly the command's embarrassment over their aircraft made them send me to Viet Nam before the *Stars and Stripes* newspaper wrote an article about it. If there had been speed dial in those days, I would have had the *Stars and Stripes* editor's number in my phone as a last resort, if complaining hadn't worked out.

For the next few years I considered that trip to be the worst experience of my life. But after a few years of relating the story it sort of evolved into a collection of amusing and absurd anecdotes, which then transformed into fond memories. I suppose time does heal all wounds...or at least mellows memories.

HEY YAH

By Charlotte Brock

"Hey Charlotte, guess what time it is?"

"Uh-oh. Don't tell me it's…

"SYSCON DANCE PARTY!" we shouted together.

"One Two Three Uh!"

As Outkast blared out of the speakers hooked up to our computers, we jumped out of our chairs and danced to the center of the small room, singing along with André and his chorus of happy partiers.

"My baby don't mess around because she loves me so…"

Teresa and I had stripped off our blouses and wore our green sweatshirts with our desert digitals and dusty tan boots; it was in the low forties at night this time of year, and the small room we had to sit in for hours on end, the "SysCon" (Systems Control), had few creature comforts. About six feet by eight, it was made of bare concrete, the walls covered with Arabic graffiti. A large steel hook hung from the ceiling, and we tried to avoid thinking what it had been used for. After all, Camp Taqqadum, or "TQ," was an Iraqi military camp before the U.S. liberation (or invasion), and it was known that some of the buildings here had held torture chambers. Teresa, a.k.a. "Little T" (she *was* a very small Marine officer) and I inhabited the SysCon twenty-four hours a day between the two of us. She had walked in a half hour before, to relieve me and take the next twelve-hour watch.

"So why you, why you, why you, why you, why you are we so in denial when we know we're not happy heeeerrreeee…"

Teresa did the Snoopy dance. I countered with the Running Man. Then she did the Muppet. I did the Hammer dance. Neither of us could dance worth a lick, of course, but hey, who was watching?

The dancing warmed me up quickly and I pulled my sweatshirt off my torso and arms, but left it hanging on my head, so that it covered my hair veil-style.

"Yo dude, what the fuck, are you going Virgin Mary on me?"

"Nah, man, it's my new hairstyle!" and I waved my head around like I was in a shampoo commercial.

332

"Oh yeah?" In response, Teresa did her best impression of Sultan Hashim Ahman Al-Tai, sinking her head into her shoulders and adopting a ridiculous, spacey smile.

Sultan Hashim Ahman Al-Tai was the ex-Minister of Defense of Iraq. Like fifty-one other former government officials, he was on America's "Most Wanted" list. I had bought the "Most Wanted Iraqis" deck of playing cards in Kuwait: each card had a picture of one of the men (and the lone woman) whom American soldiers and Marines were supposed to capture or kill. The pictures were nearly all black-and-white, fuzzy, and could have been mug shots; the villains looked like villains. Except for Sultan Hashim Ahman Al-Tai, who figured on the eight of hearts. The ex-Minister of Defense looked jovially into the camera, garbed in green, gold and red. He was either truly short and squat or the picture had been stretched somehow to make him look that way; the effect was quite humorous. He looked like a young Santa Claus (in Iraqi military uniform), with red cheeks, a full mustache, a double chin, and a face beaming with happiness. As soon as Teresa had seen the eight of hearts, she had burst out laughing.

"Dude, check this guy out!" He looked so out of place among the stern, grim henchmen that I had to laugh too. It had quickly become an inside joke in our little group of lieutenants and warrant officers. All you had to do was say "eight of hearts" and Little T would start giggling. It was so cute and funny to see her go into peals of laughter that I couldn't help laughing with her. We got many a bellyache from looking at the infamous and unfortunate (but oh-so-joyful) Sultan Hashim Ahman Al-Tai.

Teresa and I laughed so hard we had to stop dancing. We turned down the music and sat on our desks.

"Holy Shit. We are going batshit crazy!" I said when we had recovered our breaths.

"Well, I know I am..." Pause. "Hey, it's three, did you send the SysCon report to MEF?"

"Uh, no, hold on, lemme do that before I leave." Oops. I had forgotten to send the report, again. It felt silly though to send a report that no one read. If I didn't send it, nothing ever happened. Except that I would gulp guiltily when Teresa came on watch and asked me if I had sent it. I sat behind one of the six laptops in the SysCon and typed up my report.

There were two forms of email in Iraq: the regular Internet, which we called "NIPR," short for "Non-Secure Internet Protocol," and the "SIPR," or "Secure Internet Protocol." The two systems were totally separate. NIPR was the Internet as known throughout the U.S. and the world; the world-wide-web, with pages and sites and email applications. SIPR was a similar network, except that access to it was strictly limited to those who had at least a Secret clearance and a need-to-know. Stateside, very few Marines used SIPR regularly. In Iraq, we communicated with other units almost exclusively over the SIPR. NIPR was used to write back home, and for the Internet.

Ten minutes later, I had sent our higher headquarters, the First Marine Expeditionary Force (MEF) SysCon in Camp Blue Diamond, a synopsis of what had happened during the last six hours (we lost the satellite from midnight to 0130, then it came back up; the multi-channel link to Camp Rhino went down briefly at 2220, 2300, and 0210) and the current status of communications on Camp Taqqadum (SIPR is up, NIPR is SLLOOOWWW, all radio nets are good, phones are up).

I checked the SIPR for Intel updates one last time before leaving. MEF Headquarters, as well as other units, maintained sites that summarized everything combat-related that was going on in the Anbar Province. Discoveries of weapons caches were the most frequent type of event, but there were also reports of Indirect Fire (IDF) on US or allied camps, improvised explosive devices (IEDs) found on main routes, suspicious activities by local populations, shots taken at helicopters, and firefights. My eyes scanned the most recent entries for the dreaded words: "US KIA." This time, they weren't there.

I wished Teresa a good night and a quiet watch and headed over to the female head trailer to make a head call before I hit the rack. In my backpack, which I wore everywhere, I had toothbrush, toothpaste and facial soap. That way I wouldn't have to spend another twenty minutes going back to the bathroom after getting to my tent.

By the time I had walked the half-mile or so across Tent City, unlaced my boots, taken off my blouse, unhooked my bra and threaded it through my sleeve so as not to have to take my T-shirt off, rubbed my feet together to try to rid them of sand, and found my way into my sleeping bag, all in the dark, it was 4:30 a.m. Most of the women in my tent would be getting up in an hour or two to get to the DFAC (Dining Facility, Army term for Chow Hall) before it stopped serving breakfast. I lay in bed listening to the reassuring hum of the A/C. I liked the sound, but I hated how cold it was set! I had to pull my sleeping bag over my head to conserve warmth.

Light crept into the corners of the tent, past the mosquito net that hung from the top bunk, and through my closed eyelids. I tried to turn the other way and get back to sleep, but my tent mates were just getting up and dressed. Despite their best attempts to be considerate for those whose nights had just begun, they made noise. It was even louder outside. Groups of soldiers and Marines walked by on their way to chow, conversing loudly, laughing, scuffling, rifles and gear clinking. Minutes later the flap of cloth that served as a door was untied and blinding rays of light pierced the dim interior and stabbed at my brain. Ugh. I had finally fallen asleep only minutes ago, it seemed. Maybe after everyone left the tent I could get back to sleep.... But the day only got brighter and I barely managed to doze off a couple times. Finally, at 9:30, I got up. If I was going to get some PT in, I had to do it now: lunch was over at 12:30, which meant I had to be there at 12:15 at the latest, and it took about forty-five minutes for me to shower and change after PT. If I wanted to get a run and weightlifting in, I had to start before 10 a.m. In any case, I had to pee pretty badly, and there was no going back to sleep after a fifteen-minute walk to the head and back. I found my shower shoes by my cot and stood up.

Another day had begun—Heey Ya! Hey Yaah.

FIRST COMBAT CONVOY

By David Charles

Twenty plus years as an active duty Marine without spending any time in a combat zone did not prepare me for my son's first deployment to a hostile area. Growing up the son of a Marine may have made the Corps seem like the perfect choice for him but I doubt that did much to prepare him for his first combat situation either. The Corps provided a wealth of training about combat to both my son and me; however, combat and having a son in combat are two experiences for which no amount of instruction can fully prepare a person.

My son and I did not stay in touch as much as I would have liked while he was in Iraq; so, I was looking forward to getting together when he got back. He had gotten married a few months before deploying. I was the best man at his wedding, but the precious few minutes he had during satellite phone calls from Iraq were reserved for his young bride. Worse, he was never much of a writer, so letters were few.

Not until after he returned was he able to describe his experience to me in detail. I brought him to a billiard hall, one of his favorite pastimes, so he could "whup" me at a few games of eight ball and tell me about some of his experiences. He managed to do both at the same time.

I lined up a shot and my son began talking.

"We had been in-country maybe 10 days and were going on our first convoy. My friend Ben came up to me, and said, 'I thought we were coming to Fallujah to repair vehicles, not ride around in them.'

"'Dude, you're a Marine first, a mechanic second,' I told Ben. 'Why do you think we trained to shoot all those weapons and shit? We'll be doing a couple of these convoys a week.'

"We climbed up into our vehicles, armored hummers rank with sweat and dust. As gunner on the driver's side of the vehicle, I was practically standing beside the driver when I was up looking around behind my M240 machine gun.

"Engines started rumbling up and down the line and then we were on the move. The minesweeping seven-ton truck was the first vehicle in the convoy for obvious reasons, followed by several hummers: the command vehicle occupied by my new platoon commander and his radioman and gunner; the armored support vehicle I was in along with three other Marines; and the support vehicle Ben was in that was identical to mine. There were various other trucks in the convoy as well, for transporting troops and supplies.

"Soon we were moving down the roads of Fallujah heading for a place called TQ. At first, the drive wasn't much different than any other drive I had been on before. The city had a constant smell of a landfill. That wasn't surprising since there was trash everywhere I looked, along with colorfully clad people of all ages and sexes walking, and a few men driving in cars."

My son lined up his next shot, the twelve ball in the side pocket. I imagined the scene he was describing as a combination of the Arizona desert and the concrete urban squalor in certain "second world areas" we had traveled through as a family moving to a new military duty station when my son was still a teenager. My mind threw in some Middle Easterners I had seen on CNN and equipped a few of them with hidden weapons for good measure. Adam's voice brought me back to reality.

"As the convoy approached the first overpass I tensed up and remembered this was no sightseeing tour. That was the first 'this is for real' moment. We had been briefed that this was the first hot spot that we would encounter. In this case, hot meant the enemy could be up on the overpass and choose any moment to throw something down onto one of the vehicles. Whether it was an IED (Improvised Explosive Device) or just a heavy chunk of concrete, it could be damaging to man or vehicle. I kept my eyes focused on the overpass railing but never saw any motion up there.

"The next hot spot we were warned about was called 'The Pizza Slice,' a wedge-shaped divided four-lane road that merged into a simple, two-lane road leading onto a bridge. As the multi-lane road merged into two lanes, traffic slowed down to a crawl.

"I didn't even hear the first bullets whizzing by. I guess because they we coming from the other side and weren't coming that close...yet."

My son, studying the layout on the pool table, was intent on planning his next shot. There had been times when, as a child, he was so intent on what he was doing that he would be oblivious to all else. He rubbed his hands and knees raw playing on a skateboard when he was four and didn't even notice until his mother reacted to the blood.

"The radioman in my hummer grabbed under the back of my flak jacket and pulled me down. 'Watch out!' he said, 'Don't be up there when bullets are coming at ya from where ya can't shoot.'

"'I'm s'posed to watch the left,' I said.

"'Not when you can't shoot back,' he said very deliberately, 'and you aren't covered where it's coming from now.'"

Clutching a pool cue, I said a silent thank you to a Marine I'd probably never meet.

"So while the convoy inched along, I stayed down a while in the hummer and tried to figure out what was going on from the sights and sounds, which were just confusing. Fog of War. Like in Boot Camp, but nothing like Boot. Then, when I heard some fire coming from my side, I jumped back up and grabbed the machine gun again, looking for enemy so I could return fire...I saw an old man running away from the convoy with a couple young boys in tow. They'd been in the wrong place at the wrong time and were fleeing for their lives. Even though my vision narrowed, focused on the target, I noticed colorfully clad civilians scattering in several directions, as if they knew exactly what they were doing.

"Some of the other gunners let loose a few scattered rounds, but I never saw anything I should shoot at. I felt silly up there behind the machine gun, not shooting, but we're trained not to shoot unless you identify a target, because you can easily hurt innocent bystanders."

As my son ricocheted a billiard ball into a pocket with accuracy, I was proud to hear he had paid attention in training and maintained his discipline in the midst of trying circumstances.

"I don't know why, but the radioman grabbed me and yanked me down again.

"'Get your head down!'

"As my butt hit the seat, I heard 'Ping!' Paint flew off the inside of my turret cover. That was my first real 'oh-shit' moment. I stared at the newly marked up turret cover where my head had been only a moment before. If that Marine hadn't yanked me down, (hmm) would the bullets have ricocheted off my helmet or gone through my head?"

I smiled back at him as I chalked my pool cue. I was happy because we didn't have the answer to his question. He could have been wounded or shot dead at that very moment. My worst fear could easily have been realized. The recurring dread of losing my son and the nightmare of guilt was once again staring me in the face. I had practically delivered him to the Marine Corps and combat (I'm not sure I could live with it). Ignoring the fetid lump in my stomach, gulping it down, I listened to his continuing drama.

"The convoy moved on over the bridge and the fire-fight was over. Just like that. From beginning to end, I had probably been in the hot zone only a couple minutes. I hoped no one had been hurt. My senses were pinging; I was more alert than ever before. The rest of that trip was uneventful but the tension never let up. It was like that two-plus-hour drive took days to bring us within the relatively safe TQ encampment.

"While there, all the gunners who had fired off rounds went to see the JAG. They weren't in real trouble or anything but they had to explain what they saw and shot at. Those talks with the JAG were actually for our protection. The details were gathered while still fresh in the minds of the shooters. I realized how lucky it was that I didn't squeeze off a round just to be doing what I thought everyone else was doing. Actually, only a couple Marines had used their weapons that day.

"After the cargo and men were loaded, we made the trip back to Fallujah in peace. I never thought of a convoy as just another ride again. I had qualified for a Combat Action Ribbon on my first convoy. More importantly, we didn't lose anybody and I had full respect for what I had gotten myself into.

"Right after we got over the bridge, and as it all was happening, was when things changed. Everything changed. I realized and respected all of those who came before me, and all of those there with me, a lot more after that. I've had some scary moments before but never have I had an experience where I was almost more worried about the other Marines than myself.

"I was standing off to myself smoking one cigarette after another when Ben approached me.

"'Whad'ya think?' he asked.

"'Shit was crazy,' I said.

"With a grunt, he agreed. With nothing else to say we stood there a half hour or more, smoking and appreciating each other's company, even in the silence, maybe because of the silence."

My son and I did not talk much on the ride back from the billiard hall; we didn't have to. I understood being more worried about the other Marine, my son in this case, than myself. My son understood what being a Marine was all about. He seemed pleased we had shared and further bonded as both Marines and father-and-son. I was pleased and proud of the Marine he had become and thankful to God that he came home in one piece. We were just appreciating each other's company. Even in the silence. Maybe, because of the silence.

BRIGHT AND PRESSED

By Stacy Atkinson

"Mom, I need you to sign here. I'm leaving next Monday." The words popped out of my older sister's mouth. Mom's mouth and my mouth were wide open in complete and utter shock. I was 10 years old at the time and couldn't help but wonder what my sister was about to put herself through. I spent the next couple of days running around the house nagging my sister for answers to questions. "What is it going to be like?" "What are they going make you do?" My sister always responded uneasily, "I'm really not sure."

My sister left, made it through boot camp, and Mom and I traveled to South Carolina to watch her graduate. I felt the enormous sense of pride my sister had for her accomplishment. How badly I wanted to be just like her! I hadn't always wanted to be just like her. But somehow at that point in my life, I couldn't help but admire everything I imagined she had gone through to reach that point.

A few years later I spent a day on Fort Hamilton Army Base in Brooklyn, New York, watching the Marine Corps Silent Drill Team perform. It was a class trip, and all we expected as 8th graders was a really boring history lesson or a performance that would put us to sleep. Sitting there on the grass, I immediately knew I was in for much more. The Marines' pressed and bright uniforms, along with their intense movements—the "pop and lock" of the rifles, the clicking of their heels, and their coordinated movements—has stood out in my mind for years, every time I hear mention of the Marines. As a child, every time I saw one of those red, black and gold United States Marine Corps emblems, I always thought back on those Marines in their ever so bright and pressed uniforms. I had always heard that they were the best, whatever that meant, and knew that one day if I was strong enough to sign up I wanted to be a Marine.

I graduated High School in 2002 with a good scholarship to attend Saint Joseph's College in New York, and planned to become a teacher—if I earned a Bachelor's Degree. Teaching was one of those other dreams in the back of my mind, an old dream, but not as old as the Marine dream. Ready to embark on the college life, I committed myself to Saint Joe's, but after two years I still dreamed of being one of those Marine guys. No matter how much I tried I couldn't get the Marine dream out of my head. Could I make it through Boot Camp though? No way! The thought of failure often entered and exited my mind, but the desire lingered.

I convinced myself over and over again that I could never do it. I convinced myself that I wasn't even worthy of dreaming about it. In my mind becoming a Marine was just not possible for a weak 120-pound girl with no athletic orientation whatsoever. The words raced over and over in my head: "There is just no way I can ever make it."

In 2005, I put the teaching dream to the side and accepted a full time job working as a staffing specialist. With a bold salary of 41,000 dollars a year, who would ever think of refusing the offer just to finish a degree? I sure didn't. I also relocated with the company to Pittsburgh, Pennsylvania on an impulse and spent a year there.

After that first year, I became bored and my dream of becoming one of those Marine people crept up on me. As I considered my options, I bounced back and forth promising myself to go back to college and become a teacher because it was the easier of my two dreams and, as a teacher, I wouldn't have to go to Boot Camp. Looking for every excuse in the book to not sign up for the Marines, I also remained unsuccessful in returning to school to complete a teaching degree.

One Saturday afternoon in the mall, I saw him—the man who would recruit me into the Marines and help me begin my journey. Neither he nor I knew it at the time, but I would be one of only two women he recruited and shipped off to Boot Camp during his entire three year recruiting tour.

When I saw my recruiter, I was in line at the Dairy Queen in the Food Court. I stared as he passed through the Food Court, holding a cup of coffee and wearing that uniform so pressed and bright. Instantly that Silent Drill Team I had thought about for years came to mind. I couldn't help but think that I at least should talk to him. Talking to him could do no harm—he could never convince me to give up my high-paying job to join. I was way stronger that!

I followed him downstairs to his office and let him walk far ahead of me. He entered the small recruiting hub and closed the door. I chickened out and went home. If I wasn't going to join, I didn't even want to waste his time—excuses were still winning the battle in my mind.

For two months, I promised myself I would at least go talk to the recruiter. I never found the nerve to do it. Plus, my great job was keeping me busy. Besides, I didn't want to put him through all the butchering, the questioning, the interrogation I was planning. I was completely convinced that he could never ever say anything that would make me want to join. Why even bother? Boot Camp would be too tough. And aside from having the toughest Boot Camp for recruits, there were only a small percentage of female Marines, 6 percent at the time, in the whole Marine Corps. I could never make it into that elite few.

One day, despite all of those self-inflicted negative thoughts, I did it. I went into the recruiter's office to donate to the Marine Corps Reserve Toys for Tots program and scheduled an appointment for an enlistment interview. I got the "*So you want to be a Marine?*" look. That really lit me on fire. Not a fire of anger but a fire of motivation. I had long hair and long red nails. I was wearing a suit and heels—but so what? I could be a Marine, too, if I wanted. Plenty of females made it through Boot Camp before me and plenty will make it after me. Who were any of them to look at me puzzled just because I didn't exactly fit the average description of a potential Marine? I'd show them! That became my new attitude regarding the Marine Corps. It was an attitude that changed my life forever.

I met with the recruiter one evening. Before he arrived, I really thought that he was going to hate me. I was going to be that potential recruit that came in with all the questions recruiters dodge. I was going to butcher him up. He had no idea! I was just coming in to inquire about those Marine people. I wasn't joining! I don't want to go through Boot Camp!

We spoke for a good two hours. I was certain that I had the upper hand, while wondering all the while what exactly was the upper hand for a girl who willingly went and spoke to this busy recruiter. I would not let this recruiter do to me what he had done to so many others by convincing them what they should do in life. I was to be strong and ask all the questions. I wanted to make him scratch his head and convince me not to join! I left the recruiter's office and promised to look at the other services and see which would offer me the best opportunity. After all, all the recruiting branch offices were within feet of each other and I had the upper hand. Remember? The Marines needed me; I didn't need them!

I was still saying to myself that there was no way I was going anywhere, but I never even made it to the other services' recruiting offices because I knew that the Marines were the best—whatever that meant—and I knew that the uniform was always bright and pressed.

I lost touch with my recruiter for a whole two days, and then there he was, ringing my phone and begging for answers. I went into the office three times more to discuss the process of enlistment and fill out all sorts of paperwork. Each time I kept thinking to myself that this wasn't really happening. I wasn't going to give up my dog and my apartment and my really good job...NO WAY! How stupid to sacrifice all that for a low paying job where they were going to tell me where to live, what to do, and even make me run, too!

Then it happened. My recruiter called me at my job and said everything had checked out. I could enlist! He asked me when I wanted to swear in. Swear in? Was he nuts? I kept screaming in my head, "I can't make it through boot camp!" But after many talks with other Marines and researching all that I could, I became determined to make it.

Two weeks later, I spent the afternoon swearing in to become a United States Marine. What a moment that was! I couldn't even recite the oath—I was a blubbering mess: proud, overjoyed and a little bit nervous. I planned everything out in my head and promised that I would do the Marine thing and leave the Marine Corps a better person or stay in and continue on with the Marine Corps life.

Shipping out to Boot Camp evoked another round of self-questioning: "Am I really doing this?" "When will I turn around and go home?"

For 3 months, I kept thinking that one day I would wake up and be home, and none of this Marine-stuff would have ever happened. But I didn't want my enlistment to be a dream because at this point, it was already too much of a reality: hard work, sweat, pain. I was determined to make it.

Determination is what has truly carried me through this entire journey. I graduated Boot Camp on July 14, 2006. That feeling is truly indescribable. I could never really put into words what it felt like to earn a title I had denied myself for so many years. I remembered my sister's Army graduation. Now I really know what she had felt because I was feeling the same thing upon completing Boot Camp. I still thought that it couldn't be true and that none of it was happening. But with everything I had been through during Boot Camp, it had better have all been true; I better have earned that title, Marine.

With two short years in the Marine Corps, I am grateful each day for that 8th grade class trip to see the Silent Drill team and for seeing my recruiter strolling through the Food Court. I can't imagine my life any other way. It would be neither as satisfying nor as rewarding. Jobs will come and go but earning the title, Marine, is something no one can ever take away. We're motivated and we scream, we run and we are mean, but in the end, our job is to be selfless advocates of America's freedom. That's a job like none other.

My salary is way less than 41K a year, but being a Marine is worth way more than any monetary amount. Marines from all walks of life are far different than any other organized group of people I've met. There are tons of stories about how Marines actually wound up choosing this branch of service. Many did it for the self-accomplishment, the challenge, or out of patriotism. I've made up a tremendous number of cheesy reasons for my decision to join. The truth is, I don't believe I chose the Marine Corps; I'm pretty sure the Marine Corps chose me.

HAYES FOR THE DEFENSE

By Jack Hayes

It was a cold, sunny afternoon in November of 1952. In my room at the (BOQ) Bachelor Officer's Quarters at the Naval Shipyard in Portsmouth, Virginia, I was poring over the papers I needed to know "cold" for a contractors' meeting in the morning. A Reserve Lieutenant JG called to active duty from my first civilian job, I had been trained as a marine engineer and commissioned by The New York State Maritime Academy, so I knew my job. The call-up to active duty had been expected, and I was not as rankled as some were at the Navy.

My concentration was broken by a knock on the door of my room. The messenger had come from Captain Seim, my skipper, directing me to report to his room.

"What now?" I thought.

This had been a tough week with the ship in dry-dock undergoing massive overhaul from battle damage. We had received topside damage in a three-hour gun duel with shore batteries in Wonsan Harbor, and hull damage from a mine in the South China Sea while out with Task Force 77. The Japanese had fixed us up in a yard in Sasebo with a skin over the sealed forward fireroom, where three of my guys were still part of the machinery from the mine blast. We came around the world with the other three destroyers of Destroyer Division 2 in that condition.

It was winter and the dry-docked ship was not habitable. So the crew had been housed in barracks and the officers in Bachelor Officers Quarters at the yard. It was not bad living, but I had already managed to find trouble. One four striper, probably newly promoted, had taken umbrage when I did not salute his car as he went by me as I was walking one day (chicken shit). And then one afternoon I had inadvertently let the sink in my room overflow while washing my socks; I thought I had freed the drain to allow them to continue to rinse, but when I went next door to continue working with my staff on upgrading engine room orders, the sink filled and ran over. The water ran down the walls of the captain's room below mine; that one required a dress-blues appearance for the reaming out about destroying government property.

As Head of the Engineering Department on USS Barton (DD722), I already had my hands full with contractor meetings and supervising the overhaul. I didn't need a "chewing out" from the skipper to boot, I thought. But I washed my face and changed into clean khakis in preparation for his telling me how I should have been more attentive to the two captains.

But that was not what he had in mind. Instead, without a "by your leave" he informed me that I would be defense attorney for a Sailor who he had referred to a Summary Court Martial. It was a complete surprise to me. Despite my heavy workload in the yard, I couldn't refuse the Captain's assignment, of course. But what did I know about being a lawyer? I didn't even know the man whose future had been thrust into my hands. What a travesty of justice this would be, I thought.

This deck division sailor "...threw a fit in the crew's head in barracks," they said. As the crew prepared to muster for liberty one Saturday morning, he had slashed his wrists. It was considered a sham by his department chief, the cut being superficial and the man known to be missing some of his old pals who had recently received Bad Conduct Discharges (BCDs) and been mustered out. The first lieutenant put the man on report for malingering, and later for going absent without leave (AWOL). At mast the captain awarded the summary court.

But whatever my problems with contractor meetings and overhauls, the court was to be held in a few days, and I had to bone up on the Uniform Code of Military Justice rules so I could properly take on this new, unexpected assignment to defend the man, no matter what he had done. I had never met the Sailor, so I arranged to interview him at the brig. As I returned the Marine sentry's salute at the brig gate, I saw Sailors marching in dungarees—believe me, there's nothing like a prison run by the Marines for "squids" (the Marine nickname for Sailors): shaved heads; tight dungarees and properly worn white cup hats; marching in lock-step where each man is close enough to the one in front and behind in ranks to breathe down one-another's necks; and lots of loudly-barked orders by the Marine guards.

The Sailor's name was Schwartz. He had been serving in one of the deck divisions aboard ship and didn't know me. He was scared to death when we met, sitting rigidly across the table from me and hardly speaking, beyond "Yes sir" and "No sir" when I questioned him. I persisted quietly, though, explaining that I had been assigned to help him by representing him in the court. I stressed that I needed to know all the facts to be able to represent him properly.

Finally, after three interview sessions, my client opened up a little. He told me he had complained of headaches and nervousness to his division chief, but had been refused permission to report to the hospital and he had been restricted to the ship and barracks. As a result, frustrated, he "went over the hill." I thought he had jumped the base somehow and gone home.

"Where did you go?" I asked. He said he went to the hospital on the base to see a doctor.

"Whom did you see?" I got doctor's names.

I went to the hospital and interviewed the doctors. At first they were non-committal, probably seeing me as an extra problem punched into their already-busy schedules. But eventually they said they remembered having seen him and had diagnosed his problem. They had given him some medicine to calm him down.

Aha! The refusal to allow a visit to the doctor and retaliation for going anyway was evidence of his bosses having a pre-conceived notion about this guy. We had a defense! This legal stuff was not going to be so bad after all. But there was an additional problem with the court being convened at this time. The Legal Officer (prosecutor) aboard BARTON was a Lieutenant Forsythe. He was committed to making the Navy a career, and had applied for and been accepted to submarine school in Groton, Connecticut. He was to leave in a few days and had been given five days delay in reporting—time off when he could visit his Yankee relatives before reporting to the school. But I took my job seriously, and did not consider the inconvenience a long trial would impose on my friend, the Legal Officer.

The court was convened as scheduled in a cleared compartment aboard the dry-docked BARTON. The Executive Officer, Commander Denniston, a lawyer in civilian life from Mobile, Alabama, was President of the Court, the judge, so I expected it to be conducted in a professional way. When we began I became concerned. Although I had done my best to prepare a defense for my client, I was apprehensive. I guess I expected there would be "practice sessions," but what I saw when the proceedings began was amateurish.

The Commander, the prosecutor and I sat, each with a thick Uniform

Code of Military Justice book, while the accused listened, and the proceedings moved forward following the description of a trial as it was laid out as a script, page by page, line by line and word by word from the books. It seemed a sham of a trial to me. But I soon realized that the assigned court was not high enough to rate transfer to the JAG office on the base for adjudication by professionals, and we had to do our best.

I had not seen any requirement in my readings that the defense needed to inform the prosecutor in advance of what was to be presented, and we proceeded as though there would be no defense—the prosecutor calling his witnesses to lay out his case for the court. I cross-examined each witness and established that his accusers had not believed that there was anything the accused needed at the hospital and had pre-judged him.

When I visited the doctors, I had informed them that I wished for them to testify, and I had scheduled their appearance. They knew what I wanted and were prepared to testify truthfully about my client's attendance at the hospital and need for treatment. The testimony of the doctors and my client's division officers on the stand took three whole days. My days investigating and the time to set up the court took four more. The Legal Officer's five days delay in reporting to Sub School had elapsed and he was pissed. At the conclusion of the trial it was also apparent that my client was unhappy as well. He had wanted a BCD and release from the Navy like his buddies; instead, the verdict approved by the JAG was 3 months confinement back in the brig at hard labor.

Brig time would straighten him out, I figured. And although my client wasn't happy, I had saved his reputation—a BCD was not a recommendation to carry into an interview when he would apply for a civilian job after getting out. I felt I had done my duty even though no one was happy.

Save me from lawyering!

MCWS8

4 October – 1 November 2008

Guest Writer: Melinda Copp

Participants:
David
Fred
Moe
Nancy
Stacy
Shana
Monica
"N"—The Narrator

Choice Determines Destiny

—Banner hanging above the main gate at Marine Corps Air Station Beaufort, South Carolina during Fall 2008.

CARRYING ON

Pete and I brought his mother home in hospice care following her three-week hospital stay. Margaret's care required all my attention. A new rhythm became routine. We ate later and smoked earlier. Moments of dying grew stronger than moments of living, while the many strangers who helped us grew closer than friends. There was neither enough we could do nor time enough to do it. The fine yarn of days unwound as in the paws of a kitten, until those tender paws grew claws. Margaret died May 20, 2008 in her home on Coosaw Island, where Pete and I had lived next door to her for nine years.

Margaret Milne Coull Drumm came to this country as a five-year-old child from Scotland. Her first months in America were spent lying in bed recovering from Scarlet Fever in the Ellis Island hospital. Margaret spent her adult life raising six children and working as a nurse. When she arrived to Beaufort in 1974, she purchased the land beside Lucy Point Creek, where we now live. She knew me well, and her, I. Before her death, Margaret discussed with me a list of possessions she wanted her family to receive. Winding up her bequests, she said, "You'll be fine. You have your writing…and my plants." Our love of gardening had made us friends when we first met. Later, Margaret had taken interest in my writing and teaching life. Still, her comment was bittersweet, considering the amount of time spent apart from her while I was pursuing that teaching and writing life. For the first six years of my marriage, Pete, Margaret, Karen (Pete's sister), and I had been a family of four. Other family members lived hundreds of miles away. With Karen's death in 2004, we became a family of three. Now we were two, and the silence was vast. Marking our loss of mother, grandmother, and friend, a celebration of Margaret's life was held on Saturday, May 24, at Coosaw Island. A bagpiper played, strolling by the river, piping his dirge, our tears in his wake.

Eternity will not efface those dear records of transports past;
Thy image at our last embrace; Ah! little thought we 'twas our last!
Ayr gurgling kiss'd his pebbled shore, o'erhung with wild woods thick'ning green;

The fragrant birch, and hawthorn hoar, twin'd am'rous round the raptur'd scene.
The flowers sprang wanton to be prest, the birds sang love on ev'ry spray.
Till too, too soon, the glowing west proclaim'd the speed of winged day.
Still o'er these scenes my mem'ry wakes, and fondly broods with miser care.
Time but the impression deeper makes, as streams their channels deeper wear.
—From "To Mary in Heaven"[1]

On May 22, Kevin Watson, Press 53 publisher, contacted me by email and agreed to accept my proposal for a Milspeak anthology. It was iffy for a while. When he initially contacted me on March 13, 2008, Kevin had asked for a proposal for an anthology of military writing that would include Milspeak writers' memoirs and invited contributors' works of fiction, nonfiction, and poetry. Soon, Kevin, Sheryl Monks (former co-owner Press 53), and I had decided to add a fiction co-editor, Jeff Hess. A Navy Veteran, Jeff was one of three veterans, including me, who had discussed doing something with writing for veterans in a Queens University anteroom during our graduation week in May 2005. He began a writing workshop for veterans in Florida around the same time I did in South Carolina. Jeff called his workshop DD214, the official government form number for discharge papers.

On March 28, 2008, Kevin, Sheryl, Jeff, and I tried discussing the anthology project using Yahoo chat. Not everyone could hear, so we switched to a Press 53 chat room, all of us typing as fast as we could. After a while, I read the conversation and didn't offer much—the wheels were spinning. It might sound ungrateful, but I didn't want to edit an anthology written by both civilian and military people. I wanted to edit an anthology of Milspeak writing and share the Milspeak story.

I typed into the conversation: "Kevin, may I make a proposal?"

"Sure," he replied.

"Can we have two books? Jeff could edit the military fiction anthology and I'll edit a Milspeak anthology." The silence was huge. Eventually, Kevin replied that I should a write another proposal for a stand-alone Milspeak anthology. I worked up the proposal as fast as I could. That opportunity was transformed into reality upon receiving Kevin's approval to proceed on May 22—Milspeak would have its own anthology.

I had stopped writing when Margaret became ill. After she died, I couldn't think or write. The work of caring for Margaret and my grief exhausted me. I had declined teaching two fall courses at the technical college because I was worn out and knew I would need time to work on the Milspeak anthology. I chewed on design ideas all through the summer. Still couldn't write. August brought the realization that I didn't really know what Milspeak was accomplishing, and this was causing my case of writer's block. To resolve uncertainty, I asked Milspeak writers for feedback.

I had first read "Hutch" in *Poetry*, a publication of the Poetry Foundation. Harriet Monroe, who embraced the dissident poets of her age, founded *Poetry* in 1912: "They throw a bomb into the entrenched camps, give to American art a much-needed shaking up."[2] The poets' circular distributed by Harriet assured them "of a chance to be heard in their own place, without the limitations imposed by a popular magazine."[3] Although Harriet and I were born generations apart, our philosophies toward writing and writers are similar. Milspeak writers' experience of military life shared in their own words can give America and American art a "much-needed shaking up" without limitations imposed by the publishing culture or the Department of Defense. It is, of course, a coincidence that my literary life was born on a mountaintop in South America in 1996, while Harriet Monroe's life ended in 1936 on a nearby mountaintop.

After first reading "Hutch" in *Poetry*, I began sharing it with my college students and Milspeak writers. I contacted Atsuro Riley through *Poetry*, and asked Mr. Riley's permission to include his poem in this anthology as its epigram because this anthology is a "Hutch" holding Milspeak writers' stories within its cover, and "Hutch" speaks of what war veterans experience when imagination marries memory. Fed by imagination, memory grows over time, eventually taking on a life of its own. Even the smallest of daily encounters can render new meaning from an old experience hidden in the folds of memory, causing the mind to flash back upon pain and sorrow as if the wound had reopened.

Rather than write a thank you to them, I decided to invite those who had helped develop Milspeak, had served as guest writers, and had mentored Milspeak writers and me, to contribute to this anthology their thoughts on their Milspeak experience and writing as a healing art. Their responses have been generous and informing.

But my work designing and compiling this anthology is most informed by my work with Dr. Sheila Tombe. Between 2002 and 2006, I worked as a volunteer at *Apostrophe: USCB Journal of the Arts* under the guidance of Dr. Tombe, the journal's founder and one of my undergraduate professors in literature. One of the founding principles of *Apostrophe* was to publish emerging writers alongside established writers. Sheila taught me to recognize good literature; perhaps most significantly by making me read and choose "yeses and maybes" without first considering the source of the submission. She taught me that to respect the work is to respect the writer. This complements a principle I learned in the military: a general or a lieutenant might be flying the plane I controlled, but control procedures and mission accomplishment are indifferent to rank. Sheila has been one of my most important mentors by training me for the work I am doing.

Milspeak writers and I worked on a cover design. Fred Siedentopf did the work of putting our ideas together. I sent our cover to Kevin and wrote that we were willing to change the cover if something else would work better. Kevin sent back a cover he had designed that included an image of a Short Timer's Calendar recorded on someone's hand. "It's perfect," I wrote back, "I love it." I couldn't say anything else. I wasn't sure I should. Kevin knew only a little of my personal story. The last thing I wanted was to scare away our publisher with revelations about my twisted past. On November 16, a few days after Kevin delivered the cover design, I sent this email to him:

As you might know, I am in recovery from alcoholism. Have been since 1985, though I've only been sober since January 28, 1992, my first sober day. Many things led to the moment in my Okinawa barracks room when I sobered up on the evening of January 27, 1992. Suffice to say, that night I was seriously ready to die and to take action to do so. I decided to try turning it all over to a higher power one more time. I was alone in my room, terribly hung over still from the night before when a memorial service for a fellow marine was held; I felt responsible for her death. I got on my knees and asked for help, for strength to go on. A hand grasped my right shoulder. The world and my problems disappeared. I felt peace, real peace, for the first time in my life. Then it was over. But it's never really been over. From that moment, my perspective on life changed. I never drank again. From that moment till now, I've tried my best to help others recover from whatever it is they suffer. I'm no saint. I do a lot wrong. Milspeak, like my enlistment in the Corps, was an accident of chance. I've never spoken about that hand except in 12-step meetings or when I was trying to help someone suffering the ravages of alcoholism.

From the moment I was touched by that strange hand in my Okinawa barracks room, I have felt as though I have no time to waste. My understanding of that moment as a spiritual experience has grown, but I can make no claim to the stuff the hand was made of. And, as Forrest Gump would say, "That's all I have to say about that."

Kevin had found the cover image on the Internet, and knew only that a soldier's sister had taken the photograph. I hoped Kevin could find the photographer and that she would allow use of the image for the anthology cover. The Short Timer's Calendar recorded on the hand is something I recognized right away. Fred Siedentopf, a Milspeak writer, provides this explanation of the Short Timer's Calendar:

The term "short timer" has been used in the military for generations and identifies someone who is getting close to release from active duty or to the end of a tour of duty. No one knows for sure when the term entered the lexicon of the military, but it came into widespread use during the Vietnam War.

In Vietnam, each service member knew when he or she was going to be sent home...when his rotation date came around. He also knew when his enlistment was up. The closer he came to either date naturally meant his time was short, therefore anyone getting close to rotating out of Vietnam or getting close to discharge was a Short Timer. This gave birth to the Short Timer's Calendar used to count off the number of days remaining until you left Vietnam on the "Freedom Bird" and/or the number of days until discharge.

It wasn't actually a calendar; it was usually the outline of a picture marked off in little blocks with numbers in them. These numbers represented the number of days remaining until the event. A typical Short Timer's Calendar would have a picture divided into as many as 100 or as few as 30 parts, the most popular being 90. The favorite calendars were variations of an unclad pin-up girl or the short timer who is so short his helmet covers him completely.

On November 22, 2008, Kevin sent me an email. "Brace yourself," he wrote. He had forwarded the email from the photographer, Crystal Floyd, who gave us permission to use the image. But her email also included the following:

> This means more to me than I can express—as I lost my brother in September in an auto accident. After he'd braved the war zone, god closed the chapter of his young life in a motor accident. There is so much I am still processing, and learning. He's my BABY brother, yet it is HE who has taught ME much.

The cover image is, as Kevin said, a perfect metaphor for Milspeak. I don't know the name of Crystal's brother. I don't know exactly how he died. In a sense, his anonymity is appropriate. His is the loss each American feels for the Unknown Soldier and the grief they share with families who lose loved ones to war. I feel this sister's loss of her brother and am so grateful to her for allowing her photograph to grace our cover. The image represents all this anthology hopes to be, a message to the world about the military experience.

Crystal's image has been my talisman, my philosopher's stone, my inspiration while I worked to bring this anthology together. My own left hand is half numb, and has been since 1985 when my left arm was broken in the drunk driving accident that nearly killed my best friend. During my drinking career, I sent five cars to the junkyard, each the result of drinking and driving. I should have died many times during my blackout-drinking career. The Marine in Okinawa whose death I felt responsible for had died drunk after driving her car into a wall. The accident happened less than two weeks after I spoke with her about her drinking over a couple longneck Buds. I was a hypocrite, a senior Marine hiding none too well her drinking after resuming alcoholic drinking following treatment for alcoholism, and presuming to talk a junior Marine sober. I survived that talk. She didn't. I wanted to die. Alone in my barracks room, desperate for release, I got on my knees and asked for help. Help came in the form of that strange hand grasping my shoulder. That hand found me, Crystal's photograph found me, just as Milspeak writers find me, just as you have found this book. Chance or a choice presented by chance has brought us all together.

Good things have come from my initial plan for the war veterans' writing workshop that became Milspeak Creative Writing Seminars. While I was planning MCWS 1 in 2005, Lynn Freed had just published "Doing Time: My Years in the Creative Writing Gulag."[4] More than three years later, when I began working with this anthology, the questions initially raised by Freed's article remained. Had pursuing my three big projects following graduation been a waste of time? Was I wasting others' time by continuing Milspeak, writing, and teaching? Would I become what Freed's narrator implied she had become, bowed and beaten under by student writers' manuscripts? Had I taken a wrong turn on the road toward excellence?

To answer those questions, old lessons learned many times over during twenty active duty years as a training program developer, leader, and trainer, joined new lessons: I had grown into a teacher, a writer, and leader of Milspeak Creative Writing Seminars. Milspeak writers answered those questions through feedback. Guest contributors to this anthology have answered with their thoughts. Writing, teaching, and Milspeak are the boon of my search for meaning, not the end.

At its worst, the dismissive attitude of Lynn Freed's narrator toward the hard work of student writers is no different in principle from the private school headmaster and teachers who told me not to expect too much from my "country kids." No—I will not become that as a teacher or a workshop leader. I will jump up and down and dance when the days of highbrow and lowbrow educational values come to an end and we all recognize that every human being has the ability to learn. Each individual in this world has a right to the achievement of potential. Given the right learning environment that potential can be achieved, but the individual must be willing to do the work.

Life experience, not mere classroom experience, matters in developing and carrying out any type of program. My life experience played an important role in Milspeak's evolution. Only a creative writing MFA graduate could have set up a writing program like Milspeak, a model of Queens University of Charlotte's MFA program. Only a Marine could have set up and carried out an unfunded writing program—"Can Do; Make Do." My twisted journey toward excellence has proven one of my greatest strengths; being an alcoholic is equally important. Without experiencing the many challenges, pitfalls, and failures of my life, how could I have the compassion, tolerance, and empathy necessary to work with the diverse group of writers who have stepped across the threshold into The Blackbird Zone? Only a writer with military experience could and would work at length with inexperienced military writers who enter The Blackbird Zone. Only a writer with military experience could understand what military people endure in a military life. I am a writer, a human being who uses written language to share life experiences and lessons learned from the great experiment that is life. I am a worker of the work put before me: to live, to explore, and to analyze the findings of my great adventure. I am bound by the tenets of poetic faith to share my results. To reach fulfillment, my written work needs a reader. But to write for a reader instead of to myself is to determine the sum of an equation minus a factor. I must first discover my truth and strength if I am to share it. Pen and paper, memoir and essay are my gear. When I write, I write for myself *and* for a reader.

Collaboration is Milspeak's heart. If collaboration takes place with one writer, as it did in MCWS 1, the effort is worthwhile. Without the writers who sign up for workshop, there couldn't be a Milspeak. Milspeak writers bring to workshop a shared experience of living a military life and a shared dream of writing for a reader, for themselves, or for family. They learn to work together to bring the best of a story to life. Often, their stories are difficult for them to share and sometimes have never before been shared with anyone. These writers have worked together to bring something to life from the ashes of the past. Warren Slesinger's MCWS 2 talk on the work of Gregory Orr taught me that the power relationship between event and self is changed through writing. Self as poet masters the almost overwhelming disorder that is stabilized by taking charge of an imagination fueled to inferno by memory. Perhaps Dante would agree that writing is a stay against confusion as Robert Frost suggested. No matter a person's writing skills, writing can be a stay against confusion, a communication, a bridge between the conscious and unconscious contents of the mind. Through writing memoir with other military people, Milspeak writers cross that bridge, and repair it if necessary. Perhaps specialized workshops and thematic anthologies can help others from all walks of life understand each other as Milspeak has done among military people.

The life lessons our veterans can impart to each other are priceless, but become useful when seasoned veterans have a way to carry their wisdom to a new generation of veterans. Writing has long achieved this purpose, as demonstrated in Book 16 of Homer's *The Odyssey*. Odysseus and his son, Telemachus, meet for the first time since Odysseus's journey began 20 years before. Prior to their meeting, Odysseus (representing the seasoned warrior) is approached by the goddess Athena, who tells him it is time to share his truth with his son, Telemachus (representing the young warrior). Only then will the two be strong enough to win the next battle, bringing down the many suitors populating Odysseus's palace in a bid to control the kingdom.

The seasoned warrior, Odysseus, transformed by Athena into a golden vision of his former war-torn, shipwrecked self, confronts the young warrior, who does not recognize his father—he sees a god who must be worshipped. The young warrior, intimidated by this god, recognizes in the other only surface glory: the reward of battles won, the title, Hero. The young warrior cannot see himself in the seasoned warrior. Comparing himself to the seasoned warrior, rather than identifying with him and recognizing they share the same wounds of troubled memories and repressed emotions, the young warrior's intimidation grows. He sees himself as less-than the other and lacking wisdom, judgment, and experience. The young warrior fears that in showing emotion the seasoned warrior will judge him cowardly, weak and unworthy of the battle yet to be waged against the suitors.

The seasoned warrior has no such inhibition—Athena, goddess of wisdom, has demanded he share his truth. The seasoned warrior sets the young one straight by acknowledging that the younger has borne as much pain and as many trials as he. The seasoned warrior's words free the younger to release emotions long hidden during his struggle toward valiance. In a moment of clarity, the young warrior recognizes himself in his father—reality overcomes imagination. Here, then, is the message of the ancient warrior to the modern warrior: the past is not a god to be worshipped; the ability to endure emotional pain in silence is not a mark of courage—stoic silence leads to inner disquiet and untold suffering, which, when endured alone, leads to untold emotional, psychological, spiritual, and physical complications.

"N" the Narrator, like Athena in *The Odyssey*, is the communication tool Milspeak uses to bring military people together over the truths in their stories despite the differences in their experience. "N," the I on the page, is the bridge between inner and outer worlds, the neutral element that helps one human being understand the human in the other. "N" is the great equalizer, the letter that bears all things and all experience. Both seasoned and young warriors need each other's truth in order to complete the journey home. Why not give our seasoned veterans the chance to impart their wisdom to the young before the young become lost in wartime experience? Why not bring them together for dialog before the young are sent into battle and upon their return? In each other's stories, old wounds can be healed and some wounds will be prevented. Milspeak is not a perfect tool and the participant pool has been small, but if someone like me can learn as much as I have through a program like Milspeak, then similar programs in the right hands should reap even larger rewards for military personnel and civilians alike.

One of the most misunderstood wounds of military service is PTSD. By degrees the symptoms of PTSD identify themselves not as a disorder but as a syndrome. The process begins to unfold with experiencing a traumatic event that continues to work beneath the surface, making itself known over time through symptoms too often misdiagnosed as originating from other conditions. PTSD sometimes completely disables those affected by stripping away the ability to deal with problems of living. Like all processes, once the steps of PTSD progression are identified the symptoms can be addressed, and sometimes reversed or put in remission. But, like alcoholism, PTSD has no cure. PTSD is as difficult as alcoholism to diagnose and to understand, particularly for those who live with its symptoms. Like alcoholism, PTSD requires self-acceptance to overcome denial of the condition's existence and effect on human life. Only an alcoholic can diagnose him- or herself as alcoholic; only someone suffering the symptoms of PTSD can determine if he or she has PTSD. In alcoholism and PTSD diagnosis, professionals can point out symptoms and the way to recovery, but it is only upon accepting that one has either condition can healing begin. Understanding the PTSD process enhances the ability to cope in a positive way with problems of living that arise as symptoms. That alcoholism and PTSD share many symptoms is no secret. One condition often accompanies the other. It is a confounding oversight that 12-Step program methodology has not yet been applied to PTSD recovery methodology. The importance of memoir writing in dealing with the problems of living that arise from PTSD is also underestimated. However, it is my experience that writing works best if veterans write with veterans. Veterans who are living successfully with PTSD are the best candidates to work with veterans who are not. Only an interactive and interdisciplinary approach to understanding, preventing, and relieving posttraumatic stress syndrome will achieve better treatment results.

Military people often disagree whose war was worst, best, or most important. Those who serve during wartime but do not see combat are frequently put down, ignored, and left feeling as though they are incompetent, inadequate, cowards—that is a reality of military life. Just the other day I received an email joke that has been making the rounds since the 1980s. I was saddened to learn it still exists and received it shortly after posting "Scars on My Heart" on the Milspeak website. The joke takes form as a counterfeit version of the VA's application for disability benefits. The form is called, "Hurt Feelings Report." The "Whiner's Name" is requested. The "Whiner" is asked to answer when his feelings were hurt, if no post-combat brief was offered, if he wants his mommy, and if he has woman-like hormones, among many other degrading questions posed. This is but one example of how the suffering are tortured by comrades-in-arms. Use of such despicable "jokes" among military people is only one reason those suffering remain closeted more often than not. To go to war is to go to war—no matter time, place, or duration! No generation is greater than another—no war more deadly or awful than another. War is war. And, believe it or not, peacetime can be as dangerous as wartime—the Reagan-era years of conflict prove that.

Milspeak began because I felt undeserving of my disability rating and I recognized a need could be filled by my abilities. My abilities outweigh my disabilities, yet I remain unemployed, and not for lack of serious attempts to secure employment. Maybe because of disability, maybe because of social skills, maybe because I write terrible resumes and cover letters, maybe because I am unqualified to do anything other than what I am doing with Milspeak—I don't know why I have remained unemployed, but only through Milspeak, adjunct teaching, and writing have I been able to continue being a contributing member of society after my military service ended in 1998. Friends have told me to renegotiate my honesty with employers about my disability rating. The law of the land tells me I don't have to mention disability. The law of sobriety, as I understand it, doesn't allow for that. To stay sober, I must lead my life with honesty; I must live an authentic life.

The language of disability has too long disenfranchised the wounded by enforcing stereotypes. Each time we attach *dis-* to a new word or use an old term with that prefix, stigma is reinforced by placing the burden of explanation on whomsoever the *dis-* is intended to describe. *Dis*abled,

363

*dis*order—all words with this negative prefix attached and associated with the wounded should be *dis*carded, *dis*missed and changed. Changing the way we talk about *dis*ability might be the only way to begin leading civilian and military cultures toward relinquishing the negative stereotype of *dis*ability associated with PTSD and *dis*abled veterans. Our veterans and active duty warriors will continue to avoid seeking individual and family counseling until we relinquish that stereotype. The military must lead the way in this effort. Until rehabilitation programs become known as career builders rather than career enders, military people will continue to mistreat each other, stigmatizing those who seek assistance with problems of living and destroying any progress we could be making toward improving the civilian community's healthy understanding of the reality of military life.

When contemplating Milspeak's uncertain future, David Ellard and I have often wondered why seminar advertising and articles in *The Jet Stream* and *The Boot* attract so few active duty enlisted participants, the workhorses of our country's military. As an enlisted Marine, I want to reach the workhorses, the people like me. Maybe those who would consider writing with Milspeak think I am an unqualified instructor. Maybe they fear exposure on a command level. Who would want to write about their military experiences after witnessing the nation's highest-ranking general, General Peter Pace, toppled from the nation's most powerful military post for speaking his mind? Part of the answer is that most young enlisted service members would rather spend their free time with their families. They have so little free time, particularly with our country at war on more than one front. Not only do our military members deploy for longer tours in war zones than ever before, but each deployment is preceded by training that often calls for months' long separations from family. Divorce and suicide rates are climbing. Acts of violence are on the rise in military families. As the title character in the film, *Juno*, says, "I'm dealing with things way beyond my maturity level"; humanity as a whole is dealing with things way above our maturity level as proven by our inability to work together to solve common problems.

Anything Helps, even a small creative writing program like Milspeak.

Maintaining public silence about military life creates separation from self, an inner sense of unease in the outer world. This silence separates human being from human being. Breaking this silence gives birth to many voices—not only to a public voice but also to an inner voice. Milspeak writers are empowered by breaking this silence through sharing their experiences in writing. Our warriors have more than earned the right to freedom of speech, freedom from fear, freedom from want, and freedom of religion. Each American enjoys the Four Freedoms because military men and women brought this country into freedom and have kept it free since 1776. Will speaking out about military life bring discredit upon our country, our military, or the service members themselves? I don't think so. Then why do we military people so fear our own voices? Most of us fear being misunderstood by the civilian community and the military community. Many military people fear career repercussions. Open dialog will certainly create heat, but that energy will help us grow as a country and as human beings. Our leaders owe our warriors the right to exercise the very freedoms they protect. Milspeak proves this can be accomplished without destroying good order and discipline.

David Ellard has been instrumental in the development of Milspeak. From the beginning, David believed in Milspeak's potential as a tool for military people to use to understand their experience:

> It is important to note that comments, opinions and writing of any and all Milspeak writers are theirs alone and do not reflect any official opinions or positions of the United States Marine Corps or Marine Corps Community Services Institutions. That being said, I am proud that MCCS has allowed MCWS to be held at locations convenient to the military community it serves, and for allowing MCWS writers to tell their stories, their way. I am happy to be involved as a representative of Marine Corps Lifelong Learning, and Marine Corps Community Services (MCCS) at Marine Corps Air Station (MCAS) Beaufort and Marine Corps Recruit Depot (MCRD) Parris Island in providing what I see as a valuable service to our local military community. I was quickly sold on the value of MCWS and history has confirmed it.
>
> When Ms. Sally Drumm first approached me in 2005 about the concept, I was a little skeptical. The first thing that comes to mind when a "new class" is proposed to me is, "What are the angles?" Most proposals are about some teacher or company making money. The Marine Corps pays tuition assistance via local Lifelong Learning centers so that Marines can continue their

education on a voluntary basis. Tuition assistance dollars is usually what the proposition is all about.

Whatever Sally's proposition was about, it was not about money. She has not received one dime from tuition assistance and not one dime from the MCWS participants. She was a Marine Veteran who had gained an education in writing from her veteran's benefits and she wanted to give back. She had first hand experience with the cathartic value of writing about one's experiences and she wanted to share that with others, especially Marines who served in our current and recent conflicts. Being a veteran, she knew the military leaves people with experiences that can be conflicts in the psyche and that she had a way of working through those conflicts that she was willing, even eager, to share.

Sally's eagerness to provide a service to Marines was quickly expanded to the greater military community. To my knowledge, something like our MCWS has not been done before. For MCCS to support such a venture, it had to be open to all of the local military community, including all MCCS eligible patrons. Expanding the possible attendees was the right thing to do. First, all of these people potentially had military related stories and could benefit from the MCWS experience. Second, having the larger pool to draw from ultimately kept the dream alive by providing attendees. Last, the United States Marines belong to the nation and their stories are all our stories.

Over these three years, I have seen MCWS benefit many people. I met individuals who attended the seminars who were clearly touched by the positive experience they enjoyed. I've read most, if not all, of the stories written and have been blessed by them. MCWS led to the Milspeak organization and website, which in turn allows anyone with Internet access to learn more about the nuances of the military experience. This website has actually brought individuals back together, rekindling old relationships. Not everyone's story may come across as positive in itself but as a whole, the collection appears very positive to me. MCWS has provided a return from a business standpoint as well. MCCS is in the business of providing services to the Marine community on a limited budget. MCWS' aforementioned benefits are clear and many so its service is undisputed; on the other hand, the investment is a small one. The Education Services Officer's time and the classroom facilities are there anyway and even with a small expense in marketing MCWS to the military community, they are easily offset by the positive image of MCCS. Patrons feel better about using paid MCCS activities (even discounted as they basically are), like the exchanges, theaters, restaurants, clubs, etc, when they can see the free services they also enjoy. Now there is a book being written about MCWS. Even more people will learn about the Marine Corps experience, the many people that make up the Marine Corps Community, and the services provided by Marine Corps Community Services.

During MCWS 8, Guest writer Melinda Copp, an MFA candidate in Goucher College's creative writing program, gave a welcomed talk about her experience as an editor and freelance writer. Melinda answered our questions for two hours. Another of the pleasures of this workshop was learning how far returning writers have come with their work.

Shana, who had been unable to complete her work during MCWS 6 due to a change in duty stations, has written a letter to her daughter about achieving the difficult balance between duties as a Marine and a Mother. Nancy has written beautifully about her experience as a young Air Force bride in Guam during the Vietnam War. David, game for another seminar, tried something new with a story about an encounter with Iraqi insurgents, as told to him by a young Marine. From David:

When I contacted the Marine who told me this story to get his permission to include it in this anthology, he was very excited that his story was being told and that many more people would read it. He is considering submitting more stories either through myself or directly to the Milspeak website. To me, this story exemplifies what MCWS is all about. While only a small piece of this Marine's development, I am confident that the experience of telling it to me, and our going through the writing process and delving into the details, was a small part of our healing and growing process. Plus, it was fun to write and to read.

Writers returning for another seminar included Stacy, who has written about her struggle to earn her degree while on active duty, and Moe, who wrote about his first firefight in Vietnam. Moe, at heart a poet, began a mentoring relationship with Tom Sheehan—poet, writer, Korean War Veteran, and farmer—during June 2008. Stacy graduated from Embry-Riddle Aeronautical University during MCWS 8. Participating in her first seminar, Monica, a Marine wife whose husband was away on a long deployment, wrote about the many goodbyes military families must endure. Monica had this to say about her first experience with Milspeak:

It was by accident that I came across a flyer for the Milspeak program. My husband had just left for Iraq and I was searching for activities to make the months pass by quicker. The class would provide me with adult conversation and a chance to have time to myself. I love my children dearly, but I needed to find something for me. Besides, I had always loved to read and write I just didn't know how to put my thoughts into order so that they would become a story. This program seemed the perfect opportunity to learn.

When I first signed up for the class I didn't realize that we would actually have to write a story. I thought it would just be a bunch of people learning the in's and out's of writing. As nervous as I was about letting others hear my story, I knew that I needed the chance to try, if only for myself.

The first class was a little surprising. Apparently this class had been offered several times and I was just now beginning. This could have been intimidating, but Sally and the participants were so kind and open it made me comfortable enough to share my thoughts. One of the first things that Sally asked us to do was to introduce ourselves and explain what our story would be about. Listening to everyone discuss their stories I began to feel insignificant. These people had such great stories and I was soon enraptured with what they were talking about. How could my experiences compare to their stories? When my turn finally arrived I explained my story and voiced my concern regarding what type of demand there was for a story such as mine. Their replies were encouraging and made me realize that we are each unique and this uniqueness allows us to tell a compelling story.

Writing the story was hard. To really write a story you have to be honest with yourself. There were many nights that I sat at my computer crying because to write this story was to live the moments over and over again. When the crying would start I would push through to the end. Over time it became easier to put my emotions on paper, but it was still difficult to read. To think that I was hurting so much and at the same time putting a smile on my face is hard. This is where I realized that I do what I do for my family. With my husband deploying I had to be strong for my children, my mother-in-law and my Marine. I didn't want him to deploy thinking I couldn't make it. I wanted him to do his job and do it good. If he was constantly worrying about me then he wouldn't have his complete attention on watching his back. I wanted him to come home safely and if it meant smiling as he walked away from me, then I would endure the pain and wait for the joy of his return.

If I had only one chance to say something about this program, I would simply say try it. You don't lose anything by trying something new and in the end you may realize that the healing that it offers you was well worth the time you spent crying at your computer. In the end you are stronger for what you have endured and the possibility that someone can benefit from your experience is an added incentive. As always, the story of my time as a Marine Corps spouse is ongoing and I hope to be able to share more of my experiences with you.

Fred returned for a second go at the Milspeak process to write "Monkey Mountain," an account of his Vietnam War experience with the first combat Marine Air Control Squadron (MACS). Fred's "Monkey Mountain" has made its way around the MACS community. Many Vietnam Veterans from the MACS Pack began sharing their stories, so many that Fred and I founded *Milspeak Memo*, an Ezine dedicated to Freedom of Speech. Volume 1 was devoted to and describes the Vietnam War Era Experience in a montage of stories, poetry and video. *Milspeak Memo* is reaching our troops around the world. Fred writes:

I was a bit fired up after CWS7 and submitted a few of my pieces for publication, and I even wrote a piece of fiction for a creative writing contest for unpublished authors. The responses were daunting, or rather the lack of responses. I received zilch, zip, nada, zero, nothing. If it weren't for my cancelled check for the entry fee for the creative writing contest, I wouldn't have known they had received my short story.

I decided that maybe I had slept through some important part of CWS7. The tricks I didn't know that caused me to be so widely rejected could now be gleaned by attending CWS8. When the announcement came I immediately signed up, determined to learn the secret of sending out a manuscript and cashing the returning check.

I also started thinking about a story to write about. After agonizing over what to cover in CWS7 I decided to again write about a personal experience and to keep the narrative upbeat. I had found it difficult during the first class to think about those times that were less than fun, and found it impossible to put those experiences and feelings down on paper. I could hardly face them myself, let alone put them into words.

After the first class, and sharing some of the dark experiences of others, I was finally able to think about my "dark" times, although I was still unable to share them with other people. During CWS8 I was finally able to address some of that on paper and wrote a poem that wasn't presented as part of the writing assignment. I'm going to include it here.

Sally asked us to write an introduction to each of our pieces, explaining what the class meant to us, what we learned, and how we came to write what we did. I wrote "Monkey Mountain" because I lived it and I could write it in a style I was comfortable with. What I learned during both classes finally dawned on me. I learned that I had lived my entire Marine Corps career chasing after the next adventure.

Just being in Viet Nam and working on helicopters and their avionics would have been more than fulfilling to most Marines. Not me. I had to pursue guard details, flying missions as a gunner, and chasing after crashed aircraft in the elephant grass. I wasn't content on Sea Duty to be simply a sea-going Marine, I had to be part of the ships landing party, be the Commodore's Driver, and be a member of a five inch deck gun crew. I spent years volunteering for jobs that were little wanted by others and even less understood. Not living in a rut kept me from thinking about things since everything I faced was new, and not looking back on the past couldn't bother me let alone hurt me.

CWS7 and CWS8 have allowed me to start looking back and facing some of the bad things that occurred. I realize that a lot of my fear in "going back" occurred from feeling that much of what happened was my fault. I've come to realize that most of the bad things were inevitable, the course of events were such that no one could have changed the outcome. After more than forty years I'm beginning to feel good about myself again. If I never get a check for something I write, it's O.K. I've been well paid already, in self-awareness and the lifting away of a blanket of guilt.

Reading Fred's first draft of "Monkey Mountain" at home was an indescribable experience. This was a story I had always wanted to know, but no one had ever told me. Most of my twenty years in the Corps were spent with the MACS Pack; the fight for equality was grueling during those years. "Monkey Mountain" taught me the origins of many of the MACS Pack's traditions. I was especially surprised to learn that the first combat MACS so closely resembled the shaved South American mountaintop where I had injured my back in 1996. No one had ever shared stories about the MACS with me as Fred did during MCWS 8. He accepted me as a woman and as a Marine—he recognized that I could be both. During Workshop 1, I kept my emotions in check, but during Workshop 2, I broke down and lost any semblance of military bearing or of workshop leader. Like Sirens, the many griefs of my life sang from the rock in my chest, my weeping more than any human being should be asked to hear. But they did hear, and they listened—the writers understood better than I did what was happening to me. Milspeak writers brought me home to a sense of balance within myself. They were with me during some of the most difficult times in my life. They carried me home to the military family I abandoned when I retired.

During my eighth workshop, I was writing the anthology narrative, and beginning to analyze Milspeak, its effects and its potential. So much had happened during the years Milspeak was forming, far more than I ever imagined possible. I hadn't realized the Milspeak process had been at work on me just as it works on the writers. Two great losses have affected my life and will always affect my future: never having a child and never having a father; both losses are directly connected to military life, and yet, perhaps because of these losses, Milspeak has been my life's greatest gift and most important work. Milspeak writers taught me this, and showed me that my work with them was and is a calling, my way of giving back for all I've received—freedom from drink, an education, teachers, and friends. To find so many teachers and friends along the way to now is the best thing of all. When Milspeak began, I had no idea the writers would help me as much as I help them. Through Fred, I realized that mine is the generation who carried on after the Vietnam War, bearing with us the traditions of all who came before, passing those traditions on to the next generation, the men and women who are now leading troops in the Middle East, each of us a link in an unbroken chain that was forged in antiquity and leads into the future. Even I am a link in that lineage. In Fred, I found my Odysseus. Through him, I recognized the warrior in myself, and Fred recognized the poet in himself. Fred died Memorial Day 2009. Through this anthology, Fred's experience, strength and hope lives on.

Milspeak is part of that something larger than ourselves each human being strives toward. We sometimes feel alone on the journey toward excellence, but along the way we meet friends, rediscover family, and establish values. We make mistakes. The Roadmap is in a constant state of change, the future suspended in mist. Landmarks, like loved ones, pass away. At times we feel lost. We work to overcome obstacles. We struggle with demands of duty and honor. Sometimes our dreams fail us; sometimes we fail our dreams. Carrying on, we are mystified by life and the strength of human beings to help us on our way—even if, sometimes, they may stand in our way. We learn with every step taken that we, too, are human, imperfect and enduring.

Notes:
[1] Burns, Robert. *The Songs of Robert Burns*. Glasgow, Scotland: David Bryce and Son, Pearl Edition. Publication date not given. Margaret carried this tiny book from Scotland to America.
[2] Poetry Foundation. 30 April 2009. http://www.poetryfoundation.org/poetrymagazine/history.html
[3] ibid.
[4] *Harper's* vol. 311, no. 1862 (July 2005): 65.

THE RISKS OF WRITING
AND THE COURAGE TO DO IT ANYWAY

By Melinda Copp

On a cloudy Saturday morning in the fall, I arrived at the Marine Corps
Air Station in Beaufort, South Carolina, ten minutes early. As I parked
my car just inside the gate, I took deep breaths and shifted in my seat. I'm
a civilian and so I usually see the bases in my community from the outside
when I'm driving by. Inside, as I looked around at the landscape of plain
buildings, wide lawns, and uniformed personnel, I thought about the last
time I was on a military base.

About a year before, I was working on a magazine story about military
families and the systems the Army uses to support them while their spouses,
parents, and loved ones are called away. I went on base to attend an Army
family readiness pre-deployment meeting just days before this particular
division was leaving for Iraq.

The meeting was held in a theater on base. My military escort, the
magazine photographer, and I found a row of seats off to the side, and I
watched as everyone filed in. The troops, with their high-and-tight haircuts,
were easy to spot even in civilian clothing. But there were also women
shushing babies, school-aged boys with wide eyes, and little girls dressed
in pink skirts and white sandals. When the officers took the stage, they
talked about how the soldiers would be paid, how the webcams could
broadcast their images across the Atlantic, and about how the phone tree
would work if the unthinkable happened. It didn't take me long to realize
that the unthinkable was truly possible for almost everyone sitting in the
theater that evening.

In the back of the room, a baby fussed before belting out a cry. And it
didn't take me long to imagine what I would feel like, to be sitting there,
listening to this discussion on who would call to tell me that the unthinkable
had happened and have my baby start crying on my lap. This feeling of
worry overwhelmed me, and I wondered what they would do to cope with
the uncertainty of deploying to a war overseas.

When Sally pulled up, I followed her in my car around the corner to the building that held, among other things, the Milspeak meeting room. She introduced herself as we got out of our respective cars and held the door for me when we walked inside. The building was empty and barely lit, and on the walk upstairs she told me about the people who would be there to talk to me. They were soldiers, wives, husbands, mothers, fathers, and veterans—all people who had executed an inordinate amount of courage in the face of uncertainty. They were there that morning because through the Milspeak program they were learning to write their experiences as creative nonfiction—a mission that's obviously less dangerous, but still involves plenty of risk.

I've always loved writing, but it's not always been easy for me to write. I can remember feeling like everyone in my first creative writing class was so much more talented than me. They had better ideas and they understood how to craft a better story. In those earliest years of my writing life, I never dreamed of publishing my creative work. I could never send my work out so strangers could read it.

Writing can be scary and troubling to do. Creative nonfiction, personal stories in particular, are among the most difficult to write. It takes guts to look honestly at life and the experiences that upset, challenge, and even destroy us. Making meaning out of them can be a frightening pursuit. And even when the material is sorted out, it takes guts to put other priorities aside and show up at your desk to write day after day when there are no guarantees that anything will ever come of it. To toil over it day after day, and face it when it feels most awkward, then format it and send it out into the world alone for others to judge it can be terrifying, especially for new writers. But writing is also hopeful, with others encouraging us to keep working.

I felt the confidence to pursue creative writing because I had a wonderful poetry teacher that made me feel like I could. When sitting in his class one day, just before graduating, I realized that if I showed up day after day then something would eventually happen. Writing was something that I could do, anyone could do, if they put their mind to it and put work into it. Sure, it was nerve-wracking to work so hard in such a solitary way, but you can make something truthful and beautiful from whatever material life has dealt.

Sally and I climbed the stairs to the second floor. Milspeak, in its eighth session that fall, was an opportunity to encourage another new writer to that same realization—that writing about their experiences can give them a sense of clarity and understanding. Sally paused before entering the classroom and asked, "Are you nervous?"

"No," I said. And I wasn't, not anymore.

FOR LOVE AND HONOR

By Shana Tamla Willoughby

I can't believe you are already thirteen; where did the years go? I would have bet anything that time would stand still, allowing me the opportunity to spoil you as a child, forever. Funny, life doesn't operate like that, would you agree? As my daughter, you have been with me throughout my military career and I would not have asked for it to be any other way. Truly you are my rock; the one thing in my life that I can look at and have no regrets!

It is written, "there is a time for everything, and a season for every activity under the heaven" (Ecclesiastes 3:1). I write this verse because as you continue to grow, mature, and become wiser you will experience varying seasons in your life. This season of separation between you and I is a season in both our lives that has caused me to take a look at my life as a woman who happens to be a Marine, but who is a Mother first. As you continue to grow, I want to be able to share in every season of your life as a reminder that the harsh, bitter, and stormy winds of Winter will not always last; Spring will eventually come and when it does you will be able to embrace the beautifulness of your Winter season, which will enable you to become firmly planted.

Every time I look at you I am reminded of the many blessings I have been given throughout my life. I love you dearly and I will always love you. Your faith in me has been amazing and sometime unbelievable; I often wonder, do you think I am "superwoman"? Dear daughter, I hate to disappoint you, but I am not a "superwoman," and honestly I don't think that I would ever want to be; I am content with knowing that as your Mother I have flaws and these are flaws that I don't desire to keep hidden or locked away, but to allow you to always see my humanness and simply put my heart. Although you are currently living with your father, I want to communicate my thoughts towards you as I've never done before, so if you are to ever have doubts or fears you can refer back to this letter. Here's my heart to you, my precious daughter.

October 3, 2008: After talking to you on the phone, I have so many emotions going through my body at one time; I am happy that you made it to a safe place but scared that the ending could have turned out much worse than the surrounding circumstances that led you to run away. I am angry with your dad for not knowing what the hell is going on in his own household and angry at myself for not taking you with me when I changed duty stations to San Diego, CA, because this entire year and a half you've been living with your dad has been a major headache for me.

Not being able to hold you is the hardest thing for me, because every time you've hurt or were afraid I was there. I have to keep busy, I tell myself. My daughter needs me to remain strong for her; I can't fall apart, because then who will be there for both of us? How did I ever get here?

February 14, 1996: "Look at you; you are a big ball of nervousness!" Who would have thought that you would have actually said, "Yes," to his proposal? "Why do you want to marry him, anyway?" So many questions run through my mind as I prepare to pick out a suitable dress for a quickie ceremony at the Justice of the Peace, in which I will become officially married. I ignore every signal my body sends me, as I place one foot in front of the other, and make my way out the door to meet my future husband.

You can't very well runaway from your fears, because they will always hunt you down and make you confront them. A marriage out of convenience can only last as long as both parties agree to play the part, right? Looking back I know I only agreed to marry your dad because he is your father. At the time, I truly believed that everything would work itself out, but as we have moved forward in time, I now know that this has probably played a pivotal part in the strains of your father's and my relationship.

October 4, 2008: OMG, it's only 2 a.m. and I'm wide-awake, ugh! I hate when my mind is so overwhelmed with thoughts that sleep goes on vacation. Oh how my body aches for the tender arms of my lover, Sleep. Last night was an uneventful night, I didn't sleep well at all, because my mind has physically separated itself from my present location and I am with you, but it's not enough, because I want to be right beside you. Did you sleep well last night? I can't believe that I'm at this place again, where I am completely helpless! I have thought on more than one occasion of going UA (Unauthorized Absence) and dealing with the ramifications of my actions upon my return. Please don't think that I regret for one minute being in the military, because I don't. It's just that I find days where I am in disagreement with the policies and guidelines currently in place governing military personnel.

Ever since I checked into MALS-11, in lovely Miramar, California, I have been on the go; I worked at MALS-11 for approximately 2 weeks before being told that I was coming to Yuma, AZ to fulfill the role of barracks manager for WTI. Could this have come at a more inconvenient time? I mean I'm waiting on housing, which means my storage will have to be extended because my 90 day period will be over at the beginning of March, and oh, by the way, I need to find someone who can take off work to come sign for my household goods, once I play phone-tag with the individuals at the TMO office just to find out the proper process to request an extension. Great! So here I am again in lovely Yuma, Arizona for another great WTI, and after informing the Maintenance Chief and Sergeant Major last night about you running away, I find that I still have to wait. Here. I. Wait.

October 5, 2008: Today I wreaked havoc on myself for the things I can't control; it sucks, because as your Mother I have this innate ability to try and take away all your pain so you will never hurt in life. I love you so much and I want you to always remember that you are the child I prayed for, but received so much more. Never think that you are a mistake or unwanted. Unfortunately there are things we inherit because we grew up in a certain environment or household that cause us a great deal of pain and emotional baggage, but these should never define your future! Dear child, can I give you my heart as deeply as I know how; can you allow me to tell the story of me, sharing every emotion, whether good, bad, or ugly? Can you allow me the opportunity to be unveiled before you?

Being separated from you is the hardest thing for me. Even after 15 years of being in the military, it is something I don't ever get accustomed to. Some random thoughts for you to digest: before coming to CA I settled in my mind to be content with being the "other" parent, meaning I was ok with being the parent who visited during special occasions and other times, sending you gifts and letters through the mail, and sending financial support. The reason I was content with this decision is because I see how hard it is for you to be away from family, so I chose to be the one who sacrificed having you with me while I finished out my last five years in the military. I never want you to think you have to choose between your father and me, because you don't. Although I don't feel about my family and your father the way you do, this does not erase how I feel for you, and how much I want you to never feel like you're being torn between us. I guess I never really thought about the toll or stress you may deal with being a child of a single military person. As a military person, I have taken on the mindset of learning to leave old places without regret and to accept new ones for what they looked like, nothing more and nothing less. But as a child, it's probably not as easy to disassociate yourself from family and friends only to start over again in a new place. And now this is where I find myself, at another crossroads.

October 6, 2008: I talked to a friend of mine today and I feel a little better, but I hate being patient. She gave me some insight; she can truly relate to my feelings because she is a mother herself and she also grew up living with her father because her mother was in the Army. She let me know that she always wanted to live with her mother, but was never afforded the opportunity. She spent time with her mother, but this was never enough; she expressed how there were times she experienced feelings of betrayal, anger, bitterness, and total longing towards her mother. Hearing this made me afraid, but at the same time gave me ears and eyes to see from a different perspective. Being a single parent is already hard, but then you add on the fact that I am in the military and it seems to intensify the situation, and everybody always has their "two-cents" to add, which really pisses me off! I wish I could see into the future, but I can't. I can only do what I believe is best for you, and you alone. You are about to enter into high school and this brings about a whole new batch of questions and concerns that I honestly don't know if I'm prepared to handle. I will not take the coward's approach and run away leaving you to fend for yourself. I have come to terms with knowing that while in the military providing you with consistency is not a guarantee, especially now with all that is going on; deployment, long hours, inconsistent work schedules, and being on unfamiliar territory are just a few basics of being a child of the military. There are other issues that come into play as a child gets older and becomes attached to peers. Simply put most children don't like change. Who am I kidding? I'll be honest. I don't too much care for change, either! So this leaves me to come up with a solution that has your best interest at heart, because at the end of the day, I don't care what my superiors think of me. Nor do I care what individual Marines think of me. You are all that matters and I want your best, at all times.

Here we go again, I'm finding it harder and harder to get up these days. What does this mean, I suppose? I can't wait to see you, hold you, and tell you how beautiful you are. I can't wait to hear how your day progressed while at school. I can't wait 'til the separation is over, for good. I am sorry to repeat myself, but I don't know what the future holds. I trust that this season will spring forth in beauty from a heart that has completely surrendered. Today as I was on my way to work, Charles Stanley was on the radio and he was speaking on coming to the place in our lives where we are completely emptied of ourselves and our foolish gain. As I began to ponder what he said, I began to think about Proverbs 3: 5,6— "Trust in the LORD with all your heart and lean not on your own understanding, but in all your ways acknowledge Him and He will direct your paths." During this season, I have become bitter, angry, and unapproachable because I have felt unfairly treated. But as I listened to Charles' message, I began to understand that all my anger and bitterness is directed towards God. I'm unsatisfied. I'm at a place where my footing is unsure; a dry a thirsty place. A place where what used to satisfy doesn't quench my thirst anymore. Darling daughter, I'm scared and I don't know what my next move will be, but I do know that you will always be first in my life and I will never be too busy for you. Again, I want your best and your best only, so, as I set plans in motion, I would like to leave you with this simple prayer: "God grant me the serenity to accept the things I cannot change; courage to change the things I can; and wisdom to know the difference."

I love you now and for always,
Mom

JUMP IN FEET FIRST

By Nancy Whitworth

Moisture dripped from the edges of a rusting corrugated metal roof supported by four metal posts. Under this canopy sat a washing machine supported by planks sunken into the moist jungle soil of Guam. As I smiled and gestured with an armful of dirty laundry, my Filipina neighbor graciously invited me to join her. Although neither of us spoke the same language, we worked together, taking turns placing loads into the metal agitator and swinging the wringer into a locked position as needed. Unlike the old Maytag my mother used, there was no galvanized tub of fresh rinse water to catch freshly washed laundry. As the sheets were fed through the wringer, I attempted to balance myself to feed with one hand and catch with the other. As the sheets tumbled, the edges that missed my grasp rested on orange pieces of decayed metal surrounding the platform and in mud puddles formed by the dripping water.

"Dear God, what am I doing in the middle of the jungle, sharing whatever resources are available and grateful not to be wringing these clothes out by hand in the kitchen sink?"

I was very grateful that my neighbor was so generous with her time and her washing machine, but I was determined using both would be the first and last time. During our first month of married life together, I had washed the towels and sheets by hand but did not have the strength to squeeze the water out. They hung dripping from the kitchen chairs and table onto the tiled floor. Brian, my 20-year-old husband, was stationed at Andersen Air Force Base on Guam. He refused to take the laundry to the barracks. "I can't do that. I would be too embarrassed." My compromise was to ingratiate myself to my neighbor. Now another solution had to be found.

As a young, 21-year-old, bride in 1968 during the Vietnam War, I left college in Maine and joined my husband at his new duty station in Guam. As an E-3, Brian was not eligible for base housing. The struggle to join him was only the first of many challenges. I had borrowed $200 for airfare from relatives. That would get me to Hawaii. My monthly dependent's portion

($130) of Brian's military pay would more than cover my airfare of $113 from Honolulu to Guam. Already in Guam, Brian had found a new house in Yigo, the first village out the front gate, about 3 miles. We would need a car for transportation. Before leaving for Guam, I had also secured a small installment loan over 12 months for household supplies. My once-a-month $130 allotment and Brian's pay on the first and the fifteenth of each month totaled $330.00, not nearly enough to pay for all we needed.

The news did not get better when I arrived in Guam. The house Brian rented could accommodate three couples. Brian's vision was to share the house to pay the rent. The house had three bedrooms, one bath, a kitchen and a living room. The furnishings included a kitchen table and four chairs, one bed, and a couch. Unfortunately, Brian could not find two other couples to share expenses. In addition to paying $175 for a car, rent for the house was $175 a month. Neither of us were strangers to hard work so we would find a way to manage.

Brian was the oldest of five and a military brat. His father was a B-52 pilot stationed at Loring Air Force Base, Maine. The family allowance for clothes covered the basics. If Brian wanted Bass Weejuns instead of regular loafers, he worked after school to make up the difference. In fact, he had worked in the Officers Club kitchen, as a lifeguard, as a bagboy at the commissary, and was even driving a school bus on base at age 16.

I began working in the potato fields of my father's small farm at age eight. School always began in the middle of August. Classes ran for three weeks, and then recessed three weeks for potato harvest. Fall was always full of promise, hard work, fluctuating temperatures, and the anticipation of financial reward from the potato harvest. Before dawn Monday through Saturday, we would dress in layers: union suit (long johns), shirts, sweatshirts, pants, one or two pair of socks, sneakers, and brown cotton work gloves. We were paid in cash each week: twenty-five cents a barrel. A barrel held one hundred and sixty pounds of potatoes. We were each given a basket, a section of the length of the field was marked for each of us, we were handed tickets to mark our barrels, and the day began.

On Saturday afternoons, all the pickers—school children and migrant laborers from the Mic Mac Indian reservations in New Brunswick, Canada—lined up in the farmer's kitchen. Tickets were tallied and the monies due calculated. I would keep a little money for the movie and a treat. The rest was put aside for shopping and kept in a small safe in my parent's bedroom. We never had a checking account or savings account. The small safe held a few hundred dollars for emergencies such as making sure family members could get home if a death occurred.

At the end of harvest, we were each responsible for purchasing our one pair of shoes and clothes for the school year. Usually, I bought one pair of Bass Weejuns and three wool skirt and sweater sets. We made our own selections, handled any layaways, and paid our own bills. I would lay the three outfits out on my grandmother's horsehair stuffed sofa and admire them every evening. The sense of pride, accomplishment, and responsibility I felt in those days has always remained with me, along with a strong work ethic. I learned early on that when you commit to a job, you do the best you can regardless of the circumstances or the pay level.

For Brian and me in Guam survival was not a question of handling our financial obligations; we were responsible and hard working. The question was how to increase our income and reduce rental costs. Brian worked swing shifts and midnights as a K-9 handler on the flight lines. During the day he worked full time at a warehouse job on base. He also negotiated with the landlord to perform yard work, painting, or whatever needed to be finished on the house for a reduction in rent. We searched for other rentals and Brian found a cashier's position for me at the Officers Club part time until I could enroll at the University of Guam to finish my senior year. I had already applied and been granted work-study money by the University.

Until I began school, I spent a lot of time alone in a house without heat, air conditioning, radio, television, or a telephone, and neighbors who kept mostly to themselves. The island's climate, plants, and topography were new to me and it took time for my body to acclimate. Guam's environment was as different from Maine's as my Filipina neighbor's body was from my own. She was built to withstand yearlong soggy humidity and sweltering heat. I was built to withstand the snow and ice of Maine winters.

On the flight between Hawaii and Guam, the initial humidity kicked in. I went from a wavy haired, 110 pound woman who had boarded an airplane in Bangor to a frizzy headed, water swollen version of myself that walked into the terminal in Agana, Guam. Brian's first question, "What happened to you?" would be repeated many times during my thirteen months here. The shock of the heat and humidity was soon met with the unwelcome guests that accompanied the climate. Water bugs (cockroaches), water buffalo (caribou), geckos, chameleons, and large lizards greeted me during the first few weeks.

Northern Maine, known by many as "the other Maine" or "the county," was not what tourists define as Maine. We had access to neither ocean nor quaint coastal towns. The nearest large city was Bangor, about 150 miles from my hometown, Fort Fairfield. We seldom had reason to travel that far.

I loved the county's uniqueness, history and sense of permanence. The land has always soothed me. The quiet, calm exterior of rural nature asks for nothing. The openness of the fallow fields with their boundaries was a landscape in contrast to the closeness of my two sisters and me sharing a full-sized bed during our childhoods. My refuge from the confines of a large family living in close quarters was to walk up the farm road with fields on my right, woods on my left, and headlands that formed part of the border of the farm straight ahead. A light breeze, bright sunshine, and solitude were my companions. The fields were a window framed by the headlands—a spare and pure buffer from the outside world. The light to medium brown color of the land belied the richness of the pungent soil that lay beneath. The hard crust looked tough and lifeless, but once the soil had been plowed and harrowed, the turned-over soil was soft and deep chocolate brown. The dark, moist soil evoked a feeling of oneness, peace, and serenity.

On Guam, the tropical climate produced torrential downpours randomly several times a day. The saturated soil formed a pungent mud that sucked up everything in its path. Planks were needed to support foot traffic, and washing machines, from the mire. The humidity only deepened the effect. When it wasn't raining, my attempts to keep the burning sun at bay served only to preserve the muck. Yet, the life growing in the soil produced lush green fronds and brilliant floral bursts. The only cultivation required was that used to keep the roads from being overgrown and to protect small pouches cut into the jungle. Each three-sided pouch held a small wooden house lifted off the ground by wooden stilts. Wooden steps led up to the living quarters while chickens and rooster roamed beneath the house protected from the elements by the porch floor.

Guam sometimes reminded me, the way opposites that share traits could, of the many qualities of Maine that I had left behind and deeply missed. It had its own rich culture and history. Although finite in size, like

384

Maine, the variety of plants, animals, insects, and land formations presented a new world to me.

Each end of the island was occupied by a military installation: one Navy base and one Air Force base. Nearly the entire interior swath of land connecting the two bases was made up of deep, thick jungle growth. We learned after we had returned stateside, that a WWII Japanese soldier had emerged from that jungle. That someone could survive, undetected, in the jungle for over 25 years seems too implausible to believe if you've never seen that jungle.

When traveling the two-lane road that led out of the Main Gate at Andersen AFB and connected that end of the island to the Navy Base, I was often reminded of the country road I had walked in Maine. The Back Gate road traversed the other coast. The convex edges of the island had a smattering of small villages, a university, and the island capital of Agana. Andersen AFB (APO 96334) was an active outpost in the Vietnam War effort. On takeoff, B-52s rumbled off the runway and out over a cliff. While we were stationed on Guam, one of the giants did not gain the lift it needed, and we lost a crew.

Like Maine, Guam's weather, with the accompanying erosion of hard and soft rock formations, carved out beautiful beaches, offset by cliffs with caves gouged deeply into the surface. From the bluff that supported the campus of the university, an uneven collage of green fed down the steep slope to the edge of a cliff overlooking the sea. The unevenness of jungle canopy complemented the jaggedness of the rocks and the white caps beyond. The soil supported deep roots but the true richness and depth of the soil lay in its people.

In Maine, I was the oldest child in a large Irish Catholic family. Creativity, self-expression, and individualism were not conducive to the family's work as potato farmers. My role as surrogate mother, keeper of family secrets, standard setter, goal achiever, and good Catholic girl cast a long shadow on my life. I felt like a top, always in motion but someone else was controlling speed and function. Events and roles are easily understood but the emotion, anxiety, and repetition over the years wear deep grooves into memory. At times it feels impossible to record over the sublimated messages of the past.

On Guam, the native peoples were of Spanish descent. Family, religion, and celebrating their heritage were key elements of the culture. I felt a closeness and acceptance by the open, warm, generous people I met. Although I was isolated by lack of a driver's license and a vehicle, I always had transportation—to the university, to the summer work-study job on campus, and to the teaching job after I graduated. When someone went on vacation, they arranged for someone else to pick me up. Their love and generosity allowed me to explore the "self" that lay dormant. Like a rogue wave disrupting a calm ocean, their support was the soil I needed for growth. Little did I know when I began this journey that isolation, family, and financial insecurity would continue to impact my life—only on different soil.

CORPORAL J'S HOUSE CLEANING

Based on an actual account as told to David Charles

This is J and here is an experience that will never be forgotten.

On a patrol in Fallujah, my four-man fire team and I were clearing houses, kicking down doors, so to speak. We took a short break to breathe, to discuss lessons learned, and to regroup.

"Chas, you've got to stop tossing a grenade into the place as soon as we break the door," I tell the Lance Corporal who normally takes point. The wiry nineteen-year old from Ohio was the quickest man on the team.

"But Corporal J," Chas replies with too much of a whine for me, "That's the way Corporal Goose taught me." Chas looks over at the big, smiling, twenty-one-year-old Mexican whose odd name we cut short to Goose.

"Yea," adds Goose, "That way there's no way for an insurgent inside to shoot us as we go in."

"I know that sounds pretty good but it's not the way we're gonna do it," I explain. I spend as much eye contact on Marty, the green, eighteen-year-old redneck, as I do on Chas. "First, we have to account for them grenades and we're not supposed to use them that way. You don't know if there's any insurgents in there or if there's any innocents in there. Second, if you do kill an insurgent, he can't give any information. The more enemy we can detain, the more info on weapons caches and enemy strongholds we get. That saves some lives and catches the big ones."

"I still don't like goin' in without clearing it with a grenade first," Chas said.

"Look, you need a break from point. I'll go in first on the next one."

We pop the door on this house and I step one foot in. All hell breaks loose. When I enter the house I am immediately engaged by the insurgents, so I break right. For whatever reason, one of my knuckleheads yells, "Frag out!" and lobs a fragmentation grenade into the doorway.

387

It was coming right at me so I bust down the tiny cramped hallway, through a flimsy door, and right into the arms of a surprised insurgent. We smack together so hard and with so much force that we both go horizontal and I land on his head and back. In the commotion not one of us can get to our rifles. I try to reach my M-9 pistol but can't reach it because the insurgent is freaking out.

I have been practicing Martial arts since I was five years old. I go into Mushin, which means no mind, and all my training kicks in . . . eyes, breath, mobility. I don't consciously process input and make decisions. That instinctive part of the brain just takes over and reacts as efficiently as humanly possible.

I jam my hands into his face and neck and tear into him all the way down to his wrists. I start at the top because that was all I could get my hands on well with him under and low down on my much larger body, which is pinning him to the floor. I squeeze what's in my hands, starting at the top and working my way down. I squeeze and lift up my two hundred twenty pounds of muscle as I reach down lower and grab the next body part that shows under my lifting body. When his wrists clear, I grab them, pick him up, and slam him down on his face. I pull out a zip-tie and bind him without totally loosing control.

If I totally lost control I would kill him because he wanted to kill me, but it will be better if I don't kill him. Once the insurgent gets to our interrogators, he will spill everything he knows.

It gets quiet and I look around. My fire team comes walking down the hall toward me. "Clear?" I ask.

"Clear," Goose answers, "three insurgents, down for good."

With the entire situation finished, we took a look at my detainee. He looked like he had been used for a punching bag and he had my handprints all over his face, neck and arms. But he was zip-tied and we were all still alive.

Through everything, incapacitating the insurgent and capturing him was more gratifying to me than killing him would have been. All insurgents should face jail time for what they have done. Why should they get to die quickly? They all wanted to die and that was the easy way out.

CHERRY BLOSSOM TIME

By Bernard "Moe" Haagensen

With the last and final step off of the airplane's stairwell I felt like a person standing in a frying pan with the stove still on! The tarmac had been soaking under the Asian sun for at least ten hours. Man it was hot!

We new troops, or "Cherrys" as we were called, were shuffled like a deck of cards upon our arrival in Cam Ranh Bay, South Vietnam. After arriving, in country, we Cherrys were to be sent throughout this most astonishing area of the Far East as replacement troops. As replacement troops, we were put anywhere or anyplace the United States Army had an opening.

My feet were still burning as the air base gave me an elusive view of my new surroundings through a wavy mirage of heat. Suddenly my name and number bellowed from the PA system. My twelve-month tour of duty had just begun.

The very next day my body was relocated by airplane and helicopter to the northern section of the southern half of what used to be one entire country. The country had been separated by an invisible line that theoretically ran straight across it's mid-section. This line known as the DMZ (De-Militarized Zone) was also referred to as the 17th parallel.

I had been relocated to a place known as "Camp Evans," about twenty miles south of this invisible line.

I was a soldier, trained in mortar fire, and I was pretty good at it. This certain battalion of the 101st Airborne (3rd Battalion / 187th Infantry) did not have a Company with a mortar platoon and did not need any trained mortar men!

I was assigned to a three-man sniper team. Presently my team was holding their position "somewhere out in the field." What did I know about "somewhere out in the field?" I was a Cherry!

The senior NCO (non-commissioned officer) assigned my rank and file to a nightly ambush squad until I could be placed with my three-man team somewhere, out there. I now had about three hours to obtain the necessary gear such as a guns, ammo, grenades, knife, face paint, backpack, cigarettes etc. to be of service. What if it rained?

I was twenty days shy of a nineteenth birthday not knowing that all hell was about to break loose later that evening.

The sun had already begun to set when our squad exited the western gate of Camp Evans. We traveled on foot for about an hour in one direction. Darkness fell upon us ten minutes out of camp. Darkness really fell on us maybe thirty minutes later when a clouded night sky would not permit us to have any more light than was reflected by a waning moon.

Our ten man squad then circled itself to form a loose oval perimeter as some soldiers belly-crawled through four foot tall elephant grass to set trip wires attached to small and easily portable land mines known as "claymores."

The troop whose area I was to be in support of was a man from San Bernardino, California. He called himself Hooker P. Nose but his real name was Randy Leman. Inside of the tall elephant grass, Hooker said to me, using a low and stern whisper, "Cherry! You are a goddamned Cherry! Keep yer mouth shut and make yer eyes stay open cause if I hafta die for somthin' you did I'm gonna take you with me!" By this time my asshole was a little more than puckered up.

I was scared shitless when the first claymore mine exploded followed by incessant and uncontrolled volleys of gunfire, whistling, through the tall grass. Lying on my stomach in the womb created by the elephant grass, I began to pull the trigger of my weapon. One magazine clip later and the night felt darker. Relieving a bandoleer, of ammunition, from my shoulder I grabbed another clip and proceeded to do the same thing all over again. And again. And again.

In the darkness the elephant grass began to have a shape and a formation as helicopters dropped flares from the sky. An eerie and hideous hue of pale yellowish-like illumination filled the night. The womb of grass surrounding me slowly became more comforting as the night wore on, and I traded fire with the unseen.

The morning's first traces of natural light were beginning to soak through the tall elephant grass. The jungle was turning itself from night into day as Hooker P. Nose softly whispered into my ear, "Goddamn it Blondie! Can you believe this shit? A dirt mound! A fuckin' dirt mound! All night long we fired into a dirt mound!"

I replied by not making any noise.

"How many clips you got left?" he again whispered.

When Randy Leman whispered into my ear I knew I had been saved. I wasn't a "Cherry" anymore.

The new sun began to rise in the eastern sky. Gazing gently toward the west, then looking directly overhead, I closed my eyes for the longest second of my life and said thank-you to the One above us all, while holding out two fingers for Randy to see.

THE TITLE BEYOND THE TITLE

By Stacy Atkinson

Going to college was a goal I grew up wanting to achieve. I promised myself many times that I would be a college graduate no matter the effort. I never put much thought into just how much effort becoming a graduate was going to take. I attempted college twice before I made my third time a charm.

I sat in a Marine Corps recruiter's office wondering to myself "What am I doing here?" Wasting his time is what. I really didn't think I could go through with becoming a Marine and earning that title. I was only curious. Great! How was I going to get up and leave now? He's going to follow me, and worse yet, he is not going to stop calling me.

Well, I was right about some of my thoughts that day and dead wrong about others. The recruiter, to my relief, did not stop calling me and I sure was going to earn that title. On July 14, 2006, I did. I became a United States Marine.

After graduating from 13 weeks of boot camp, I went on to Marine Combat Training. I then moved on to my military occupational school in avionics located in Pensacola, Florida. I liked school, but this just seemed like it was never going to end. I relearned my hatred for numbers and whoever the demon was that invented them. Finally, I was assigned to my final school in Oceana, Virginia where I received the hands-on training in my job as an Avionics Technician. This would complete all of my military occupational schools.

At each of those schools, I remember always being scared of the Fleet Marine Force, commonly known as just the Fleet. The thought of being on my own in the Marine Corps frightened me. No senior Marine would care about my well being the way my school instructors had. I was shaking in my boots when I checked into my new duty station at Marine Aviation Logistics Squadron Three One. This was the fleet I had heard so much about in boot camp and in school. The fleet that I never really believed existed. This fleet I became a part of was filled with great times and great Marines and tons of work and long working hours. I felt as if I was ready, but I was still really nervous.

I had been in school for a very long time and was excited not to be cramming for tests or attending those study groups where nothing really ever got accomplished. What I didn't know is that I would be bored. I was eager to go to work everyday and learn about my job, but once I did, I felt like I was doing the same exact thing day after day. I yearned for something else to occupy my mind as work became monotonous.

I thought back often to the evening I spent in my recruiter's office. I could hear him tell me the things I wanted to hear. Well, the ones he thought I wanted to hear. I remember the motivating poster about the Marines and just how wonderful and tough they all were. On many occasions throughout the day at work, I thought back to that night and wondered why I was sitting in that work center in this uniform.

I can't deny the fact that I was proud to be a Marine. I worked hard for that title and worked hard to wear that uniform. I was proud to be able to serve my country but still there was something more. What now? Was there something else beyond this title, Marine?

Again thinking back on that very memorable night in that tiny recruiter's office I remembered these colorful tags my recruiter laid out for me. He called them benefit tags. I thought of them as sales pitches in small rectangle shapes with big font and bright colors. He laid them in front of me and said, "Ok, pick the three that mean the most to you." What kind of a question is that? I couldn't possibly pick three benefit tags right then. I expected to take them home and have time to think about the question. This was important, and I could never make such a quick decision.

There were tags with tangible things on them and others with intangible things. Things like leadership and a challenge. Those were important but I didn't feel as though I needed the Marines for that. The opportunity to travel was one I remembered. That was nice and all but I didn't really desire to leave the place I already knew. I looked down and saw one that really hit home.

At the time of my visit to the Recruiter, I was working full time to pay for school and spending all my time at work and little time focusing on school. So in a nutshell, I was working full time, going to school in between, getting bad grades and paying an enormous amount of money for the whole thing. I picked up the tag that read "Educational Opportunities" and said, "This one is the benefit most important to me."

He went on and on about the educational benefits the Marine Corps offered. He spoke about things like tuition assistance and the Montgomery GI Bill. He mentioned how convenient it was to transfer credits from one college to the next when changing duty stations. All around it sounded like the Marine Corps, as an institution, was very pro-education.

I decided to join. My strong desire to obtain a college education was one of the reasons why I swore that oath.

I enrolled in school immediately upon my check in to MALS 31. My shop was little. 650 they called us. I saw one familiar face and hoped for some more. Slowly they trickled in and I felt like we were all a family. I enjoyed working at 650. It was a fun place filled with great people, great leaders and lots of work, just as promised to me by the instructors back at MOS school.

I quickly found myself balancing a full-time Marine Corps job and schoolwork at the same time. Being a Marine didn't make it any easier; it was actually harder. It didn't cost me any money but the stress I dealt with was higher than any amount of tuition fees. I was lucky to have somewhat of a support system. One amazing Staff Sergeant I worked for was so considerate of my school situation. He told me he'd support me in anything I decided to do and would never ever stop a Marine from bettering themselves. Turned out he was a student, too, and we would help each other through working full time while attending school.

Unfortunately, there were some Marines who did not support me. These I encountered more often, as there were more of them. Some Marines immediately thought I would require special treatment or some sort of special accommodations. Without even knowing me, people would label me as the Marine who only cared about school. These labels hurt me, but I never let them get me down. I worked hard to become a Marine and I worked hard to be a student, too. Neither title was compromised for the other.

I found that some Marines centralized their life around the Marine Corps and embraced the idea that being a Marine is the only thing they were responsible for. It seemed that they thought that anything outside of their MOS, formations, Physical training, rifle qualifications and safety briefs would negatively impact the Marine they were supposed to be. This mentality was not one I possessed. All of that was important, but what about the person underneath that uniform? What significance did their goals and dreams have? For me, the significance was great, but I can't deny that it was difficult dealing with those hard charger Marines. They always made me feel like I was doing something wrong by going to school. I never neglected my duties as a United States Marine. I never put my education in front of my title, Marine. I knew that the fleet would be a tough place to be, without adding more to my plate, but the sacrifices were worth it to me. I knew that I was inflicting more work upon myself. Being a student was important to me. Becoming a graduate was part of my dream. It was that simple. I just had to do it no matter what it took.

Regardless of the struggles I faced attending college, I graduated on October 18, 2008. I realized that dream. I had to grow a very thick layer of tough skin. I had to shrug my shoulders often and ignore the snide comments from other Marines. But I couldn't be stopped. I knew what I wanted and I knew how to get there.

Graduation represented something huge for me. Walking across that stage was one of the proudest moments of my life. The Master of Ceremonies read my name and read what I did in the Marine Corps. He announced that with a 3.781 Grade Point Average, I was a distinguished graduate with Summa Cum Laude Honors. I could barely believe it was me they were announcing. That moment made every single one of my struggles worth it. I did it. I obtained a Bachelor of Science in Professional Aeronautics from Embry-Riddle Aeronautical University. For just a moment, as I took those steps on and off the stage, nothing else mattered. I was grateful for every single person that stood by me and appreciated every one else who made it difficult for me. They helped make the struggle worth it.

My dreams will not end here. My personality will never allow me to stop the fight for success. Graduation felt like a door was closing. Everyone knows what they say about closing doors. Another door opens. For me, it's the door that leads to a graduate degree. I have already heard the comments and seen the eye rolls when I talk about my plans. But when it's all said and done, and I am walking across another stage listening to my name through the speakers at commencement, nothing else will matter. The struggle will once again be well worth it.

The benefit tag Educational Opportunities is one of the strong reasons I became a United States Marine. It doesn't make me a better Marine but it surely doesn't make me a worse one. Every single credit hour represents something greater than I could ever put into words. That moment on stage was priceless. It all represented the dream of a girl who sat in a recruiter's office and picked the benefit tag that mattered most to her. She took the tag and ran with it, giving herself a title beyond the title Marine.

MONKEY MOUNTAIN

By F. P. Siedentopf

When I landed at Da Nang yesterday morning it was in the low 80's and humid...just like I remembered from my previous tour of duty. At sea level in Southeast Asia you don't expect anything else but heat and humidity even when it isn't monsoon season. The only time I'd ever felt a chill in the air in Viet Nam was flying as a gunner on a UH-34 helicopter at 3000 feet.

Now it was about 2:00 AM and I woke up shivering with only a sheet wrapped around me. I turned on the table lamp and blinked my eyes to see clearer. The blurriness was due not to a problem with my eyes but what seemed to be fog was creeping in through the screen on the open window. In fact, water was dripping off the locker, condensation like that on a frozen mug of beer at the beach.

I stepped towards my locker to get the blanket I never thought I'd need. After all, this was Viet Nam and I'd never really needed a blanket before when I was in country. Hell, even in January you could work up a sweat walking to the showers.

I opened my locker, rummaged under my boots, cartridge belt, and magazines and found my blanket. It felt cold and damp, but I presumed it would dry out from body heat long before I caught pneumonia. As I started to close the locker door, I saw a little sign glued just under the vent. I didn't see it earlier because I had my utility jacket hanging over the door. It told me to keep the locker plugged in and use only 75 or 100-watt bulbs. I had wondered why there was an electrical cord sticking out of my locker and now I knew. The light bulbs generated heat, which kept the inside of the locker dry...or drier than the ambient air in the room. It's the military version of a Hasbro Easy Bake Oven, and as long as you kept enough room between your gear and the light bulbs there was no chance of a fire. I decided to wait until tomorrow to see if it worked.

I went back to bed, turned out the light, and formed a cocoon of cold, damp sheet and blanket around me. For the first time ever I appreciated the nearly 36 hours of travel time I'd spent getting from New York City to Da Nang...I was so bushed I went right to sleep.

My previous tour in Viet Nam found me stationed at the Marble Mountain Air Facility or at a forward aviation staging area at Dong Ha. In those earlier days I was an Avionics Technician assigned to Headquarters and Maintenance Squadron-16 (H&MS-16), but like everyone else pulled my share of security details; perimeter guard, convoy security, and my favorite, helicopter gunner. At Dong Ha we also took turns on aircraft recovery detail. We'd go to an aircraft crash site and try to recover as much of the bird as possible. Time permitting we'd try to evacuate the engine(s), and fuselage. We'd first make sure that all documents, frequency cards, and personal crew data was recovered. If we couldn't lift aircraft components out or they were too damaged, we'd set explosive and incendiary charges to destroy the aircraft totally when we left. That was even more fun than being a gunner.

In 1966 the Marine Corps began replacing our workhorse UH-34 helicopters with the CH-46. The UH-34 was a proven and nearly indestructible aircraft. It had a reciprocating piston engine that could take a .50 caliber round and still get you home leaving a trail of smoke and oil behind. The CH-46 had twin jet turbine engines that at the beginning of its service life were considerably less reliable.

In the first two months that CH-46's were operating out of Marble Mountain Air Field there were three crashes and maintenance problems caused them to be grounded. (Another six were shot down shortly afterwards operating out of the Dong Ha staging area). Sand, dust, and dirt kept being sucked into the engines causing them to seize up; if you were airborne at the time, you crashed. The engines needed to be synchronized to operate efficiently. If they got out of synchronization the vibrations would cause the transmission to separate from the engines and the aircraft would split into pieces. Another problem was in the electronics system. In some cases keying a radio would cause the Power Management System (PMS) to stutter and one or both of the engines would quit. This is a highly undesirable trait when flying. It's ironic that decades before PMS became a valid medical diagnosis it was already giving guys fits.

After I left Viet Nam in the fall of 1966 I was looking for a way to disassociate myself from helicopters. I didn't trust the CH-46 and I didn't want to fly in them. In 1967, while assigned to Headquarters and Maintenance Squadron-26 at New River, NC, I was tasked to accompany a CH-46 squadron to Viegues, Puerto Rico to provide their Intermediate Avionics support. While in Viegues, all the CH-46's were grounded again because of crashes and I immediately volunteered for retraining as a Tactical Air Operations Center (TAOC) Technician. I had no idea what the school or the specialty was about, but it was a way out and even students in this new military occupational specialty (MOS) were eligible for proficiency pay at a higher rate than I was currently authorized. To my amazement, I was accepted.

The TAOC Technicians Course was given at the Marine Corps Communications Electronics School at Marine Corps Base, 29 Palms, California. I was pleasantly surprised by my desperation choice for re-training. Since the MOS was new, every student in the class was re-training, with no advancement from repairman to technician possible that early in the game. No one would have a leg up in the classroom or in the lab classes on the equipment.

The course lasted a year...we were learning the intricacies of computer operations, computer repair, data displays, operator interfaces, and data link operations on a purpose built computer system. Much of the programming was "hard wired" with electronic switching from one wire bundle to another to change modes of operation. There was no "Geek Squad" to call for help, and no Internet to search for those ubiquitous FAQs we're all used to. Even the company technical representatives had no idea how some things worked or what caused certain symptoms when there was a failure.

After graduation from Tech School I spent nearly a year at Marine Corps Air Station, Yuma AZ, getting to know the equipment and learning the nuances of being a Staff Non Commissioned Officer (SNCO). Although I was promoted while in school I was still a student, with no responsibilities other than minding my Ps and Qs and not failing. Leading as a SNCO technician and as a SNCO Marine required different skills but the same determination. Thankfully failures were few and I was honored with orders to Viet Nam.

On this trip to this land of enchantment, I was assigned to a Marine Air Control Squadron (MACS). No aircraft to work on; just radars, radios, missiles, and computers. The unit was MACS-4, the first automated, computer equipped Air Control Squadron deployed to a combat zone.

Personnel were issued orders to MACS-4 based on merit, not merely to staff the Table of Organization. The mission of MACS-4 was to provide air defense around Da Nang. A Hawk missile battery provided close-in threat elimination if our air controllers were unable to vector interceptors to take out enemy aircraft at long range. Without giving away any secrets, we had data links to the Airborne Warning and Control System (AWACS) and the Navy Tactical Data System (NTDS) that enabled our Tactical Air Operations Center (TAOC) to monitor and control air defense well beyond our own radar range. Enough said; think "Star Wars," think anything, but forget what you just read. Much of what is written about those systems is still so classified, there are notifications on the documents that say "Burn Before Reading."

The MACS was positioned on the highest point of the Son Tra peninsular, which is north east of Da Nang. Our compound was spread out wherever there was a bit of level land to put a building, emplace a radar set or situate a generator. It covered about three quarters of a mile east to west, and there were several hundred feet separating our lowest point from the highest. In width we sprawled several hundred feet north and south to the narrowest point of the camp, which was only the width of a one-lane road with no shoulders. The squadron was at the end of a long often one lane road that started at the gates to the Air Force compound at the base of the mountain (sea level) and ran across the crest of the ridge that eventually became the high point of the mountain, about 700 meters (2300 feet) up. This entire mass of rock, not just the high point that was part of our site, was referred to as Monkey Mountain.

We Americans named it Monkey Mountain because of the large colony of macaques or rock apes that inhabited the slopes of the peninsular. There seemed to be two species, one with no tail and one with a short bobtail. During the construction of our squadron's site, an abandoned and injured juvenile macaque was found. Corpsmen nursed it back to health and "Chipper" became the squadron mascot. She was kept on a tether at sick bay and would greet all who entered with a little bark and hand stretched out like a Kasbah beggar, looking for a treat of nuts or sunflower seeds. Chipper however, was a perfect Marine mascot—she much preferred beer.

At night the guard would often call an alert when the macaques would "probe" our concertina perimeter defenses. In the moonlight and through the clouds that often gathered around the mountain like London fog, the Rock Apes looked like little people in gray pajamas. Since they often threw rocks at the guards, the possibility of the commotion being a VC grenade attack had to be taken into consideration. Sirens, flares, and searchlights were a common occurrence. Why they would throw rocks at the guards or try to get through the concertina wire was a mystery. I suspected that the guards threw soda cans and other garbage off the hill that disturbed the macaques. It's also possible that our compound was built on a trail that they had used to get from one side of the mountain to the other for generations. Since little is known about Asian macaques, we could have had their queen tied up at sickbay and they were trying to get her back.

The 8 foot by 8 foot room I was shivering in at 2:00 AM was one of the perks of being a SNCO and it was a lot better than sharing a wood frame, hard backed tent with eleven other guys. Compared to my living conditions as a mere Corporal and Sergeant on my previous visit to this Asian wonderland, a damp chilly private room was the height of luxury. The next morning there was pounding on our doors about a quarter to six, which I soon learned was the Monkey Mountain version of reveille. I was reluctant to leave my warm and cozy cocoon, but three things forced me to plant my feet on the floor and get moving. First was fear. I didn't want to start my first day in my new unit being late. Second was hunger. I could smell the bacon cooking in the mess hall (that was before the politically correct term of "dining facility" was foisted off on the military) that was only a few hundred feet away. Third was physical. I could no longer ignore my bladder.

After resolving my bladder issue, brushing my teeth, and a quick shave, I headed for the mess hall. (I still refuse to use "dining facility.") Even though the mess hall was a few hundred feet away looking straight at it, there was a tough walk of about a quarter mile to get to it. During that walk I learned two things. First it wasn't fog that had been the problem I encountered earlier that morning; Monkey Mountain was in the clouds. Second, with everything located on different levels, paths wound back and forth to get you up or down hill on a grade that would not require rappelling techniques, or navigating dangerous steep and treacherous wooden stairways.

The mess hall was well worth the climb to reach. About three weeks after I arrived, the stairs from the living area to the Mess Hall were repaired. Even with the stairs in place it was a tough climb—53 wooden steps that were slicker than snot when wet, and that was every morning and every night when the cloud rolled in, and all day when it rained. Everywhere you went in the compound you encountered slippery wet wooden stairs and decks, and even the asphalt paving was very slippery when the cloud rolled in.

Finally arriving at the mess hall, I filled a plate with food, found a good spot to sit and eat, and to watch the door. I dug in. Those 36 hours of travel that let me sleep through last night's arctic fog also left me with quite an appetite. When traveling I can't eat much. I get too nervous to eat a meal without getting sick, so I tend to munch on saltines and nibble beef jerky or Slim Jims instead. Now that I was relatively relaxed my body was ready to make up the four or five thousand calories it had missed.

I was one of the first "customers," and as I sat there devouring my morning repast I spotted spot some friends I knew when they came in and invited them to join me. It's always beneficial when reporting aboard for a new tour of duty to have friends already there. You can quickly get the lay of the land; the do's and don'ts; who to know and who to avoid; what recreation is available; what services are available; and what you have to go off base to get. Learning all of that by trial and error can lead to anguish and angst in equal measure. I've always found that the expression, "It's a small world" is more than applicable to the Marine Corps family. After a few years of service, it's difficult to go anywhere and not find a friend or two.

Two of the people who joined me at breakfast had been in my tech class at 29 Palms. We trekked up the hill to our equipment site together. They filled me in on our OIC and NCOIC, and briefed me on the SNCOs and Officers in the Communications, Radar, Communications & Maintenance, and Tactical Data Control Center sections we worked with. When I reported to my new bosses we sat and chewed the fat for awhile, feeling each other out while I waited for a call to report to the Squadron Sergeant Major (SgtMaj) who'd introduce me to the Commanding Officer (CO).

My NCOIC took me on a tour of our equipment, showing me how it was laid out and where the interfaces with the other equipment were located. We also stopped in at the other sections and introduced me around. Each stop meant another cup of coffee. After we had completed our rounds, my need to reduce bladder pressure was extremely strong. My new boss pointed out where the "rest room" was and admonished me strongly to slam the door a few times before entering and to stomp my feet when I got inside. Puzzled, I asked him why. The short response chilled me just like that fog the night before: "Pit vipers" he said. No one had given me a warning before that...I could just imagine my tour of duty ending earlier that morning when I had relieved my bladder before breakfast. I could have died from a snake bite or died from shame holding and squeezing a snake bitten portion of my anatomy, attempting to slow the spread of venom, while duck-walking to sick bay yelling, "Corpsman, Corpsman!" It was a treacherous trek down to the "two-holer."

For the next few weeks, things progressed smoothly. We worked two twelve-hour shifts and I was on the day crew. That meant I had a chance to visit our joint SNCO and Officer club for an hour or two and relax. It wasn't a very large club, but we had a large fireplace that helped drive away the "shivers" and "chilblains" while sipping a drink and telling sea stories. A sea story is quite similar to a fairy tale. The main difference is that a fairy tale begins with, "Once upon a time...." A sea story however, begins with, "This is no shit...."

There was a fairly large and well-stocked bar, and a small stage area for the infrequent USO show. We also had a small slot machine room with five machines, but they were hardly ever used. As you can imagine, the club was the gathering place for most social activity. Reading was done in your room, watching TV or a movie was done at the club. Playing cards was done in our rooms if any money was at stake; pinochle, hearts, and rummy were enjoyed at the club by players and kibitzers alike. USO Shows and the occasional USO or Club system sponsored band packed the house. We much preferred the bands since they were usually from the Philippines and always had a gorgeous young lady as part of the group. Even if she wasn't a stripper (we had those on occasion), she'd usually be dressed in the style of the times—knee high boots and a miniskirt. The boots were made for walking, but the skirt was made for staring!

The area over the stage and to the immediate right and left was our "Trophy Wall." It was a tradition that when you went on a Rest and Recuperation (R & R) run, you'd bring back a trophy depicting the high point of your vacation. Some brought back pictures or knick-knacks but most brought back a skimpy pair of panties. If you met your wife or fiancé on R & R you were exempt from tacking up a pair of panties. The wall was a riot of color and shimmering silk and lace.

Our Squadron Sergeant Major was John McGinnes. He was a short, chubby, crusty, loud spoken, often vulgar Boston Irishman on the down side of fifty. Every day at noon he'd enter the club, pound on the bar, and yell, "Rum for the Sergeant Major!" He'd remain there guarding the entry to the club until one hour after the club's "official" opening when he'd retire to quarters for the day. He knew exactly who, officer or enlisted, was supposed to be at work and would run you off if you tried to sneak in.

McGinnes, an irascible curmudgeon who tolerated no breach of Marine Corps tradition or ethics, had about 35 years of service at the time, having served during the Banana Wars in the 1930s in Nicaragua, all through WW II, and through Korea. He said he got out of the Marine Corps twice but couldn't stand civilians and had to come back in. We called him "Loveable John" behind his back and not as a derisive appellation. Loveable John was the only R & R returnee to bring back a pair of panties from his wife who he called "Rotten Rube." They were the largest pair of panties I have ever seen and were prominently displayed over the stage at the center. At first glance it looked like a Chilean Condor was swooping in for a landing.

The best part of the club was the porch/patio area on the side. There were huge windows on either side of the fireplace that formed the back wall of the porch/patio area. From the porch/patio we had an unobstructed view of Da Nang all the way south to Chou Lai. On a clear night, you could see the aircraft taking off from Chou Lai, or at least their lights and afterburners. We had a view of the deep-water piers, the Tien Sha base, China Beach, I Corps Headquarters, and Marble Mountain. We could watch the activity at Da Nang air base. We could also see the tracers when there were firefights anywhere around Da Nang or follow any air strikes in those contested areas.

But the best part of the porch/patio was our Sunday Steak cookouts. Our mess hall staff served a remarkable breakfast every day. Lunch and supper always were adequate, but not exceptional. We very rarely had pot roast but could always count on meatloaf. We very rarely had pork chops, but could always count on hamburgers, big fat juicy ones, but still hamburgers. We rarely had ham or chicken, but always had ground beef as meatballs, meat sauce, as stock in stew, or as Salisbury steaks or fricadillas. We often joked that the Mess Chief had a cookbook titled "1000 ways To Cook Chopped Meat" and he was only half way through. In fact, each week when drawing rations, our Mess Chief would take a lot of the lesser desirable chopped meat to ensure he got a double ration of steaks. That way every person was sure to get a steak on Sunday and there were enough extras to feed our guests if there were any.

We shared Monkey Mountain with the Air Force who had an Air Defense site lower down and who provided the security to get on the road that ran the length of the peninsular. Half way between the Air Force and us was the Armed Forces Viet Nam (AFVN) Radio and Television Service Transmitter site. Adrian Cronauer, who was in turn made famous by Robin Williams in the film "Good Morning, America," made AFVN famous. There were always a few of these entertainment folks invited to Sunday steak cookouts. There was also a standing invitation to the nurses on the hospital ships USS Repose and USS Sanctuary when they were in port. Hell, there was a standing invitation to nurses in general to join us for a cookout. We always had a few takers. The cookout would start at noon and end at 2000 so everyone could get back home before curfew. As luck would have it, sometimes a nurse or two would miss the bus and would be forced to spend the night. There was never a shortage of berthing space for a stranded nurse.

There were only three "tourist" attractions on Monkey Mountain, other than the rock apes. There was AFVN, MACS-4's Steak Cookouts, and the jet from the *USS Bon Homme Richard* that crashed into the side of the mountain in 1967. The pilot apparently misjudged how high the mountain was and flew straight in, dying instantly. There was no transmission of any sort indicating if there was a problem or not, and as far as I can determine the actual cause of the crash remains unknown.

In addition to The SNCO and Officers Club, there was a separate club for the NCOs (corporals and sergeants) and an Enlisted Club for the privates, privates first class (PFC), and lance corporals. In I Corps, all clubs came under a club system. Food, drink, and supplies were purchased by the club system and each club drew what supplies were needed weekly. Bartenders, waitresses, cooks, cashiers, accountants, and janitorial staff were all Vietnamese nationals hired and vetted by the club system. Each club had a crew assigned.

Club managers were military personnel who were assigned club management occupational specialties and were part of the club system staff. There were also "duty" managers who oversaw operations when the club manager was not available or after his working hours. These "duty" managers were regular military that were "moonlighting" for a salary, usually minimum wage. Regular club managers also were paid a salary, usually minimum wage plus 50%.

Clubs were located at the different bases and served all tenant units, with one exception. Our clubs on Monkey Mountain were exclusively MACS-4's. Instead of having club managers assigned by the club system, our managers were assigned by the Squadron CO. Once assigned, they worked for the club system but all administrative control remained with the Squadron. It was similar to being on Temporary Additional Orders (TAD) without having orders written. The Enlisted Club was about to make this tour of duty one of the most memorable times of my life.

After nearly two months in country, I was told to report to the CO. I left my work area trying to figure out what I had done wrong and why I was being called on the carpet. Other than staying in the club after closing to finish my drinks one night, I couldn't think of a thing. I worried about Red Cross notifications. Someone back in the states might be dead or dying. I was nearly a wreck when I got to the SgtMaj's office. Loveable John, closemouthed as ever, took me to the CO with no explanation. I proceeded to the CO's desk, centered myself in front of it, came to attention, and said, "Staff Sergeant Siedentopf reporting as ordered, Sir!" He waved his hand casually towards a chair and said, "Have a seat, Sied."

That was a quick indication of two things; there would be no ensuing Courts Martial and it wasn't a lead-in to a Red Cross casualty notification. I thought about a line from Macbeth, "Present fears are less than horrible imaginings." I had worked myself into a froth with all sorts of wild thoughts when whatever was going to come would be benign.

I sat, and the CO asked me if the rumors were true that I had worked at a private club in North Carolina as a manager. Hadn't I had also worked at bars in Yuma, Arizona, as bartender and manager? I admitted that I had. He then informed me that the current manager of the Enlisted Club was being short toured (sent home early) and that I was going to be the new manager. Since I was relatively new in my TAOC Technician's MOS,

I begged off so I could learn the system. The CO promised that the assignment would be temporary, and as soon as a suitable replacement arrived, I would be relieved. Having little choice, I accepted.

The Enlisted Club was one of many standard prefabricated warehouse buildings, 100' by 75', which were built by a Texas contractor all over Viet Nam. This one was modified with regular wall sections in lieu of roller doors, and had standard single and double doorways. The short wall on one end held a bar and a doorway leading to four refrigerated shipping containers. The short wall at the other end supported a small stage and an entrance to my new office. In between these walls resided a motley collection of folding tables and chairs, the sort of tables churches use for pot luck dinners, only these had some unholy looking stains on them.

For diversions we had three wall mounted TV sets all tuned to the same station, AFVN TV, the only station broadcasting in English; and two pool tables, each with a chipped cue ball and an average of 13 object balls per table when the club closed at night. There was a box of spare balls in the office so the racks could be filled each morning before opening. Billiard balls constantly disappeared. After nearly forty years of contemplation about what happened to those billiard balls, I've finally come to a conclusion. Since they were never found in the trash or in anyone's possession during a "shakedown" for contraband, they had to have been disposed of in some other manner. Undoubtedly the troops tossed them off the hill to stir up the rock apes to attack the wire.

Another diversion was an inoperable Foosball table that was probably the most sought after recreation item in the club. The rods and kickers had long since been removed and green felt had been glued to the table top and sides forming a more than adequate "craps" table. Two sheets of plywood had been placed together over a 2' X 4' frame that nested tightly onto the top of the table. It had been trimmed into an octagon and covered with green felt also to form a very functional poker table. Since gambling wasn't legal, the table was used to play engineer dice, or an occasional hand of Crazy Eights or Bid Whist.

Besides the coolers behind the bar (only beer and soft drinks were on the menu), there were three small pizza ovens, just like those in the 7-11 convenience stores of the era. Several racks of potato chips and other similar snacks were on a shelf behind the bar. The last items contributing to the bar décor were a dozen large galvanized garbage cans strategically placed to hold the beer and soda empties. In the morning every can was full with a nearly equal number of empties on the floor that missed the toss and bounced off the walls. This was not a Michelin Guide 5 Star tavern; it was a classic Marine Corps Slop Chute.

Leaving the CO's office, I went to the Enlisted Club to find the manager Steve; and get briefed, take a tour, and get introduced to my new duties. I had three days before he left for home and part of that time involved Steve checking out. It was just a little after 0800 and I got the grand tour of the club. We sat down in the office to go over the daily and weekly schedule. With that done, we proceeded to go through the paces of a normal day's routine. Steve had it all hand written down on three pages of yellow legal pad paper, front and back, and there was a lot to do. The workday started at 0800 and ended at about 0200 the next morning. Steve tossed me a small ring of keys and said, "Here's the keys to your truck, let's go." I told him I didn't have a government driver's license, but had an international license picked up while on Sea Duty. He told me not to worry; we'd get it taken care of at the Club System offices. Somehow that never happened. We got into the slightly battered Dodge D-200 crew cab pick-up and my new adventure began.

I could hardly believe the schedule:

0830: Leave the compound and drive to the Air Force main gate at the bottom of the mountain. Pick up the club day workers and janitorial crews. Drive back to the compound and drop off workers at clubs. 0900–1100: Get club cleaned up, re-stock coolers, re-stock snack racks and pizza cooler. Recount previous day's receipts and prepare deposit. Make up shopping list for supplies to draw from club system and what was needed to be purchased at Hill 327 PX from petty cash.

1100–1130: Lunch!

1130: Stop at other two clubs and pick up managers for run to Club System/PX. If they couldn't make the run get their deposits/ shopping lists and find a "shotgun" passenger for security. Return to compound and distribute purchases. [At this point there should be an hour of free time for a shower]

1600–1630: Get club set up for the evening, get duty manager started.

1630: leave the compound, drive to the Air Force main gate at the bottom of the mountain, and pick up the nightshift club workers. Drive back to the compound and drop off night workers.

1700 and 1715: Eat supper.

1730: Pick up day workers and take them to the Air Force front gate at the bottom of the mountain. Return to the compound.

1800–2330: Keep the Club from being torn apart; catch up on paper work; give duty manager a break! If things are quiet, take a nap.

2300: Close the club. While duty manager and night workers are shutting everything down, work up the register receipts and lock all in safe.

2330: Pick up the night workers, a shotgun (co-driver and/or guard) or two depending on the security level and leave the compound. Drive the night workers to their homes since it would be after curfew before they arrived and they couldn't travel on their own. Return to compound.

Add to that, on Thursdays, have a 2 1/2 ton or flatbed semi scheduled for beer, soda, wine, and hard liquor pick-up with a driver and three guards for the truck and a shotgun for the pick-up that led our mini-convoy. Thursday's also required combining the daily deposit run with the liquor supply convoy.

Being club manager made for 12–15 hour days. Once or twice a week I could get the SNCO & Officer Club manager to take the evening run so I could get to sleep by midnight. Once or twice a week I could get the NCO club manager to make the deposit run. That still had me clocking over 60 hours a week. But there was a financial benefit involved in the job. I was paid $1.50 per hour by the club system, a nickel over minimum wage for the first 40 hours, time and a half ($2.25 per hour) for the next 20 hours, and double time ($3.00 per hour) for anything over 60 hours. That put a weekly check in my pocket for $105.00 to $120.00! That was close to $500.00 a month that I had no time to spend. My military pay, with all extras, was tax-free and was $795.00 a month. To put that in perspective, a SSgt in 2008, with the same time in service earns $2930.00 a month, not counting combat pay or other extras. While I worked at the club I drew no military pay, letting it ride on the books. In fact, I let my military pay ride until I rotated back to the States. My club earnings ran to a little over $1,500.00 before I finally was relieved as club manager. I still had $1,300.00 of it to live on until I rotated back to the States. I had ten months military pay to draw when I got back home which meant a brand new Mustang! I put a few thousand in the bank and with the several hundred I had left of my club earnings, I spent three months at Marine Corps Air Facility, Santa Ana, California absolutely enjoying myself bar hopping from beer joint to beer joint.

Two other noteworthy things occurred while I was with MACS-4, one of which was a typhoon in October. We knew that Da Nang would take a direct hit which meant Monkey Mountain would get hit with full force winds straight off the ocean. We knew that troop safety was a concern and personnel were evacuated to lower ground. All squadron records and all classified documents were also evacuated. But the equipment had to stay behind. The decision was made to leave the equipment in place with power available but not running. The commercial generators that supplied power would be kept on line and a skeleton crew of the contracted Koreans would stay behind. Four Marines were chosen to stay behind to provide security.

I was one of the four SNCOs that remained behind. We were to provide security only for the Koreans and the operational site: the plateau with our radars, computers, generators and other electronic equipment. If Charlie tried to breach the perimeter and the four of us couldn't hold or repel them, we were to set off explosives and thermal charges to destroy the equipment.

Between you, me, and the lamp post, there was no way the four of us with .45 caliber pistols, 12 gauge shotguns, M-16 rifles, one M-60 machine gun, and a collection of hand grenades were going to be able to stop any determined penetration. About ten hours before the typhoon hit it was raining hard enough and the wind was gusting strong enough that you couldn't see crap ten feet away! We got soaked to the skin taking turns patrolling the limited perimeter, but luckily Charlie was probably hunkered down for the storm too.

The next noteworthy event occurred when the squadron had just about repaired all the damage caused by the typhoon. We received word that the squadron would deploy to the States and be deactivated. This was the end of 1970, and the U.S. pull out from Viet Nam was in full swing. We immediately went into stand down and started packing everything up for embark aboard Navy shipping. Getting off the hill by truck would probably have taken weeks since the road to our site could only accommodate only one semi-trailer moving either up or down at a time. There just wasn't room for two to pass. A Six-by (2 ½ ton truck) could only pass another Six-by in a few places if they timed their runs correctly—almost everything had to be helicopter lifted to the deep-water piers for embark.

Amazingly there was only one load that didn't make it. Naturally our CO was quite concerned with getting all of our unique equipment back home in one piece. We had electronic shelters worth several millions of dollars, some of which only a handful of copies existed and couldn't be replaced. Some of these shelters cost more than the flyaway cost of a brand-new F-4 Phantom II jet. We decided to set the CO up for a disaster—an accident that he'd think might end his career. We liked the guy, but we were vicious imps!

We had an old supply shelter that had been designated for scrap that we loaded up with scrap metal to give it weight. We got the pilot of one of the CH-53's to go along with our plan. He cut the load that the CO thought was a multi-million dollar shelter from 3000' over the ocean just north of China Beach. It was tricky getting the CO to the LZ when our designated load was to take off. He had no idea what was about to happen. We had him believing the load was the main computer shelter of the TAOC System. When the pilot pickled the load, I thought the CO was going to have a heart attack.

That was the start of a minor tradition in the MACS units, the "staged" disaster before, after, or during every deployment. There were four requirements to pull it off. First, no actual damage to equipment or people could occur. A dark, spreading, wet stain in the trousers was acceptable. Second, the perpetrators had to be able to remain anonymous—Don't ask, don't tell. Third, only an officer or senior enlisted could be the pigeon. Fourth and last, the maximum number of squadron personnel had to be able to bear witness to the disaster and the pigeon's response.

There were twenty-three of us who had nine months or more in country who would accompany the equipment back to the States. We were to off load it to MCAF Santa Ana and stand by to turn the gear over to the Marine Corps Tactical System Support Activity (MCTSSA), and,

411

subsequently, to the supply system for overhaul. The unit, MACS-4, deactivated. The rest of the troops would either go to Okinawa to join MACS-8, or if they had enough time in country, they would fly back home on the freedom bird.

The evening of the day that the last piece of equipment left, all that remained were two radars, motor transport equipment, the base generators, the buildings, and the clubs. The next morning everything would be turned over to the Vietnamese. The Enlisted Club and the NCO Club were stripped of all beer and soda for a troop "binge" at deep water piers, a goodbye party that left very few sober. Four of us stayed behind again to provide security, and dispose of the hard liquor in the SNCO and Officers Club.

We weren't told how to dispose of it, and there was a lot of booze...twenty full cases and a few partial cases. Most of the evening went this way: Open a bottle. Make a toast. Take a swig. Make a toast. Take a swig. Throw the bottle at the rock apes. We conscientiously disposed of every bottle of beer and wine in that club and did a fairly good job of knocking off the hard liquor, too. I remember having tears in my eyes throwing bottles of Bonded Beam and Crown Royal down on the rocks. We did such a good job tossing back and tossing off that in the morning we had to trade a jeep to a Vietnamese Army sergeant to get him to drive us down to the deep water piers. If anyone of us had tried to make the drive we would have ended up like the jet that had crashed into Monkey Mountain, a tangled mass of metal with all aboard dead.

I can't say that militarily the tour at Monkey Mountain either boosted my career or hurt it. Promotions that followed were timely, so I suppose the hiatus from being a Staff Sergeant working in my MOS and instead running a club can simply be chalked up to one hell of an experience and a damned good time.

GOOD-BYE

By Monica C. Greer

I can hear the alarm clock in the distance, but to open my eyes would be to welcome the day that I have been dreading for the past nine months. With the country currently in the midst of determining a president, I am dealing with the fear of my loved one deploying to fight in Operation Iraqi Freedom. Once awake, my fear would become a reality.

As the alarm clock continues to encourage me to wake up, I roll over and look at the place where my husband would normally be. He's not there, having risen earlier to be at the squadron by the designated time prior to their departure. Over the years we had gotten used to the early arrival time for the Marines, even though the actual departure time could be five hours later. With departures scheduled before daylight, we always made the decision for him to go first, with the kids and me arriving later to say good-bye.

Today would only be slightly different than past good-byes. Our two boys had made the decision to leave early with Dad. Our oldest, Cody, felt that at the ripe age of eleven he needed to be there when Dad was issued his service rifle. I think he was trying to show how he could handle the responsibility of being the man of the house while Dad was gone. Our middle child, Colton, was still naive to the fact that Dad was leaving and simply said that he wanted to go "...because I ain't ever been up that early, except to go huntin' with Dad."

Anyone who has been around the Marine Corps knows that their motto is "Hurry up and wait." It always seemed that there was some reason for the Marines to be delayed. Either the plane would be late, they would have to refuel or something as silly as the plane having to wait on the arrival of toilet paper. Departures just never seemed to go as planned, but today could be the day. This deployment could go just as scheduled. Today could be the day that they would actually leave on time.

Suddenly wide awake, I rush to get dressed then wake our two year old daughter, Taylor, and tell her that we have to go and see Daddy get on the plane. Making sure to grab my camera, to capture the moments, I quickly usher Taylor out the door and into the car. Once buckled into our seats I pause to take a deep breath. I can do this. Everything will be just fine. I still have a couple of hours before he leaves and he will be gone only seven months. With the thought of making it on my own for seven months, I start the car and begin the ten-minute trip to the Air Station, all the time wondering how twelve weeks became seven months.

My life changed forever with the words, "Baby, I joined the Marine Corps." In stunned silence I turned from washing dishes to look at my husband. Who was this man standing before me? "You did what?" I said.

"Instead of going to the unemployment office today, I went to see a recruiter. I signed the papers and the only thing left to do is for you to sign some paper saying you can financially make it without me for 12 weeks. The recruiter is coming over tomorrow night to go over the paperwork. I should leave for boot camp in about four months." This was the only explanation my husband gave.

Was he kidding me? I knew that in our town, with the Steel Plant going bankrupt, a job would be hard to come by. But to join the Marine Corps? I don't know what shocked me the most, the fact that he had done something without discussing it with me or the fact that he had signed his life over to Uncle Sam for the next four years. We had just built a new house, I had just earned a promotion at work, I had finally found some good friends to talk to, and now he had joined the Marine Corps. Not to mention the fact that he was 27 years old. Did they allow people that old to join the Marine Corps?

The next night my husband and I sat on the sofa listening as the recruiter spoke of the benefits of being a Marine and the pride of wearing the uniform. In all honesty, it didn't sound that bad. We would have a steady paycheck, insurance and housing. Moving from duty station to duty station would allow us to see different parts of the country, and the schools on base that our kids would be attending were some of the best. Not to mention the people I would meet and the family environment that I would become a part of. Listening to the recruiter speak, I began to understand some of the reasons why my husband wanted to join. Who wouldn't want these things for their family?

When handed a pen, I knew that the final decision would be mine. I could support my husband and join the Marine Corps Family the recruiter had talked about, or I could refuse and my husband would have to find another way to help support us. I quickly signed on the dotted line.

Never once did I think about the time that I would have to spend raising our children on my own. After all, the recruiter only spoke of the twelve weeks we would be separated while my husband trained at boot camp and I was naïve enough not to think to ask about future separations.

That weekend we began to discuss what we were going to do. What needed to be done to put the house on the market? Should we take a quick trip with the kids as a special family outing? What job would he go to school for? Where would we be stationed? How were we going to explain to the boys that daddy was leaving? How would we tell his parents, and mine, about the decision we had made? We were excited for the future and just assumed it would all work out. We had four months to get everything in order, and we would use every chance we had to do something special with the boys.

Little did I know that one phone call would quickly show me the reality of not only being a Marine, but also of being a Marine Corps spouse. Six weeks after we had signed the papers for my husband to join the Marine Corps, I arrived home from work and was met at the door by my husband.

"The recruiter called," he said.

"What did he want?"

"A spot opened and I'm leaving tonight for boot camp."

By now, he was searching through the washer for the jeans he had just washed.

I simply stood there looking at him. So many thoughts ran through my mind—

I thought he wasn't leaving for at least another two months! The house was not even on the market yet.

What about our boys? At ages three and six, how would we explain to them that Daddy was suddenly leaving?

What did he mean he was leaving tonight? Why not tomorrow? What could he possibly do over the weekend?

Had he told his mother? What about his dad? When will he say good-bye to them?

What are you taking with you? We are so unprepared for this!

Eventually, my mind wrapped around the fact that he didn't have a choice. Rather than whine and cry, I chose to be supportive of the decision we had made. After all, the final decision had been mine. Without my signature, he would never have been able to join. As he packed his bag and made phone calls, I sat on our bed stunned. Finally with a nod of disbelief I thought, "Welcome to the Marine Corps."

Five years later, as I prepare to walk into the hangar, where our squadron is located, I wonder if I will ever get used to saying good-bye. My husband leaving early for boot camp was just the beginning of our good-byes. Over the past years I have had to say it often, not only to him, but also to friends and family. Looking now at my two year old daughter, who is wide awake and jabbering to anyone who will listen, I smile to myself at the thought of being as carefree as she, and opened the door to yet another good-bye.

When first walking into the hangar, I can't help but feel overwhelmed by the activity around me. My first priority is to find my Marine, but to find him I must make my way through a sea of people. Everywhere I look, a different scene seems to be taking place.

To my left is the Commanding Officer's jet. The Marines have parked the jet in the hangar to allow families to take pictures of it, because this is a symbol of who they are. Our squadron is VMFA-122, the Werewolves, and they are excited to be able to go into a war zone, for the first time in many years, and do what they were trained to do. This tactical fighter aircraft, which is only one of many within the squadron, has a fierce picture of a werewolf painted on the tail and will soon be in a country flying missions specific to Operation Iraqi Freedom. Our Marines will be the ones maintaining the squadron's jets, flying the jets and when needed, helping to destroy those who oppose them. The pictures the families are taking show something of beauty, but in reality, this is a force to be reckoned with. I wonder to myself if the smiling families realize what it is they are standing before. If not, then I hope they at least understand the pride that our Marines will feel when they launch our jets into battle.

Directly in front of me are chairs for families to sit together before their Marine leaves. So many emotions dance over the faces of the people around me. Some of these emotions I can relate to, others I can only imagine. A wife sits weeping while her Marine kneels before her comforting her, as best he can. A mother stands beside her husband as they watch their son talk with a fellow Marine, all the while keeping a hand on the service rifle slung across his breast. A Marine sits holding her infant son, knowing that by the time she returns from war she will have missed his first steps.

For the emotions on their faces, I can only imagine what they must be thinking.

The wife I can sympathize with. I've been there and am facing the same situation again today.

The mother I can only feel for. How do you send off your son to a land where you cannot touch him if he is hurt, hold him if he is scared?

The Marine who is a mother, how do you leave your child to go and do what you are trained to do? With my emotions close to the surface I acknowledge that this is the reason I am not a Marine.

Then there are those who are smiling and laughing. It's not that they are happy about the deployment; it's just that these are the Marine Corps Family members that my husband's recruiter had spoken of. These are the friends who come to support someone whose Marine is deploying and they are here to make us smile. They are here to help take our minds off what is about to happen. They are here to be a shoulder for us to lean on when our Marines have left. These are the close friends that we have made and the people who are now our family sharing in our good-byes. Just seeing them makes me smile and lightens my mood. With this final thought I wipe the tears from my cheek and continue my search for my Marine.

To my right are the activities that will catch the attention of my boys. The squadron wanted to help keep the children occupied, so at 5:00 am there are bounce houses, music, nachos and snow cones already in place. Occupied and hyper is what the kids would be later, but I am thankful for the distraction they will offer.

As I walk to the bounce houses I side step around the Marines who are fast asleep on the floor with only their backpacks as a pillow. Only a Marine can fall asleep on a cement floor. I assume that this is yet another skill that is taught during boot camp.

Finally I catch a glimpse of my boys, but still no husband. Where can he be? I am feeling a little nervous about the fact that I can't find him. The time for the departure is drawing closer. Pulling my phone out of my pocket, I quickly punch in his number and wait for his answer.

"Hello?"

"Where are you at?" I ask, and try to keep my tears from falling yet again.

"I'm right here next to the bleachers."

"Where? I don't see you."

"I'm right here in front of you. Don't you see me?" he calmly replies.

"No, I can't find you."

"Dummy, look right in front of you. I'm right here."

My eyes lock onto him smiling and my rising hysteria slowly diminishes. I quickly put my phone away and we meet each other half way. Before I can do more than touch him, Taylor is jumping into her Daddy's arms and I am blocked from holding him by the service rifle slung across his breast.

"I couldn't find you and I was getting worried," I tell him.

"Yeah. Things are crazy."

At this point, his attention is captured by our two-year-old calling for her Bubba and Coco, the nicknames given to her brothers, Cody and Colton. Of course, the boys are being entertained by Tux the Clown and the wonderful balloon swords he is creating for them.

As my husband and daughter start toward the boys, I look out the hangar doors and catch a glimpse of the commercial aircraft sitting on the tarmac. It sits there waiting to take our Marines away from us. The aircraft represents another good-bye, and once said I will have to endure the next seven months alone. The time for good-bye will come, but for the moment I want to enjoy the time we have together—

Turning toward my family, I put a smile on my face and turn my back on the good-bye.

THE DYING TIME

The sea breeze brings a bit of chill as the darkness settles in, or perhaps it's the chill of fear.
There's light from a drifting mortar flare, an omen that the Dying Time is near.

We've set our mines and crouch low in the bunkers under a star filled tropic sky.
Will Charlie lose, or will it be me who calls false tails now that the Dying Time draws nigh?

Each night the landscape flickers with the flares and our tracers slay the shadows.
Morning sweeps find no blood, but Charlie is out there somewhere, we know.

Mortar rounds found our camp in his early hit-and-run 'cause Charlie needs his sleep.
In his day job he cuts our hair or cleans our huts and those are jobs he means to keep.

In daylight war moves away from camps and Charlie hides in plain sight.
He relaxes until once again he starts the clock for the Dying Time at night.

Each night we suffer little deaths, each time a mortar strikes, each time a round is fired.
The Dying Time can kill you quick, but most die slow, worn out, and tired.

That was forty years ago and I left without a wound, but I left there twice as old.
I still feel the Dying Time in the night, at my shoulder dark and cold.

—F. P. Siedentopf

CONTRIBUTOR BIOGRAPHIES

Stacy Atkinson, an active duty Marine, lives in Beaufort, South Carolina and works aboard MCAS Beaufort. She graduated October 18, 2008 from Embry Riddle Aeronautical University, after earning a BS in Professional Aeronautics. She is currently enrolled at University of South Carolina and is pursuing a Master of Arts in Teaching. Stacy is also a Marine wife. Her husband is an Air Traffic Controller aboard MCAS Beaufort. They are currently expecting their first child.

Vivian I. Bikulege was born and raised in Pittsburgh Pennsylvania. Her father was a Navy veteran, and she married a first lieutenant in the United States Marine Corps in 1986. Her husband later retired as a lieutenant colonel. Vivian writes *Whatever*, a column published in *The Lowcountry Weekly*, distributed in Beaufort, South Carolina and surrounding areas. Her columns have been featured on *Your Day*, an ETV radio program broadcast on local NPR stations. Vivian also writes feature articles for *Hilton Head Monthly*, and *Lowcountry Monthly*. She was one of the winners in the 2004 Piccolo Fiction Open (PFO) for her piece *Right Credo*. PFO is a literary component of the Piccolo Spoleto Arts Festival in Charleston, South Carolina. Essays presented by Vivian in the Milspeak anthology are unedited. Currently, Vivian is working to develop her work as a book-length memoir, *Yucca Sluts*.

Born in Washington, DC, **Gerard Boe** was raised on the East coast in a military family. Boe graduated from W.V. Wesleyan College with BS degree, from Ohio State University with a MS and Texas A&M University with Ph.D. He served a tour in the USMC as an Air Intelligence Officer, and then transferred to the US Army. Boe retired after 21 years service in the US Army. Following retirement, Boe worked at Medical College of Georgia, and owned and operated a management consulting business. He sold the business to accept a position as Executive Director, American Medical Technologist in Chicago. Boe retired from AMT to Beaufort, and has been writing poetry and nonfiction for several years.

Charlotte M. Brock was a Marine Officer from May 2002 to July 2008. Born in Kingston, Jamaica, of a French mother and American Foreign Service Officer father, she spent most of her childhood overseas. Charlotte attended the University of North Carolina at Chapel Hill and participated in Naval Reserve Officers Training Corps. While on active duty, she was stationed in Camp Pendleton, California, and Parris Island, South Carolina. She deployed twice to Iraq: with the 1st Force Service Support Group in 2004 and with Multi-National Corps-Iraq in 2005. She is currently an editor at the Center for Strategic and Budgetary Affairs, a Washington DC-based think tank.

Major General Matthew P. Caulfield was commissioned in 1958 and retired in 1992. He currently resides in Oceanside, CA.

David Ellard writes under the penname David Charles. Born and raised in a small town in the South, David joined the US Marine Corps as a teenager during the Cold War period. Having joined for law enforcement training, his first Marine job after "recruit" and "student" was as a military policeman. Once he cut his teeth guarding gates and on patrol, David became a Marine criminal investigator. Most of his career was in military law enforcement minus some out of specialty assignments, including three years on recruiting duty. Most of David's writing is drawn from his direct military experience, but his interest in sharing the military story has led him to help others share their stories, as can be seen in "First Combat Convoy" and "Corporal J's Housecleaning." David's military decorations (in order of precedence from lowest to highest) include the Marine Corps Recruiting Service Ribbon, Navy and Marine Corps Overseas Service Ribbon, Sea Service Deployment Ribbon, Humanitarian Service Medal, Global War on Terrorism Service Medal, National Defense Service Medal, Marine Corps Good Conduct Medal, Navy Meritorious Unit Commendation Ribbon, Navy Unit Commendation Ribbon, Navy & Marine Corps Achievement Medal, Navy & Marine Corps Commendation Medal, and the Meritorious Service Medal. David has been married for over a quarter century to a supportive, loving wife and has two children. His son is currently a US Marine and his daughter is a college student. He credits MCWS for making his dream of becoming a writer come true.

Melinda Copp is a freelance writer based in Bluffton, South Carolina. In 2005, she started an editorial consulting business, The Writer's Sherpa, to help aspiring authors achieve their writing and publishing goals. In August of 2009 she will earn her MFA in creative writing in Goucher College's nonfiction program. You can read more about her at www.MelindaCopp.com and www.WritersSherpa.com.

Bob Cowser, Jr.'s first book, *Dream Season*, was a New York Times Book Review "Editor's Choice" and "Paperback Row" selection and was listed among the *Chronicle of Higher Education's* best-ever college sports books. He is also the author of *Scorekeeping*, a collection of coming-of-age essays, and his essays and reviews have appeared widely in American literary magazines, including *Missouri Review, Prairie Schooner, American Literary Review, Sycamore Review, Brevity, Sonora Review, Fourth Genre,* and *Creative Nonfiction.* He is Associate Professor of English at St. Lawrence University, where he teaches courses in nonfiction writing and later American literature, and an adjunct member of the faculty of Ashland University's Low-Residency MFA program. He also serves as associate editor of *River Teeth: A Journal of Nonfiction Narrative.*

Jo Ann Doane served six years in the Marine Corps before entering the Order of Cistercians of the Strict Observance as a trappistine nun. She left the monastery after nine years and returned to Beaufort, South Carolina where she now resides. Jo Ann works with animals and writes poetry from an esoteric perspective. Jo Ann and Sally's friendship has continued since January 22, 1983 when they served together at Marine Air Control Squadron 5 at MCAS Beaufort.

Melissa Ellis was born and raised in the small Virginia town of Spotsylvania. After graduating high school, life took her to various places, including Maryland, Virginia Beach and eventually South Carolina. It was there, in 2002, that she began working as a civilian for the United States Marine Corps at Parris Island Recruit Depot. She currently works there, for the Sixth Marine Corps Recruiting District, handling Human Resource and performance management issues for civilian personnel. The youngest of five, family is extremely important to her as reflected in her piece, "Hair Today, Gone Tomorrow."

Monica Greer was born and raised in Gadsden, Alabama and graduated from Coosa Christian High School in 1994. She married her best friend in 1999 and together they are raising their three children. Life in her hometown was the only thing that Monica knew until her husband surprised her by joining the United States Marine Corps. Monica is the Family Readiness Officer for VMFA-251 at Marine Corps Air Station Beaufort.

Yvonne Rivers Green was born and raised in Big Estate, a small community within Beaufort, SC. Yvonne has 12 siblings and graduated from Battery Creek High School in 1977. She has two adult children. Yvonne has been employed by the Federal government for twenty-two years at Marine Corps Recruit Depot, Parris Island, SC. Yvonne thanks Milspeak for the opportunity and inspiration, and gives thanks to her Lord and Savior Jesus Christ for the gift.

Bernard "Moe" Haagensen, a veteran of the Vietnam conflict, 101st, Airborne Air Mobile 1970-71, was born in western New York and settled in South Carolina's Lowcountry. Milspeak creative writing workshops have given this ex-soldier a new communion with which he may regenerate life. The Milspeak experience has allowed Moe to unravel rock hard memories and cast them to the wind.

Jack Hayes and his wife, Frances, are both retired from business and live on Dataw Island, a gated community near Beaufort, South Carolina. Originally a New Yorker, Jack graduated from New York State Maritime Academy with an engineering license in the Merchant Marine and commission in the Navy, a Baccalaureate from State University of New York, and Master of Business Administration from Fairleigh Dickenson University. He began writing memoir to provide his son and five grandchildren with a record of his life experiences.

Michael Kobre is the Dana Professor of English at Queens University of Charlotte and On-Campus Director of the Queens Low-Residency MFA Program. He's the author of *Walker Percy's Voices* (University of Georgia Press, 2000). His essays and fiction have appeared in *Tin House, West Branch, Mississippi Quarterly, Critique,* and other journals.

Rebecca McClanahan has published nine books, most recently *Deep Light: New and Selected Poems 1987-2007* and *The Riddle Song and Other Rememberings*, which won the 2005 Glasgow prize in nonfiction. She has also authored four previous books of poetry and two books of writing instruction, including *Word Painting: A Guide to Writing More Descriptively*. McClanahan's work has appeared in *The Best American Poetry*, *The Best American Essays*, *Kenyon Review*, *Georgia Review*, *Gettysburg Review*, and numerous other publications. McClanahan, who lives in New York, has received the Wood Prize from *POETRY*, a Pushcart Prize in fiction, and (twice) the Carter prize for the essay from *Shenendoah*. Rebecca's website is www.mcclanmuse.com.

Sondra Meek was born and raised in Lakeland, Fl. She joined the Marine Corps in 1990 and is currently a Master Sergeant serving with III Marine Expeditionary Force, Okinawa, Japan. She is also married to a Marine and has two daughters, ages 13 and 8. She has served in support of Operation Iraqi Freedom, and her husband has served in support of Operation Enduring Freedom.

Dinty W. Moore is the author of the memoir *Between Panic & Desire* (University of Nebraska). His other books include *The Accidental Buddhist, Toothpick Men, The Emperor's Virtual Clothes*, and the writing guide, *The Truth of the Matter: Art and Craft in Creative Nonfiction*. He has published essays and stories in *The Southern Review*, *The Georgia Review*, *Harpers*, *The New York Times Sunday Magazine*, *Gettysburg Review*, *Utne Reader*, and *Crazyhorse*, and teaches in the creative nonfiction PhD program at Ohio University.

Kathryn Evans Parker went to work with Marine Corps Community Services (MCCS) at Parris Island, South Carolina in August 1976 and is still working there. The work she does is varied, but always involves details. Currently her position is in the Review and Analysis department where she manages programs and audits. Kathryn grew up in a small town, Salters, South Carolina, where her Mother still lives. During high school her first real job was typing and bookkeeping for a small Western Auto Store, then went on to become a "Soda Jerk" at a local "Drug Store." Her parents could not afford to send her to college, but she wanted to continue her education so badly that they sacrificed everything for her to attend Columbia Commercial College in Columbia, SC. She promised her parents that she would pay them back and is blessed to have her Mother, age 86, to continue to pay back in wonderful ways. Her majors were accounting and IBM Automation. Shortly after college, she moved to Charleston, SC where her first job was in data processing and accounting with Data Processing Service Company. This job offered her great training in both of her career choices. In December 1964, she married Bertis Reed Parker, Jr. of Beaufort, South Carolina. They moved to Beaufort in February 1976 where they still live with their two beautiful cats, Frank and Jesse James.

Richard Peabody, a prolific poet, fiction writer and editor, is an experienced teacher and important activist in the Washington, D.C. community of letters. He is editor of *Gargoyle Magazine* (founded in 1976), and has published a novella, two books of short stories, six books of poems, plus an e-book, and edited (or co-edited) nineteen anthologies including: *Mondo Barbie, Mondo Elvis, Conversations with Gore Vidal, A Different Beat: Writings by Women of the Beat Generation*, and *Kiss the Sky: Fiction and Poetry Starring Jimi Hendrix*. Peabody teaches fiction writing for the Johns Hopkins Advanced Studies Program. You can find out more about him at: www.gargoylemagazine.com or www.wikipedia.org.

Debra A. Pochie traveled the world as a military child before settling in her father's hometown, Beaufort, South Carolina. She is employed by Marine Corps Community Services at Marine Corp Air Station Beaufort and Parris Island Recruit Training Depot. Debra has three children and two and a half grandbabies that are proud enough to call her Mother as well as Goobergaa.

Ian Pounds began his education traveling ten thousand miles on the angle of a genetically transmitted hitchhiker's thumb. He sailed around the world with Semester at Sea, a shipboard campus devoted to global studies. He acquired his B.A. in creative writing from The Evergreen State College, and later studied Elizabethan literature at Oxford University. For three years he practiced Vipassana meditation, and for three years he homesteaded an otherwise deserted island in Southeast Alaska. His plays have been showcased at Seattle's New City Theatre and Olympia's Black

Box. He's been a stonemason, a performance poet, a counselor of runaway teens, and led workshops with the Association for Experiential Education and the Vermont Stage Company. He was a scholar at the Bread Loaf Writers' Conference, where he served over ten years on the admissions committee and coordinated the Bakeless Literary Prizes. He has recently completed a memoir, *The Hippie and the Marine: an American journal.* He hails from Ripton, Vermont.

Lisa Annelouise Rentz lives and gardens in Beaufort with her husband Irby Rentz, and works as the editor of *ArtNews*, the print magazine of the Arts Council of Beaufort County. Her essays, short stories, and illustrations have been published by *Skirt*, *Salon.com*, *night rally*, *Noshi Knitting*, *Charleston Magazine*, *Boston Public Radio*, and accepted into the University of South Carolina-Beaufort's permanent collection.

Atsuro Riley is the author of *Romey's Order*, forthcoming in 2010 from the Phoenix Poets series of The University of Chicago Press. His work has appeared in *POETRY, The Threepenny Review,* and *McSweeney's,* and has been awarded the Pushcart Prize and *POETRY*'s Wood Prize. Brought up in the South Carolina Lowcountry, Riley lives near San Francisco.

Debra Sharkey enlisted in the Marine Corps in December 1984. Now a First Sergeant soon to retire, Debra originally trained as a heavy equipment operator. She has served as a heavy equipment operator instructor and as a Drill Instructor, Senior Drill Instructor and Series Gunnery Sergeant. After leaving the Parris Island drill field in April 1998, she reported to Marine Corps Base, Quantico, Virginia, where she spent a summer serving as a Sergeant Instructor at the Officer Candidate School. First Sergeant Sharkey deployed to Operation Iraqi Freedom from February 2003 until June 2003 with 180 Marines and Sailors under her charge. In October 2004 in preparation for deployment to Operation Iraqi Freedom 04-06, she completed SASO Training and deployed to Desert Talon 1-05 with 250 Marines and Sailors in her company. At her present duty station, she has served as a First Sergeant for a Female Training Company at 4th Recruit Training Battalion and is currently serving as a First Sergeant for Service Company Headquarters and Service Battalion, which has 284 Marines.

Jillian Schedneck taught Literature and Creative Writing at the American University in Dubai for the 2007-2008 academic year. In 2006 she was a professor at Abu Dhabi University. Jillian holds a Master of Fine Arts in Creative Writing from West Virginia University. She is currently working on a travel memoir about her experiences in the United Arab Emirates titled "Abu Dhabi Days, Dubai Nights." Her creative work has been published in literary journals such as *The Common Review, Brevity,* and *Fourth River.*

Tom Sheehan's latest books are *Brief Cases, Short Spans,* November 2008 from Press 53 of NC; *From the Quickening,* January 2009 from Pocol Press of VA; a proposal for a collection of cowboy stories, *Where the Cowboys Ride Forever,* is in the hands of a western publisher; other in-process works are *Epic Cures II,* and novels *Murder from the Forum, Death of a Lottery Foe, An Accountable Death, The Keating Script,* and *Death of the Final God.* His work is currently in or forthcoming in *Ocean Magazine, Perigee, Rope and Wire Magazine, Qarrtsiluni, Green Silk Journal, Halfway down the Stairs, Ad Hoc Monadnock, Hawk & Whippoorwill, Eden Waters Press, Milspeak Memo, Milspeak Mentoring, Ensorcelled, Canopic Jar, SFWP, Eskimo Pie, Lock Raven Review, Indite Circle, Northville Review, Pine Tree Mysteries,* and in the anthology *Home of the Brave: Stories in Uniform,* edited by Jeffery Hess for Press 53. He has 10 Pushcart nominations, a Noted Story of 2007 nomination, the Georges Simenon Award, and a selection for inclusion in the *Dzanc Best of the Web Anthology for 2009.*

Lisa Kahn Schnell served as a Peace Corps Volunteer in Ghana, West Africa, from 1998-2000. Her essay "Circling," which first appeared in *Brevity,* will be anthologized in *Online Writing: The Best of the First Ten Years* (Snowvigate Press, 2009). She lives in Kutztown, Pennsylvania with her husband and their two daughters.

F.P. Siedentopf retired from the Marine Corps after serving thirty years on active duty. Starting as a Reservist "grunt" in 1959, he integrated into the Regular Marine Corps upon graduation from recruit training and opted for aviation training as an avionics technician. After aviation training at NAS Memphis, TN he was assigned to Sea Duty aboard the USS Boxer,

LPH-4. After Sea Duty, he had various postings to aviation units in North Carolina, Okinawa, and Vietnam. In 1968 he retrained as a technician on the Tactical Air Operations Center (TAOC), a tactical data computer for aircraft interception. Until his retirement in 1990, he served in various technical billets and in logistics billets as both a Supply Officer/Supply Chief and Logistics Officer/Logistics Chief. His personal decorations include the Good Conduct Medal, The Navy Achievement Medal (2 awards), The Navy Commendation Medal (2 awards), and the Meritorious Service Medal. He was a contributing writer at Bruce's Really Good Quotes at http://www.reallygoodquotesonline.com/about/, writing the column, "Imp-Revised News" as "The Bad Sied." Sadly, Fred passed away on Memorial Day 2009, only weeks before the publication of this book.

Warren Slesinger was a university press editor for several years and teaches part-time at the University of South Carolina-Beaufort. In 2008, Finishing Line Press published his chapbook, *A Word For It*. Warren edited *Spreading the Word: Editors on Poetry* and *The Whole Story: Editors on Fiction*, both books published by The Bench Press and used in creative writing courses. His poetry and his "definitions" have been published in numerous magazines, including *The Georgia Review, New Letters*, and *South Carolina Review*. In 2003, the SC Commission on the Arts awarded Warren a poetry fellowship.

Shawne Steiger is a social worker in the Syracuse VA, where she works as the PTSD Clinical Team Lead. She earned an MSW from Syracuse University in 1991 and an MFA in Fiction from Vermont College in 2006. Her work has appeared in *The Berkshire Review, The Portland Review, Trillium Literary Journal, upstreet 3* and *Segue Online Literary Journal.*

Nancy Whitworth was born and raised in Fort Fairfield, Maine. She received a BA from the University of Maine in International Affairs and an MBA from the Whittemore Business School at the University of New Hampshire. Nancy works for Marine Corps Community Services aboard Marine Corps Air Station, Beaufort, SC. She and her husband reside in Beaufort. "Jump in Feet First" is the beginning of a longer memoir Nancy is writing for her family.

Shana Tamla Willoughby was born in Raleigh, NC. She is in the Marine Corps, stationed in Miramar, California, and has one daughter. During 16 years in the military, Shana has experienced a lot and has grown a lot. Writing is cathartic for Shana, who uses her words to create a canvas of beauty. Revealing her deepest thoughts or the fun side of her imagination allows a look into the heart of her words as she unveils her soul. Her most precious assets are the wisdom and foresight gained through different experiences that cause her to glean certain priorities in her life. She chooses to live her life with no regrets from the past or present, or from future decisions, but to overcome these seasons of her life through many blessings bestowed and to blossom where she's planted.

A. M. Yallum has been on active duty in the Marine Corps more than twenty years and is currently stationed in Okinawa, Japan. He writes fiction and studied journalism for three years before enlisting in the Corps.

ABOUT THE EDITOR

Sally Drumm earned an MFA in creative writing from Queens University of Charlotte, NC, in May 2005 and founded Milspeak in September 2005. A Cold War Veteran and Marine Corps retiree, Sally received her education through a Veterans Administration's rehabilitation program for disabled veterans. Sally's writing has appeared in *Gargoyle*, *The Gettysburg Review*, *Mythic Passages* and other venues, including *Milspeak Memo*, an online journal dedicated to freedom of speech and sharing military life in the words of those who live it. Visit *Milspeak Memo* to read or to share your writing at www.milspeak.org.

A portion of proceeds from *MILSPEAK: Warriors, Veterans, Family, and Friends, Writing the Military Experience* is being donated to Chaplain's Helping Hands Fund (CHHF), which is administered by the Chief of Chaplains office at Walter Reed Medical Center. CHHF provides spiritual and financial aid to wounded service members from all military branches and their families. This donation does not represent an endorsement of Milspeak by CHHF or the Chaplain Corps, but is a gift from all anthology contributors to continue the good works of military chaplains.

the trees

the trees i see are big and tall
some of them are very small
the leaves on the trees will soon be gone
then it is time to move along

where will i go what will i see
all of this is not new to me
i will just walk and soon i'll find
another place to ease my mind

—Jo Ann Doane, Cold War Veteran
1974 - tenth grade

CPSIA information can be obtained at www.ICGtesting.com
Printed in the USA
BVOW05s1558180714

359474BV00003B/125/P